Fearing Burr, George Lincoln

The Town of Hingham in the late Civil War

Fearing Burr, George Lincoln

The Town of Hingham in the late Civil War

ISBN/EAN: 9783337132798

Printed in Europe, USA, Canada, Australia, Japan

Cover: Foto ©ninafisch / pixelio.de

More available books at **www.hansebooks.com**

THE

TOWN OF HINGHAM

IN

THE LATE CIVIL WAR,

WITH

SKETCHES OF ITS SOLDIERS AND SAILORS.

ALSO

THE ADDRESS

AND OTHER EXERCISES

AT THE

Dedication of the Soldiers' and Sailors' Monument.

PREPARED BY

FEARING BURR AND GEORGE LINCOLN.

PUBLISHED BY ORDER OF THE TOWN.
1876.

RAND, AVERY & CO., PRINTERS, BOSTON.

At the Annual Meeting of the inhabitants of Hingham, held Monday, March 6, 1871. it was —

"*Voted*, That the Report of the Committee on the Soldiers' and Sailors' Monument be accepted, and their recommendations be adopted, and that the report be recommitted to the Committee for publication in accordance with their report."

HINGHAM, May 15. 1871.

At a meeting of the Committee on Soldiers' and Sailors' Monument, it was

"*Voted*, That Messrs. George Lincoln, Fearing Burr, John Cushing, and Col. Hawkes Fearing be a committee to compile a report of the doings of the Committee on Soldiers' and Sailors' Monument for publication, including the report made to the Town at the last March meeting.

"*Voted*, that the Committee have power to fill vacancies."

[Signed]   JOHN M. CORBETT, *Secretary*.

HINGHAM, June 19, 1871.

At a meeting of the Committee chosen to prepare for publication the proceedings at the Dedication of the Soldiers' and Sailors' Monument, it was

"*Voted*, That the subject matter, and the work of preparation, be left with George Lincoln and Fearing Burr."

At a meeting of the inhabitants of Hingham, held Nov. 10, 1871, it was

"*Voted*, That the Soldiers' and Sailors' Monument Committee be authorized to publish an account of the action of the Town, and a record of its Soldiers and Sailors during the rebellion, in connection with the Dedicatory Exercises which they were authorized to have printed by a vote of the Town at the meeting in March last."

IN

Commemoration of the Sacrifice

MADE BY

THE SONS OF HINGHAM

FOR FREEDOM

AND THE CAUSE OF A UNITED
COUNTRY.

PREFATORY REMARKS.

THIS volume has been prepared by the undersigned at the request of the Committee on the Soldiers' and Sailors' Monument. It was understood to be the wish of this Committee that the work should embrace, in addition to the address and general exercises relating to the dedication of the Monument, a record of the services of all connected with the Town of Hingham who took part in the suppression of the rebellion, and a memorial sketch of that portion who fell for the cause they were striving to support and defend.

At the time the commission was placed in our hands, the Committee could scarcely have realized the magnitude of the labor they had thus imposed. It was certainly not foreseen by us. We had but entered on our work, ere it became evident, that, in order to a faithful history, much more should be comprised than was at first contemplated. The action of the Town at its numerous meetings; the frequent, less formal gatherings of our citizens; the efforts for filling the quotas required of the town; the draft; the patriotic co-operation of the ladies in their noble labors for the supply of comfortable apparel for those engaged in the service, and for providing the numerous articles needed for the relief and sustenance of the sick and wounded, — these, and a vast amount of historical facts of a more general character, we were soon convinced could not be omitted without greatly impairing the interest and value of the publication.

The collection of so much material was a matter not readily accomplished. The sources of information, even when known, were not always easily reached, and the particulars obtained often proved partial or unreliable. In addition to this, the difficulties attendant on revising, selecting, and arranging, made the fulfilment of our task slow, laborious, and oftentimes discouraging.

But earnestly desiring to answer the expectations of those more directly interested, as well as to meet the wishes of our citizens generally, we have given to the work committed to us our best endeavors. No available sources of information have been neglected that might aid in any degree to render the volume more complete and accurate. We have addressed a call to every surviving soldier and seaman, — native, resident, or otherwise associated with the Town, — for a statement of his experience in the great conflict. Correspondence has been opened with almost every section of the Union. Every document in possession of the Town has been not only carefully examined, but literally transcribed.

The sketches of the heroic dead are the results of our unwearied care and solicitude. To present, in full, the details of their history, their privations and sufferings, and the incidents connected with the one great sacrifice made for their country, we have personally appealed, for facts, to relatives, comrades, and friends.

Our progress has thus been unavoidably slow ; and it was natural that the public, perhaps not understanding the actual extent of the work in which we were engaged, or fully realizing that it was being gratuitously performed, should have become somewhat impatient at the seemingly unnecessary delay. From the one hand came the general appeal for the early appearance of the volume ; while, on the other, it was evident that time was slowly giving accuracy, fulness, and interest to the work as it steadily progressed toward completion. We feel it, however, but just to add, that to avoid apparent remissness, and to meet the calls of those who looked upon the publication as too long deferred, we have devoted — and not infrequently — a measure of time, duty to ourselves and those dependent on us would seem to have suggested should have been elsewhere bestowed.

For any errors, which, notwithstanding the strictest care and diligence, may have found their way to the pages of the volume, we ask the indulgence of the public. Inaccuracies met us at almost every step, and to avoid them we were early convinced would be an impossibility. They were found in the pages of official documents published by the State, as well as among the papers in possession of the Town; and they not infrequently occur in the journals and periodicals of the time. They were communicated by correspondents, and given in verbal answers to applications made for facts, or the verification of names and dates. They will be found in the literal transcripts of narratives, designed and believed on the part of the authors to be true and accurate, and they will be noticed by surviving compeers in the records of the heroic dead.

But having steadily labored with an earnest desire and purpose to present the history of each soldier and seaman in strict accordance with the facts known to us, and having conscientiously aimed to bestow on every act of courage and heroism the acknowledgment and meed of praise to which it may be justly entitled, we claim the kind forbearance of those — if such there be — who may think their record impaired either by errors of omission or commission, as well as from any who may feel that like experience has failed to receive like commendation.

Finally, our fellow-citizens are assured that a reviewal of the acts of the Town during the rebellion will afford every truly patriotic heart the most unalloyed gratification. There is no page of its history that bears not ample testimony to the single-heart-edness of the people of Hingham in their fidelity to the integrity of the Union. Promptly responding to the call of the executive for military aid, the citizen soldiers of Hingham were among the first to take arms, as they were the first to leave the State for the seat of war. No subsequent occasion created a need which the liberality of our people did not supply ; and no appeal, however exacting, was made by our common country which did not enlist the heartiest sympathy and co-operation. Kindred, friends, substance, were offered for the cause by cheerful hands. Reverses, however numerous or severe, never for an instant gave rise to despair. The faith in the final success of a cause deemed most dear and sacred, if at times weakened, was never broken. It was this faith which stimulated and inspired the public heart at the beginning ; and we believe, under Providence, it was its sustaining power and influence which in the end secured the final triumph for the Union, and for the establishment and perpetuity of universal freedom.

FEARING BURR,

GEORGE LINCOLN.

ACKNOWLEDGMENTS.

—

It remains for us to express our acknowledgments to the several gentlemen, who, cheerfully co-operating in our labors, have rendered us much valuable aid in the preparation of the volume for publication.

To Hon. Benjamin W. Harris, our Representative in Congress from the Second District, we are under especial obligations. Our numerous calls for time and services have uniformly received attention, and could scarcely have been answered with greater promptitude, or more fully and acceptably. He has won our esteem as a faithful public servant, and is tendered our heartiest thanks.

Our acknowledgments are also due to Capt. Lemuel Pope, of Hingham, for assistance rendered in revising the portion of the volume relating to the Navy; a work to which he devoted much valuable time, and one which a large experience in this department of the service during the war eminently fitted him to perform.

John D. Long, Esq., will please accept our thanks for his ready and cheerful compliance with our request that he would provide the introduction to the chapter on the dead.

Arthur Lincoln, Esq., also is tendered our acknowledgments for a like ready service in supplying the memorial sketch of President Lincoln.

We would further express our obligations to Henry Siders, Esq., chairman of the Board of Selectmen, for facts required

from the records of the Town ; and also to Mr. Hosah G. Goodrich, of the West Grammar School, for acceptable services.

To these expressions of our indebtedness for personal favors,
it is but just to recognize the assistance derived from the publi-
cations of the adjutant-general of Massachusetts, and particularly
for the facts supplied by the columns of "The Hingham Journal."

FEARING BURR,
GEORGE LINCOLN.

HINGHAM, Jan. 1, 1876.

CONTENTS.

CHAPTER I.

THE MONUMENT.

CHAPTER II.

PROCEEDINGS OF TOWN AND CITIZENS' MEETINGS.

CHAPTER III.

DRAFTS AND SUBSTITUTES.

CHAPTER X.

THIRTY-SECOND REGIMENT.

CHAPTER XI.

THREE YEARS' MEN CONTINUED.

CHAPTER XII.

THREE YEARS' MEN CONTINUED.

CHAPTER XIII.

THREE YEARS' MEN CONCLUDED.

CHAPTER XIV.

CHAPTER XV.

CHAPTER XVI.

CHAPTER XVII.

THE NAVY.

CHAPTER XVIII.

IN MEMORIAM.

CHAPTER XIX.

APPENDIX.

HINGHAM IN THE CIVIL WAR.

HINGHAM IN THE CIVIL WAR.

CHAPTER I.

THE MONUMENT.

THE first proposition relating to the establishment of a suitable memorial to the deceased soldiers and sailors of Hingham was brought before the inhabitants of the Town at the annual meeting held March 3, 1868, when, by unanimous consent, Col. Charles W. Seymour offered the following resolution, viz. : —

"*Resolved*, That the Town of Hingham cause marble tablets to be placed on the walls of the Town Hall, and that the names of all soldiers and sailors, both native and resident, who gave their lives in the country's defence in the late rebellion, be engraved on the tablets placed on the end of the hall, and that the names of all enlisted men (volunteers and those who were drafted) to the several quotas of the town be engraved on those placed on the side walls." The resolution was favorably considered ; but, as it could not legally be acted upon at the time, the subject was referred to the selectmen.

Among the articles in the warrant for the annual meeting March 8, 1869, were the following : —

"31. To hear the Report of the Selectmen to whom was referred the subject of procuring tablets to be placed in the Town Hall."

"32. What action will the Town take toward the erection of a suitable monument in memory of those soldiers and sailors, citizens of this town, who gave their lives in support of the cause of liberty and union during the late war against rebellion."

Action upon article thirty-one was indefinitely postponed. Upon article thirty-two, it was " voted that the sum of five thousand dollars be appropriated by the Town for a suitable monument, to be erected to the memory of the soldiers and sailors, who during the rebellion, representing the Town of Hingham, died in the service of their country ; and that the matter be placed in the hands of a committee, consisting of E. Waters Burr, Amasa Whiting, John K. Corthell, John Todd, Samuel J. Henderson, William J. Nelson, William Thomas, Elijah Shute, and John Cushing, with power to procure a design, contract for the Monument, locate, and, when finished, to cause the same to be dedicated with appropriate ceremonies.

Voted, That, in addition to the sum appropriated by the Town, the citizens be requested to subscribe and give the sum of one dollar each, and the children ten cents each, that all may contribute to so noble a cause.

Voted, That the Committee cause the names of all the soldiers and sailors representing the Town who died or were slain during the rebellion, also those who in the service of other towns, but natives of Hingham, died in the service, to be engraved on the Monument ; and, should the Committee deem it expedient, to inscribe thereon the names of all natives of Hingham who died in the service of their country during any former wars.

Voted, That the names of the officers and members of the Lincoln Light Infantry who answered the first call for troops, in April, 1861, the names of all soldiers and sailors who represented the town during the rebellion, the names of the Com-

mittee chosen to cause the Monument to be erected, and of
the citizens and children who make donations to this object, be
engrossed on parchment by the Town clerk, and that the same
be placed in or under the corner-stone."

The Committee began at once the work assigned them. Mr.
John M. Corbett was invited to meet with them, and to act as
secretary. Having organized, and appointed sub-committees,
they held frequent meetings for the purpose of completing the
business they were chosen to accomplish.

In addition to the five thousand dollars appropriated by the
Town, the sum of eight hundred and eighty-one dollars and forty-
four cents was subscribed, in accordance with the preceding
vote, by the citizens and children. A complete list of the subscribers appears in the appendix.

It only remains here to insert a copy of the agreement made
between the Committee, and the Proprietors of the Hingham
Cemetery, as an accessible and convenient source of information.

INDENTURE.

This Indenture made and executed this eleventh day of April, A. D.
eighteen hundred and seventy, by and between the Town of Hingham and
the " Proprietors of the Hingham Cemetery,"

Witnesseth. That whereas the said Town, at a meeting held on the eighth
day of March, A. D. eighteen hundred and sixty-nine, voted to erect a suitable monument " to the memory of the soldiers and sailors who, during the
late rebellion, representing the Town of Hingham, died in the service of
their country," and did place the matter in the hands of a committee then
chosen, which said committee, acting for and in behalf of the Town, have
procured a monument, and have decided what names and inscriptions shall
be placed thereon, and have determined to place and erect the same within
the grounds of said cemetery, on the lot and upon the terms hereinafter
described and set forth : and whereas the said Proprietors, in consideration
thereof, have agreed to furnish said lot upon which said Town may erect and
maintain said monument upon the terms aforesaid :

Now, in consideration aforesaid, it is hereby mutually agreed by and between the parties hereto as follows, to wit : —

First. That the said Proprietors shall, and they do hereby, grant to the
said Town, upon the terms and stipulations hereinafter set forth, the right
to erect and to forever maintain said monument on the following described lot
within their cemetery : to wit, an irregular lot situated on the summit of that
part of their cemetery which was purchased of Atherton Tilden, by Adam

Wallace Thaxter, and presented to said Proprietors, and which said lot contains about twenty-five rods, and is entirely surrounded by a road or avenue, and lies about ninety-three feet north of land late of said Tilden, and now of Albert Fearing, and about one hundred and fifteen feet west of land now or late of Hannah Hinckley : —

Second. That said Town shall place and erect said monument, so procured as aforesaid, on said lot, upon a suitable and proper foundation, and shall properly grade off the grounds in said lot during the present year, and shall always keep and maintain said monument and the foundation thereof on said lot in good repair and condition, and all at its own expense : but said Town shall never be called upon to contribute any thing towards the care or improvement of the grounds in said lot after they shall have been graded off as aforesaid.

Third, While said monument remains upon said lot, no part thereof shall be appropriated or used for any other purpose whatsoever : but if, from any cause, said monument shall be destroyed or cease to be maintained on said lot, then the rights of the Town in said lot shall terminate, and this agreement be at an end.

Fourth. The said " Proprietors " shall have and retain the entire control of said lot, and of the care and management thereof : and no alteration, improvement, or embellishment thereof shall be made, except with their assent and under their direction, and they shall always keep the grounds in said lot in a neat and orderly condition, without any cost or charge to the Town. In testimony whereof, the said parties have caused this instrument to be signed, — the said " Proprietors " by Daniel Bassett and Enos Loring, a committee thereto duly authorized, and the said Town by the said committee so chosen as aforesaid the day and year first above written.

THE PROPRIETORS OF THE HINGHAM CEMETERY, by

           DANIEL BASSETT,   }   *Committee.*
           ENOS LORING,   }

THE TOWN OF HINGHAM, by

           E. WATERS BURR,
           AMASA WHITING,
           JOHN K. CORTHELL,
           JOHN TODD,   *Town*
           S. J. HENDERSON,   *Committee*
           WM. J. NELSON,   *of nine.*
           WM. THOMAS,
           ELIJAH SHUTE,
           JOHN CUSHING.

From the Transactions of the Committee, as recorded by their secretary, we make the following extracts relating to the preliminary arrangements for the dedication of the Monument.

May 9, 1870. — A communication from Hon. Solomon Lincoln was laid before the Committee, accepting their invitation to deliver the address.

At the same meeting Col. Hawkes Fearing was chosen to act as chief marshal on the day of the celebration.   Mr. E. Waters Burr, the chairman of the Committee, being absent, Mr. John Cushing was chosen chairman *pro tem.*

May 16. — The committee voted, " That the Monument be dedicated on the 17th of June next." They subsequently appointed Hon. Albert Fearing, President of the Day, and Rev. Calvin Lincoln, Chaplain.

June 15. — At a meeting of the Committee held on the Monument lot, it was " voted, that the Monument be accepted, and that the thanks of the Committee be presented by the acting chairman, to Mr. F. J. Fuller of Quincy, the architect and builder, for the very satisfactory manner in which the work had been performed." This vote being communicated to Mr. Fuller, he replied briefly, thanking the Committee for the compliment paid him, and expressing great pleasure that his work so fully met their approbation.

Printed notices relating to the exercises for the dedication of the Monument were issued as follows : —

CHIEF MARSHAL'S NOTICE.

ORDER OF PROCESSION AT THE DEDICATION OF THE SOLDIERS' AND SAILORS' MONUMENT,

Erected by the Town of Hingham, June 17, 1870.

Police.

A detachment of the constabulary force of Hingham, under the direction of Constable Charles Spring.

Military escort,

consisting of

Weymouth Brass Band;

A battalion composed of Co. D, First Regiment and Co. I, Seventh Regiment, M. V. M., Major Charles E. Spaulding, commanding,

accompanied by Drum Corps of Seventh Regiment.

Aid.   Chief Marshal.   *Aid.*

FIRST DIVISION.

Aid.   Division marshal.   *Aid.*

Hingham Brass Band.

Chairman of Monumental Committee, president, orator, and chaplain of the day.

Marshal.   Selectmen of Hingham.   *Marshal.*

Invited guests.

Clergymen of Hingham.

Town clerk, treasurer, and school committee.

Marshal.   Other Town officers.   *Marshal.*

Officers of the Hingham Cemetery Corporation.

Officers of the Hingham Agricultural and Horticultural Society.

Marshal.   Trustees of Derby Academy.   *Marshal.*

Trustees of the Hingham Public Library.

President, directors, and secretary of the Hingham Mutual Fire Insurance Company.

President, trustees, and treasurer of the Hingham Institution for Savings.

President, directors, and cashier of the Hingham National Bank.

Old Colony Lodge of F. & A. M.

Board of fire-wards.

Marshal.   Fire companies.   *Marshal.*

Extinguisher No. 1; Torrent No. 2; Niagara No. 3; Constitution No. 4.

Citizens on foot.

SECOND DIVISION.

Aid.   Division marshal.   *Aid.*

South Hingham Cornet Band.

Marshal.   Edwin Humphrey Post. No. 104, G. A. R.   *Marshal.*

Lincoln Post. No. 40, G. A. R.

Reynolds Post. No. 58, G. A. R.

Marshal.   McPherson Post. No. 73, G. A. R.   *Marshal.*

Hartsuff Post, No. 74, G. A. R.

Paul Revere Post. No. 88, G. A. R.   •

Gen. Charles Griffin Post, No. 112, G. A. R.

Commander and Staff of the Department of Mass., G. A. R.

Marshal.   Orphans of deceased soldiers.   •   *Marshal.*

THIRD DIVISION.

Aid.   Division marshal.   *Aid.*

Marshal.   Pupils of the public schools, in carriages, in   *Marshal.*

charge of their respective teachers.

Teachers and pupils of private schools.

Teachers and pupils of Derby Academy.

Marshal.   Citizens in carriages.   *Marshal.*

The Monumental Committee, president, orator, chaplain, selectmen of Hingham, invited guests, and clergymen of the Town, are invited to assemble at Room No. 2, Public Library Building, at 1½ o'clock, P.M.; and all other bodies designated as a part of the first division are requested to meet at Niagara Hall, at the same hour, where marshals will be in attendance to impart all needful information.

The procession will form at 1½ o'clock, P.M., on the Green near the Public Library, — the escort on Short Street; the first division on School Street; the second division within the Square; the third division on Middle Street, right resting on the Avenue extending from Middle to School Street; and will move by the following route: up Middle to Pleasant, Main, and Leavitt Streets to Agricultural Hall, where an address will be delivered by Hon. Solomon Lincoln, and other appropriate exercises will be held; after which the procession will re-form, passing over Leavitt, Main, and South Streets, to the main entrance of Hingham Cemetery, thence to the Monumental Grounds, where exercises will be held pertaining to the formal transfer of the Monument by the Committee, and the acceptance of the same in behalf of the Town by the selectmen.

Marshals of the several organizations are requested to report to the chiefs of their respective divisions at the earliest practicable moment, in order to facilitate a prompt formation of the procession.

Assistant marshals not specially detailed will report for duty at 9 o'clock, A.M., at the chief marshal's headquarters, on Main Street, opposite Short Street.

The following named gentlemen are appointed assistant marshals; viz., Theophilus Kilby, Josiah M. Lane, William Cushing, David Cushing, jun., Levi B. Ripley, William H. Leavitt, Wallace Corthell, John Stephenson, Arthur A. Burr, Thos. J. Leavitt, Marcellus C. Cloudman, Thos. Stephenson, Benjamin F. Meservey, Jos. Ripley, Eleazer P. Dunbar, Lyman B. Whiton, Luther Stephenson, jun., Henry F. Siders, George E. Siders, Charles F. Whiton, Joseph B. Thaxter, Benjamin Andrews, Frank W. Hatch, Thomas Weston, Edmund Hersey, 2d, Hosea B. Hersey, Webster Hersey, E. S. Tirrell, Thomas Humphrey, Daniel Perkins, Francis M. Stowell, Joseph A. Newhall, Simeon J. Dunbar, Caleb G. Beal, H. Burr Crandall, Edward T. Bouvé, Albert Leavitt, and E. T. C. Stephenson.

Luther Stephenson, jun., Benjamin F. Meservey, and Simeon J. Dunbar, are designated as chiefs of divisions, first, second, and third, respectively, and will be respected accordingly.

Aids to the chief marshal, John C. Whiton and John C. Hollis.

The following are assigned for special duty, —

1. Marshal Levi B. Ripley, assisted by Marshal Marcellus C. Cloudman, is charged with the execution of that part of the programme pertaining to the national salutes. He will procure transportation for the guns, provide rations and furnish quarters for the gunners, and, on the receipt of this, will report for instructions.

4

2. The arrangement of carriages on the Agricultural Grounds will be under the direction of Marshal John Stephenson.

3. Marshals Jos. Ripley, Wallace Corthell, Thos. Stephenson, Wm. Cushing, Francis M. Stowell, Frank W. Hatch, Webster Hersey, and Thos. Humphrey, will be in attendance at Agricultural Hall, to receive and assist in seating the procession.

4. Marshals Theophilus Kilby, E. T. C. Stephenson, Josiah M. Lane, Chas. F. Whiton, Arthur A. Burr, and Henry F. Siders, are assigned to duty at Public Library Building.

5. Marshals Lyman B. Whiton, Thos. J. Leavitt, E. S. Tirrell, Albert Leavitt, Hosea B. Hersey, and Wm. H. Leavitt, are detailed for duty at Niagara Hall.

HAWKES FEARING, *Chief Marshal.*

ORDER OF NOTICE.

The day will open with firing a national salute on Liberty Pole Hill at sunrise, at Hingham Centre at noon, and at Broad Bridge at sundown.

Concert by the South Hingham Cornet Band, at 8 o'clock, A. M., at Fountain Square : and also by the Hingham Brass Band, at the same hour, at South Hingham.

Reception of the various Posts of the G.A.R. by detachments of Post 104.

Dress parade by the military on Broad Bridge, at 10½, A.M.

Review of the military and Grand Army of the Republic, on the Common at Hingham Centre, at 11 o'clock, A.M.

Military and G. A. R. will partake of a collation at Agricultural Hall, at 12 o'clock, M.

At 1 o'clock, P.M., the services at the hall will consist first of prayer and singing, after which the audience will listen to an address by Hon. Solomon Lincoln. The singing during the day will be under the direction of Mr. E. B. Whitcomb of South Hingham, and original hymns are expected by Hingham poets for the occasion. After the services at the hall have been completed, the procession will form, and march to the Hingham Cemetery, where services appropriate to the occasion will be held.

It is expected the Monument will be tastefully decorated with flowers and bunting by John Todd, Esq., whose artistic skill the people of Hingham have so often witnessed. During the unveiling of the Monument, minute guns will be fired from Cobb's Hill. A number of young ladies, corresponding to the number of names upon the Monument, will pay their tribute of respect to the memory of the fallen, by each placing a bouquet of flowers at the base of the Monument. It is intended to make the whole service pleasant and impressive, and one that will be remembered by the youth.

The citizens of Hingham generally are requested to lay aside their common avocations, and join in rendering this memorial to the fallen one of interest and profit.

JOHN CUSHING, *Chairman pro tem.*

Friday, the 17th of June, was a day to be remembered in the annals of Hingham. Although the morning was cloudy, and rain fell in showers during a portion of the afternoon, yet the weather was not unfavorable for the celebration. The temperature was comfortable, the streets were free from dust, and the rain did not descend till the exercises were far advanced.

The bells on the various meeting-houses were rung at sunrise; and salutes were fired at morning, noon, and night, in accordance with the preceding order of notice, the services of a detachment from the Second Battery Light Artillery, M. V., having been secured for the occasion.

At eight o'clock, A.M., the South Hingham Cornet Band gave an open-air concert at Fountain Square, and at the same hour the Hingham Brass Band furnished a musical entertainment to the people of the south part of the town.

Throughout the day the Town presented a lively and festive appearance. Business generally was suspended, and the streets were thronged with people. Many residents of the adjoining towns, and a large number of military guests from other places, were present; and the whole morning teemed with music, military evolutions, marching, and counter-marching.

The chief interest of the day centered of course in the procession, which in length, character, and brilliancy, was probably never surpassed in this Town upon any occasion. It began to move over the route prescribed by the chief marshal at about two o'clock, P.M., and proceeded to Agricultural Hall. After the large audience was seated, the president of the day, Hon. Albert Fearing, arose, and welcomed the assemblage in a few well chosen words. The South Hingham Cornet Band followed with a voluntary. Prayer was then offered by the chaplain of the day, Rev. Calvin Lincoln, of the First Parish.

The following ode, written for the occasion by James Humphrey Wilder, and read by Rev. Henry W. Jones, pastor of the Orthodox Congregational Society, was then sung by a select choir, conducted by Mr. E. Barker Whitcomb.

AIR — "*Star Spangled Banner.*"

Glory, glory to God for the fathers of old,
   A home on these shores for sweet *Freedom* who founded, —
Who to battle with famine and foemen were bold,
   While that home with stanch bulwarks they bravely surrounded.
         And the tree planted here,
         Nursed by storms wild and drear,
Is now spreading its branches all nations to cheer.
Oh! their memory shall live, their names ever be bright,
For the earth and the heavens in their praise will unite.

And honored be they, worthy sons of stern sires,
   Who, linked heart and hand in resistless communion,
Declared Freedom their birthright, and lighted the fires
   That should weld North and South in a glorious *Union.*
         Then bright to the world
         The dear flag was unfurled,
'Neath whose stars to the dust old Oppression was hurled.
Oh! their memory shall live, their names ever be bright,
For the earth and the heavens in their praise will unite.

Dark, dark, was the day, sad and fearful the sight,
   When traitors to nought these rich blessings would trample :
When they madly and blindly, with infamous fight,
   Strove to blot from its view the world's peerless example.
         And all shrouded in gloom,
         Stood a shadowy tomb,
Though for Liberty meant, it was Slavery's doom.
Ah! their memory is pain, and their names dark as night,
And the heavens with the earth in their shame must unite.

Glory, glory to God for the brave hearts and true,
   Who sprang to the rescue when peril impended ;
Ay, who counted not life dear such foes to subdue,
   And gallantly Freedom and Union defended.
         And the laurels they won,
         As the ages roll on,
Ever greener shall grow, — till the last setting sun ;
And their memory shall live, and their names shall be bright,
For the earth and the heavens in their praise shall unite.

Now, all honor to them, the young heroes *our own*,
  Who left their loved homes, to return, alas ! never:
Who, forgetting themselves, thought of country alone,
  And died that their land might be Freedom's forever.
     While the world shall endure,
     Their glory is sure,
More lasting than granite, no crystal more pure ;
And their memory shall live, and their names shall be bright.
For the earth and the heavens in their praise shall unite.

The address was then delivered by Hon. Solomon Lincoln.

ADDRESS

DELIVERED AT THE DEDICATION OF THE

Soldiers' and Sailors' Monument in Hingham,

June 17, 1870,

By SOLOMON LINCOLN.

ADDRESS.

FRIENDS AND FELLOW-CITIZENS, — We have assembled to-day
with mingled emotions of sorrow and joy, — sorrow for the
patriot dead who gave their lives to their country, and joy in the
triumph of the cause for which they fought.

This is a historic day. It is the anniversary of the first great
battle for freedom which electrified a continent, and was felt
throughout the civilized world. That was one of the series of
great actions which culminated in the Declaration of Independence, — that noble instrument, written in words of immortal truth
by Thomas Jefferson, and defended on the floor of Congress and
before the world by the matchless eloquence of John Adams ;
Virginia and Massachusetts uniting in laying deep and strong
the foundation of our great temple of freedom, which has now
withstood the assaults of foes within and foes without for nearly
a century. The heroes of the Revolution cemented the union
of these States with their blood.

Every section, every State, every village, sent its quota of brave
men to maintain the rights which were claimed by the people
for themselves and their posterity. In the providence of God,
victory crowned their noble sacrifices, and the United States
achieved an independent rank among the nations of the earth.

The traditions, the history, of this day are all on the side of
freedom. It is a glorious and immortal day.

We have assembled to do honor to the brave men who, inspired
with the spirit of the Revolution, and animated by the sentiment

of American Independence, rallied around the flag of their country to defend it from the treasonable attacks of a gigantic rebellion. The power of the people was equal to the emergency. Their patriotism rose with every fresh demand upon it. Defeat could not subdue it, treason could not destroy it. Victory only stimulated to higher effort. Our fair fabric of freedom was preserved. It stood, and will stand we trust forever, in greater strength and with increased beauty.

But, fellow-citizens, we are painfully sensible, on this day, of the sacrifices which were made to obtain that great result. We know too well the blood and treasure which were poured out like water to maintain the glorious institutions which our fathers gave their blood and treasure to establish.

We cannot look around us, and not perceive in the tears of sympathy for the noble dead, the terrible losses which this and every other village of our land have suffered by the parricidal attempt to overthrow the Union and Constitution, which are so dear to us all.

The causes of the rebellion are matters of history. Statesmen have discussed them. The highest powers of eloquence were exerted in the councils of the nation, and before the people, to check and control the operation of those causes. But in vain. The mistaken confidence of politicians in their ability to effect a peaceable separation of the States of the Union, and thus gratify the pride and establish the power of sectional ambition, so soon as it was developed in action, and sounded the first gun of rebellion in the harbor of Charleston, revealed the might that slumbered in the arms of freemen and the weakness of their foes. A thrill of patriotic enthusiasm ran through the free North and West. Citizens of all ranks and parties rallied with Revolutionary ardor around the flag of their country, to defend the fortresses and Capitol of the Union. Armies sprang into existence as if by magic. Forces, such as had not been seen in modern times,

were organized under the lead of gallant chiefs, and marched to
the battle-field to defend what they felt to be truth, freedom,
right. I saw much of these exciting scenes. But no poor words
of mine can describe them. My voice is powerless to utter fitting terms of eulogy, the majesty of the popular uprising. I
felt it all. And it was then, and is now, a source to my mind of
the proudest satisfaction, that I saw among those military corps
who earliest left home and families, with wives and children, a
gallant company from my native town, bearing an honored Revolutionary name, threading their way by tap of drum through the
crowded streets of the metropolis to the State House, there to
receive the outfit which a spirit of prophecy had prompted an
ever vigilant and patriotic governor to have in preparation for
them, and that I had the privilege of standing by his side, and to
listen to his farewell words to one regiment, uttered with all that
simplicity, tenderness, fervor, and beauty which seemed like the
words of inspiration to all who heard them.

The scenes of the war, the actors in those scenes, the mighty
armies which sprang from the people, and whom the people
honored and sustained, the gatherings of the women of the land
to provide every thing which thoughtful kindness could suggest
for the comfort of those who were dear to them, the profuse liberality of men of wealth, the large contributions of those of
more moderate means, the patriotic action of the governments
of States and Nation to give energy and power to the popular
will, — all these subjects have passed into history, and fill the
brightest pages of our public annals.

Glorious scenes, glorious men! noble efforts in the cause of
humanity and freedom! They live in our memories, and sink
deep into our hearts.

It would be to me a gratifying service, if I could narrate, even
in a summary manner, the events of the war, the parts which
were performed by brave men upon the land and the sea, and

especially those which we associate with our native Town, where
both authorities and citizens worked in harmonious action to
leave no duty undone which patriotism called on them to do;
but the mass of facts which press upon the memory on this
occasion almost bewilders the imagination, and must be dealt
with in a more careful and deliberate manner by the historian. It
would be a very desirable work to be accomplished, if a special
account of the services of each officer and soldier and sailor,
natives of this town, as forming a part of its quota, could be prepared for the gratification of the living and the instruction of
posterity. Our indefatigable Town clerk has many of the facts,
systematically arranged, which would be necessary to effect such
an object. The narration of the services and sacrifices and brilliant achievements of men of Hingham, in the army and navy,
written with exact truth, taste, and discrimination, would make a
volume of surpassing interest to relatives, friends, and to all
classes of citizens.[1] A collection of such volumes from all parts
of the country, and giving to each its distinctive claims to public
gratitude, would compose an extensive national library, unexam-
pled in the history of literature. Much of this work has been
done; and the histories of regiments, corps, expeditions, and of
the war generally, which have been prepared with great labor and
expense, are but beginnings of what remains to be accomplished.

By the aid of the printing-press, a monument may be constructed which will be more durable than bronze or granite or
marble.

But perhaps the time may not have arrived for the preparation
of such works in the most satisfactory manner. For it is true
that for an impartial, philosophical, instructive history of events
of deepest interest to the human race, time is necessary to
soften asperities, to remove prejudices, and to do justice to all
parties and all sections of the country.

[1] This volume is intended to supply the want above described.

During the war of the rebellion, as may be inferred from what I have already said, this Town furnished its full quota of several hundred men.

The whole number of men called into service during the war was 2,656,553. Of these 1,490,000 were in actual service ; of this number nearly 60,000 were killed on the field, and about 35,000 were mortally wounded. Disease in camps and hospitals slew 184,000. It is estimated that at least 300,000 Union soldiers perished during the war. Full that number of Confederate soldiers lost their lives ; and the aggregate number of men, including both armies, who were crippled or permanently disabled by disease, was estimated at 400,000. The actual loss to the country of able-bodied men, in consequence of the rebellion, was full 1,000,000.

But notwithstanding these painful facts, carrying sorrow and calamity into so many families, and cutting down the flower of the young men of the land, we are permitted to rejoice in the success of the great struggle for which they gave their lives to their country. In the providence of God, the great cause of the rebellion was irrevocably removed, and every inhabitant of the land thus redeemed can enjoy the pure air of freedom. Our martyred president seemed to have been an instrument in the hands of the Almighty to purify this nation, and by his emancipation proclamation to breathe into it the breath of life, and to stamp his own with immortality.

The number of soldiers and sailors, natives or residents of this Town, or who formed a part of its quota, whose lives were sacrificed in consequence of the rebellion, was eighty. Of these many were slain on the field of battle, and were buried where they fell. Others died from wounds or disease ; and to some it was the hard fate to perish in the prisons of Salisbury, Belle Isle, and Andersonville. Besides these, were those who survived the fields of battle, and who bear the marks of wounds received in the service of their country. Many of the dead have been buried in the cemeteries of this Town, where the hand of friendship has had the privilege of placing appropriate memorial stones to designate the places of their interment. But a few days since the beautiful service was performed of decorating their burial places with flowers. This form of remembrance of the fallen heroes was a fresh expression of affection and gratitude, honorable to the living and to the dead. It touched the sympathies of the young as well as the old, and taught in the language of nature the duty of cherishing the highest sentiments of an enlightened patriotism and a profound homage for the nation's benefactors. But this affecting service addressed itself to the living, while it brought to mind those equally dear to us all, whose remains repose in unknown graves on the fields where they fell.

Influenced by the sentiment that a permanent form of record of the names of all our heroes wherever they died, and wherever buried, would speak to posterity in language not to be mistaken, this Town, acting in its corporate capacity, with many of its inhabitants acting upon the most generous impulses, have caused the erection of a monument of granite, in one of our ancient cemeteries, in a conspicuous position, where its mute eloquence will address future ages, and commend the example of those whose names are inscribed upon it to succeeding generations. Thus may they be taught, by a perpetual remembrance, to appreciate the services and sacrifices of the gallant men whose lives were laid upon the altar of our Union, that they might transmit to posterity, a happy, united, and free country.

I have said that this is a historic day. The erection of the Monument to the memory of our soldiers and sailors in the place where it stands, has an appropriateness which harmonizes well with our local historical associations. It stands amid the graves of our ancestors, the first settlers of the Town, whose valor was displayed at an early date in our history, in defending

our infant settlement from hostile attacks. The men who, in
Provincial times, united with the forces of the mother country to
repel the incursions of the French, repose almost beneath its
shadow. The heroes and patriots of the Revolution, in considerable numbers, found their final resting-place within its
limits. That distinguished general whose name is conspicuous
in our annals, and who merited and enjoyed the confidence of
Washington, rests in this consecrated ground. The elegant yet
simple and appropriate monument over his remains, speaks no
word of eulogy. But Revolutionary services, his history and his
life, are his highest eulogy. There, also, are the graves of many
who bore arms in the war of 1812, by some called our second
war of Independence.

The names of many of those whom we this day commemorate,
are to be found upon the memorials which friendship has placed
to designate their burial places, within the limits of the cemetery, and in view of the noble Monument upon which we have
sought to hand them down to posterity, with those of the noble
army of martyrs who perished with them.

It stands near the grave of the great governor, whose mortal
remains are at rest in the soil of the town which he loved so
well, — he whose whole soul and thought was bestowed upon
his country, who blended the brilliant talent of a statesman with
the lofty sentiment of a patriot and the true honor of a man.
As we read the names upon the Monument, our eyes will turn
upon the grave of him whose warm heart inspired them to deeds
of valor, and who so tenderly cared for the dead heroes who fell
victims as the first martyrs in the rebellion. His own life
was given to his country, as truly as the soldier's who fell upon
the field of battle ; and his monument, we trust, will yet rise in
simple beauty, to designate the grave of one whose history is so
intimately associated with that of our own Town, our beloved
Commonwealth, and of the United States.

I have said that this was a day of sorrow as well as of joy. The thoughts which I have expressed, indicate how deeply many hearts will be affected on this occasion. Our sympathies are with them. And the lesson of the hour teaches us all how tenderly every honorable effort should be made to alleviate the burthens which their sacrifices have brought upon them. We have also living heroes to remember, as well as the dead to commemorate. The flowers of yesterday were for the living, — the Monument of to-day is for posterity. Hereafter gratitude will remember both ; and when, hereafter, we shall with increased interest scatter beautiful flowers upon the graves of the dead, shall we not take care that the graceful Monument which we this day dedicate to our fallen heroes shall be hung with garlands and wreaths of *immortelles.*

The ancient Greeks decorated the graves of their illustrious heroes with fresh flowers, and also called into requisition the highest talent of the sculptor and the artisan to rear permanent statues and monuments to their memory. We imitate the customs of antiquity, not on account of their origin in nations of an advanced civilization and refinement, but because they spring from the highest impulses of our nature, and are the natural expression of humanity and patriotism.

The service, therefore, which we perform to-day, is done with joy and not with grief. We rise above the depressing thoughts which would invest our solemnities with gloom and despondency, and read in the glorious events which crowd upon our memories, and elevate our feelings, the brightest hopes for the future of our country. We rejoice in the victory over rebellion, chastening our joy by subduing every emotion of sectional pride or ambition, and glorying in the triumph not for the North alone, not for the West, but for the South as well, and for freedom and humanity to all.

While, therefore, we devote this day to commemorate the

patriot dead, we will rejoice that our country is free, that the Union is preserved, that our institutions are safe, that time, the great arbiter, will heal all animosities, and conquer all prejudices, that justice will reign, that the rights of every citizen will be secured, and that amid the trials and perplexities consequent upon a state of civil war, the nation will rise above all adverse influences, and animated by a spirit of patriotism, the love of freedom, and a just regard for the rights of every citizen, will commence a new career of true glory and renown.

The monuments which we raise in honor of the dead, shall remind the living of their duty to themselves, to their country, and to posterity.

Our excellent governor recently stated that "the Legislature has but carried out the will of the people in renewing for three years the State Aid law, which is so beneficial in assisting the needy families, and those whose service in the war has left them feeble and dependent" And he adds, "It is to the honor of our good old Commonwealth that she provides *far more abundantly for those stricken ones than any other State in the Union.*

This is indeed a proud record for Massachusetts. It shows that the people are true to the principles of the founders of the Republic, that ingratitude to public benefactors is not a stain upon their patriotism, and that, whether in prosperity or adversity, the true glory of the State is the object, as it is the reward, of the highest sentiments of patriotism.

Let us go hence, then, with hearts animated and refreshed by these reflections upon our national and local history, to the consecrated spot so rich in ancestral associations, with the young and old, the soldier and the citizen ; to dedicate the graceful Monument erected in honor of our fallen heroes, by the solemn anthem, the devout prayer, with poetry and music, amid the rich foliage and beautiful flowers of summer, in the cause of patriotism, philanthropy, freedom, truth.

At the close of the Address, the following ode, composed for the occasion by Miss Almira Seymour, was read by Rev. Jonathan Tilson, of the Baptist Society, and sung by the choir to the tune, " America."

> Darkness o'er all the land,
> An outstretched, red right-hand
>   Menaced the blow,
> A nation's life the aim;
> Surrender all but name !
> From Massachusetts came
>   The first firm No !
>
> A voice from Sumter spoke :
> From desk and workshop broke
> ·   Our young and brave ;
> The darkened air flushed bright
> With freedom's symbol-light,
> As forward in their might
>   They rushed to save.
>
> Forward ! o'er fortress bound,
> Forward ! o'er leagues of ground,
>   O'er surging wave :
> Through wilderness and fen,
> Through Hunger's ghastly den —
> Repulsed — forward again
>   They rushed to save.
>
> They fought, they fell, they *saved !*
> Deep be their names engraved
>   On changeless stone ;
> Names lettered now in light,
> Truth's monogram of might,
> With theirs who fell for right
>   In years far-flown.
>
> Baptized in infancy
> With life-blood of the free,
>   O holy land !
> Confirmed in manhood's prime
> By the same rite sublime,
> To higher heights yet climb,
>   Led by God's hand.

Our Country — with acclaim
Shout, coupling each loved name —
Our Country *free !*
From Gulf to Arctic shore,
Ocean's to ocean's roar,
UNION *forevermore*
IN LIBERTY!

The services at the hall were closed with a benediction by the chaplain.

After the procession was re-formed, it proceeded to the Hingham Cemetery. A platform, tastefully decorated with flags and flowers, had been erected a few yards west of the Monument, upon which the gentlemen having the services in charge were seated.

The Monument itself presented a most attractive appearance. Running evergreen encircled the entire shaft, and the die was covered with a large American ensign to veil it. When all was in readiness, the exercises were introduced with a musical performance by the five bands consolidated.

The president of the day then arose in his place, and addressed the large assemblage as follows : —

Beneath these over-arching heavens, with the sun partially veiled, and the clouds dropping tears of sympathy with the scene, and surrounded by ancestral graves, and Monuments of distinguished men, we meet to dedicate this imposing monument, erected by the citizens of Hingham to the memory of the heroes, who, in the late contest, gave up their lives in defence of the Constitution, and to sustain the integrity of the Union. It would be an agreeable privilege to speak of the virtues and patriotic sacrifices of the men whose names are inscribed upon this Monument : but this duty was appropriately assigned to a distinguished citizen, and most eloquently has it been discharged.

In paying this grateful tribute to the memory of the dead, let us not forget the living, whose amputated limbs and deep scars daily remind us of the magnitude of the conflict and the importance of the result.

We cordially welcome to this occasion our young friends, who are so soon to fill the places we now occupy, and to reap all the blessings secured by the great struggle for liberty. We welcome, too, this band of citizen soldiers, representing that great and noble army, the pride and glory and safety of our country. No name is more honorable than that of a citizen soldier, ready to discharge all the duties of civil life, and as ready to take up arms to defend the country from foreign and domestic foes. Far distant be the day when they shall cease to be cherished and sustained! Welcome, thrice welcome all to a participation in the services of this hour!

We raise this Monument in no vain-glorious spirit, nor in any disposition to exult over a fallen foe, but as the expression of our admiration for bravery, and our appreciation of the value of the services rendered by these men to our common country.

And now that many of the causes of dissension have been removed, let us all unite in cultivating a spirit of charity and love between all sections of the country, and thus cement this Union of the States, and do what we can to make it perpetual. And may we not hope, that long before the moss shall gather upon this beautiful Monument, and beneath the hand of time it shall crumble into fragments, wars and rumors of wars shall cease, and the influence of the Prince of peace shall be felt in every land, and the people of every nation shall dwell together in harmony and love.

Prayer was then offered by the chaplain; after which the following original ode, composed for the occasion by Mrs. C. L. P. Stephenson, was sung by a choir of young ladies, to the tune, "Auld Lang Syne."

> We've whispered words of gratitude,
>   Sweet memories told in flowers,
> And we have raised an obelisk.
>   For fame in future hours,
> To the brave *men* who nobly fought
>   Our Union to restore.
> Who died beneath the "Stars and Stripes,"
>   The heroes of our war.
>
> The sound of words will pass away,
>   The fairest flowers will fade;
> But long this work of art shall stand
>   Within this sacred shade,
> To the brave *men* who nobly fought
>   Our Union to restore,
> Who died beneath the "Stars and Stripes,"
>   The heroes of our war.
>
> Though some afar are sleeping still
>   Beneath an humbler sod,
> They all will wake within the smile
>   Of glory from their God,
> The noble *men* who bravely fought
>   Our Union to restore,
> Who died beneath the "Stars and Stripes,"
>   The heroes of our war.

But while we give our absent friends
   The honor and the tear,
We also fold within our hearts
  ` Their hero-comrades here;
For they were men who left their homes,
   And many burdens bore,
Who fought to save the " Stars and Stripes."
   Brave heroes of our war.

This granite pile will tell the tale
   Of martyrs now asleep,
When we have left the ranks of time,
   And others vigil keep.
'Twill téach to them the lesson true,
   Which we to-day should heed, —
Each life for *freedom* sacrificed
   For *future peace* will plead.

While the youthful choir were singing, the flag which had
veiled the Monument was removed, the detachment of artillery
fired a series of minute guns from Ward Hill, and the base of
the Monument was decorated with flowers by the hands of the
children.

Mr. John Cushing, acting chairman of the Committee, then
presented the Monument to the Town authorities, with the
following remarks : —

MR. PRESIDENT AND CITIZENS OF HINGHAM, — I stand before you to-
day to perform a duty which I gladly would have avoided. Our worthy
chairman, whose voice should have cheered us here to-day, is seeking for
health on the Pacific Coast. His untiring industry to see this work completed entitles him to our gratitude and esteem. My prayer is, and I doubt
not it is the prayer of you all, that he may return in due time to his family
and friends fully recruited in bodily strength and vigor.

At a meeting of the legal voters of Hingham, held May 8, 1869, it was
voted that the sum of five thousand dollars be appropriated towards building
a Monument to the memory of the soldiers and sailors who died or were
slain during the rebellion, and that a Committee of nine be appointed to
cause the same to be erected, and when finished to be dedicated with
appropriate ceremonies.

The Committee having discharged the duty intrusted to them, it seems fitting and proper at this time to give you a brief account of their doings, and of the motives which have actuated them in this sad but pleasant undertaking.

In April, 1869, the Committee met for the first time at the residence of Mr. E. Waters Burr; and, after organizing and choosing Mr. Burr as chairman, we invited Mr. John M. Corbett as our secretary, which he cheerfully accepted, and the duty he has faithfully performed.

Two questions naturally came before this meeting, viz., what shall be the design of the Monument? and, second, where shall it be located? I need not go into particulars in regard to the labor spent to procure a suitable design: suffice it to say, that the Committee contracted with Mr. F. J. Fuller of Quincy, to build and erect just such a monument as you see before you to-day; and it is for you, citizens of Hingham, to decide whether or not the Committee have met your expectations. Let me say, however, that the Committee have given it as *their* opinion that the work is done in a neat and workmanlike manner, and reflects great credit upon the character and capacity of the workman and the contractor.

In locating this Monument, it is not to be supposed the Committee have met the expectations of you all. I think the Town never contemplated a union of feeling when they committed the whole subject to the hands of a committee, not only to erect, but to locate the Monument. The Committee visited various localities which had been suggested as suitable places to erect a Monument; but at last, after much deliberation, they decided unanimously that this was the most fitting and proper place the Town afforded for the location. It is certainly true that this spot has more than a common interest to all the citizens of Hingham. Here lie the remains of some of the first settlers. A monument to their memory was erected by the Town some years ago. Here on these grounds lie two distinguished patriots, — one of the revolution of 1775, the other of 1861. One fought to break the British yoke; the other to break the yoke in our own country. We love to look at the marble slab that records the death of Major-Gen. Benjamin Lincoln, a great and good man, and one that served his country in an hour of peril and distress.

We trust the day is not far distant when the lovers of impartial liberty will erect a monument to the memory of that other good and great man, John A. Andrew, who fell a sacrifice to the tyranny in our own country.

I am told there are sixteen of the number of those whose names are on the Monument who lie interred in this place, two at Liberty Plain, two at

South Hingham, three at Centre Hingham, and five at Fort Hill. Most of the others lie in unknown graves upon Southern soil. What more fitting place, then, than this to erect a public Monument? Surely you would not consecrate your play-ground for an object so painful and sad.

In this quiet retreat, away from the noise of the street, with the bay so finely in view, truly this place is one of rare beauty and fitness. In standing on this spot the other day, I could not help thinking of the account in Maccabees, of Simon building a monument on the sepulchre of his father and his brethren who were slain by their enemy, Tryphon. On this monument were ships carved, that they might be seen of all that sail on the sea.

The practice of adorning the monuments of those slain in battle is nothing new, but was practised by the ancients to a much greater extent. The object was to inspire the living with resolution by commending the courage of the slain. We trust we have a higher and better purpose in view than to inspire merely physical courage and daring. It is gratitude for what they have done for us that moves our hearts to deeds of this kind.

I trust we have come here to-day with no other feeling than thankfulness that our feet now stand on that everlasting rock of liberty and peace.

Mr. Chairman of the Selectmen of Hingham, — This Monument we here dedicate to-day is cheerfully and trustingly committed to your charge, believing that the cause for which it was erected will forever be a guarantee that it will suffer no detriment from the idle and thoughtless, and that the ground will always be kept in such a condition that it will reflect honor to the Town, and to those who may come after us.

This deed, which I present to you from the Committee in behalf of the proprietors of the Cemetery, conveys a certain irregular lot of land, giving the boundaries thereof in full. It was certainly an act of generosity on the part of the proprietors in relinquishing so valuable a spot of land gratuitously for the erection of this Monument. You will see that provision has been made for keeping the lot forever in a neat and proper manner, without any expense to the town. But, should the Monument be destroyed or removed for any cause, the land reverts back to the corporation.

Henry Siders, Esq., chairman of the selectmen of Hingham, in behalf of the Town, received the Monument, and said, —

This gathering before me is a testimony of the general interest which this occasion has awakened. This large concourse of people, with faces glowing with sympathy and joy, proclaims that the *day*, the *place*, and the *occasion* have made a deep impression upon their hearts.

We are standing among the resting-places of many of the fathers and mothers of this great company. We are standing near the remains of the lamented Gov. Andrew. Blessed spot!

The object of the citizens of this ancient Town in erecting this Monument, is to show to the country their sense of the value and services of our fellow townsmen, who in our country's danger, at the firing of the *first* gun on Sumter, and at every call afterward, left their homes and families, and buckled on their armor, and marched forth to meet the foe. To those whose names are inscribed upon that tablet is this Monument erected; and long may it stand as a memorial to those brave men, who, in defending their country, sacrificed their lives!

And to you soldiers and sailors, who have been allowed to return to your friends, and whom we are happy to meet in this consecrated place to partake in the ceremony of dedicating this beautiful Monument, I extend a hearty welcome ; and may the same hand that led you through the late struggle be with you to the last!

Mr. CHAIRMAN OF THE MONUMENT COMMITTEE, — As Chairman of the Selectmen of this Town, I would say, in receiving this Monument from you, that we cherish every memorial of those brave men. We admire their courage in their country's dangerous hour. May this Monument stand after you and I and this great company shall have passed away! And may these young children learn the purpose of its erection from maternal lips!

Finally, I would say, may this country itself become one splendid monument, not of oppression and terror, but of wisdom, of peace, and of liberty, upon which the world may gaze with admiration forever!

At the conclusion of the remarks by Mr. Siders, the following original ode, written by a lady, and read by the president of the day, was sung by the audience to the tune, " Old Hundred."

> God of our noble sires that dared
>   A realm from tyrant hands to wrest !
> Who oft in danger's hour has spared
>   A land by threatening ills distressed, —
>
> To worthy sons thou didst intrust
>   This heritage of blood and tears,
> And childrens', with the fathers' dust,
>   Shall share the fame of future years.

They fought, they fell, for freedom's sake.
  Spring's sweetest flowers their graves shall strew,
And storied marbles long shall wake
  Within our hearts the grateful glow.

God of our country! in her cause
  Let every pulse beat true and high,
Strong to maintain her righteous laws,
  Strong, like her brave, for her to die!

The benediction, by Rev. M. P. Alderman, pastor of the Methodist Society, closed the exercises of the day.

The Monument is of Quincy granite. It rests upon a solid foundation, ten feet square by six feet deep, laid in regular courses of split stone and cement. The mottoes, mouldings, and embellishments upon it are skilfully wrought, and the general outline of the whole structure is neat and pleasing in appearance. The proportions are as follows : *Lower base*, eight feet nine inches square, by one foot five inches in height. *Plinth*, six feet eight inches square, by one foot five inches in height. *Upper base*, moulded, five feet eleven inches square, by one foot two inches in height. *Die*, four feet six inches square, by seven feet one inch in height. *Shaft*, two feet nine inches square at base, by nineteen feet in height. Whole height, thirty feet.

The die bears these inscriptions : —

7

[South Face.]

ERECTED BY THE TOWN.
—— 1870. ——

CAPT. EDWIN HUMPHREY.
LIEUT. NATHANIEL FRENCH, Jr.
SERGT. HENRY C. FRENCH.
" PETER OURISH.
CORP. JACOB GILKEY CUSHING.
" W. IRVING STODDAR.
" NELSON F. CORTHELL.
" WILLIAM BREEN.

PRIVATES.

DANIEL L. BEAL.
WILLIAM H. H. BEAL.
WILLIAM B. CUSHING.
JAMES T. CHURCHILL.
CHARLES E. FRENCH.
JOHN W. GARDNER.
JOHN Q. HERSEY.
BENJAMIN LINCOLN.
WILLIAM J. STOCKWELL.
DEMERICK STODDER.
ALBERT WILDER.

HONOR TO THE BRAVE.

[East Face.]

REST THROUGH LIBERTY.

MAJOR. BENJAMIN C. LINCOLN.
LIEUT. FRANCIS THOMAS.
" ELIJAH B. GILL, Jr.
SERGT. LEAVITT LINCOLN.

PRIVATES.

HORACE D. BURR.
THOMAS CHURCHILL.
ANDREW J. DAMON.
WILLIAM DUNBAR, Jr.
JAMES FITZGERALD.
MICHAEL FEE.
RICHARD J. FARRELL.
GARDNER JONES.
HENRY B. LIVINGSTONE.
JOHN S. NEAL.
EDWARD A. F. SPEAR.
DENNIS SCULLY.
JOSEPH SIMMONS.
THOMAS TINSLEY.
FRANK H. TILTON.

[North Face.]

EVER FAITHFUL.

LIEUT. GEORGE W. BIBBY.
SERGT. JAMES M. HASKELL.
    "   WILLIAM H. JONES, Jr.
    "   CHARLES S. MEADE.
    "   MICHAEL THOMPSON.
CORP. JEREMIAH J. CORCORAN.
    "   ALBERT S. HAYNES.
    "   HENRY F. MILLER.

PRIVATES.

GEORGE D. GARDNER.
WALLACE HUMPHREY.
WILLIAM H. JONES.
SEWALL PUGSLEY.
SAMUEL SPENCER.
HORACE L. STUDLEY.
THOMAS SPRAGUE.
ALVIN TOWER.
CHARLES E. WILDER.
HORATIO P. WILLARD.
DON PEDRO WILSON.

[West Face.]

FOR OUR COUNTRY.

CORP. CHARLES W. BLOSSOM.
  "   HIRAM W. HENDERSON.
  "   CHARLES D. KILBURN.

PRIVATES.

JAMES BALLENTINE.
JOHN B. CREASE.
PEREZ F. FEARING.
DANIEL D. HERSEY.
CHARLES H. MARSH.
DANIEL MURPHY.
JOHN L. MANUEL.
CONRAD P. YAEGER.
HOSEA O. BARNES.
SAMUEL M. LINCOLN.
HOLLIS HERSEY.
HIRAM NEWCOMB.
CALEB GILL.
ACT. MAS. COM. THOMAS ANDREWS.
ENSIGN. EDWARD W. HALCRO.
SEAMAN. GEORGE H. MERRITT.

FINAL REPORT OF THE MONUMENT COMMITTEE.

The following abstract of the Final Report of the Monument Committee to the Town, affords a full account of their proceedings, as well as of the magnitude and responsibility of the duty they performed.

The Committee to whom the whole subject of the erection of a monument was referred respectfully submit a full report of their doings to the Town, with such remarks and explanations as are deemed proper and necessary.

On entering upon this duty, the Committee felt the magnitude and responsibility of the undertaking they assumed; it being no temporary or transient work, to be changed or altered at any convenient time, but a lasting memorial of sufferings and sacrifices endured for a cause which has no parallel in the history of ancient or modern warfare.

The Town, in committing this subject to the judgment and discretion of the Committee, evinced a confidence which we trust the Committee duly appreciated in their desire to meet, as far as they were able, the wishes and expectations of the citizens.

In locating the Monument, we fully realized the various conflicting views held by the residents of the several sections of the Town, who were honestly and faithfully aiding by sympathy and co-operation in this most desirable work. It was, therefore, a subject of anxious solicitude that this branch of their duty should be entered upon with deliberation, and with a full knowledge of the different sites which had been suggested by persons interested in this memorial. Hence your Committee, on the afternoon of April 9, visited the various places which had been named as suitable and proper for the location of the Monument: and upon consultation, it was voted to refer the subject to the next meeting, deeming it wise to deliberate further before taking a final vote upon the subject.

At a subsequent meeting (at which all were present) held at the Town Hall, April 15, to further consider the subject of location, and also of a design suitable for the Monument, it was agreed unanimously to locate it on the grounds of the Hingham Cemetery; it being understood at the time, and afterwards agreed to, that the proprietors of that cemetery would cheerfully give to the Town a desirable lot of land for that purpose, with all the rights and privileges necessary for their convenience, and to forever keep the grounds in a neat and proper condition, without any expense to the Town.

The Committee, in giving their final and hearty approval to its being located in the Hingham Cemetery, perceived various and weighty reasons for so doing. There seemed to be but two places which could be obtained desirable for its location, — one on the Common at Hingham Centre, and the other at the Hingham Cemetery.

With regard to its location on the Common at Hingham Centre, different opinions appeared to prevail among those living in its immediate vicinity. Some strongly objected to its being placed there, for the reason that it would destroy its usefulness as a place for rural and pleasurable sports; others thought it the proper and only place, being the most central and the most desirable spot for its location. Your Committee did not believe it to be desirable to place the Monument where a considerable number of the inhabitants, living near by, strongly objected.

The Hingham Cemetery offered peculiar attractions as a place for the Monument to be erected. It was somewhat remote from the public gaze, and yet one to which visitors could retire without annoyance from the public travel. It was deemed that this would be in accordance with the taste and feelings of a majority of our citizens. This cemetery is emphatically one in which the whole people of Hingham are deeply interested to preserve and beautify. And it must ever remain so, as long as revolutionary heroes and defenders of the republic mingle their dust with those of their friends in this place.

Having at length, after much deliberation, decided upon the spot, the next step was to procure a design and issue proposals for building and setting the Monument. The Committee visited several monuments, and procured various designs or plans, which were duly examined; but the present design was thought the best, considering the sum of money the Town felt able and willing to spend in its erection.

At a meeting of the Committee, held April 15, a sub-committee was chosen to issue proposals, with plans and specifications for building and setting it. The Committee immediately entered upon their work; and at a meeting of the whole Committee, held June 8, responses to their proposals had been received from four gentlemen to build and set the Monument, according to the design and specifications issued. The gentlemen proposing to build the Monument were men of integrity and uprightness, and could be relied upon to do, in a faithful and workmanlike manner, whatever work they undertook. But the great disparity in the estimates of these gentlemen made it imperative on your Committee to accept of the proposal of Mr. F. J. Fuller of Quincy, as the builder, for the sum of five thousand dollars, the whole to be completed by the 15th of October. Mr. Fuller entered at once upon the work, but soon perceived the time was too limited, which induced him to ask of the Committee an extension to the 1st of November. This proposition was brought to the attention of the Committee at their meeting, Sept. 4; and they at once, in view of the lateness of the season, voted to extend the time to the first of May, the Committee being assured that some additions and improvements would be made if that time was allowed for its being finished.

We believe Mr. Fuller has acted honestly and conscientiously in the matter, and has given us a piece of work which is an honor to the Town, and one that reflects great credit upon himself and upon his fame as a skilful artisan.

It will be seen by reference to the vote of the Town, that they instructed the Committee to "cause the names of all the soldiers and sailors representing the Town who died or were slain during the rebellion, also those who in the service of other towns, but natives of Hingham, died in the service, to be engraved upon the Monument."

The Committee have endeavored to adhere strictly to the wishes of the Town in this regard, not only causing the names of all native born citizens to be inscribed upon the Monument, and also those representing the Town, but they felt confident of the public approval of their act in causing the names of all *residents* who served in the rebellion to be inscribed thereon. Nearly half of those who left Hingham for the war were residents, some of them for many years, and were surely entitled to that consideration and respect which we had proposed to bestow upon native born citizens. The vote of the town would seem to imply that the names of none were to be inscribed upon the Monument, except those "who died or were slain during the war."

There is a large class of those whose lives were sacrificed in the cause of the rebellion who lingered, some of them a long time, after the advent of peace. Though they died after the rebellion ended, they were martyrs to the cause of the Union, as well as those who died upon the field of battle. Your Committee did not hesitate to have the names of all such inscribed upon the Monument, firmly anticipating the Town's hearty approval of this seeming deviation from their instructions in this matter.

The Town directed, "Should the Committee deem it expedient, to have inscribed thereon the names of all natives of Hingham who died in the service of their country during any former war." The records, and even the families, of many of these soldiers have passed away in the march of time, making it impossible to obtain any thing like a reliable list of them. Your Committee, therefore, deemed it inexpedient to have the names of this class inscribed upon the Monument for the reason above stated.

The following contents were placed under the Monument by a vote of the Town, viz. : —

The names of the officers and members of the Lincoln Light Infantry who answered the first call for troops in April, 1861.

The names of all soldiers and sailors who represented the Town during the rebellion.

The names of the Committee chosen to cause the Monument to be erected.

The names of the citizens and children who have made donations for this object.

These have been engrossed on parchment by the Town clerk, Charles N. Marsh, Esq., and placed under the corner-stone of the Monument.

By a vote of the Committee passed May 9, 1870, the following docu-

THE MONUMENT.57

ments were added to the list, and all enclosed in a metallic box, and placed under the Monument : —

Reports of the Selectmen of the Town for the years 1868 and 1869.

Report of the Hingham Agricultural and Horticultural Society for the year 1869.

Copy of the Hingham Journal of June 10, 1870.

The name of the orator of the day; names of the chief marshal and his aids; names of the officers and members of Post No. 104 of the Grand Army of the Republic; name of the architect and builder of the Monument.

Copies of the seals of the Hingham National Bank; also those of the Hingham Institution for Savings, and the Hingham First Parish Society.

Specimens of silver and copper coins, fractional currency, revenue stamps, and postage stamps of the United States.

A piece of oak from the meeting-house of the First Parish.

A piece of hard pine, taken from one of the deck-planks of Minot's Ledge Light (destroyed in the gale of 1851).

Photographs of Children's Mission building, Boston.

Some wheat which was used at the laying of the corner-stone of Bunker Hill Monument, at the laying of the foundation-stone of the statue of Warren, the corner-stone of the Minot's Ledge Light-house, the corner-stone of the two monuments at Plymouth.

It was the intention of the Committee to have the whole work completed and dedicated some time in the month of May, but the unavoidable delay in the completion of the Monument rendered it impossible to do so. Consequently your Committee fixed upon the 17th of June, as a fitting and proper time; it being a day of historic fame in the annals of liberty and American Independence. The Monument on Bunker Hill tells of deeds and sacrifices for national and individual liberty. The Monument we have erected will tell alike of noble and generous deeds, sacrifices and privations, to perpetuate the blessings we inherited from those whose name and fame will ever be sacred to hearts wherever beating in the cause of human freedom.

Early in the summer of 1869, your Committee invited the Hon. Solomon Lincoln to address the citizens of Hingham at the dedication of the Monument. It was not the Committee alone whose voice was heard in this matter. The citizens, one and all, expressed a desire that Mr. Lincoln's services should be secured for that occasion, if not at too great a sacrifice to himself and others. The Committee corresponded with Mr. Lincoln several times, with a view to this object. Being active in sympathy and co-operation with the soldiers during the war, and also in the proposed testimonial to their services, he finally consented, although amid pressing daily duties and ill-health, to respond to the wishes of his fellow-citizens. We need not say that the address was listened to with the closest attention, and was expressive of the feelings and sentiments of those who heard it. We recommend that the Town take such measures to publish it, with a full account of the doings of the dedication, as in their minds the importance of the occasion demands.

8

Having performed the work intrusted to them, and seeing the Monument properly placed upon the grounds selected for that purpose, the chairman *pro tem.*, in behalf of the Committee, and in presence of the assembled citizens of Hingham and her guests from abroad, formally delivered it over to the authorities of the Town. The chairman of the selectmen responded in a few appropriate remarks, accepting the trust, and with other ceremonies the exercises of the day were brought to a close. The unfavorable state of the weather made the out-of-door exercises somewhat embarrassing, yet we believe they were generally of such a nature as to leave a deep and lasting impression upon the minds of all who were present.

Much credit is due the president of the day, for the able manner in which he presided at the dedication; and also the chief marshal and his assistants, for the ability shown in the discharge of so important a duty.

The Hingham Post should not be forgotten, affording as they did substantial aid to the Committee in furthering the objects of the dedication.

The Muses, also, which are usually evoked on such occasions, were not silent, as was evinced by many patriotic and soul-stirring pieces.

The singing, under the direction of Mr. E. B. Whitcomb, was conducted in a manner to reflect credit upon those who represent the musical portion of our Town.

The financial account of the Committee is as follows: Received from the citizens of Hingham, whose names have been engrossed on parchment and placed under the Monument, according to a vote of the Town, eight hundred and eighty-one dollars and forty-four cents. Six hundred and fifty-seven persons paid from one dollar to fifty; two hundred and sixty-four paid ten cents and upwards. This sum was considerably reduced by the expenses necessarily attending the erection of the Monument.

The Committee, desirous of dedicating the Monument in an appropriate and suitable manner, with such services as should be lasting and impressive, especially on the youth of this Town, found their funds inadequate to meet the expenses of the occasion. Several of our liberal and enterprising citizens cheerfully responded to the wants of the Committee, by placing in their hands the sum of six hundred and sixty-five dollars for the furtherance and completion of this object. The Hingham Post contributed seventy-five dollars towards the expenses of the dedication.

The whole sum received by the Committee, including the five thousand dollars received from the town for the Monument, was six thousand six hundred and twenty-one dollars and twenty-one cents.

The Committee paid Mr. F. J. Fuller of Quincy, for building and setting the Monument, five thousand dollars.

The expenses of the Committee before and for the dedication were fifteen hundred and eighty dollars and fifty-two cents, leaving a balance in the hands of the Treasurer, Mr. John Todd, of forty dollars and fifty-two cents, which sum has been given to the "Charity Fund" of Post 104 of the Grand Army of the Republic.

In concluding this somewhat lengthy and imperfect report of our doings, the Committee beg leave to say, that the utmost harmony has existed in their deliberations, and no feeling has prevailed other than one of disinterestedness and true devotion to the object for which they were chosen.

The Committee have held twenty-three meetings. They visited the work as it progressed, several times, with a view to perfecting every part; and while they do not claim perfection in their doings, they flatter themselves that the industry and perseverance they have manifested will entitle them to the charitable judgment of their fellow-citizens.

Respectfully submitted,

E. WATERS BURR,
AMASA WHITING,
JOHN K. CORTHELL,
JOHN TODD,
SAMUEL J. HENDERSON,
WILLIAM J. NELSON,
WILLIAM THOMAS,
ELIJAH SHUTE,
JOHN CUSHING.

HINGHAM, March 6, 1871.

CHAPTER II.

PROCEEDINGS OF TOWN AND CITIZENS' MEETINGS.

Relief for the Families of the Lincoln Light Infantry — Meetings held by the Ladies to make Garments for the Soldiers — Appropriation by the Town — Committees appointed — Public Reception of the Lincoln Light Infantry on their Return from Fortress Monroe — Aid to the Families of Volunteers — Bounty to Volunteers — Committee chosen to encourage Enlistments for Three Years — Increase of Bounty offered to Volunteers for Nine Months — Liberality of the Citizens — The Second Battle of Bull Run — The Ladies meet on Sunday to prepare Hospital Supplies — War-Meetings — Earnest Call for Enlistments — Companies of " Exempts " formed — Parade of the " Home Guards," and Address by Rev. Joseph Richardson — Appropriations for Town and State Aid — More War-Meetings — Letter from Gov. Andrew — Meetings of Citizens liable to Draft — Rallying Committee appointed — Citizens' Subscription — Individual Acts of Generosity — Recruiting Money to be refunded — Town Assistance in obtaining Recruits — The Great National Calamity — Meeting of Citizens — Expressions of Grief — Funeral Ceremonies.

THE facts presented in this chapter have been obtained from the Records of the Secretary, and Treasurer of the Citizens' Recruiting Committee; from private diaries, Town documents, and the columns of " The Hingham Journal."

April 19, 1861. — A meeting of the citizens of Hingham was held at the Town Hall for the purpose of devising measures for the relief of such families of members of the Lincoln Light Infantry as might need assistance during the absence of the company. The meeting was called to order by Capt. John Stephenson, who stated, that, in consequence of the sudden departure of the Lincoln Light Infantry for Fortress Monroe, a number of families in town were left without their usual means of support ; and in closing he gave the number of persons that would probably need assistance for the next three months.

Caleb Gill was chosen chairman of the meeting, and Henry C. Harding, secretary.

Remarks appropriate to the occasion were then made by Revs. Calvin Lincoln, E. Porter Dyer, and Jonathan Tilson ; and also by Luther Stephenson, Capt. Jairus B. Lincoln,

Isaac Barnes, Bela T. Sprague, Elijah Whiton, Robert W. Lincoln, and others. Subsequently a subscription was suggested ; and by the unanimous vote of those present, a committee, consisting of Messrs. John Todd, John Stephenson, and Joseph Jacob, was chosen to carry the same into effect. A paper was immediately circulated in the hall, from which was realized the sum of eight hundred dollars. The meeting was large and very enthusiastic.

Sunday, P.M., *April* 28. — A large number of ladies met at Masonic Hall, in Lincoln Building, for the purpose of making clothing to be sent to the members of the Lincoln Light Infantry at Fortress Monroe. Mrs. Solomon Lincoln acted as principal superintendent of the work, and under her direction it was completed in time for shipment by steamer "Cambridge." The labor of pressing and finishing was performed by Messrs. Lincoln Burr, John K. Corbett, John Todd, and Loring Jacob, who gratuitously proffered their valuable services for the occasion.

During the war, the ladies of the various sewing-circles held frequent meetings in the different sections of the town for the purpose of preparing comfortable raiment for our men in the service. These meetings were generally held at Loring, Torrent, Niagara, Union, Constitution, and Liberty Halls. But there were also other gatherings for this purpose at the residences of mothers, sisters, daughters, and friends who were unable to leave their homes ; and thus the good work found willing hands and patriotic hearts among the daughters as well as the sons of Hingham.

April 30. — At a Town-meeting, Charles W. Cushing, Esq., in the chair, it was

"*Voted*, That the Town appropriate $6,000, for the purpose of furnishing such supplies as may be wanted by the families of those who have been, or may be, called into the service of their country ; and that the money be expended under the direction of a committee of six, consisting of John Todd, David Cain, John Stephenson, Demerick Marble, Joseph Jacob, and Albert Whiting." Should more troops be called from this Town, the committee were instructed to furnish them with clothing and other necessaries.

July 10. 1861. — A citizens' meeting was held for the purpose of making arrangements for the reception of the Lincoln Light Infantry on their return from the seat of war. Col. Charles W. Seymour was chosen moderator, and Henry E. Hersey, Esq., secretary. Addresses by Melzar W. Clark, John Cushing, James S. Lewis, Esq., Luther Stephenson, Col. Seymour, and others were made ; and a committee was chosen to make the necessary arrangements for their reception.

COMMITTEE OF ARRANGEMENTS.

John Todd, John Stephenson, Joseph Jacob, William Fearing, 2d, David Cain, E. Waters Burr, Elijah L. Whiton, Daniel Bassett, David Leavitt, Demerick Marble, Abner L. Leavitt, John K. Corthell, John Cushing, David Cushing, jun., E. Barker Whitcomb, Charles W. Seymour, Henry E. Hersey, Joseph B. Thaxter, jun., Thomas F. Whiton, and Albert Whiting.

The *Marshals* appointed were, Albert Whiting, Seth C. Dunbar, Joseph Jacob, jun., Ezra Wilder, George Cushing, 2d, Solomon Lincoln, jun., Henry C. Harding, Charles Spring, William C. Lincoln, George Lincoln, jun., John D. Gates, Robert W. Lincoln, Charles W. Cushing, Erastus Whiton, Hiram Gardner, Ezra T. C. Stephenson, Joseph H. French, George H. French, Albert E. Thayer, Joseph A. Newhall, Benjamin Thomas, and Enos Loring.

Aids. — Daniel Bassett, David Cushing, jun., John K. Corthell, Edwin Wilder, 2d, and Thomas Stephenson.

July 18. — At a meeting of the Committee of Arrangements, it was decided to provide a collation at the Town Hall ; and the following ladies and gentlemen were chosen to carry the same into effect : viz., Mrs. Albert Whiting, Mrs. John Cushing, Mrs. E. Barker Whitcomb, Mrs. B. S. Hersey, Miss Elizabeth L. Cushing, Mrs. Lucy Sturtevant, Mrs. David R. Hersey, Mrs. William Thomas, Mrs. Thomas J. Leavitt, Mrs. John S. Souther, Mrs. E. Waters Burr, Miss Sally Thaxter, Mrs. Joseph A. Newhall, Mrs. Walton V. Meade, Miss Sarah L. Marsh, David Leavitt, David Cushing, jun., Daniel Bassett, Abner L. Leavitt, and Thomas F. Whiton.

Nov. 15, 1861. — At a meeting of the inhabitants of Hingham, in Town meeting assembled, Col. Charles W. Seymour in the chair, it was

"*Voted*, That the sum of three thousand dollars be raised in aid of the families of volunteers, and that the selectmen be authorized to apply the same as their judgment shall dictate."

March 3, 1862. — At a Town-meeting, the Committee previously chosen to direct the expenditures of money appropriated for aid to the families of volunteers, and for furnishing clothing and other necessaries to volunteers which might be called into service at a future time, reported that they had expended for Company I, Fourth Regiment M. V. M. (the Lincoln Light Infantry), for uniforms, under-clothing, caps, shoes, &c., $1331.27, and to volunteers in other companies $18.50.

July 5, 1862. — At a Town-meeting held this day, at four o'clock, P.M., Capt. John Stephenson moderator, it was

"*Voted*, To raise five thousand dollars for the payment of State aid to the families of volunteers enlisted in the service of the United States, and one thousand dollars as Town aid to volunteers and their families, the same to be appropriated under the direction of the selectmen.

July 11. — A large and enthusiastic meeting of the citizens of Hingham was held this Friday evening, at the Town Hall, in response to the call of the selectmen to take action in reference to furnishing the Town's quota of recruits as called for by the commander-in-chief. The following officers were chosen, viz.: President, LUTHER STEPHENSON; Vice-Presidents, EDWARD CAZNEAU, CALEB S. HUNT, DEMERICK MARBLE, JAMES S. LEWIS, CROCKER WILDER, and SETH SPRAGUE.

Charles N. Marsh was chosen Secretary, but, not being present, Henry C. Harding was chosen Secretary *pro tem*.

Animating and encouraging addresses were made by the presiding officer and other gentlemen, urging enlistments, and recommending that a liberal bounty be paid by the Town to volunteers, and offering to contribute generously, if need be, to prevent the necessity of a draft.

Voted, Unanimously, to recommend to the Town that an appropriation be made sufficient to pay a bounty of seventy-five dollars to each person who may volunteer to make up the quota of men required of this Town. It was also

Voted, That a committee of twelve be chosen to co-operate with the selectmen in procuring enlistments, and the following persons were chosen, viz.: Rev. Jonathan Tilson, Rev. J. L. Hatch, Edward Cazneau, Seth Sprague, Demerick Marble, Albert Whiting, Charles Sprague, Ezra Wilder, Elijah L. Whiton, George Hersey, jun., Andrew W. Gardner, Abner L. Beal, E. Barker Whitcomb, Edmund Hersey, Thomas Fee, and John Stephenson.

July 15. — Agreeably to a call issued by the committee chosen July 11, the citizens met at the Town Hall to consider the great and important question of the day, — the call for volunteers.

The meeting was called to order by Col. Cazneau, and organized by the choice of the following officers, viz.: President, Hon. Solomon Lincoln. Vice-Presidents, Jairus B Lincoln, George P. Hayward, Charles Siders, J. Sturgis Nye, William Whiton, Isaac Barnes, Robert W. Lincoln, Joseph B. Thaxter, jun., James S. Lewis, Joseph Ripley, Alfred Loring, George M. Soule, Luther Stephenson, Crocker Wilder, Charles W. Seymour, John Lincoln, James L. Gardner, Anson Nickerson, Orr F. Jerald, and Elijah Whiton. Secretaries, Charles N. Marsh, and Henry C. Harding.

The President, upon taking the chair, stated the object of the meeting, and urged upon all present the duty of responding promptly to the necessities and demands of the present crisis. He then called upon Revs. Calvin Lincoln, J. L. Hatch, Daniel Bowen, John E. Davenport, E. Porter Dyer, and Jonathan Tilson, who responded in short, patriotic, and pertinent addresses. E. S. Tobey, Esq., of Boston, being present, was also called upon; and, although not a citizen of Hingham, he offered to contribute, if necessity required, towards furnishing the means to induce young men to enlist.

On motion of George Hersey, jun., it was

Voted, To recommend to the Town, that a bounty of one hundred dollars be paid to each volunteer. The meeting then adjourned.

July 19. — At a Town meeting held this Saturday evening, Col. Cazneau was chosen moderator.

Voted, To pay volunteers who may be accepted, and mustered into the service of the United States, to the number of fifty-one, — that being the quota of this town, — a bounty of one hundred dollars each ; and the Town treasurer was authorized to hire money for the payment of the same.

The citizens' meeting, adjourned from Tuesday evening last, was held immediately after the Town-meeting. Col. Cazneau made the opening remarks ; and in the absence of Hon. Solomon Lincoln, the president, Luther Stephenson was called to the chair. Brief addresses were made by Caleb Gill, Caleb T. Bassett, Rev. Mr. Davenport, George Hersey, jun., Caleb Stodder, John Cushing, and the presiding officer. Several young men then came forward and signed the enlistment papers. On motion of Col. Cazneau, the meeting adjourned to meet at the same place the Tuesday following.

July 22. — An adjourned war-meeting was held at the Town Hall, for the purpose of obtaining volunteers. Luther Stephenson presided. Col. Cazneau spoke of the services rendered by Capts. Stephenson and Humphrey, of Lieuts. French, Whiton, and Bouvé, and also referred to the noble young men who had gone from this Town as privates and in other capacities. Revs. Messrs. Hatch, Tilson, Davenport, and Dyer followed. The meeting was further addressed by Capt. John Stephenson, Melzar W. Clark, and Capt. Peter N. Sprague.

On motion of Col. Cazneau, Capt. John Stephenson, and Peter Hersey, jun., were chosen to nominate a committee of ladies, whose duty it shall be to call the next meeting at such time and place as they may decide upon, with authority to procure speakers, music, and whatever else may be wanted to insure a grand gathering. The ladies chosen upon this committee were, Mrs. Jairus B. Lincoln, Mrs. Jonathan Tilson, Mrs. E. Porter Dyer, Mrs. J. L. Hatch, Mrs. Alfred Loring, Mrs. Job S. Whiton, Mrs. Charles W. Cushing, Mrs. John Lincoln, Mrs. David R. Hersey, Mrs. Alfred A. Rouel, and Mrs. John E. Davenport. The meeting then adjourned to meet at the call of the committee of ladies.

Aug. 6, 1862. — A meeting appointed by the ladies of Hingham, to encourage the enlistment of volunteers to fill the quota of the Town, was held at the Town Hall. It was largely attended.

Capt. Jairus B. Lincoln called the meeting to order, and read the names of the persons selected for president, vice-presidents, and secretaries.

Luther Stephenson, having been mentioned as president, took the chair. After a few complimentary words to the ladies, he called upon Rev. E. Porter Dyer, who responded in his usual happy manner. Mr. Southworth, of Scituate, followed.

Edward S. Tobey, Esq., of Boston, also gave an earnest and forcible address.

Rev. E. Porter Dyer then read an original poem. Rev. Calvin Lincoln and others followed ; after which several recruits came forward, and signed the enlistment papers. The meeting was then adjourned to the next evening.

Aug. 7. — At a citizens' meeting held in the Town Hall, it was " *Voted*, To recommend the Town to increase the amount of bounty to volunteers from one hundred, to two hundred dollars."

Aug. 11. — At a meeting of the citizens, it was " *Voted* to request the selectmen to offer a bounty of one hundred dollars to all volunteers who will enlist upon the second call, the same being for nine months' service." This meeting was enlivened by the fine performances of the Weymouth Band, who volunteered their services for the occasion.

Aug. 15. — At a Town-meeting, Luther Stephenson being moderator, it was

" *Voted*, To give one hundred dollars in addition to the sum already authorized to be paid to volunteers for three years, for the first quota.

Aug. 27. — A meeting of the citizens was held to aid in the enlistment of volunteers for nine months. Addresses were made by several individuals present ; and it was " *Voted*, To recommend the Town to pay fifty dollars additional bounty," thereby raising the amount to one hundred and fifty dollars for nine months' men.

Aug. 29. — A Town-meeting was held this evening, to fix upon the amount of bounty to be offered for recruits, who will volunteer upon the quota of Hingham for nine months.

Crocker Wilder, Esq., was chosen moderator; and it was " *Voted*, To add fifty dollars to the one hundred recommended at the meeting held on the 15th inst. ;" making, in all, a bounty of one hundred and fifty dollars for each volunteer upon the second quota.

A citizens' war-meeting was held immediately after the Town-meeting last mentioned. Luther Stephenson occupied the chair, and Henry C. Harding acted as secretary.

After vocal music by the Whitcomb Family, Rev. Mr. Round of Boston was introduced, and, being himself a recruit, was able to enforce his eloquence by saying to the young men about him, *Come!* Rev. Mr. Hinckley, Messrs. George Hersey, jun., and Caleb T. Bassett, followed. Rev. E. Porter Dyer, being the next speaker, took the opportunity to introduce Mr. E. Waters Burr, who made a brief but highly patriotic speech ; and in closing, he generously pledged himself to give ten dollars each to the ten men who would first come forward and enlist. Mr. George P. Hayward also offered to pay the family of the first married man who would enlist, if he should be accepted, the sum of twelve dollars the first month, and eleven dollars for each of the subsequent eight months. Another gentleman would give five dollars each to the first five men who would enlist that night. These generous offers were received with hearty and prolonged applause, and several names were added to the list of recruits.

Aug. 31. — News of the second battle of Bull Run, and of the immediate need of hospital supplies at Washington, D.C., having reached town by telegraph this Sunday morning, the usual afternoon service at the churches was generally omitted, in order that the ladies of the different societies might devote their time either to making hospital garments or in preparing bandages, lint, &c., for the wounded soldiers.

The next day (Monday) several packages, containing the necessary articles for the wounded, were sent to the Sanitary Rooms in Boston by the ladies of Hingham, to be forwarded to Washington.

Sept. 8, 1862. — A very full meeting of the citizens was held at the Town Hall this Monday evening. Col. Cazneau, chairman of the board of selectmen, presided. After the opening remarks, Capt. Rounds of Boston was introduced. Rev. Mr. Hatch followed. Edward S. Tobey, Esq., then eloquently appealed to the young men to come forward and enroll their names.

Luther Stephenson, Quincy Bicknell, and Col. Seymour made earnest and stirring addresses, after which the meeting was adjourned.

Sept. 12, 1862. — An adjourned meeting of the citizens was held at the Town Hall, with Col. Cazneau in the chair, and Israel Whitcomb as secretary.

The following persons were chosen a committee to canvass their respective districts for the purpose of obtaining the signatures of exempts from military duty, and organizing the same into a company or companies viz. ; Joseph Jacob and Seth Sprague in the south school district ; John Stephenson and John Leavitt in the middle district ; John Todd and Elijah L. Whiton in the north district ; Quincy Bicknell, Caleb Gill, and Edward Cazneau in the west district. Appropriate addresses were made by Col. Cazneau, Quincy Bicknell, Caleb Gill, Luther Stephenson, Rev. E. Porter Dyer, Col. Seymour, and others.

Subsequently two companies of " Home Guards," numbering in all about one hundred men, paraded as a battalion the 22d of October, and, after marching through the principal streets of the Town, partook of a collation at Loring Hall. Rev. Joseph Richardson, the senior pastor of the First Parish, and others, addressed the assembly. A second parade occurred on the afternoon of the annual election, Nov. 4.

Dec. 2, 1862. — At a Town-meeting held this evening, Quincy Bicknell, Esq., in the chair, it was

" *Voted,* To authorize the selectmen, should they deem it expedient, to increase the bounty from one hundred and fifty dollars to a sum not exceeding two hundred dollars, for volunteers to fill up the quota of the Town."

" *Voted,* That the use of the Centre School House of the west district be granted to the ' Home Guard ' for drill purposes, subject to the regulation and control of the School Committee."

March 9, 1863.— A Town-meeting was held, with Col. Charles W. Seymour as moderator.

" *Voted,* That the sum of $9,000 be placed at the disposal of the selectmen for the payment of State aid to the families of volunteers, if needed."

"*Voted*, That the sum of $800 be raised by taxation as Town aid to the families of volunteers, if needed, to be expended under the direction of the selectmen."

April 6, 1863. — Town-meeting ; Caleb Gill, Esq., moderator.

" *Voted*, That the Town treasurer be authorized, under the direction of the selectmen, to hire such sums of money as may be required to carry into effect the 1st and 2d sections of chapter 79 of the Acts of the General Court for 1863, relating to the paying of State aid to the families of deceased and disabled volunteers."

Aug. 14, 1863. — At a Town-meeting held this evening, James S. Lewis, Esq., moderator, it was " *Voted*, That the sum of $15,000, for State and Town aid, be raised by the Town, and be and hereby is appropriated, under the direction of the selectmen, for the aid of the wives, children, parents, brothers, and sisters of those inhabitants of the Town who may be drafted into the army of the United States, and serve therein, under the law passed by Congress entitled " An Act enrolling and calling out the National Forces, and for other purposes," approved March 3, 1863, provided no more than $200 shall be paid to or for any one person, in addition to State aid."

"*Voted*, That the treasurer be authorized to hire the sum of $15,000, to carry the above vote into effect, under the direction of the selectmen, should they deem it necessary."

Nov. 3, 1863. — Town-meeting. The subject of allowing to David H. Champlin the aid granted to drafted men according to a vote of the Town, Aug. 14, 1863, was referred to a committee consisting of Samuel L. Fearing, John Todd, and Melzar W. Clark, to report thereon at a future meeting.

Dec. 7, 1863. — At a war-meeting of the citizens of Hingham, held at the Town Hall this Monday evening, Edward Cazneau was chosen president, and Charles N. Marsh, secretary.

The meeting was addressed by Rev. Calvin Lincoln, Rev. Joshua Young, Luther Stephenson, Col. Charles W. Seymour, and the chairman.

Dec. 11. — An adjourned meeting of the citizens of Hingham

was held this Friday evening, to aid in filling up the quota of
the town.   Col. Cazneau presided, and Charles N. Marsh offici-
ated as secretary.   Addresses were made by Col. Seymour, Rev.
E. Porter Dyer, Messrs. Benjamin Thomas, Luther Stephenson,
Caleb T. Bassett, and Revs. Messrs. Lincoln and Hatch.   The
secretary then read a communication from Rev. Joshua Young,
which among other good things contained a sentiment relating
to " Our Armies," and one also to " Old Hingham."

The following letter was received from Gov. Andrew, in reply
to an invitation to be present and address the meeting : —

BOSTON, Dec. 1, 1863.

EDWARD CAZNEAU, ESQ., *Chairman of Selectmen, Hingham.*

Dear Sir, — In reply to yours of Nov. 28, I can only say that it is impossible for me to attend the meeting at Hingham on Monday, Dec. 7, as you
request, although I need not assure you what pleasure it would give me
to meet my friends and neighbors, or to aid in the labor of recruiting there,
if it were in my power to do so.

Very respectfully your friend and servant,

JOHN A. ANDREW, *Governor of Massachusetts.*

This meeting was enlivened by the excellent performances of
the Weymouth Band.   On motion of Capt. John Stephenson, a
rallying committee was chosen to aid the selectmen in obtaining
recruits.   The names of the committee were as follows :
Crocker Wilder, Amasa Whiting, Alfred Loring, Ezra Wilder,
John Cushing, Andrew W. Dunbar, John Stephenson, David
Leavitt, John K. Corthell, Fearing Burr, jun., J. Sturgis Nye,
Ezra Stephenson, George Hersey, jun., Joseph Ripley, Joseph B.
Thaxter, jun., Charles W. Seymour, Benjamin Thomas, William
J. Nelson, Isaac Barnes, and Israel Whitcomb.

Dec. 14. — At a meeting of the citizens liable to draft, George
Hersey, jun., was chosen chairman, and Israel Whitcomb,
secretary.

" *Voted,* That a subscription paper be circulated among those
persons present who are liable to a draft, to ascertain the amount
of money that can be raised towards securing recruits for the
quota of Hingham under the last call of the President of the
United States.

" *Voted,* To choose a committee of twelve to solicit subscriptions from persons who are liable to draft, and not present at this meeting. The committee chosen were as follows: Amasa Whiting, George Dunbar, and William Cushing, of the South Ward. Henry Stephenson, Henry Merritt, jun., and Joseph T. Sprague, of the Middle Ward. Charles N. Marsh, Samuel M. Beal, and Isaac Gardner, of the North Ward; and Edmund Hersey, 2d, William F. Harden, and Isaac W. Our, of the west district of the North Ward.

"*Voted*, To choose a committee of twenty-five, to solicit subscriptions from the community at large, for the purpose of filling the quota of Hingham under the call of the President of the United States, dated Oct. 17, 1863." The persons chosen upon this committee were: Amasa Whiting, Albert B. Loring, Alfred Loring, William C. Wilder, Ezra Wilder, E. Barker Whitcomb, Samuel Lincoln, Israel Whitcomb, Joseph T. Sprague, Charles B. Boyd, David Leavitt, John Stephenson, John B. Lewis, Samuel L. Beal, J. Sturgis Nye, William J. Nelson, Henry C. Harding, Andrew J. Gardner, George Hersey, jun., Gridley F. Hersey, George Lincoln, jun., Henry Stephenson, Joseph Ripley, Caleb S. Hersey, and George Tilden.

David Cushing, jun., was added to the committee at large, to solicit subscriptions from Hingham persons who were residing in Boston.

Adjourned to meet the next evening.

Dec. 15. — At a meeting of the citizens liable to draft, held this evening, Col. Seymour was chosen treasurer. "*Voted*, That the whole matter of recruiting for the quota of the Town be recommitted to the former committee of twenty, chosen by the citizens of Hingham."

Dec. 30. — A meeting of the citizens of Hingham liable to draft, and of others interested in filling the quota of the Town, was held this evening. Crocker Wilder, Esq., was chosen chairman, and Israel Whitcomb, secretary.

Col. Seymour, treasurer, reported that he had received from the soliciting committee the sum of $4,685, and had paid to persons for recruiting purposes $1,391.34; leaving a balance on hand of $3,293.66.

"*Voted*, To hold a war meeting at this place to-morrow afternoon, commencing at two o'clock, and that the citizens be requested to close their places of business at twelve o'clock ; also to cause the bells on the meeting-houses to be rung half an hour before the meeting.

"*Voted*, That all citizens present be requested to act as a rallying committee to persuade persons who are liable to draft to attend the meeting to-morrow afternoon." Adjourned.

Dec. 31. — A meeting of the citizens of Hingham was held this Thursday afternoon, with Crocker Wilder, Esq., as chairman, and Israel Whitcomb, secretary. After passing several unimportant votes, it was adjourned to meet at seven o'clock, P.M.

At the evening meeting, Luther Stephenson was chosen to preside, in the absence of Mr. Wilder. Eloquent remarks were made by the chairman, by Revs. E. Porter Dyer, and J. L. Hatch, Col. Seymour, Isaac Barnes, and others. Subsequently it was " *Voted*, To dissolve, with three cheers for the Union."

Feb. 12, 1864. — At a meeting of the citizens of Hingham, held at the Town Hall this Friday evening, Crocker Wilder, Esq., was chosen chairman, and Israel Whitcomb, secretary.

Col. Seymour, treasurer of the Citizens' Recruiting Committee, presented his final report, which was read and accepted.

SUMMARY OF THE REPORT.

RECEIVED OF THE SOLICITING COMMITTEE, $6,093.50.

Of this amount,	one person gave	$250.00	$250.00
"	one person gave	150.00	150.00
"	five persons gave	100.00	500.00
"	one person gave	60.00	60.00
"	ten persons gave	50.00	500.00
"	three persons gave	40.00	120.00
"	two persons gave	30.00	60.00
"	forty-two persons gave	25.00	1,050.00
"	twenty-one persons gave	20.00	420.00
"	twenty-five persons gave	15.00	375.00
"	one person gave	13.00	13.00
"	one hundred and thirty-two persons gave	10.00	1,320.00
"	three persons gave	8.00	24.00
"	one person gave	7.00	7.00
"	two hundred and twenty-one persons gave	5.00	1,105.00
"	twenty-five persons gave	3.00	75.00
"	one person gave	2.50	2.50
"	twenty-seven persons gave	2.00	54.00
"	eight persons gave	1.00	8.00

$6,093.50

This amount does not include any portion of the two thousand dollars previously offered by Hon. Albert Fearing, or of the generous gift of five hundred dollars by Edward S. Tobey, Esq., of Boston. Neither does it take in the proceeds of any fair or entertainment, or of the several collections taken up at war meetings prior to the appointment of the Citizens' Recruiting Committee.

The credit side of the report shows in detail the amount paid for thirty-eight new recruits, and for twenty-six veterans who re-enlisted upon the quota of Hingham, with the necessary expenses of recruiting the same.

The meeting was adjourned to Monday evening, 15th inst.

Feb. 15. — An adjourned meeting of the citizens liable to draft, and of others interested in filling the quota of the Town, was held at the Town Hall. Col. Seymour gave some additional information relating to the receipts and expenditures of the Citizens' Recruiting Committee ; after which the thanks of the meeting were presented to the Committee of Twenty for their services in filling the quota of the Town under the call of Oct. 17, 1863.

" *Voted,* To choose a recruiting committee of seven ; and the following persons were appointed, viz. : Israel Whitcomb, David Leavitt, Edmund Hersey, 2d, Elijah Shute, Jason W. Whitney, William Fearing, 2d, and Charles N. Marsh."

" *Voted,* To choose a soliciting committee of thirty to canvass the Town for subscriptions to aid in securing recruits for the quota of Hingham under the call of the President of the United States, dated Feb. 1, 1864."

March 7, 1864. — At the annual Town-meeting, James S. Lewis, Esq., moderator, it was

" *Voted* That eight hundred dollars of the money raised for Town expenses be appropriated, under the direction of the selectmen, for Town aid to the families of volunteers.

" *Voted,* That the treasurer be authorized to hire eight thousand dollars for paying State aid, under the direction of the selectmen.

" *Voted,* To accept the minority report of the committee to whom was referred the subject of allowing David H. Champlin the aid granted to drafted men." The report recommends that he receive the same benefits granted to drafted men.

" *Voted*, To choose a committee consisting of Seth Sprague, Demerick Marble,George Hersey, jun., James S. Lewis, and Caleb Gill, to audit the accounts of the recruiting officer, agreeably to order No. 32, from the Governor of the Commonwealth.

" *Voted*, That the treasurer be authorized to hire the sum of one thousand dollars to defray the expenses of recruiting in anticipation of premiums for volunteers enlisted under said order" (32).

April 11, 1864. — At a Town-meeting held this Monday afternoon, James S. Lewis, Esq., in the chair, it was

" *Voted*, That the Town refund the money contributed by individuals, and applied for the purpose of procuring its proportion of the quota of volunteers in the military service called for from the Commonwealth, under the orders of the President of the United States, dated Oct. 17, 1863, and Feb. 1, 1864, so far as it can be done legally, and that no part of said money shall be refunded before the first day of August next.

" *Voted*, To raise eight thousand dollars for the purpose of carrying the above vote into effect, provided such amount shall be required.

" *Voted*, That the treasurer be authorized, with the advice of the selectmen, to hire a sufficient sum of money for the purpose of procuring the Town's proportion of the quota of volunteers as may be called for from the Commonwealth, under any order or call from the President of the United States, issued after the first day of March, 1864, provided such sum shall not exceed one hundred and twenty-five dollars to each volunteer obtained under such call or order."

As an expression of the citizens of this Town, it was

" *Voted*, That the selectmen be authorized to take action in procuring and interring the bodies of officers and soldiers belonging to this Town that may hereafter die in the service.

" *Voted*, That the selectmen be requested to petition the Legislature, that authority be granted to raise money for defraying the expenses of obtaining and interring the bodies of such officers and soldiers belonging to this Town as may die in the service during the rebellion."

June, 17. — Omitting several citizens' meetings which were unimportant in their results, an adjourned war-meeting was held this evening.

" *Voted*, That the enrolled men of this Town be requested to pay the sum of fifteen dollars each, for the purpose of securing a sufficient number of recruits to fill the quota of the Town in anticipation of a call by the President of the United States for three hundred thousand men.

" *Voted*, To appoint a committee to solicit subscriptions from persons liable to draft and from citizens generally. The committee were also to take into consideration the correcting of the enrolment by reporting all cases of permanent disability, &c."

The following persons were chosen a committee to solicit subscriptions, viz. : —

North Ward. — Andrew J. Gardner, Isaac Gardner, Elijah D. Tilden, Albert E. Thayer, Thomas J. Hersey, Edmund Hersey, 2d, and George Lincoln, jun.

Middle Ward. — Demerick Marble, Elisha Burr, Joseph T. Sprague, George Bailey, Loring Jacob, De Witt C. Bates, and Reuben H. Corthell.

South Ward. — Elpalet L. Cushing, William Cushing, Joshua D. Turner, William C. Wilder, Elijah Shute, Edmund Hobart, Edwin Tower, and Joseph H. Wilder.

July 30. — A meeting of the citizens liable to draft was held for the purpose of making arrangements to fill the quota of the Town under the last call. By vote of those present De Witt C. Bates was chosen to solicit subscriptions.

Aug. 8, 1864. — At a meeting of the citizens liable to draft, and others interested in filling the quota, a subscription paper was circulated from which was realized upwards of one thousand dollars. Several gentlemen present expressed their intention of procuring substitutes, and it was voted to allow all such persons the sum of $250 from the recruiting fund. Up to this time the committee appointed to solicit subscriptions reported that they had succeeded in raising between five and six thousand dollars towards obtaining recruits.

Aug. 13. — A citizens' meeting was held for the purpose of obtaining home recruits for coast defence for one year's service.

Aug. 20. — An adjourned meeting of those liable to draft, and

of all others interested in filling the quota of the Town, was held
this evening. It was announced as "*the last meeting* (unless
more encouragement be given) that will be held before the
draft." A statement was made showing the number of men
required to fill the quota of the Town. To meet this demand, a
deposit had been made with the State to secure a proportion
of the number required. Eight substitutes, also, had recently
been furnished by persons who were liable to be drafted, and
fifteen or more credits were expected from enlistments in the navy.

Dec. 29, 1864. — In accordance with an Act of the Massachusetts Legislature concerning the Militia, approved May 14,
1864, a meeting of the citizens of Hingham liable to military
duty was held at the Town Hall for the purpose of forming a
company and choosing a captain. Henry Jones was unanimously elected to the office, but the Act was shortly afterwards
suspended, and the company never met for parade or military
drill. Capt. Jones was well qualified for the honor conferred
upon him, having seen three years of active service *at the front*
with the Eighteenth Regiment M.V.I., of the Army of the Potomac.

March 6, 1865. — At the annual Town-meeting, James S.
Lewis, Esq., moderator, it was voted that the treasurer be authorized to hire $9,000, with the approbation of the selectmen,
for the payment of State aid, and that $800 of the amount raised
for Town expenses be appropriated, under the direction of the
selectmen, for Town aid.

The Town treasurer, with the advice of the selectmen, was
also authorized to hire a sufficient sum of money for procuring
the Town's proportion of volunteers called for from the Commonwealth, or under any call or order from the President of the
United States, issued after the first day of March, 1865, provided
such sum shall not exceed one hundred and twenty-five dollars
to each recruit obtained under such call or order.

"*Voted*, That $1,000 of the money raised for Town expenses be
appropriated for recruiting purposes if necessary."

THE GREAT NATIONAL CALAMITY.

April 17, 1865. — Monday evening, a meeting of the inhabitants of Hingham was held at the request of the selectmen, "to decide what action the Town will take in relation to the great national calamity. The meeting was called to order by Demerick Marble, Esq., chairman of the board of selectmen, who read the address issued by the acting secretary of state to the people of the United States, inviting them to meet in their respective places of worship at the hour of the funeral services of the late lamented Chief Magistrate for the purpose of solemnizing the occasion with appropriate ceremonies."

James S. Lewis, Esq., was chairman of the meeting, and De Witt C. Bates, secretary.

Rev. Calvin Lincoln addressed the throne of grace in words befitting the occasion.

Remarks by Rev. Jonathan Tilson, Rev. Calvin Lincoln, Rev. Joshua Young, Messrs. Bela T. Sprague, Luther Stephenson, and Edwin Wilder, 2d, followed.

The meeting voted unanimously to adopt measures for a proper observance of the day ; and a committee, consisting of Messrs. Edwin Wilder, 2d, Demerick Marble, John Stephenson, Joseph Jacob, jun., John Cushing, and Charles N. Marsh, was chosen to report a plan of action for the consideration of those present.

The committee subsequently reported, recommending that on Wednesday, in conformity with the request of the secretary of state, a union service be held in the meeting-house of the First Parish ; and that a committee of nine be chosen to make the necessary arrangements. The report was adopted, and the following persons were appointed a committee ; viz., John Todd, Joseph Ripley, Charles N. Marsh, John Stephenson, David Leavitt, John K. Corthell, Andrew W. Dunbar, Elijah Shute, and Ezra Wilder. The selectmen were added to the committee.

THE FUNERAL CEREMONIES

took place at the old meeting-house, Wednesday, April 19, commencing at 12 o'clock, M. The exercises consisted of prayer, reading of the Scriptures, singing by the choir, and a funeral discourse by Rev. Mr. Young of the Third Parish. All the clergymen of the Town took part in the religious exercises. The church was appropriately draped in mourning, and pews and aisles were filled to overflowing. The galleries were reserved for the scholars of the public schools.

At the conclusion of the services in the church, a procession was formed, consisting of the scholars, followed by a funeral car, and a large number of the inhabitants of the Town. The procession moved first to Fountain Square, and thence to the cemetery in the rear of the church, where, near the spot on which the Soldiers' and Sailors' Monument has since been erected, the last sad duties of the hour were performed, including appropriate vocal music by the children, and remarks by the clergymen and others.

The day was mild and pleasant. In the different parts of the Town, flags and bunting were displayed at half-mast, and the public buildings, as well as many private residences, were draped with the emblems of mourning. Bells were tolled at morning, noon, and night, and minute-guns were fired from the hill in the rear of the north school-house at the time of the services. It was a solemn day, and one long to be remembered. Never before were the people called upon to grieve for one on whom they placed greater reliance as a statesman, or for one whom they loved and respected more than Abraham Lincoln.

CHAPTER III.

DRAFTS AND SUBSTITUTES.

The Drafts — Act of Congress regulating Enrolments — Number of Persons enrolled in Hingham — The Draft at Taunton — List of the Drafted — List of Persons exempted by Payment of Commutation — Copy of Notice to Persons drafted — Copy of Receipt for Money paid for Commutation — Copy of Certificate of Non-Liability given by Board of Enrolment — Opening of Recruiting-Office — Re-enlistments from the Thirty-second Regiment — Substitutes.

DURING the Civil War four drafts were appointed by the national government, and enforced throughout the loyal States as follow, viz. : —

First in July, 1863.[1] This draft was for *one-fifth* of the whole number registered under the *first class*.

The second draft took place in April, 1864, for deficiencies under calls for seven hundred thousand men.

The third, in September, 1864, for deficiencies under the call of July 18, 1864, for five hundred thousand men.

The fourth, in February, 1865, for deficiencies under the call of Dec. 19, 1864, for three hundred thousand men.

Though admitted to be equitable and just, yet in no section of the country did the "draft" find hearty sympathy or approval in the popular mind. The prevailing love of freedom forbade a coerced or unwilling service ; and so averse was public sentiment to acts of conscription, that the most determined and persevering efforts were everywhere made to avoid the draft, and fill the quotas required by voluntary enlistments. To a large extent, these efforts were crowned with the most gratifying suc-

---

[1] Congress had passed an Act requiring that enrolments be made in two classes; the first embracing those liable to do military duty between twenty years and thirty-five years of age ; and all unmarried persons liable to military service over thirty-five years and under forty-five years of age.

The second class included all married persons liable to do military duty between thirty-five years and forty-five years of age.

cess, and the proportion of men forced into the ranks through the unavoidable decree of the draft must have been small indeed.

In order to the proper apportionment of the number of men to be furnished, an enrolment was made of all male citizens in the State, in accordance with the Act of Congress before mentioned. Charles N. Marsh, Esq., was appointed Enrolling Officer for the town of Hingham, and entered upon his work in June, 1863.

The result was as follows, viz. :—

Whole number of persons enrolled, 679.

First class, including all between the ages of twenty and thirty-five, and all single men and widowers from thirty-five to forty-five years of age, 341.

Second class, including all married men from thirty-five to forty-five years of age, 175.

Third class, including those now in the service or discharged, 163.

Sixteen claimed residence in other cities or towns, and sixty-three claimed exemption as aliens.

With a single exception, all the quotas of Hingham were filled by voluntary enlistments. The draft for a deficiency was made at Taunton, July 20, 1863, when one hundred names, enrolled under the first class, were drawn as follow, viz. : —

Reuben Sprague,
William Fearing, 2d,
John C. Fearing,
Morallus Lane,
Ebenezer C. Ripley,
Alanson Crosby,
Charles C. Hersey,
Francis H. Stowell,
Samuel Lemon,
Caleb C. White,
Don Pedro Wilson,
Hosea B. Hersey,
William K. Gould,
Benjamin Thomas,
George Fox,

Caleb Marsh,
John F. Welsh,
John O. Remington,
Ambrose Leach,
Josiah Q. Gardner,
Smith Richardson,
Atkinson Nye,
Thomas McGlone,
John Lemon,
Edwin W. Beal,
Andrew C. Cushing,
Edward Pyne,
Edward O. Farmer,
Joseph H. Litchfield,
Thomas Stephenson,

Henry W. Ripley,
Levi Hersey,
George Hobart,
William C. Miller,
John Hines,
Ebenezer C. Hobart,
George Lang,
Patrick Fee,
George R. Ripley,
Thomas Bacezil,
Leonard Birch,
Albert T. Hutchins,
Hiram T. Howard,
George W. Young,
Warren Remington,
Timothy Shea,
William H. Starr,
Leavitt Sprague, 2d,
Caleb F. Gardner,
David Fearing, jun.,
Edwin Wilder, 2d,
John White,
Joseph Curtis,
Edward S. Cushing,
William Coughlan,
Henry Hobart,*
Theophilus Cushing, jun.,
Edmund Hersey, 2d,
David Thaxter,
Joshua Jacob, jun.,
Charles Stephenson,
Joseph H. Lincoln,
William C. Wilder,
Seth S. Hersey, jun.,
Matthew Clynch,

Daniel W. Sprague,
Sewall Pugsley,
Richard Staples,
Benjamin L. Cushing,
Lincoln B. Bicknell,
Josiah S. Remington,
Peter McGlone,
Edward C. Wilder,
James K. Young,
John Pyne,
George W. Tilden,
William T. Nelson,
Laban O. Beal,
Elijah W. Burr,
Barzillai Lincoln,
John Wilder,
Charles H. Eldredge,
Daniel Bowen,
Thomas Murray,
Ebed Sprague, jun.,
Edwin H. Bates,
Thomas L. Sprague,
Howard Litchfield, jun.,
Stephen P. Gould,
Redmond Welsh,
George A. Newhall,
James M. Garland,
Albert Whiton,
Isaac B. Miller,
Freeman Pugsley,
Charles Mayhew,
James S. King,
Willard Snow,
Thomas J. Hersey,
George R. Turner.

So far as known, three only joined the army under the requisition of this draft ; viz.,William K. Gould, Sewall Pugsley, and Don

Pedro Wilson. A very large majority was excused for disability; and the remainder either exempted by provisions of the law, or by payment of the sum required for commutation. Among the latter were the following : —

Alanson Crosby,	Henry Hobart,
Andrew C. Cushing,	James S. King,
Edward S. Cushing,	Edward Pyne,
William Fearing, 2d,	Willard Snow,
Josiah L. Gardner,	William H. Starr,
Seth S. Hersey, jun.,	George W. Tilden,
Thomas Jones Hersey,	George W. Young,
Ebenezer C. Hobart,	

Of natives, but at the time non-residents of Hingham, the draft included, —

Gustavus Abbott,	Amasa Lincoln,
Charles W. Bassett,	Solomon Lincoln, jun.,
Elijah Beal,	Thomas W. Lincoln,
Robert Burr,	David Ripley,
Henry Damon,	Levi B. Ripley,
Henry L. Fearing,	Joseph S. Sprague,
Timothy Foster,	Leonard Sprague,
Henry Kenerson,	Samuel Sprague,
George Lane,	Levi Stearns,
Parker E. Lane,	James Tilden,
William Lane,	Albert T. Whiting,
Weston Lewis,	Dexter B. Whiton.

COPY OF THE OFFICIAL NOTICE ADDRESSED TO THE PERSONS DRAFTED.

[Form 39.]

PROVOST MARSHAL'S OFFICE, SECOND DISTRICT, STATE OF MASS., July 20, 1863.

To A. B., HINGHAM.

Sir, — You are hereby notified that you were, on the twentieth day of July, 1863, legally drafted in the service of the United States for the period of three years, in accordance with the provisions of the Act of Congress, for " enrolling and calling out the National Forces, and for other purposes," approved March 3, 1863. You will accordingly report, on or before the 8th of

August, at the place of rendezvous, in Taunton, or be deemed a deserter, and be subject to the penalty prescribed therefor by the Rules and Articles of War.

Transportation will be furnished you on presenting this notification at Hingham Station, on the S. S. R. R., or at the station nearest your place of residence.

[Signed]   J. W. D. HALL,
Provost Marshal, Second District of Mass.

COPY OF RECEIPT FOR THE SUM PAID FOR COMMUTATION.

[No. 44.]

SECOND MASSACHUSETTS COLLECTION DISTRICT.

Received at Milton on the thirteenth day of August, 1863, from A. B., of Hingham, who was drafted into the service of the United States, on the second day of July, 1863, from the Second Congressional District of the State of Massachusetts, the sum of three hundred ($300) dollars, to obtain, under Section 13 of the "Act for enrolling and calling out the National Forces, and for other purposes, approved March 3, 1863," discharge from further liability under this draft.

Signed in Triplicate.
C. P. HUNTINGTON, *Receiver of Commutation Money.*

[Form 31.]

CERTIFICATE OF NON-LIABILITY TO BE GIVEN BY THE BOARD OF ENROLMENT.

We, the subscribers, composing the Board of Enrolment of the Second District of the State of Massachusetts, provided for in Section 8, Act of Congress "for enrolling and calling out the National Forces," approved March 3, 1863, hereby certify that A. B., of Hingham, Plymouth County, State of Massachusetts, having given satisfactory evidence that he is not properly subject to do military duty, as required by said Act, by reason of having paid three hundred dollars, is exempt from all liability to military duty for the term of this draft.

[Signed]   J. W. D. HALL,
Provost Marshal and President of Board of Enrolment.

Dated at Taunton, this thirteenth day of August, 1863.

Members of the Thirty-second Regiment, who enlisted as veteran volunteers, and who were counted on the quota of the Town of Hingham, being regularly mustered into the service of the United States for three years from Jan. 5, 1864:—

Ephraim Anderson,	William Breen,
Otis L. Battles,	John C. Chadbourn,

Jacob G. Cushing,	Frank H. Miller,
William L. Dawes,	Peter Ourish,
John W. Eldredge,	Harvey M. Pratt,
Thomas L. French,	William Riley,
Edwin Hersey,	Charles H. F. Stodder,
Wallace Humphrey,	Edgar P. Stodder,
Gardner Jones,	Washington I. Stodder,
James McCarty,	Nathaniel Wilder, 2d,
Charles S. Meade,	George A. Wolfe.

Under date of Oct. 27, 1863, the President of the United States issued a call for 300,000 volunteers to serve for three years, or during the war. Of this number, the State of Massachusetts was to furnish 15,126, the quota of the town of Hingham being 50. The general order provided, "that, in case this number was not raised by voluntary enlistment, a draft would be ordered to supply the deficiency, which draft would commence on the fifth day of the January following."

To fill the quota, and avoid the draft, our citizens labored with indefatigable perseverance. In addition to the bounty of three hundred and twenty-five dollars offered by the State, money was appropriated by the Town, and contributed by private subscriptions. A recruiting office was opened in Lincoln's Building, Col. Edward Cazneau was appointed recruiting officer, Town and Citizens' meetings were frequent and spirited, a Citizens' Committee was raised, a recruiting agent was appointed in Boston, and every exertion made to secure the end desired. Before the time assigned for the draft, the quota was full. The recruiting officer had forwarded forty-two volunteers to camp, and the re-enlistment of twenty-two soldiers from the Thirty-second Regiment swelled the total beyond the number required.

The draft in April, 1864. — The quota of Massachusetts on the last call of the national government for 200,000 men was 10,639. There was a deficiency on the part of the State, up to March 1, amounting to 9,953 men, making the total required 20,592. Of these, 33 were to be furnished by the Town of Hingham. This number was materially reduced by the balance standing in our favor ; and the remainder, through the labors of the recruiting officer, and the committee chosen by the citizens, was soon obtained.

In May, 1864, the Enrolment Act was amended by Congress, allowing no exemption because of social relations, and consolidating the first and second classes ; thus making all between the ages of twenty and forty-five equally liable to the draft.

The draft in September, 1864. — Under this draft the quota of Hingham was seventy-two. Credit being allowed for naval enlistments, the number required from Massachusetts was soon obtained, with a balance of 21,675 in its favor. This surplus was apportioned among the several towns and cities as far as practicable, and the balance remained credited to the State at large.

Through the successful labors of the recruiting officer, Charles N. Marsh, Esq., and the Citizens' Committee, with the aid derived from numerous enlistments from the Town in the navy, and the share of the surplus men due from the State at large, the quota of Hingham was filled before the day appointed for the draft.

To date of Oct. 1, 1864, the aggregate of the quotas and deficiencies of the Town, from the time of the call in February, 1864, was 189 : the number actually furnished was 200 ; leaving a surplus of 11 men, which, on the 1st of December, was increased to 26 men.

SUBSTITUTES.

The Conscription Law provided that any man desiring a discharge for three years might furnish a substitute, the average cost of such being about seven hundred dollars. A portion of this amount, however, was afterwards refunded.

The law also made provision for a class termed " representative substitutes." Any enrolled man, after examination at the office of the provost marshal, and being pronounced physically unfit for military service, was authorized to provide a " representative substitute," and obtain his discharge for a term of three years. When a recruit was thus furnished, the sum of one hundred and twenty-five dollars was contributed by the Town, and seventy-five dollars from the enrolment fund.

The order from the provost marshal provided further, that

any person not liable to a draft might deposit one hundred and twenty-five dollars with the State treasurer, and be entitled to a representative recruit, who should be credited to the Town in which the person resided, unless such Town might be already credited with one-fourth the number required to fill its quota ; in which case the representative would be credited to the State at large. Ladies were authorized to furnish substitutes under similar conditions.

Substitutes, voluntary or representative, were furnished by the following persons, viz. : —

PRINCIPAL.	SUBSTITUTE.
Amos B. Bates,	John M. Whittier,
DeWitt C. Bates,	Dennis Riley,
Caleb G. Beal,	John Manill,
Ambrose Beech,	
E. Waters Burr,	
Isaac Gardner, 2d,	Adolph Wagner,
Tobias O. Gardner,	
W. Allan Gay,	
Theodore R. Glover,	
George P. Hayward,	
David R. Hersey,	Vernon W. Andrews,
Charles Howard,	John Stuart,
David Jacob,	Joseph T. King,
Joseph Jacob, jun.,	Martin Callahan,
Loring Jacob,	John H. Buxton,
Arthur Lincoln,	John Domick,
George Lincoln, jun.,	Christian Veil,
Solomon Lincoln, jun.,	
Enos Loring,	Jerry Hurley,
Thomas F. Whiton,	
William C. Wilder.	Job Nicholas.

ABRAHAM LINCOLN.

THE Compilers of this volume have thought it would be appropriate to its object to embrace in it a brief sketch of ABRAHAM LINCOLN, our great leader in the war of the rebellion. Believing that we have a local interest, also, in all that pertains to his life and character, and that a brief tribute to his memory will be in harmony with our work, we have requested Mr. ARTHUR LINCOLN of this town to prepare such a sketch, which is subjoined.

CHAPTER IV.

ABRAHAM LINCOLN.

NO name in American history can be mentioned which more quickly excites the tenderest emotions of our hearts than that of Abraham Lincoln. How deep the affection, how strong the sympathy it awakens, and how kind the thought it inspires! We revere the name of Washington, and are grateful for his noble services for his country's good; we honor the name of Franklin for his profound wisdom and strong practical sense; we are proud of the name of Webster, and admire his gigantic intellect and transcendent eloquence; but we love the name of Lincoln, and cherish his memory for the martyrdom he suffered for us. We realize that he was a part of our very selves, and appreciate the many virtues of his mind and heart.

There seems more or less of chance in the life of every man; and it is undoubtedly true, so far as Mr. Lincoln's nomination to the Presidency was concerned, that he was selected for his "availability," and favored by fortune. Tried by the test of experience, how could he have expected the honor, in competition with the chiefs of the nation, who had served the public for many years, and whose names were known throughout the land! Up to the time of his nomination, there was little of chance in his life; but by toil, through trial and adversity, under the most discouraging circumstances, he worked his own way, with few teachers, few books, and few companions, from obscurity to the front rank among men.

There is, however, less of chance in the lives of most men than we commonly suppose. All are, to a great extent, self-made, and hold their destinies in their own hands. It was peculiarly so with Abraham Lincoln. No man was ever more entitled to the distinction of being called a self-made man than

he, and no one among us has raised himself to so high an eminence from so humble a beginning. The story of his life is a
remarkable one, so romantic withal, and yet so real. It very
naturally finds.its place in any record of the soldiers and sailors,
whom he regarded with so much interest, and with whom he
was so intimately associated and worked so faithfully during the
nation's great struggle for existence. If it be a fact (for which
our historians assure us we have strong presumptive evidence
for believing), that the blood of the Pennsylvania Lincolns
flowed in his veins, and that the Lincolns everywhere are of
the same stock, and all descended from the settlers of Hingham,
how appropriate it seems to set apart a portion of these pages
to honor his name, in connection with the history of the services
of our own soldiers and sailors !

It becomes, therefore, an interesting fact that the names of
the two great chief magistrates, John Albion Andrew and Abraham Lincoln, the head of our own Commonwealth and the head
of the Nation, who so closely resembled each other in many great
qualities, should be so intimately connected with our own town.
We are proud to record the names of two such patriots and
martyrs in this volume.

Abraham Lincoln, the son of Thomas and Nancy (Hanks)
Lincoln, was born in that part of Hardin County, Kentucky,
now embraced by the lines of the recently formed County of
Larue, Feb. 12, 1809. The history of the first twenty-one years
of his life is soon told, and, as he himself said, is perfectly
characterized by a single line of Gray's Elegy.

" The short and simple annals of the poor."

He was born in a rude log-cabin, and lived in one for the first
seven years of his backwoods life. In his eighth year his father
removed to Indiana, and settled near the present town of Gentry-
ville. Here the boy was engaged chiefly in farm-work, labor for
hire, clearing forests and similar occupations. Here he remained
for thirteen years. The monotony of his life was only once
broken by a voyage by river to the sugar plantations around New
Orleans, whither he went in charge of a flat boat and cargo. At
twenty-one years of age, the family removed to Macon County,

Illinois, where they again constructed and lived in a log-cabin. During all these years he had no advantages of education. His mother died in his tenth year. His father could neither read nor write, and Abraham himself had only learned to read, write, and cipher. Yet in these years he had laid the foundations for that high eminence to which he afterwards attained. He had been a constant reader of the Bible, and from its pages and a few volumes of American biography, — the lives of Washington, Franklin, Clay, and a few others, — he had learned the lessons which enabled him to reach to the highest statesmanship.

After the removal to Illinois he started out on a new life, although his occupation for a while was of the humblest kind. He was engaged in splitting rails, acting as clerk in a country store, and became a soldier and captain in the Black Hawk War. Hitherto his life had flowed on like a tranquil stream, though growing wider and deeper as it neared the great centres of civilization ; and now with rapid strides he pushes his way on to fame. He had become very popular as a political debater, when, in 1834, he was elected to the Legislature of Illinois. He began to study law about the same time, and, in 1836, was admitted to the bar. He was married, in the thirty-third year of his age, to Miss Mary Todd of Lexington, Kentucky. On Dec. 6, 1847, he was elected a member of Congress. On Jan. 17, 1851, his father died. In 1858, he went through his memorable political campaign with Hon. Stephen A. Douglas. They canvassed the State in their contest for the senatorship. In his debates with Mr. Douglas, Mr. Lincoln was the victor, in popular estimation, and received a majority of the popular votes, although he lost the election on the ballot in the legislature, in consequence of a peculiar apportionment of the legislative districts. But the battle was to him a Bunker Hill fight, — a defeat with all the elements of victory. In June, 1860, the new Republican party assembled in convention in Chicago, and Mr. Lincoln was nominated for the Presidency. Now for the first time he is conscious of the great mission which awaits him. Truly the hand of God seems to have been in the selection. For what could have dictated the choice, which was made, to the minds of men, in the presence of the tried and trusted statesmen and leaders of the

nation who were gathered on that platform   His course seems
to have been thus far directed by some invisible hand ; for un-
consciously he had pushed his way from the humblest obscurity,
steadily and persistently, through the greatest trials, into national
recognition, as if destined for the sceptre now to be placed in his
hand.   He pauses under the new and great responsibility which
presses upon him, and in sad and serious thought and fervent
prayer awaits the issue, and prepares for the work to come.

The triumphant election of Nov. 6, 1860, soon followed ; and
in March following, Abraham Lincoln was inaugurated President
of the United States.   What a spectacle is this in the National
Capitol at Washington !   Senators, representatives, judges of
the highest courts of judicature, foreign diplomates, governors,
— the eminent and distinguished men of the land, assembled to
witness the august ceremonies, and the central figure of them
all, — he, the humble citizen from the back-woods, who has
passed half of his life in the wilderness.   The President now
fully recognized the fact that he was an instrument in the hand
of God to accomplish a great purpose.   He believed himself a
pilot at the ship's helm.   He knew not what storms would rock,
nor what tempests assail her ; but, apprehending danger, he had
bidden adieu to the peaceful scenes of home, and firmly set his
hand to the work, and plunged into the trial and turmoil of
official life, and the struggle of the great rebellion.   How sad
seem now his parting words to his neighbors in Springfield,
" My friends, I know not how soon I shall see you again " !

How nobly he did his work we all know.   The history of Mr.
Lincoln's life during the four succeeding years is the history of
the war itself, and is largely told in the sketches of the soldiers
and sailors whose names are recorded in this volume.   The first
gun from Sumter roused the people to arms.   The President's call
for men, the quick response of our own great war Governor, and
the march of our troops to the seat of war, the clash of arms, the
bloody battles, the tedious waitings, the sickness, imprisonments,
and deaths that followed, the reverses, the successes, and the
final overthrow of the rebellion that brought peace and victory to
our arms, all are fresh in our minds ; and how faithful and honest
and patient through the whole was our leader ! How confident in

the justice of our cause, how hopeful in the result, and how devoted to the soldiers and sailors who fought for it! How grand to him must have been the language of his own emancipation proclamation, "ALL PERSONS HELD AS SLAVES . . . ARE, AND HENCEFORWARD SHALL BE, FREE!" And how great the privilege of freeing four millions of African bondmen, upon which action he invoked the "CONSIDERATE JUDGMENT OF MANKIND, AND THE GRACIOUS FAVOR OF ALMIGHTY GOD"! How gratifying to him, in the midst of all these gigantic military campaigns, must have been his overwhelming re-election, and how glorious to him the final success of our arms!

But the bells had scarcely rung out to the nation the glad tidings of our great joy,—the fall of Richmond, the surrender of Lee, and the end of the rebellion,— when they tolled a nation's grief for the death of the great and good President, struck down by the hand of an assassin. He died on the fourteenth day of April, 1865; and the blood that flowed from his wounds sealed deep in our hearts the love and affection we bore him, and closed the lips of his traducers forever. The whole world rose up in sympathy, and exclaimed, he

"Hath borne his faculties so meek, hath been
So clear in his great office, that his virtues
Will plead like angels, trumpet-tongued, against
The deep damnation of his taking off."

So ended the life of Abraham Lincoln. He had fought a good fight; he had fulfilled his mission; he had seen the successful end of his work. As his funeral procession moved in silence across the land, the nations of the earth paid solemn tribute to the dead. Kings and queens sent sympathetic lines from their own hands, and all races and classes of men were moved to words of reverence and respect. His name is now in the affectionate keeping of mankind.

Mr. Lincoln was not regarded as a man of genius, and certainly not of the highest culture; but he had sound common sense, and a strong and decided purpose; he was fertile in practical expedients; simple, yet grand; kind, yet firm; rough somewhat in exterior, yet gentle and sympathetic in action; sagacious, and, above all, honest and pure in heart.

" His life was gentle, and the elements
So mixed in him, that Nature might stand up,
And say to all the world, *This was a man !* "

His speeches were singularly terse and effective. His admin-
istration was wise and practical. No suspicion of his integrity in
office ever entered the mind of friend or foe. He had the tact —
nay, the power as if inspired — of seeming to lead while he followed the people's will. This was especially marked in his
course with regard to issuing the emancipation proclamation.
He knew the people were ready for it, and would sustain him in
issuing.it. More sagacious than they, he anticipated their wants,
and insisted at last, against the judgment of many wise men, in
delaying the proclamation no longer. The result showed how
wisely he had interpreted their own will, and how he really followed, though seeming to be in advance of, their own opinion. It
was well, perhaps, for the republic, that, during the war, it had so
genuine a son of the soil to direct its armies and guide its coun-
sels. It indicated more fully to despotic governments abroad the
strength of our institutions and the worth of our men. Our
duty now is to insist that this Union, which he did so much to
preserve, must and shall be maintained. If every one works, as
he did, for the common good, we cannot fail ; and future generations will enjoy the blessings of a government " of the people,
by the people, and for the people," which " shall not perish from
the earth ; " and, as they look back through the centuries, will
find no brighter name to mark this period of our country's
history than that of Abraham Lincoln.

CHAPTER V.

THE LINCOLN LIGHT INFANTRY.

Introductory — The Lincoln Light Infantry — Telegraph Despatch from Gov. Andrew — Roll of Members and Volunteers — Public Exercises and Incidents on leaving Hingham — Arrival in Boston — Departure — Passage to Fortress Monroe — Additional Volunteers — Leave Hingham, and embark at Boston by Steamer "Cambridge" — Arrival and joining of the Company at Fortress Monroe — Five Weeks at Fortress Monroe — Newport News — Expiration of Term of Enlistment — Embark at Fortress Monroe for Boston — Reception in Boston — Arrival and Reception at Hingham — History of the Company.

I T is no part of the object of the present volume to discuss the causes which, in the process of time, slowly but steadily co-operated in bringing upon our country the late civil war. It is sufficient to say, that from the time of the attack on Fort Sumter, on the 12th of April, 1861, to the surrender of Gen. Lee, on the 9th of April, 1865, — a period of nearly four years, — one section of the United States was arrayed in deadly hostility against the other. The North saw in the issue national life or national death ; and, with all the earnest patriotism of the fathers in their first great struggle for liberty, every thing dear was brought to the altar of freedom and an undivided Union.

The rich gave of their wealth without measure ; and the poor in the same liberal spirit from their limited savings, — the result of the toil and self-denial of years. To this — and more than all else — was added the blood of her sons, her hope and pride, counting nothing dear when offered for an inheritance free and undivided.

With the local events of these years of darkness and trial we are now to deal. Instances of marked heroism in battle, the giving up of life by wounds or disease in the hospital, the dying by sickness or starvation of the prisoner in the hands of the foe, the trials and sufferings of the wounded, the wearisome march, the privations of camp-life, sustained on the part of the sons of

Hingham, and those who enlisted in the Town's behalf, make up
the brilliant record to the preservation and perpetuity of which
the following pages will be devoted.

As before stated, the attack on Fort Sumter was made April
12 ; and on Tuesday, April 16, occurred the first warlike movement in Hingham, from which the history of the Town in its
relation to the civil war must bear date.   It was on this day that
the field and staff officers of the various regiments of the M. V. M.
in the vicinity of Boston met in council at the Governor's room
in the State House ; and the situation of the nation, condition of
the military of the State, movement of troops, &c., were there
fully discussed.

THE LINCOLN LIGHT INFANTRY.

On the dissolution of the meeting, Lieut.-col. Hawkes Fearing
of the Fourth Regiment M. V. M., who had been present and
taken part in the deliberations, came directly to Hingham, and
caused to be called and attended a meeting of the Lincoln Light
Infantry at the armory in the evening.   He then immediately
returned to Boston, and reported for duty at headquarters, Faneuil Hall.

The situation was critical, and the needs of the moment immediate and imperative.   The call for aid was the call of the country ;
and it was soon apparent that the alternative presented was but
a simple unit.   It was a claim on the patriotism of the company
that a sense of honor forbade the setting aside.   They were
bound to respond to the summons, and a vote was passed accordingly.

Tuesday night and the forenoon of the following day was the
only time allowed for the arrangement of their affairs, the completion of the necessary preparations, and the taking leave of
their friends.   The captain was sick ; but the remaining officers,
in a spirit of the most genuine patriotism, came promptly forward and offered, for the extremities of the hour, any service
which might be required at their hands.   With a young family
relying on him for support and counsel, the situation of Lieut.
Stephenson in accepting the command thus suddenly and unex-
pectedly imposed was one of peculiar trial.   Between the ties

of kindred and the claims of affection on the one hand, and the call of the country for support on the other, he and his band of noble men, with true patriotism, decided to do battle for freedom and their native land. As they went from home, their destination was wholly unknown, the time of absence uncertain, the nature of their service could not be foreseen, and the future was shrouded in darkness and doubt.

During the day the following official despatch was received by telegraph : —

" April 16, 1861.

LUTHER STEPHENSON, JUN.,

Capt. Sprague is discharged. You will report in Boston with the Hingham company by first train.

JOHN A. ANDREW.

The Stars and Stripes waved from the public buildings, and uniformed soldiers were hastening to and fro in busy preparation for their departure. At one o'clock, P.M., of Wednesday, the members and volunteers assembled at the armory at Hingham Centre, where they were met by Rev. Calvin Lincoln, who commended them to the care and protection of the God of their fathers in earnest and impressive prayer. At four o'clock the line was formed ; and the company, forty-two in number, took up their line of march, passing down Main Street, attended by hundreds of men, women, and children, amid the ringing of the church-bells, the waving of handkerchiefs from the dwellings as they passed, and cheered by the frequent and hearty huzzas of the gathering multitude. As they halted near the depot, each man was presented with a wreath of flowers by the scholars of the North School. They were also addressed by Col. Charles W. Seymour, Rev. E. Porter Dyer, James S. Lewis, Esq., and Mr. Joel B. Seymour. Rev. Joseph Richardson offered in their behalf a fervent and affecting prayer; when, stepping on board the waiting train, prepared to meet whatever the future might decree, they left the town, followed by the tears, cheers, and benedictions of the assembled multitude.

The following is the roll of the Regular Members and the Volunteers of the Company, which left Hingham Wednesday afternoon, April 17, 1861, for active duty, in response to the call of the President of the United States. 13

REGULAR MEMBERS OF THE COMPANY.

RANK.	NAME.	RESIDENCE.
Captain	Luther Stephenson, jun.	Hingham.
Lieutenant	Charles Sprague,	"
"	Nathaniel French, jun.,	"
Sergeant	Peter N. Sprague,	"
"	Joshua Morse,	"
Corporal	Henry Stephenson,	"
"	Lyman B. Whiton,	"
Fifer	Samuel Bronsdon,	"
Private	George W. Bibby,	"
"	Jacob G. Cushing,	"
"	Henry S. Ewer,	"
"	Levi Kenerson,	"
"	Josiah M. Lane,	"
"	George R. Reed,	"
"	Benjamin S. Souther,	"
"	James S. Sturtevant,	"
"	William S. Whiton,	"
"	Joseph N. Berry,	Weymouth.
"	Parker E. Lane,	"
"	Daniel W. Lincoln,	"

VOLUNTEERS.

Private	George M. Adams,	Hingham.
"	Charles H. Bassett,	"
"	Andrew J. Clarke,	"
"	John Creswell,	"
"	Fergus A. Easton,	"
"	John W. Eldredge,	"
"	George A. Grover,	"
"	James M. Haskell,	"
"	George E. Humphrey,	"
"	John Q. Jacob,	"
"	Benjamin L. Jones,	"
"	George Miller,	"
"	William T. Nelson,	"

RANK.	NAME.	RESIDENCE.
Private	Ebenezer F. Roberts,	Hingham.
"	John S. Souther,	"
"	William J. Stockwell,	"
"	Alvan Tower,	"
"	Isaac G. Waters.	"
"	George Wolfe,	"
"	Elijah Prouty,	Weymouth.
"	Theodore Raymond,	"
"	Alfred W. Stoddard,	Marshfield.

Boston was not reached till late in the afternoon. The Fourth Regiment, to which the company was attached, assembled at Faneuil Hall, but had marched to the State House, where the Lincoln Light Infantry joined it. Equipments, articles of clothing, and camp necessities, including provisions, had been distributed among the troops earlier in the day; but, in the hurry and excitement of the hour, these articles of comfort were not fully shared by the Hingham soldiers.

A brief address was made by Gov. Andrew; after which, amid universal cheers, the Fourth and Sixth Regiments took up their line of rapid march together, the weather being cloudy and unpleasant, and the streets wet and muddy.

The Fourth Regiment proceeded by the Old Colony, and the Sixth by the Worcester Road. The Fourth Regiment left the city some ten minutes prior to the departure of the Sixth, and was in reality the first body of troops which left Massachusetts for the seat of war, although they did not reach their destination as soon as some others.

At Fall River the regiment embarked on board the steamer, " State of Maine," — a vessel which at the time was considered by the officers and troops generally to be unsafe or unseaworthy. She had been laid up for some time, and had nothing whatever on board, except what the soldiers had taken with them. The machinery was not in good order, the vessel was poorly ballasted, and they were eighteen hours in reaching New York City; being all that night and the next day on board, with a large proportion of the rations provided, totally unfitted for use by reason of the odor communicated from the rubber sacks in which they had been conveyed.

At New York the agent promised, and brought about, a better state of things. The steamer was put in better order, provisions were taken on board, and she left the city in a more seaworthy condition. The passage to Fortress Monroe — the point to which at last they proved to be destined — was more comfortable, and the place was reached in safety on the morning of Saturday, the 20th of April.

At the time of the departure of the company, such was the urgency of the call from the State authorities, that no opportunity was allowed to enlist the men required to make up its full quota. Immediate action was had to supply the deficiency; and thirty-seven new recruits were soon enrolled, drilled, and uniformed.

On Saturday morning, May 18, 1861, these soldiers met at the armory, at Hingham Centre; and after a brief drill, a prayer in their behalf for the protection and blessing of Heaven by Rev. E. Porter Dyer, and the exchange of farewells with their friends, took up their line of march to the music of fife and drum for the landing of the steamer "Nantasket." Under the temporary command of Capt. John Stephenson, assisted by Lieut. William Fearing, they proceeded down Main Street, by way of Broad Bridge, to the boat, where the wharf was found crowded with interested citizens, including friends and connections. Parting salutations were brief and hurried, and three times three cheers were given "betwixt ship and shore" as the steamer moved from the wharf with her burden of patriotic soldiers.

The following is a list of the volunteers who left Hingham May 18, 1861, to join Company I of the Fourth Regiment, then stationed at Fortress Monroe.

NAMES.	RESIDENCE.
Henry F. Binney,	Hingham.
James B. Bryant,	"
John W. Burr,	"
Thomas A. Carver,	"
Silas H. Cobb,	"

NAMES.	RESIDENCE.
Charles Corbett,	Hingham.
Jerry J. Corcoran,	"
Isaac M. Dow,	"
Levi H. Dow,	"
George Dunbar,	"
George W. Fearing,	"
Henry C. French,	"
Albert S. Haynes,	"
Edwin Hersey,	"
William H. Jacob,	"
William H. Jones,	"
Alfred A. Lincoln,	"
Daniel S. Lincoln,	"
William H. Marston,	"
Jacob Ourish,	"
Albert L. Peirce,	"
Charles H. F. Stodder,	"
Demerick Stodder,	"
William Taylor,	"
Charles H. Damon,	West Scituate.
George C. Dwelly,	Hanover.
Hosea Dwelly.	"
Francis W. Everson,	Weymouth.
Charles A. Gardner,	West Scituate.
Henry C. Gardner,	" "
John D. Gardner,	" "
Herbert Graves,	" "
William B. Harlow,	Hanover.
E. A. Jacob,	West Scituate.
John H. Prouty,	" "
William Prouty, jun.,	" "
Alpheus Thomas,	South "

On their arrival in Boston, they proceeded at once to the State House, where, after being equipped and supplied with clothing and other articles needed in the experience of the life of a soldier, they were addressed by Gov. Andrew, in words replete with hope and encouragement, exhorting them as true patriots to go forth for the cause of their country in this her hour of trial and danger. Dining at the Quincy House, they embarked at half-past four o'clock on board the steamer "Cambridge," which was to convey them to their port of destination. Here, as at Hingham, a large company of relatives and friends had assembled to take their leave; and many were the adieus and heartfelt farewells exchanged between those about to depart and those who were to be left behind. The voyage proved a stormy one, and the steamer was somewhat driven from her course; but the harbor was finally reached without accident, and at noon of the 22d of May all were safely landed at Fortress Monroe, the roll of the Lincoln Light Infantry being thus increased to seventy-nine men.

While at Fortress Monroe, the troops were actively engaged in mounting guns, and in the general work of putting the situation in thorough repair, as well for its defence as for offensive operations, should such become necessary.

On the 27th of May, after a stay of five weeks, the Fourth Regiment, including the Lincoln Light Infantry, by order of Gen. Butler, left Fortress Monroe for Newport News, which was reached the next day, May 28. A regiment from Vermont, and a regiment, mostly Germans, from Pennsylvania, accompanied them.

Looking over the new position, it was soon apparent, that whatever the troops might require, — whether of food, shelter, or protection from the enemy, to which they were fully exposed,— they were expected in some way to provide for themselves. As may be supposed, after the labor expended at Fortress Monroe, and just as the means of comfort and security had been well provided, the change created no little dissatisfaction. There was, however, no alternative. The neighboring farms were called in requisition for the needed supplies, intrenchments were begun, and in a few days they were prepared for the enemy.

The Point, commanding as it did the mouth of James River, was considered an important one; and early in June, from various sources, the number of available troops had been increased to more than four thousand men.

On the 9th of June the company made an expedition into the enemy's country, to ascertain, if possible, the situation and strength of the forces gathered in the vicinity. The heat was great, the journey long and wearisome; and the company returned to camp at night thoroughly exhausted and unfit for duty.

On Sunday, June 11, occurred the disaster at Big Bethel, the particulars of which need not here be given. In making up the quota of troops required for the service, it was found, that, of the Lincoln Light Infantry, but forty men were in condition to join the expedition ; all being more or less enfeebled, and still suffering from the results of the heat and fatigues experienced on the previous Thursday. Thus unfitted to take part in the enterprise, their place was supplied by Company F, Capt. Sheppard; all, however, being desirous to join the party.

Through the early part of the month of June the weather was oppressively warm, and the health of the company was somewhat impaired. Indeed, the general healthful condition of the men was scarcely regained up to its close ; and the order for removal to Hampton was received with hearty satisfaction. This change was made on Tuesday, July 2. Better shelter, better accommodations, soon told on the men in a marked improvement of health and spirits. Their stay at this locality was necessarily brief, as the term of enlistment was rapidly drawing to its close. For two weeks, quartered in private residences left tenantless by rebel citizens, or in the churches of the town, our friends of the Lincoln Light Infantry found immunity from severe labor, exposure, or fear of attack from the enemy.

The term of enlistment having expired, the Fourth Regiment, including the Lincoln Light infantry, returned to Fortress Monroe, where it embarked on board the steamer " S. R. Spaulding," and, after a pleasant passage, reached Boston, Friday, July 19. The landing was made at Long Island, and they were there ordered into camp ; the general health of the troops, notwithstanding the change of climate and the severity of the service through which they had passed, being good.

After being mustered out, the regiment moved up to the city, where a hearty reception was given it by the authorities. A dress-parade took place on the Common ; the apart-

ments of the " Tigers " were opened for the accommodation of the
Lincoln Light Infantry: Mr. E. Waters Burr generously provided
entertainment at the Parker House; and the night was passed in
comfortable quarters.

THE RECEPTION AT HINGHAM.

On the following morning, Wednesday, July 23, the Lincoln
· Light Infantry, accompanied by the Boston Brigade Band and a
detachment of the Second Battalion of Infantry in new Zouave
uniform, under Capt. John C. Whiton, took passage on board the
steamer "Nantasket" for Hingham. As they came to the landing, they were greeted by a multitude of citizens, — men, women,
and children, from every section of the town, — anxious to express
their respect and gratitude for the patriotic spirit displayed on
the part of their fellow-townsmen, and to give them a hearty
welcome home.

A procession was formed on the wharf, consisting of the
Home Guards, " Extinguisher," " Torrent," and " Niagara " fire-
companies, a numerous cavalcade, and a large company of citizens. Amid the ringing of the church-bells, the band played
" Home Again," and led the procession, under command of Capt.
John C. Whiton, from the landing to Water Street, where, in
front of the residence of Capt. Luther Stephenson, Major
Cobb's Light Battery, numbering one hundred and fifty horses
and six guns, was in waiting to head the escort. The entire
body then passed down Main Street to Broad Bridge, and
halted in front of Lincoln's · Building, where three months
before they gave the parting hand, and left for the seat of war.
Here they were surrounded and welcomed by a large concourse
of citizens ; and, after a service of thanksgiving and benediction
by Rev. Calvin Lincoln, they were addressed by Henry Edson
Hersey Esq., in the public behalf, as follows : —

"With emotions of thankfulness and joy too deep to find full expression in words, your fellow-citizens and friends welcome you to your homes.
As champions of the great cause of constitutional liberty, as pioneers of
the grand army of loyal Americans, you left at a moment's warning your
peaceful pursuits, and the dear objects of your love, to stand with your com-

patriots in arms, for the defence of the national capital, for the preservation of the nation's life; and with God's blessing the nation's life shall be preserved. Reverses, however unexpected and disastrous, shall not dishearten us. The justice of our cause remains; ay, and its ultimate vindication is as sure as the final triumph of God's truth; and they who lay down their life in its defence are martyrs in the holiest cause for which, in our time, it is permitted men to die.

"Soldiers, from the time of your departure from this spot until this moment, we have followed your fortunes and watched your every movement with an interest such as Hingham has never before felt in any company of her sons. Knowing that your position, although a glorious one, had its inevitable hardships and its grave perils, we have done what we could to sustain and encourage you. The care of your families we have regarded as a sacred trust, which we could not too conscientiously fulfil. By municipal provisions, and by private offerings, we have striven to relieve you in some measure from anxiety about your domestic interests, and to show that we appreciate the magnitude of the debt which we owe to you as the defenders of civil rights against the most infamous band of conspirators that ever bade defiance to the wrath of men and the avenging justice of Heaven.

"When you went out from among us, we felt that to you was committed the honor of our town. Knowing that the life of the camp and the garrison has never been regarded as favorable to the preservation of good morals, and how strong is the temptation to those who take up arms for lawful ends to use their power sometimes unworthily, we could not but feel some solicitude, lest even the safeguards of a New England education might at times prove insufficient. But you are returned to us with your honor as you went. And we assure you, that, glad as we have been to hear of your general good health, and of your faithful performance of all military duty, what has most rejoiced our hearts has been the reports which have reached us from time to time, that every man among you has been equal to the best in steadiness and honesty; that, in putting on the armor of soldiers, you have laid off none of the obligations which rested on you as men; that even the 'sacred soil of Virginia' has not been polluted by your presence, and that some of her chivalric sons may possibly have learned from you how to be gentlemen.

"Welcome, then, and again welcome, citizen soldiers, sons of Massachusetts, defenders of the Republic! Welcome to these family scenes,

14

where war's devastation has not come! Here no fortress walls environ you, but you are girt about with proud and grateful hearts. Not here, as in the Old Dominion, are the loyal sons of America greeted by murderous vollies from hostile batteries: here you need deploy no skirmishers as you advance, for not even the sight of a retreating rebel shall remind you that treason is anywhere abroad. The flags that wave above you have not one stripe erased or polluted, not a single star obscured, and shall not have forever.

"We congratulate you that no sad or discordant note mingles with these greetings. No traitor's bullet, nor accident, nor disease, has deprived you of a single life. No parent nor wife nor child nor brother nor sister shall blush that any man of you has tarnished his honor, or came tardy off in duty. In the hour of our imminent peril, your country summoned you to her defence, and with alacrity you responded to the call. To the latest hour of your lives shall memory delight to dwell on this patriotic scene; and the priceless blessings of the American Union shall have new value in your eyes, who thought not the sacrifice of your lives too great, if thereby that Union might be preserved.

To these remarks, Capt. Stephenson responded as follows: —

"MY FRIENDS AND NEIGHBORS, — I hardly know what to say, to properly express my thanks in behalf of my command, for this warm and enthusiastic reception, the kind and earnest greeting you have extended to us to-day. You have added one more obligation to the many that are due our friends for the constant succession of favors, for the numberless expressions of friendship and sympathy we have received during our absence; and I assure you that the knowledge that we were watched over and cared for by our friends at home has lightened many a load, and revived many a drooping spirit, worn out almost with labor and disease.

"Friends, we bring to you no laurels won on the battle-field; for although always placed in the post of danger, although there seems always to be assigned to Massachusetts men to form the advance guard in every expedition of danger and of labor, we have passed through unharmed: and, when I look around on this happy gathering, I thank God that it is so! I thank God that no wife will look in vain for the form of one she loves; no father or mother will search in vain for their son: that no child has been bereft of the care and love of a father; but that they are all here (many of us worn and weary I know) that every fireside shall be made glad by the return of husband, parent, and son, who had been so tremblingly watched, so anxiously waited for!

"And yet, although we have not been called upon to face the cannon's mouth, I know from their bearing when danger threatened, and the conflict seemed inevitable, that they would have met the enemy without flinching, and have nobly sustained the honor of old Massachusetts, and the good name of our dear town.

" No one can estimate the amount of blood and of treasure that has been saved by the prompt action of our Massachusetts militia. In all probability, had we arrived at Fortress Monroe two days later, that important post would have been lost. The key of Virginia, more important at this crisis, perhaps, than even the capital itself, would have been in the possession of traitors and rebels, and a million of treasure, and thousands of precious lives, would have been sacrificed to regain what was saved by the prompt action of eight hundred men, who left their homes, their families, and their business, to answer the call of their country, to support the government, and to enforce the laws.

" Therefore, if we have not in the field of battle been called upon to meet the foe hand to hand, we feel that we have acted an important part in the great drama; and, for myself, I am glad it has fallen to my lot to join in this second great struggle for our independence, believing that my children, and my children's children, will remember it with gratitude when I shall have passed away.

" My friends, allow me once more to thank you for your kindness towards us, and your presence here. These green fields and pleasant homes of our dear town, the church spires, the forms of these reverenced men whose voices we have missed so much at each returning sabbath, this happy re-union with our parents, wives, children, and friends, almost make us forget our toils and trials, and more than repay us for what we have done for the great cause in which we have been engaged.

At the close of these exercises the procession reformed, and marched through North, West, South, and Main Street, to the Town Hall, the Hingham soldiers leaving their guns at the armory on the way. Two guns from Major Cobb's Battery, stationed on land of Capt. James Stephenson, fired salutes as the procession passed up Pear-tree Hill.

At the Town Hall, an excellent collation had been prepared by a committee of ladies and gentlemen chosen for the purpose. The tables were spread in superabundance with almost every procurable luxury, and were beautifully adorned with the choicest flowers of the season.

The Light Battery left their guns, carriages, and horses on the grounds of the Agricultural Society, and repaired to the Town Hall.

The engine companies "Extinguisher" and "Torrent" accepted the invitation of the "Niagara" company at Hingham Centre to a collation in their hall.

At five o'clock, P.M., the Light Battery returned to camp at Quincy, and the Second Battalion of Infantry, with the band, left at 4.30, P.M., by steamer "Nantasket" for Boston.

The soldiers embraced the earliest opportunity afforded to return to their homes, where wife, children, parent, and friends were anxiously waiting to greet and welcome them.

Throughout the day flags were numerously displayed from the public buildings and from private residences in every part of the town; and the streets were thronged with carriages, and with men, women, and children.

The day and the occasion were truly eventful. The prompt and patriotic response of the Town of Hingham to the call of the country is a source of congratulation, and will form one of the brightest pages in its history. That the early re-enforcement of the garrison at Fortress Monroe by loyal troops was the means of retaining this important station on the side, and in support, of the Federal Government, there can scarcely be a doubt; and the expedition must be set down as followed by the best results, and crowned with the most desirable success. As the attending circumstances are reviewed, there is little, from first to last, that could be omitted or changed; and the whole will reflect lasting honor on every man who took part in the enterprise.

It would be ingratitude not to acknowledge the divine goodness, that, sparing all, gathered anew the ranks at home unbroken by death from disease, or by violence from the hand of man on the field of battle.

COMMITTEE AND ORDER OF PROCESSION.

Committee of Arrangement. — The Committee of Arrange-
ments for the reception were Messrs John Todd, John Stephen-
son, Joseph Jacob, William Fearing, 2d, David Cain, E. Waters
Burr, Elijah L. Whiton, Daniel Bassett, David Leavitt, Demerick
Marble, Abner L. Leavitt, John K. Corthell, John Cushing,
David Cushing, jun., E. B. Whitcomb, Charles W. Seymour,
Henry E. Hersey, Joseph B. Thaxter, jun., Thomas F. Whiton,
and Albert Whiting.

ORDER OF PROCESSION.

Aids to the Chief Marshal.
Maj. Cobb's Full Battery.
Aid. Chief Marshal. *Aid.*
Past and Honorary Members of the Lincoln Light Infantry, as a military
escort under command of Lieut. William Fearing, 2d.
Committee of arrangements.
Invited guests.
Brigade Band.
Lincoln Light Infantry.
Firewards.
The several engine companies in the order of their numbers.
Citizens generally.
Cavalcade.

Marshals. — Albert Whiting, Seth C. Dunbar, Joseph Jacob,
jun., Ezra Wilder, George Cushing, 2d, Solomon Lincoln, jun.,
Henry C. Harding, Charles Spring, William C. Lincoln, George
Lincoln, jun., John D. Gates, Robert W. Lincoln, Charles W.
Cushing, Erastus Whiton, Hiram Gardner, Ezra T. C. Stephen-
son, Joseph H. French, George H. French, Albert Thayer, Joseph
A. Newhall, Benjamin Thomas, and Enos Loring.

Aids. — Daniel Bassett, David Cushing, jun., John K. Corthell, Edwin Wilder, 2d, and Thomas Stephenson.

HISTORY.

The Lincoln Light Infantry was organized Oct. 19, 1854.
The first preliminary meeting was held Oct 14; and on the 28th
of the month, the company adopted the title of " Lincoln," in
honor of Benjamin Lincoln, a major-general in the army of the
Revolution, and a native of Hingham.

On the 20th of June, 1855, pursuant to a warrant from his Excellency, Henry J. Gardner, governor of the State and commander-in-chief, the members met for the election of officers ; and Hawkes Fearing, jun., was chosen captain.

The first parade was made July 4, 1855. Aug. 18, 1860, Joseph T. Sprague was elected captain, vice Hawkes Fearing, jun., promoted lieutenant-colonel, Fourth Regiment, M. V. M.

April 17, 1861, the company with forty-two men, in command of Lieut. Luther Stephenson, jun., left Hingham for three months' active service at Fortress Monroe and vicinity.

April 19, 1861, Lieut. Stephenson was chosen captain, vice Capt. Joseph T. Sprague.

April 23, 1861, the company was mustered into the service of the United States for three months, to date from April 16, 1861.

May 18, 1861, thirty-seven additional volunteers left Hingham to join the company, and the number was increased to seventy-nine men.

Mustered out of service July 22, and returned to Hingham July 24, 1861.

Feb. 17, 1862, Joshua Morse was elected captain, vice Luther Stephenson, jun., honorably discharged.

May 26, 1862, the company, then numbering forty-two men, was ordered to report at once on the Common at Boston for active service, on account of the rumored defeat of Gen. Banks and the Union army.

May 28, 1862, returned to Hingham, the services of the company not being required.

June 23, 1862, Peter N. Sprague was elected captain, vice Capt. Joshua Morse resigned ; and on the 29th of the September following, the company was disbanded, and the officers honorably discharged.

CHAPTER VI.

ONE HUNDRED DAYS' MEN.

THE term of enlistment of those who first entered the service for three years expired in the summer of 1864. The situation at the time was critical: the National Capital was believed to be in danger from an advance of the enemy, and the reduction of the numerical force of the army a matter of serious importance. To provide against this reduction, a furlough was offered by the government as an inducement for re-enlistment; and this was accepted by a large number of the discharged troops, who at once left for home to enjoy the vacation, to which in consideration of a long, wearisome, and perilous experience, they were so justly entitled.

A call was then issued for 85,000 troops to serve for one hundred days; and a requisition was made on the State of Massachusetts for five regiments of this class, to take the place of those temporarily absent, and also, by furnishing men for garrison duty, to strengthen the effective force then in the field. It was understood that these soldiers were not to be reckoned on the quota of the State, but were to be exempted from liability to the draft then pending, which involved a service of three years.

The number of troops actually supplied by Massachusetts under this requisition was 5,461. The number who enlisted from Hingham appears to have been limited. The records received include the following : —

FIFTH REGIMENT.

This was among the first military organizations that left Massachusetts for the seat of war, in April, 1861, and took part in the first battle of Bull Run. It afterwards, in the autumn of 1862, volunteered for nine months, and was assigned to the Department of North Carolina. July 28, 1864, it was again mustered into service, this time for the period of one hundred days. Connected with the regiment during this last term were the following persons from Hingham, viz. : —

PRIVATES.

ROBERT CUSHING.

Born in Hingham.

Enlisted at Boston; mustered at Readville, in Co. F, July 16, 1864; mustered out Nov. 16, 1864, by reason of expiration of term of enlistment.

Robert Cushing died in Hingham Sept. 26, 1869, of consumption, aged 27 years, 8 months.

REVERE LINCOLN.

Born in Hingham, Dec. 2, 1846.

Enlisted at Readville, Mass., July 12, 1864; mustered in Co. F, July 28; served at Fort McHenry, Baltimore, Md., on garrison duty, and in guarding prisoners, and new recruits who were being sent to their regiments. Mustered out at Readville, Nov. 16, 1864, by reason of expiration of service.

FORTY-SECOND REGIMENT.

This regiment originally left Boston in November, 1862, to serve for the period of nine months; and, proceeding to New York, was assigned to the Department of the Gulf. After returning to Massachusetts, it was re-organized in 1864, to do guard-duty in or near Alexandria, Va., for the term of one hundred days. In this regiment were, —

LIEUTENANTS.

JOSEPH M. THOMAS.

Born in Hanson, Aug 24, 1841.

Enlisted at Boston. Mustered in July 14, 1864, as second lieutenant of Co. A, for one hundred days. Mustered out Nov. 11, 1864, by reason of expiration of term of enlistment. Lieut. Thomas was also in the service for a period of nine months, as will be seen by referring to the proper chapter.

FERGUS ANZLE EASTON.

Born in Langham, Scotland, Sept. 24, 1842.

First, A volunteer in the Lincoln Light Infantry, and left Hingham with this company, April 17, for Fortress Monroe, serving three months.

Second, Enlisted Aug. 1, 1861, as orderly sergeant in the Sixth Regiment N.Y. Vol. Cavalry. Promoted second lieutenant, June 27, 1862, and commissioned first lieutenant March 22, 1863. Resigned at Warrenton, Va., July 29, 1863, on account of sickness.

Third, Re-enlisted as sergeant in Co. E, of the Forty-second Regiment, M. V. I., one hundred days, and was mustered in July 22, 1864. Mustered out Nov. 11, 1864.

Whole term of service two and a half years.

While connected with the Sixth New York Regiment, Lieut. Easton participated in all the variations of cavalry service. Fully at the front, he was in the engagements at South Mountain, Antietam, Wheatland, Kelly's Ford, Spottsylvania, Chancellorsville, Beverly Ford. Gettysburg, Boonsboro', Funkstown,

Williamsport, and Falling Waters, besides others of less importance. He is reported as being an accomplished and popular officer. His resignation was tendered on account of ill health.

Lieut. F. A. Easton formerly resided at South Hingham.

CORPORAL
GEORGE DUNBAR.
Born in Hingham, Nov. 14, 1838.

Enlisted at Readville, Mass., and was mustered July 20, 1864, as corporal in Co. D.

At the commencement of this service, Mr. Dunbar was detailed by special order No. 38, of Gen. Slough, to Headquarters Provost Marshal Defences South of the Potomac, under Col. Henry Hunt Wells of the Twenty-sixth Michigan Infantry, to the duty of receiving statements from prisoners, refugees, deserters, and also of preferring charges, forwarding reports from scouts, &c., until the Forty-second returned to Massachusetts.

Nov. 11, 1864, he was discharged at Readville by reason of expiration of term of enlistment.

Mr. Dunbar was also with the Lincoln Light Infantry at Fortress Monroe; and for a short time in 1862 was under orders, having been commissioned by Gov. Andrew, second lieutenant of Co. I, Fourth Regiment, M. V. He was honorably discharged Sept. 10, 1862, by reason of the disbandment of the company.

PRIVATE
JOHN HENRY STODDER.
Born in Hingham, Nov. 14, 1845.

Enlisted July 9, 1864, at Readville, Mass., as private in Co. D, and was mustered in July 11, 1864.

While in service he was engaged in provost-duty at Alexandria, Va., and was also employed in picket-duty in Maryland. Four weeks were spent at Slough Barracks Hospital, Alexandria, Va., where he was confined with typhoid fever.

After the expiration of his term of enlistment, he was mustered out at Readville, Nov. 11, 1864, having been in service four months.

SIXTIETH REGIMENT.

This was a new military organization, although many of its officers and privates had previously seen service. It was commanded by Col. Ansel D. Wass, an experienced officer of Boston, and stationed at or near Indianapolis, Ind., to perform guard-duty. There was but one enlistment from Hingham in this regiment, viz. : —

PRIVATE

ANDREW WALLACE GARDNER.

Born in Hingham, Dec. 1, 1844.

Enlisted at Quincy. Mustered in Co. B, on Hingham quota, July, 16, 1864. Mustered out at Boston, Nov. 30, 1864. (See chapter for one year's service.)

LIST OF ONE HUNDRED DAYS' MEN.

Robert Cushing.
George Dunbar.
Fergus A. Easton.
Andrew W. Gardner.

Revere Lincoln.
John H. Stodder.
Joseph M. Thomas.

CHAPTER VII.

ON the 4th of August, 1862, three hundred thousand additional men were called for by the government, to serve for a term of nine months, eleven days being allowed for recruiting the number required. Failing to answer the requisition, a draft was ordered to take place on the 15th, to make up the deficiency.

Of the number thus called for, nineteen thousand and eighty were to be furnished by the State of Massachusetts; the quota for the town of Hingham being eighty-three.

Under this class, regiments were formed as follows: viz., Third, Fourth, Fifth, Sixth, Eighth, Forty-second to the Fifty-third inclusive, and the Eleventh Battery.

Of natives or residents of Hingham known to have enlisted under this call, nearly all were included in the Forty-third, Forty-fourth, and Forty-fifth Regiments. It should, however, be stated in this connection, that a number of men were borrowed from the towns of Plymouth, Middleboro', and Quincy, to fill up the quota; and the names of such occur among the papers of the Town. Many of these men were soon after returned, and the bounty money advanced subsequently refunded.

FOURTH REGIMENT.

The Fourth Regiment was first mustered into service in April, 1861, for three months, and ordered to Fortress Monroe, Va. It was commanded by Col. Abner B. Packard of Quincy, and included among its companies the Lincoln Light Infantry (Co. I) of Hingham. When the call was made, in 1862, for 19.080 men for nine months, the Fourth again volunteered, and was sent to Camp "Joe Hooker" to receive recruits. It was placed under the command of Col. Henry Walker, and ordered to join the forces under Maj.-Gen. Banks in the Department of the Gulf. So far as known, there were but two Hingham persons in the regiment, viz. : —

CORPORAL

TILSON FULLER.

A resident of Hingham.

Enlisted at Taunton Mass., mustered in Co. K, Sept. 15, 1862, at Camp "Joe Hooker," Lakeville, Mass.; was in the battles of Vermillionville and Port Hudson, La., also detailed as clerk to Adj. Crocker of third brigade, commanded by Gen. Ingraham. Mustered out at Lakeville, Aug. 28, 1863.

Mr. Fuller gives the following additional particulars : —

"The Fourth Massachusetts Regiment sailed from New York in the ship 'George Peabody.' After a long passage, just avoiding the 'Alabama,' and narrowly escaping being ship wrecked on the rocks off the Florida coast, her passengers were safely landed at Carrollton, La., having been on ship-board forty-seven days. Camping here some weeks, we were ordered to Baton Rouge. We then marched to the rear of Port Hudson, the navy co-operating on the river, and making an appearance of attacking. In the mean time Admiral Farragut succeeded in running several of his vessels past the fort, though losing the "Mississippi," which accidentally was run aground, and subsequently blown up.

Securing a lot of cotton, we returned to Baton Rouge; then passing down the Mississippi River, crossed over opposite New Orleans to Algiers, and commenced our march to Alexandria. At Vermillionville we were opposed by the rebels; and a sharp battle ensued, lasting two days, when they retreated. After recruiting ourselves at Alexandria, we returned by forced marches, crossed the Mississippi River to the other side of Port Hudson, and were there engaged in the siege until the garrison surrendered. In one of the charges on the garrison, Capt. Bartlett and several of the company were killed, and a number wounded.

After the surrender, we remained for several weeks performing garrison duty, and were then ordered home.

PRIVATE

CALEB BEAL MARSH.

Born in Hingham, Jan. 1, 1832.

Enlisted at Canton, Mass; mustered in Co. A, Sept. 17, 1862, at Lakeville; was in the first attack at Port Hudson, and at the battle of Bisland, La.; taken prisoner June 23, 1863, and sent to Brashear City, La.; thence, July 4, to Donaldsonville, but never exchanged; afterwards with the regiment at Port Hudson; embarked on steamboat "North America" for Cairo, and from thence by railroad to Boston. Mustered out at Lakeville, Aug. 28, 1863, having, in common with other members of the regiment, served upwards of eleven months.

FIFTH REGIMENT.

The Massachusetts "Fifth" was one of the regiments called into the United States service for three months at the commencement of the war. It bore an honorable part at the battle of Bull Run, July 17, 1861, and was especially commended for steadiness and bravery.

When the call was made for nine months' men, Aug. 4, 1862, the regiment again entered the service, and was sent to Newbern, N.C. Its muster roll bears the name of —

SERGEANT

JAIRUS LINCOLN, Jun.

Born in Hingham, May 27, 1831.

Enlisted at Yarmouth, Mass.; mustered at Camp Lander, in the town of Wenham, Sept. 16, 1862, as sergeant in Co. E.

Mr. Lincoln was with the regiment at Newbern, performing guard and picket duty. He also took part in the various expeditions from that point; participated in the engagements at Goldsboro' Bridge, Kinston, and near Washington, N.C.; and was mustered out at Wenham, Mass., July 2, 1863, by reason of expiration of service.

SIXTH REGIMENT.

This was the "Old Sixth" Regiment which went through Baltimore, April 19, 1861, under Col. Jones. It was recruited again in 1862, under Col. Albert S. Follansbee, for nine months' service, and stationed in the Department of Virginia, being most of the time upon outpost duty. Its muster-roll includes the name of —

PRIVATE

GEORGE SMITH.

A resident of Hingham since the war ; born in Brighton, Mass., Jan. 20, 1832.

Enlisted for the Town of Newton. Enrolled in Co. F, Sept. 8, 1862. Was wounded slightly in the head during one of the nine battles in which he participated. Mustered out June 3, 1863, by reason of expiration of service.

FORTY-THIRD REGIMENT.

The Forty-third "Tiger" Regiment, Col. Charles S. Holbrook, was recruited at Camp Meigs, Readville, in September and October, 1862. On the 24th of the latter month, it embarked at Boston, to co-operate in the Department of North Carolina, and, on arrival at Newbern, encamped just without the limits of the city, on the banks of the Trent River. It joined the expedition to Goldsboro', and was engaged at Kinston on the 14th of December. On the 16th it was present in the battle at White-hall, and detailed the next day for an expedition to Spring Bank Bridge, which they burned, and succeeded in routing a body of the enemy stationed at this locality. Returning to Newbern, they here remained in camp until the 17th of January, 1863, when the march was made on Trenton.

From the 21st of January to the 13th of March, no further movements were made, and the regiment continued in camp. On the 14th it marched to Rocky Run for the relief of the Twenty-fifth Massachusetts Regiment, and on the 15th advanced to the junction of the Pollockville and Trent Roads. Not meeting the enemy, it again entered camp at Newbern, and continued at this station till April 7, when it joined the expedition for the relief of Little Washington.

On the 9th it was engaged at Blount's Creek, and after a short advance on the enemy from the artillery, which the regiment supported, fell back, and by a very severe march reached camp the next afternoon. April 17 it again took steamer, and embarked for Little Washington, where it was engaged in garrison and picket duty till the 24th, when camp was broken, and they proceeded to Newbern. Engaged in the construction of roads, fortifications, &c., they remained at this locality till the 24th of the following June, when all embarked for Fortress Monroe; soon after, however, leaving for White House, but shortly returning again to Fortress Monroe.

On the 2d of July orders were received to proceed to Baltimore, which they reached at noon of the next day, and on the morning of the 4th went into quarters at Camp Bradford, just without the city.

It was here that some dissatisfaction arose on account of the expiration of the term of enlistment; and an order was thereupon issued, leaving it optional with the men "to go to the front, or to return home." Two hundred and three, officers and men, including all those from Hingham, voted "to go to the front."

Proceeding to Sandy Hook under Lieut.-Col. John C. Whiton, the regiment continued to perform provost duty until July 18, when, after being highly complimented for the patriotic spirit displayed in the faithful manner in which the duties required had been performed, it was ordered to Boston to be mustered out of service.

Leaving Sandy Hook July 18, it reached Boston July 21, and was mustered out of the service of the United States July 30, 1863.

The following list includes such of the Forty-third as were natives or residents of Hingham. The record of their services has been sketched in the foregoing narrative of the general expe_ rience of the regiment.

COLONEL

JOHN CHADWICK WHITON.

Born in Hingham, Aug. 22, 1828.

His general record will be found in connection with the history of the Fifty-eighth Regiment, M. V. I., three years.

SERGEANT

DEXTER GROSE.

Co. F.

Two brothers of Sergt. Grose were also in the service.

CORPORAL

GEORGE WILLIAM FEARING.

Born in Hingham, Aug. 16, 1837.

Co. K.

At the outbreak of the rebellion, Mr. Fearing entered the service as a volunteer in the Lincoln Light Infantry, and left Hingham on the 18th of May, 1861, to join this company, then stationed at Fortress Monroe.

On the 8th of May, 1862, credited to the town of Dover, Mass., he re-enlisted as private for nine months in Co. K, of the Forty-third Regiment, and while in camp at Readville was promoted corporal.

On the march from Newbern to Goldsboro', N.C., in the month of December, 1862, he was accidentally disabled, and compelled to retire from active service; but, being retained as commissary, he continued with the regiment until the expiration of his term of enlistment.

In consideration of the permanent character of the injury sustained, a small pension has been allowed.

PRIVATES.

LORING HERSEY CUSHING.

Born in Hingham, April 3, 1840.

Co. K.

ISAAC FRANCIS GOODWIN.

Born in Lebanon, Me., May 4, 1836.

Co. K.

* HOLLIS HERSEY.

Born in Hingham, May 3, 1833.

Co. K.

PETER LORING.

Born in Hingham, Nov. 6, 1837.

Co. K.

DANIEL McKENNA.
Since deceased.

Co. K.

SAMUEL CUSHING SOUTHER.
Born in Hingham, July 8, 1824.

Co. K.

THOMAS SOUTHER.
Born in Hingham.

Co. K.

CHARLES TOWER.
Born in Hingham, May 10, 1844.

Co. K.

WILLIAM WATERS SPRAGUE.
Born in Hingham, Nov. 1, 1844.

Co. A.

The regiment also included the following, as belonging to the quota of the town : —

ROBERT M. CUMMINGS.
Braintree, 23 years of age.

Co. B.

FREDERICK W. COTTON.
Town records say " Hingham ; " State records, " Boston," age 20.

Co. K.

FORTY-FOURTH REGIMENT.

The Forty-fourth, or "New England Guard Regiment," Col. Francis L. Lee, was gathered at "Camp Meigs," Readville, Mass.; and a large proportion of the recruits were there mustered on the 12th of September, 1862.

After a few weeks spent in preparatory service, the regiment left for the "Department of North Carolina," embarking at Boston by steamer "Merrimack," and arriving at Newbern on the 26th of October. Four days after landing, it started on the Tarboro' expedition, and Sunday, Nov. 2, took part in the skirmish at Smitherick's Ford and Rawles' Mills. Returning to Newbern, it remained at this post till Dec. 11, when Cos. D and H shared in the advance towards Goldsboro'. On the 14th, these companies were engaged at Kinston; on the 16th, at Whitehall Bridge; on the 17th, in reserve at the battle of Goldsboro'; and on the 20th retired again to Newbern.

No further operations were made until early in February; when they left for Plymouth, N.C., for the purpose of seizing provisions and army supplies stored for the use of the enemy.

This being accomplished, they returned to Newbern, and remained in camp until the middle of March, when, with others, they left for Washington, N.C., the siege of this place being laid on the 30th of the month.

On the first of April, the bombardment commenced; and this was continued, with short intermissions, until the 15th, when the enemy fell back, and the siege was raised.

On the 17th, several companies, including D, under the protection of gun-boat "Com. Hull," were detailed to land at Hill's Point, and destroy and build up such intrenchments as might be found necessary to guard against attacks from the land side. Having finished the work, they left once more for Newbern, and there relieving the Forty-fifth M. V. M., continued to perform provost duty till June 6, when they embarked for Boston, Mass. On their arrival, they entered camp at Readville, where they were regularly mustered out of service on the 18th of June, 1863, their term of enlistment having expired.

During the campaign, neither Co. D nor H suffered seriously from disease, nor sustained loss from the casualties of the field, though the loss to the regiment in killed and wounded was thirty-seven, and fifty-three died from disease, or were discharged for disability.

On the 14th of July the regiment was again called out for the suppression of a draft-riot in the city of Boston, and dismissed after a service of one week.

Included in this regiment, were eight residents or natives of Hingham, viz. : —

PRIVATES.

ALVIN BLANCHARD, Jun.
Born in Hingham, March 18, 1844.
Co. D.
Died of consumption, March 8, 1874.

JAMES LEWIS HUNT, 2d.
Born in Hingham, Jan. 20, 1844.
Co. H.
Also performed duty as Regimental and Company Clerk.

WILLIAM JONES.
Born in Hingham, June, 1838.
Co. D.

LEVI KENERSON.
Born in Hingham, Feb. 21, 1838.
Co. D.

JOHN HENRY LITCHFIELD, Jun.
Born in Cohasset, Jan. 28, 1844.
Co. D.

JOHN ALBERT REED.
Born in Hingham, June 13, 1842.
Co. D.

EZRA T. C. STEPHENSON.
Born in Hingham, Feb. 18, 1842.
Co. D.

WILLIAM LORING STEPHENSON.
Born in Hingham, Dec. 22, 1838.
Co. D.
Died in Hingham, Oct. 27, 1875.

FORTY-FIFTH REGIMENT.

The Forty-fifth "Cadet Regiment," Col. Charles R. Codman, was recruited in the autumn of 1862, and, in common with the Forty-third and Forty-fourth, was mustered at Camp Meigs, Readville, Mass.

Assigned to the Department of North Carolina, the regiment embarked at Boston on board the steamer "Mississippi," Nov. 5, 1862; arrived at Morehead City, N.C., on the 14th, and the same day proceeded to Newbern. Here it remained in camp until early in December, when Co. G, which included such of the natives or residents of Hingham as were in the regiment, was detached and sent to Fort Macon, to form a part of the garrison of that post. Towards the close of April, being relieved from duty at Fort Macon, they were ordered to Fort Spinola, near which the regiment was then stationed. There the company remained until June 24, when camp was broken, and they left for Morehead City, where they embarked for Boston, touching at Fortress Monroe on the passage home. Arriving on the 30th, they proceeded to Readville, and were there mustered out of service, July 8, 1863. Of those reckoned upon the quota of the town, the Forty-fifth included the following, viz. : —

PRIVATES.

ROBERT BURNSIDE.
Of Boston.

Co. I.

ERNST F. EICHBORN.
Hingham, age 34.

Co. G.

EDWIN G. EVANS.
Dorchester, age 31.

Co. B.

JACOB A. EWELL.
Dorchester, age 44.

Co. B.

FRANCIS HERSEY.
Born in Hingham, Jan. 20, 1835.

Co. G.

HENRY O. LITTLE.
Born in Hingham, age 28.

Co. G.

WILLIAM LOWRY, Jun.
Hingham, age 27.

Co. G.

JOSIAH LANE MARSH.
Born in Hingham, March 17, 1830.

Co. G.

JOHN R. MAYHEW.
Born in Hingham, age 21.
Co. G.

* DANIEL W. PENDERGAST.
Roxbury, age 27.
Co. G.

JAMES SOUTHER.
Born in Hingham. Nov. 9, 1822.
Co. G.

ARTEMAS SPRAGUE.
Born in Hingham, age 29.
Co. G.

EDWARD TRABBITTS.
Boston, age 31.
Co. G.

HERBERT J. TULLEY.
Roxbury, age 23.
Co. G.

DANIEL J. WALLS.
Hingham, age 22.
Co. G.

FIFTIETH REGIMENT.

Recruited at Camp Stanton, in Boxford. The regiment left the State Nov. 19, 1862, for New York City; and from thence was ordered to Long Island, where it went into quarters at Camp Banks. Early in December, by various vessels, the regiment embarked for New Orleans, and was there assigned to the command of Gen. Dudley of the first division, third brigade, Nineteenth Army Corps.

It took part in the expedition of Gen. Banks to Port Hudson, and participated in the strategic movement by which Admiral Farragut was enabled to pass the batteries at this locality. Continuing in the vicinity of Port Hudson, co-operating in the various means employed for the siege of the place, it was not only present in the assaults directly made to reduce the fort, but was much of the time engaged in supporting the batteries during the bombardment, until the final surrender on the 9th of July.

It arrived in Boston Aug. 11, and was mustered out at Wenham, Aug. 24, 1863.

The only enlistment from Hingham, so far as known, was

PRIVATE

CHARLES H. BROWN.

Age 21.

Enlisted Sept. 19, 1862; member of Co. E, and was mustered out Aug. 24, 1863.

ELEVENTH LIGHT BATTERY.

This was the only battery of nine months' men which Massachusetts had in the field. It was mustered into service Aug. 25, 1862, attached to the Twenty-second Army Corps, and assigned to duty in and around Washington. The only person connected with the battery from Hingham was

PRIVATE

JOSEPH M. THOMAS.

Born in Hanson, Aug. 4, 1841.

Enlisted from Hingham, Aug. 7, 1862. Mustered in at Readville Aug. 25th, for the period of nine months; mustered out May 29, 1863, by reason of expiration of service. (See chapter for one hundred days' men.)

LIST OF NINE MONTHS' MEN.

Alvin Blanchard, jun.,
Charles H. Brown.
Robert Burnside.
Ernst F. Eichborn.
Edwin G. Evans.
Jacob A. Ewell.
George W. Fearing.
Tilson Fuller.
Isaac F. Goodwin.
Dexter Grose.
Francis Hersey.
Hollis Hersey.
James L. Hunt, 2d.
William Jones.
Levi Kenerson.
Jairus Lincoln, jun.
John H. Litchfield, jun.
Henry O. Little.
Peter Loring.
William Lowry.
Caleb B. Marsh.
Frederick W. Cotton.

Robert M. Cummings.
Loring H. Cushing.
Josiah L. Marsh.
John R. Mayhew.
Daniel McKenna.
Daniel W. Pendergast.
John A. Reed.
George Smith.
James Souther.
Samuel C. Souther.
Thomas Souther.
Artemas Sprague.
William W. Sprague.
Ezra T. C. Stephenson.
William L. Stephenson.
Joseph M. Thomas. ——
Charles Tower.
Edward Trabbits.
Herbert J. Tulley.
Daniel Walls, jun.
John C. Whiton.

CHAPTER VIII.

Enlistments from Hingham — Sixty-First Regiment, M. V. I. — Sixty-Second Regiment —
Fourth Regiment Heavy Artillery, M. V. — Miscellaneous Assignments.

THE number of persons connected with Hingham who served for the period of one year was thirty-eight. Of these, thirty-five were enrolled by recruiting-officer Charles N. Marsh. The record of all, residents and non-residents, was alike creditable to themselves and the town they represented.

A brief sketch of the history of the regiments, with the names of the Hingham men connected therewith, is here appended.

SIXTY–FIRST REGIMENT.

The "Sixty-first," recruited in the autumn of 1864 and winter of 1864–5, was under the command of Col. Charles F. Wolcott, and has a good record. After being employed in erecting fortifications to cover City Point, Va., and doing picket-guard duty on the left of the army, it was attached to Gen. Collis's brigade, then operating with the Ninth Army Corps. It conducted itself with distinguished bravery in the action before Petersburg, the 2d of April, having re-captured Fort Mahone, and forced the enemy into the inner line of his work. First. Lieut. H. Burr Crandall wrote an interesting letter to Gov. Andrew, giving a description of this engagement, which has since been published. The regiment afterwards participated in the grand review at Washington.

The following members were accredited to the quota of Hingham, viz. : —

CORPORALS.

JAMES W. GRAY.
Age 24.

Enrolled in Co. K, Jan. 20, 1865. Mustered out July 16, 1865.

JOHN E. WILSON.
Age 24.

Enrolled in Co. E, Sept. 22, 1864. Mustered out June 4, 1865.

PRIVATES.

WILLIAM H. ALLEN.
Age 19.

Enrolled in Co. F, Oct. 10, 1864. Mustered out July 16, 1865.

THOMAS S. BRIGHAM.
Age 19.

Enrolled in Co. G, Nov. 19, 1864. Mustered out July 16, 1865.

WAKEFIELD CARVER.
Age 19.

Enrolled in Co. F, Oct. 3, 1864. Mustered out July 16, 1865.

JAMES DALEY.
Age 36.

Enrolled in Co. I, Jan. 20, 1865. Mustered out July 16, 1865.

JOHN R. DONAVEN.
Age 18.

Enrolled in Co F, Oct 7, 1864. Mustered out July 16, 1865.

GEORGE C. DUNHAM.

Age 23.

Enrolled in Co. I, Jan. 20, 1865. Mustered out July 16, 1865.

MICHAEL FRANEY.

Age 39.

Enrolled in Co. K, Dec. 30, 1864. Mustered out July 16, 1865.

JOHN H. HAYES.

Age 20.

Enrolled in Co. K, Jan. 6, 1865. Mustered out July 16, 1865.

JOSEPH H. HILTON.

Age 20.

Enrolled in Co. I, Jan. 6, 1865. Mustered out July 16, 1865.

WILLIAM HILTON.

Age 41.

Enrolled in Co, F. Oct. 7, 1864. Mustered out July 16, 1865.

PATRICK J. KELLEY.

Age 18.

Enrolled in Co. C, Sept. 15, 1864. Mustered out June 4, 1865.

JAMES McNAMARA.

Age 18.

Enrolled in Co. F, Oct. 18, 1864. Discharged for disability Nov. 4, 1864.

GEORGE W. R. PUTNAM.

Age 20.

Enrolled in Co. H, Jan. 5, 1865. Mustered out July 16, 1865.

GEORGE L. RICH.

Age 22.

Enrolled in Co. H, Jan. 5, 1865. Mustered out May 15, 1865.

JOHN A. WATSON.

Age 21.

Enrolled in Co. F, Oct. 2, 1864. Mustered out July 16, 1865.

SIXTY-SECOND REGIMENT.

This regiment was being recruited at the time Gen. Lee surrendered, but was mustered out before its organization was completed, by order of the War Department, dated April 29, 1865. It had one man only from Hingham, viz. : —

PRIVATE

ANDREW WALLACE GARDNER.

Born in Hingham, Dec. 1, 1844.

Enrolled in Co. C, March 31, 1865, for one year's service. Mustered out at Readville, Mass., May 5, 1865. (See also chapter for One Hundred Days.)

FOURTH REGIMENT HEAVY ARTILLERY.

This regiment was composed of twelve unattached companies that were recruited for one year. The companies were mustered into service at Gallop's Island, Boston Harbor, during the month of August, 1864, and afterwards consolidated into a regiment by Special Order No. 395 of the War Department dated Nov. 12, 1864. The regiment was commanded by Col. William S. King, formerly lieutenant-colonel of the Thirty-fifth Mass. Vols., and was principally on garrison duty in the defences near Washington. The adjutant-general of Massachusetts, in his report of 1865, says this regiment was noted for its good drill and soldierly conduct during the entire period of its service.

Among the enlistments were the following : —

PRIVATES.

JAMES MADISON CLEVERLY.

Born in Hanover, Mass., Dec. 17, 1848; enlisted in Hingham.

Enrolled in Co. G, Aug. 27, 1864. Mustered out June 30, 1865.

JOHN A. FARRINGTON.

Age 23.

Enrolled in Co. C, Aug. 12, 1864. Mustered out June 17, 1865.

GEORGE JACOB FEARING.

Born in Hingham, Feb. 7, 1834.

Enrolled in Co. G, Aug. 16, 1864. Mustered out June 17, 1865.

WILLIAM MASON GILMAN.

Born in Boston, Feb. 17, 1847.

Enrolled in Co. G, Aug. 27, 1864. Mustered out June 17, 1865.

HENRY HART.

Age 18.

Enrolled in Co. C, Aug. 11, 1864. Mustered out June 17, 1865.

CHARLES HELMS.

Born in Northwood, N.H., Oct. 1, 1825.

Enrolled in Co. G, Aug. 22, 1864. Mustered out May 21, 1865. Was four months in Mount Pleasant Hospital confined by rheumatism.

MICHAEL LANDERS.

Age 19.

Enrolled in Co. G, Aug. 18, 1864. Mustered out June 17, 1865. Since deceased.

MICHAEL ROACH.

Age 18.

Enrolled in Co. G, Aug. 17, 1864. Mustered out June 17, 1865.

CHARLES SHUTE.

Born in Hingham. April 24, 1822: resident of Worcester, Mass.

Enrolled in Co. D, Aug. 18, 1864. Mustered out at Fort Richardson, Va., June 17, 1865.

MELZAR VINAL.

Age 24.

Enrolled in Co. C, Aug. 16, 1864. Mustered out June 17, 1865.

HENRY B. VOGELL.

Age 18.

Enrolled in Co. G, Aug. 16, 1864. Mustered out June 17, 1865.

JOSEPH N. WALLS.

Born in Ireland, Dec. 27, 1836; resides in Hingham.

Enrolled in Co. G, Aug. 16, 1864. Afterwards connected with the Twenty-third Regiment, unattached service, and lastly transferred to, and consolidated with, Co. G, of the Fourth Regiment Massachusetts Heavy Artillery, in which he first enlisted, and from which he was mustered out June 17, 1865, by reason of the close of the war.

18

MISCELLANEOUS ASSIGNMENTS.

The following were enrolled for the term of one year, and assigned to three-year regiments whose term of service had' not expired, viz. : —

WILLIAM M. CARTER.

Age 23.

Enrolled in Co. H, Fifty-eighth Regiment, M. V. I., Aug. 18, 1864. Mustered out July 14, 1865.

OWEN MURPHY.

Age 28.

Enrolled in Co. C, Seventeenth Regiment, M. V. I., Sept. 20, 1864. Service terminated June 30, 1865, order W.D., in Co. H.

WILLIAM CARTER.

Age 43.

Enrolled in Co. G, First Regiment Heavy Artillery, M. V., Sept. 28, 1864. Mustered out May 3, 1865.

FRANCIS MAYHEW.

Age 18.

Enrolled in Co. A, Third Regiment Heavy Artillery, M. V., Sept. 10, 1864. Mustered out June 14, 1865.

GEORGE PEACOCK.

Age 20.

Enrolled in Co. A, Third Regiment Heavy Artillery, M. V., Sept. 28, 1864. Mustered out June 14, 1865.

DAVID PETTINGELL.

Age 35.

Enrolled in Co. C, Seventeenth Regiment, M. V. I., Sept. 24, 1864. Service terminated June 30, 1865, order W. D., in Co. B.

PHILIP SULLIVAN.

Age 22.

Enrolled in Co. C, Seventeenth Regiment, M. V. I., Sept. 23, 1864. Service terminated June 30, 1865, order W. D, in Co. B.

AARON D. SWAN.

Age 40.

Enrolled in Co. M, Third Regiment Heavy Artillery, M. V., Aug. 27, 1864. Mustered out June 17, 1865.

LIST OF ONE-YEAR MEN.

William H. Allen.
Thomas S. Brigham.
William Carter.
William M. Carter.
Wakefield Carver.
James M. Cleverly.
James Daley.
John R. Donaven.
George C. Dunham.
John A. Farrington.
George J. Fearing.
Michael Franey.
Andrew W. Gardner.
William M. Gilman.
James W. Gray.
Henry Hart.
John H. Hayes,
Charles Helms.
Joseph H. Hilton.

William Hilton.
Patrick J. Kelley.
Michael Landers.
Francis Mayhew.
James McNamara.
Owen Murphy.
George Peacock.
David Pettingell.
George W. R. Putnam.
George L. Rich.
Michael Roach.
Charles Shute.
Philip Sullivan.
Aaron D. Swan.
Melzar Vinal.
Henry B. Vogell.
Joseph N. Walls.
John A. Watson.
John E. Wilson.

CHAPTER IX.

THREE YEARS' MEN.

SOON after the call of the National Government, issued on the 15th of April, 1861, for seventy-five thousand volunteers, to serve for a term of three months, it was apparent that the war-cloud which had risen in the South was rapidly growing darker and more threatening. The States were no longer a unit. Thousands were gathering to the support of the standard of rebellion, and the indications of a severe and protracted struggle were unmistakable.

To meet coming exigencies, it was at once decided, not only to place a numerous and efficient force in the field, but to enlist this force for a term of years. Accordingly on the 3d of May, 1861, a call was made for eighty-two thousand seven hundred and forty-eight men, divided between the regular army, volunteers, and the navy, — the same to serve *for three years* unless sooner discharged.

Again, towards the close of the month of July following, another call was issued by the government for five hundred thousand men of this class, followed successively by calls July 2, 1862, for three hundred thousand ; Oct. 17, 1863, three hundred thousand; Feb. 1, 1864, two hundred thousand ; and March 14, 1864, two hundred thousand men.

In addition to these, a call was made on the 18th of July, 1864, for five hundred thousand men ; and on the 19th of December, 1864, for three hundred thousand men, a portion only being for a term of three years.

In a very large majority of the regiments of volunteer infantry, as well as in the regiments and companies of cavalry and heavy artillery, the town of Hingham was to a greater or less extent represented.

A few words seem to be needed in this connection by way of explanation. The discrepancies between the statements given by those in the service, and the facts published by the State authorities, were found to be not only numerous, but often marked and important. Indeed, the instances of perfect conformity appear to have been the exception rather than the general rule. It will therefore be understood, that where the age, time or place of birth, date of muster or discharge, or other particulars relating to time or locality, may be at variance with the published records, they are given in strict accordance with the facts supplied under the signature of the individual interested.

Deceased soldiers and sailors are designated by an asterisk (*), and their records will be found in the chapter "In Memoriam."

FIRST REGIMENT INFANTRY.

The First Regiment, Col. Robert Cowdin, was mustered into the service of the United States on the 15th of June, 1861. Immediately on the call for volunteers for a service of three years, Col. Cowdin visited Washington, and tendered himself and regiment for that period; and this is understood to be the first regiment in the United States, armed and equipped, which was so tendered.

It left the State on the day of muster, and on the 17th marched through the streets of Baltimore, — the first Massachusetts regiment which had passed through these streets to the seat of war since the massacre of the 19th of April, as it was also the first three years' volunteer regiment that reached the city of Washington.

After an active career, and leaving a noble record of bravery, it was mustered out at the expiration of the term of enlistment, May 25, 1864.

It took part in the following engagements, viz.: Bull Run, Williamsburg, Fair Oaks, Glendale, and other battles on the Peninsula, Kettle Run, Second Bull Run, Chantilly, Fredericksburg, Chancellorsville, Gettysburg, Locust Grove, Wilderness, and Spottsylvania. Of natives or residents of Hingham, the Massachusetts First included the following: —

LIEUTENANT

*ELIJAH B. GILL, Jun.

Co. I.

PRIVATES.

*WILLIAM H. BEAL.

Co. K.

JOHN W. CHESSMAN.

Enlisted from Hingham. Mustered Sept. 4, 1861, in Co. H. Transferred to Veteran Reserve Corps, Nov. 15, 1863.

*JOHN WILLIAM GARDNER.

Co. I.

*GEORGE P. KILBURN.

Co. I.

JOSEPH M. POOLE.

Enrolled from Hingham. Mustered Aug. 13, 1862, in Co. F. Discharged at expiration of term of service, May 25, 1864.

*THOMAS TINSLEY.

Co. K.

SECOND REGIMENT.

On the authority of the Adjutant General's Report, the Second was one of the Massachusetts regiments in Gen. Sherman's army, and followed him from the mountains to the sea.

It was mustered into the service of the United States May 25, 1861 ; left for the seat of war July 8, 1861 ; and was mustered out July 14, 1865.

Its list of engagements includes Jackson, Front Royal, Winchester, Cedar Mountain, Antietam, Fredericksburg, Chancellorsville, Gettysburg, Atlanta, Raleigh, and many others.

Of enlistments connected with Hingham, it contained one only, viz. : —

ISAAC B. DAMON.

Born in Scituate, age 35.

Resident of Hingham. Enrolled from Weymouth, and Feb. 17, 1862, mustered as private in Co. I.

In early life he came from Scituate to Hingham, and was an apprentice with David A. Hersey, harness-maker. Soon after entering the army, he was appointed head of the brigade harness department, but during the march through South Carolina to the seaboard, took part in the more active, as well as more hazardous duties required for the success of the great enterprise. Escaping casualties and disease, he returned home with the regiment, and was mustered out March 27, 1865, having been in the service three years.

So far as known, Mr. Damon was the only person from Hingham connected with the army of Gen. Sherman, who made the journey through "from the mountains to the sea."

SEVENTH REGIMENT.

This regiment, recruited principally in Bristol County by Col. afterwards Major-Gen. Darius N. Couch, was mustered into the service of the United States at Taunton, Mass., June 15, 1861, and arrived at Washington, D.C., the 15th of July. It took part in the battles of the Peninsula, Fredericksburg, Chancellorsville, Gettysburg, Wilderness, Spottsylvania, North Anna, and Cold Harbor.

While in the service, it was almost constantly engaged in important duties at the front. Upon return to Taunton, June 20, 1864, it met with a welcome reception, and was mustered out the 4th of July. There were two Hingham persons in this regiment, viz. : —

PRIVATES.

*WILLIAM DUNBAR, JUN.

Co. K.

EBENEZER FLINT ROBERTS.

Born in Hingham, Aug. 28, 1837.

Mustered into the United States service at Cambridge, Mass., Aug. 11, 1862; joined Co. A, of the Seventh Regiment, M. V. I., at Sugar Loaf Mountain, Md.; was on picket-duty with the regiment on the last day of the battle at Antietam; took part in the battle of Fredericksburg, Va., in December, 1862 ; also in the " Mud March" expedition.

May 2, 1863, the regiment crossed the Rappahannock River, marching by night to Fredericksburg. The next day advanced up the Heights, and occupied the crest of Mary's Hill, captured two pieces of rebel artillery, and planted its colors upon a portion of the works from which the enemy had been driven. Continuing the pursuit towards Salem Church, the enemy was again met in strong force, and successfully encountered in a contest which lasted until dark of that day. During the fight Mr.

Roberts received a gun-shot wound in the left hand, which disabled him for duty. He was ordered to the rear, and afterwards sent to Campbell Hospital at Washington, from which place he obtained a furlough of thirty days, and came home. June 16, 1863, he reported at the hospital in Washington, and shortly afterwards was sent with six hundred others to Chestnut Hill Hospital, Philadelphia, where he remained till Nov. 15, 1863; being then transferred to the Veteran Reserve Corps, Capt. Dillon, and appointed "orderly" to the executive officer at the hospital. In this capacity he continued till the regiment came home, and was mustered out the 7th of July.

Mr. Roberts also served as a volunteer in the Lincoln Light Infantry at Fortress Monroe, Va.

NINTH REGIMENT.

The Ninth, composed principally of men of Irish birth or descent, was recruited by Col. Thomas Cass, and mustered into the United States service June 11, 1861. After being organized, the regiment was encamped at Long Island in Boston Harbor, until it embarked for Washington, where it arrived the 29th of June. Participating in most of the important engagements that took place between the Army of the Potomac and the Confederate forces in Virginia, the Ninth won a high reputation for endurance and soldierly bearing, as well as for its discipline and bravery.

Col. Cass was mortally wounded before Richmond, June 27, 1862; and after being removed to Boston, died July 12, at his residence on North Bennet Street. Col. Patrick A. Guiney of Boston afterwards commanded the regiment.

The Adjutant-general of Massachusetts, in his printed report for 1864, says, "*The Ninth was one of our best regiments.*" It was mustered out on Boston Common, June 21, 1864, by reason of the expiration of its term of service.

Of the three men who were recruited in Hingham for this regiment, only one was permanently connected with it, viz.: —

JOHN JOYCE BREEN.

Born in Hingham, Feb. 22, 1844.

Enlisted in this town July 28, 1862 ; mustered into the United States service at Camp Cameron, Cambridge, Aug. 12, as private ; promoted corporal Jan. 19, 1863.

Early in September, 1862, he joined Co. K, then at Miner's Hill ; was in active service with the Army of the Potomac, taking part in the battles of Fredericksburg, Chancellorsville, Gettysburg, Mine Run, Wilderness, and Spottsylvania ; also in the engagements of Botler's Mill, Aldie Gap, Williamsport, Wapping Heights, Bristoe's Station, Rappahannock Station, &c.

Corp. Breen was in the service twenty-two months and nine days. During this period he marched about twelve hundred miles ; was wounded by a gun-shot in the right arm at Spottsylvania, May 12, 1864 ; was then sent to Mt. Pleasant Hospital at Washington, D.C., and thence to the Satterlee Hospital at West Philadelphia, Pa. He was mustered out at Boston, Mass., June 21, 1864, by reason of expiration of service.

ELEVENTH REGIMENT.

The Eleventh Regiment, Col. George Clark, jun., was organized through the enterprising spirit and liberality of a few citizens of Boston, and may justly be termed a " Boston Regiment." It was gathered at Fort Warren ; afterwards moved to Camp Cameron, and left the State for the field of conflict on the 27th of June, 1861.

Whether the extent of its service be considered, or its sanguinary nature, the record of the Eleventh will be surpassed by few, if any, of the regiments from the State. Commencing with the battle of First Bull Run, which took place a few weeks only after leaving Boston, it was successively engaged at Yorktown, Williamsburg, Fair Oaks, Savage Station, Glendale, Malvern Hill, Bristoe's Station, Second Bull Run, Chantilly, Fredericksburg, Chancellorsville, Gettysburg, Kelly's Ford, Locust Grove, Wilderness, Spottsylvania, North Anna, Tolopotomy, Cold Harbor, Petersburg, Strawberry Plains, Deep Bottom, Poplar Spring Church, and Boydton Road.

The organization as a regiment ceased June 12, 1864, when the original members who had served three years were mustered out.

The following are the enlistments of natives or residents of Hingham : —

CAPTAIN .

* EDWIN HUMPHREY.

Co. A.

SERGEANTS.

JAMES JACKSON HEALEY.

Born in Boston, June 9, 1846.

Enlisted at Boston, May 9, 1861, as drummer in Co. E, Capt. James R. Bigelow, and was mustered June 13, 1861. Afterwards, at his request, transferred as private to Co. K of the same regiment.

Promoted corporal, next sergeant, and also served as mounted orderly to Gen. J. B. Carr. He was in every important engagement of the regiment, was twice wounded, first at Laurel Hill, next at Spottsylvania, and for a time confined in Bellevue Hospital, and also in the Campbell Hospital at Washington, D.C.

Mustered out at Boston, Mass., by reason of expiration of term of service.

* LEMUEL S. BLACKMAN.

Co. K.

* DANIEL HORACE BURR.

Co. K.

JAMES S. DUSTIN.

Enrolled from Hingham, age 40.

Mustered June 13, 1861. Included in the list of men returned by town authorities as being on the quota of Hingham.

* NATHANIEL GILL.

PRIVATES.

WILLIAM TODD BARNES.

Born in Hingham, July 5, 1836.

Enlisted at Boston for three years, and was mustered in Co. K, June 13, 1861. For some time after the close of the war he was in the insane hospital at Taunton, Mass. Since deceased.

* CHARLES H. MARSH.

Co. K.

WILLIAM CORNELIUS MILLER.

Born in Salem, Mass., Nov. 29, 1836.

Enlisted at Boston, Jan. 2, 1862, and the same day was mustered as private in Co. B. In the battle at Williamsburg, May 3, 1862, Mr. Miller was severely wounded in the shoulder, and was obliged to lie upon the field through the night. The following day, weak and suffering from loss of blood, he was removed to the field hospital, next to hospital at Baltimore, and finally sent to his home at Hingham. For a year his wound was the source of much pain, and he was finally mustered out at Boston for disability, Sept. 23, 1863. The sympathy and kindness extended on the part of his friends during his confinement are gratefully acknowledged.

WALLACE THOMAS.

Enlisted from Roxbury, Nov. 14, 1863, as private in Co. K, and was mustered out near Washington, D.C., July 14, 1865, having served to the close of the war.

Mr. Thomas was present in most of the engagements included in the record of the Eleventh Regiment. In the battles of Chancellorsville and Wilderness, — at one time victorious, and again repulsed, — the conflict was carried on in a spirit the most determined and heroic. Among the wounded, was the subject of this notice. Declining to enter the hospital for surgical aid, he manfully held his place in the ranks, and discharged his duties until perfect recovery.

At the time of mustering out, chronic diarrhœa, that universal scourge of the soldier, had already begun its work. Lingering for nearly six years, he died at Waltham, Mass., March 14, 1871, and was buried in the cemetery at Hingham Centre.

He was the son of William and Rachel (Beal) Thomas, and was born in Hingham, April 2, 1834.

UNASSIGNED RECRUITS.

WILLIAM BURTES.

Enrolled from Hingham, 21 years of age.

Mustered May 9, 1864; Transferred to Navy, June 6, 1864.

CHARLES RICHARDSON.

Enrolled from Hingham, age 21.

Mustered May 16, 1864.

TWELFTH REGIMENT.

The Twelfth Massachusetts was raised by Fletcher Webster of Marshfield, who was commissioned colonel, and commanded the regiment until he was killed at the second battle of Bull Run, Aug. 30, 1862. It was afterwards under the command of Col. James L. Bates of Weymouth, Mass. This regiment originated as follows : —

The Sunday after our troops were attacked in Baltimore, Md., a mass meeting was held in State Street, Boston, in response to a call for volunteers issued by Fletcher Webster. The meeting was addressed by William Dehon, Esq., Edward Riddle, Hon. Charles L. Woodbury, Mr. Webster, and others. After reading the proclamation of Gov. Andrew, Mr. Webster said he had offered his services for the purpose of raising a regiment to serve the United States during the continuance of the existing difficulties. " I shall be ready on Monday," said Mr. Webster, " to enlist recruits. I know that your patriotism and valor will prompt you to the path of duty, and we will show to the world that the Massachusetts of 1776 is the same in 1861."

The regiment was mustered into service June 26, 1861, and left the State July 23. It was engaged at Cedar Mountain, Second Bull Run, Antietam, Fredericksburg, Chancellorsville, Gettysburg, Wilderness, Spottsylvania, North Anna River, Cold Harbor, and Petersburg. July 8, 1864, it was mustered out of service at Boston.

Connected with this regiment were the following natives or residents of Hingham, viz. : —

CAPTAIN

*ALEXANDER HITCHBORN.

Co. F.

CORPORAL

GEORGE GARDNER.

Born in Hingham, Aug. 27. 1845.

Enlisted at Boston, June 26, 1861, in Co. E ; afterwards promoted corporal.

Was present in the engagement at Cedar Mountain (where he was corporal of the color-guard), Second Bull Run, Antietam, Fredericksburg, Chancellorsville, Wilderness, and other noted battles of the Twelfth Regiment.

After the expiration of his term of service, he returned to Boston, June 25, and was there mustered out with the regiment, July 8, 1864.

Mr. Gardner has since deceased. He was son of Aaron and Persis (Cushing) Gardner ; and died of disease of the brain, at Hingham, Feb. 21, 1871, aged twenty-five years.

*JOHN H. BLACKMAN.

Co. H.

LABAN F. CUSHING.

Born in Hingham, age 30.

Enrolled in Co. K, June 26, 1861, as a resident of Manchester ; termination of service Aug. 27, 1862, by reason of disability.

JAMES D. DUNBAR.

Born in Hingham, age 24.

Enrolled in Co. H, June 26, 1861, as a resident of Weymouth ; mustered out July 8, 1864, by expiration of service, as prisoner, having been confined ten months.

JOHN J. EDMONDS.

Age 20.

Enrolled in Co. G, June 26, 1861 ; transferred Jan. 15, 1864, to V. R. C.

*JAMES FITZGERALD.

Co. G.

JACOB GARDNER, Jun.

Born in Hingham, age 35.

Enrolled in Co. H, July 12, 1861 ; termination of service, Feb. 11, 1862, on account of disability.

*SAMUEL SPENCER.

Co. E.

*HENRY SWEARS.

Co. H.

*FRANCIS THOMAS.

Co. H.

THIRTEENTH REGIMENT.

This regiment was mustered into service July 16, 1861 ; left the State July 30, and was mustered out Aug. 1, 1864.

Its record includes the following engagements, viz. : Second Bull Run, Antietam, Fredericksburg, Chancellorsville, Gettysburg, Wilderness, Spottsylvania, North Anna, Cold Harbor, and Petersburg. Of those connected with Hingham, there were —

PRIVATES.

WILLIAM WALLACE SPRAGUE.

Born in Hingham, age 19.

Enlisted from Boston, and mustered July 20, 1861, as private in Co. B. Taken prisoner at Gettysburg, and carried to Richmond, Va. He was confined for eight months in Belle Isle : afterwards paroled with six hundred others, and came to Annapolis, Md.

Mr. Sprague states that the sufferings experienced in this prison from hunger, cold, and neglect were beyond description, and could only be known to those who had the misfortune to be confined there. " It were far better," he says, " to fall upon the battle-field, than to be taken prisoner, and slowly die from starvation and disease."

He was afterwards detailed as clerk in the quartermaster's department.

Mustered out Aug. 1, 1864, by reason of expiration of service.

GEORGE WASHINGTON STODDER.

Born in Hingham, age 29.

Enlisted at Boston, and mustered as private in Co. H, July 28, 1862.

Mustered out with the regiment, Aug. 1, 1864.

FOURTEENTH REGIMENT.

The Fourteenth, generally recognized as the "Essex Regiment," was composed entirely of companies from Essex County. On the 25th of June, it was ordered to Fort Warren; July 5 mustered into the service of the United States, and left Massachusetts Aug. 7, 1861.

Jan. 1, 1862, by orders from the War Department, the regiment was changed from an infantry to heavy artillery.

It included two enlistments from Hingham, viz., Privates

WILLIAM CARTER, and

(For record of Mr. Carter, see First Regiment Heavy Artillery.)

ANTON TAPP.

Enrolled from Hingham, age 35.

Jan. 1, 1862, mustered out for re-enlistment, and transferred to Co. L, First Regiment Heavy Artillery. Mr. Tapp was a good soldier, and left the service with an honorable record. He has since deceased.

FIFTEENTH REGIMENT.

This regiment was mustered into the service of the United States July 12, 1861; left Massachusetts Aug. 8, 1861; and was mustered out July 28, 1864.

Its list of engagements includes Ball's Bluff, battles on the Peninsula, Antietam, Fredericksburg, Chancellorsville, Gettysburg, Bristoe's Station, Robertson's Tavern, Wilderness, and all the battles from the Rapidan to Petersburg, in which the Second Army Corps took part.

Those soldiers whose term of service had not expired at the date of muster-out of the regiment were transferred to the Twentieth Regiment.

It included the following enlistment from Hingham : —

JOHN E. MORSE.

Resident of Hingham.

Enlisted from Fitchburg, Mass., July 12, 1861, as private in Co. B ; discharged July 28, 1864, by reason of expiration of term of service.

Taken prisoner at Ball's Bluff, and was four months at Richmond ; rejoined his regiment ; then, being disabled by sickness at Harrison's Landing, was sent to hospital at Little York, where he continued for some time acting as ward-master.

For bravery and meritorious conduct was promoted captain of a company belonging to the Invalid Corps. The organization, however, was soon after dissolved, its services not being required.

In May, 1864, he was wounded in the wrist, and being again disabled, returned home on a furlough.

At the time of his capture, he was connected with the Twentieth Regiment under Col. Lee. When the retreat commenced, he, in company with Col. Lee and others, hastened to the banks of the river, but found no means for crossing the stream. Failing in their attempts to construct a raft, and seeing no prospect of escape, Col. Lee advised the party to give up. Capt. Morse and one or two others decided not to yield without compulsion, and started off in another direction. They had proceeded but a short distance, when they were met by a number of mounted rebel pickets, to whom they made peaceful surrender. Being ordered to mount the horses, they obeyed forthwith, rode to the enemy's camp, and thence to Richmond. As prisoners they received kind treatment, and their captors were represented as gentlemen.

SIXTEENTH REGIMENT.

The Sixteenth Regiment, Col. Powell T. Wyman, was mustered into the United States service by companies at Camp Cameron in North Cambridge, a large proportion of the enlistments being from Middlesex County.

Among the enrolled were four men reckoned upon the quota of Hingham, viz.: —

*DENNIS MEAGHER.

Co. A.

*DON PEDRO WILSON.

Co. A.

*MICHAEL FEE.

Co. E.

*CHARLES W. BLOSSOM.

Co. I.

All were either killed or died in the service, and their records will be found in succeeding pages of the volume.

SEVENTEENTH REGIMENT.

The Seventeenth Regiment was organized at Lynnfield, Mass. The enlistments were largely from the County of Essex; though, as at first constituted, it contained one company from the County of Middlesex, and one from Suffolk.

It left the State Aug. 23, 1861; for a short time was stationed at Baltimore, and then moved to Newbern, N.C.

It was present in the engagement at Kinston, Goldsboro', and Bachelder's Creek.

Mustered out at Greensboro', N.C., July 11, 1865, and finally discharged from the service of the United States at Readville, Mass., July 26, 1865.

The number killed in battle was eleven, and one hundred and forty-two died from wounds or disease.

The enlistments from Hingham, so far as known, were three, viz. : —

SERGEANT

OWEN MURPHY.

Age 23.

First enlisted from Danvers, Mass., July 22, 1861, as private in Co. C; discharged Aug. 3, 1864, by reason of expiration of term of enlistment; Sept. 20, 1864, re-enlisted as sergeant from Hingham in Co. C; and June 30, 1865, was mustered out by order of War Department, being at the time member of Co. H.

PRIVATES.

DAVID PETTINGELL.

Age 35.

Enlisted for one year. Served on the quota of Hingham.

PHILIP SULLIVAN.

Age 22.

Enlisted for one year. Served on the quota of Hingham.

EIGHTEENTH REGIMENT.

To the loyalty and patriotic spirit of the citizens of Duxbury, Middleboro', Hanover, Dedham, and Wrentham, is due the origin of this notedly excellent regiment. Companies, previously formed and drilled in these towns, were ordered into camp at Dedham, Mass., by the governor, in July, 1861, and thus made the nucleus for the Eighteenth. To these were soon added companies from Taunton, Quincy, and Plymouth, and in November a company from the town of Carver, swelling the number to nine hundred and ninety-six men.

The regiment was mustered into the service of the United States on the 27th of August, 1861, but, as a battalion of eight companies, left Massachusetts Aug. 26, under orders for Washington.

The adjutant-general states, that during the following autumn opportunity was offered, and favorably improved, for the instruction and drilling of the regiment; and the command, thus obtaining a high degree of discipline, and a commendable proficiency in military drill and exercise, was complimented by the general of the division, George McClellan, with a new and complete outfit of uniforms, camp-equipage, &c., imported from France by the government, being the same worn by the *Chasseurs à pied*.

The subsequent history of the regiment was as brilliant as it was active and sanguinary. It shared in the battles on the Peninsula, and was engaged at Second Bull Run, Shepardstown, Fredericksburg, Chancellorsville, Gettysburg, Rappahannock Station, Wilderness, Spottsylvania, Cold Harbor, Petersburg, and Weldon Railroad. The casualties were numerous, and the regiment suffered severely; the killed and wounded numbering nearly two hundred and fifty.

Made up largely by enlistments from Plymouth County, the Eighteenth may be justly termed the "Old Colony Regiment." Few organizations have made a better record, as the following sketches of those who shared in its experiences will serve to show : —

- COLONEL

THOMAS WESTON.

Age 34.

Enrolled from Middleborough ; entered the service as captain, Co. E, Aug. 20, 1861 ; promoted major Oct. 15, 1863. Brevet lieutenant-colonel, Sept. 2, 1864, at expiration of service.

Col. Weston has been a resident of Hingham since the war.

MAJOR

BENJAMIN F. MESERVEY.

Born in Hallowell, Me., July 16, 1833.

At the commencement of the war Major Meservey was a resident of Quincy ; and upon the first call for Massachusetts troops left, April 16, 1861, with the company from that town (Co. H, Fourth Mass. Volunteer Militia), in the capacity of second lieutenant. During the three months' service, he performed all the duties required in the most efficient manner. He was engaged with his company in the first battle of the war at Big Bethel. At the expiration of his term of service, he proceeded to recruit a company for three years, which was attached to the Eighteenth Mass. Volunteers ; was commissioned as captain, and started again for the seat of war on the 2d of August, 1861, only a month having elapsed after the expiration of his first term of service.

The Eighteenth Regiment formed a part of the Army of the Potomac. It was engaged at the Battle of Hanover Court House, performed efficient service during the siege of Yorktown, and was engaged at the Battle of Gaines' Mill. Major Meservey was present with his command in these several engagements, and also at the battles of Antietam and Shepardstown Ford. At the battle of Second Bull Run the regiment suffered severely, and Major Meservey was wounded in the head.

The Eighteenth was again engaged at the battle of Fredericksburg, where in the charge on St. Mary's Heights the loss sustained was great, having advanced nearer the works of the enemy than any other troops during that terrible engagement. This regiment participated in the battles of Chancellorsville, Gettysburg, and the expedition to Mine Run, in all of which Major Meservey sustained an active and honorable part. He was also present at the battles of the Wilderness and Laurel Hill, and commanded the regiment during the campaign under Gen. Grant, from Spottsylvania to Petersburg, which included the battles at North Anna, Bethesda Church, Cold Harbor, and in front of Petersburg. He was also engaged in the fight at the Weldon Railroad.

The regiment returned to Massachusetts at the expiration of its term of enlistment, and was mustered out Sept. 2, 1864. Few organizations from our State can show so clean a record as the Eighteenth Massachusetts. Major Meservey's service was closely identified with his regiment, and was marked by bravery and efficiency.

At the time of mustering out, he received promotion to brevet-major for gallant and meritorious conduct.

Major Meservey became a citizen of Hingham soon after the close of his military service.

HENRY JONES.

Born in Hingham, March 4, 1841.

In July, 1861, enlisted at Duxbury, where he resided at the time, and on the 24th of August was mustered at Readville into Co. E, Capt. Thomas Weston. Promoted sergeant in January, 1864.

On the 1st of September he joined the Army of .the Potomac, and for the entire winter of 1861-2 was stationed at the front for outpost duty.

In April he was engaged before the defences of Yorktown, acting as skirmisher, and in support of the batteries ; and from the middle to the close of the month, or for nearly three weeks, there were few days in which he was not to a greater or less extent exposed to the fire of the enemy.

On the 30th of August, after a series of marches the most protracted and exhausting, he arrived at Bull Run, and took part in an engagement which proved one of the most disastrous of the war. During the battle he was unfortunately wounded in the hand; and, being thus incapacitated for service, three months were spent in the Fourteenth-street Hospital at Washington before complete recovery.

In the long list of battles, including Second Bull Run, Chancellorsville, Gettysburg, Rappahannock Station, Mine Run, Wilderness, Spottsylvania, Cold Harbor, and Petersburg, following as they did in rapid succession, he witnessed a reduction from the ranks of 250 men. In a single struggle more than one-half of the men were killed or wounded.

While in front of Petersburg, Serg. Jones was seriously wounded by a Minnie ball from the rifle of one of the enemy's sharpshooters. Lying down at the time, the missile entered his cheek, shattering his jaw, and at last found a lodgement in the side of the body. Thus completely disabled, he was conveyed to the City Point Hospital, and shortly after removed to the hospital at Alexandria, where he remained for some weeks until the expiration of his term of enlistment, when, in an enfeebled condition, he returned with the remnant of the regiment to Boston, and at Readville was honorably discharged from service.

SERGEANT

*WILLIAM HENRY JONES, Jun.
Co. K.

CORPORAL

*NELSON FRANCIS CORTHELL.
Co. A.

PRIVATES.

*THOMAS CHURCHILL.
Co. A.

JAMES M. DOWNER.
Enrolled from Hingham, age 21.

Mustered Aug. 25, 1863, in Co. A. Included in the official list returned by the selectmen, of soldiers serving for the quota of the town. Service terminated Jan. 9, 1864, by reason of disability.

JOHN Q. JACOB.
Enrolled from Hingham, age 21.

Mustered Aug. 24, 1861. Private in Co. K. Afterwards transferred to Veteran Reserve Corps.

*WILLIAM HENRY JONES.
Co. K.

SAMUEL THAXTER MEARS.
Born in Hingham, Aug. 1, 1837.

May 23, 1861, enlisted at Duxbury, Mass., and was mustered July 26, 1861.

He was at the battle before Yorktown, in the engagement at Charles City Court House, and at the bombardment at Harrison Landing. In the seven days' fight he was sun-struck ; and being thus disabled, was for more or less of the time confined to the hospital at Frederick, Va., and at Baltimore, Md., for ten months. Prompted by feelings of patriotism and a sense of duty, he several times rejoined his regiment, but was as often obliged to return to the hospital.

On the 23d of May, 1864, he was mustered out at Washington, D.C., by reason of expiration of term of service.

*WILLIAM WESLEY ROBINSON.
Co. K.

JEREMIAH SPENCER.
Enrolled from Hingham, age 20.

Mustered in Co. K, Aug. 24, 1861 ; mustered out Sept. 2, 1864, by reason of expiration of term of enlistment.

GEORGE E. SMITH.

Enrolled from Hingham, age 22.

Co. G.

Mustered Aug. 24, 1861 ; discharged Sept. 2, 1864, by reason of expiration of term of service.

EDWARD L. TRACY.

Enrolled from Hingham, age 18.

Mustered in Co. K, Aug. 24, 1861 ; time of discharge from service unknown.

ROBERT TUFTS.

Enrolled from Hingham, age 18.

A member of Co. K, and mustered Aug. 24, 1861 ; time of discharge from service not received.

NINETEENTH REGIMENT.

The Nineteenth Regiment, Col. Edward W. Hincks, was organized and recruited at Camp Schouler, Lynnfield ; a large proportion of the enlistments being from Essex County. It left the State on the 28th of August, 1861, and includes in its list of engagements nearly every battle which occurred in the Army of the Potomac during the war.

The Hingham men in this regiment, were

MUSICIAN

SAMUEL BRONSDON.

Born at Milton, Mass., Nov. 29, 1819.

Resides in Hingham. Enlisted at Boston, Oct. 14, 1861, on Hingham quota, and was mustered into the United States service the same day as first-class musician of the Nineteenth Regiment Band.

Mr. Bronsdon joined the regiment Nov. 4, 1861, while encamped near Edward's Ferry, about two miles from Poolsville, Md. Here he remained until Dec. 4, when the regiment was ordered to Muddy Branch, Md. March 12, 1862, the Nineteenth was sent to Harper's Ferry to join a brigade then on its way to re-enforce Gen. Banks in the Shenandoah Valley. Marched to Berryville. On the 15th, had orders to return to Harper's Ferry; and the 24th was transported by rail to Washington, thence to Fortress Monroe, arriving there the 1st of April. Marched to Hampton, and joined the Grand Army of the Potomac at the commencement of the Peninsular Campaign under Gen. McClellan. Proceeded up the Peninsula to Yorktown; thence sailed, May 6, for West Point, reaching it in the night. The next morning a light engagement occurred.

During McClellan's retreat in the seven days' fight, the Nineteenth was actively engaged at the battles of Fair Oaks, Peach Orchard, Savage Station, White Oak Swamp, Glendale, and Malvern Hill; and its loss of officers and men was very severe.

In all these engagements Mr. Bronsdon was called to perform an important service; it being the duty of a musician on the battle-field to assist in removing the wounded, to aid the surgeons in camp hospital, and to bury the dead of the regiment. For the performance of these duties, which required so much of nerve as well as of forbearance and gentleness, Mr. Bronsdon was eminently qualified.

He was mustered out at Harrison's Landing, Aug. 10, 1862, by reason of an act of Congress discharging all regimental bands.

Mr. Bronsdon was also an original member of the Lincoln Light Infantry, and served three months with the company at Fortress Monroe.

PRIVATE

JAMES McKAY.

Age 24.

A resident of, and accredited to, Hingham; enrolled Aug. 21, 1861, in Co. I; discharged Dec. 15, 1861, on account of disability.

TWENTIETH REGIMENT.

The Twentieth Regiment, Col. Robert L. Lee, was recruited at Camp Massasoit, Readville, and left Massachusetts Sept. 4, 1861. In its list of engagements are included twenty-seven of the most noted battles which occurred in and about Virginia during the civil war. The casualties were numerous : one hundred and ninety-two were killed in action ; and what may be regarded as a somewhat remarkable fact, a similar number died from wounds or disease, making a total loss of three hundred and eighty-four men.

The regiment was mustered out after the close of the war, July 16, 1865.

The enlistments from Hingham in the Twentieth were limited. They were as follows : —

MUSICIAN.

EDWARD O. GRAVES.

Enrolled from Hingham, age 43.

Enlisted July 23, 1861, in Co. K, and was discharged for disability April 11, 1863. After recovery, re-enlisted in Fifty-ninth Regiment ; then transferred to the Fifty-seventh. Mr. Graves is included in the list officially returned by the selectmen of Hingham as being on the quota of the town.

PRIVATES.

DANIEL DALEY.

A resident of Hingham, age 25.

Enrolled from Boston ; mustered Aug. 30, 1862, as private in Co. H. Was wounded at Fredericksburg, and discharged Aug. 6, 1864, by reason of expiration of term of service. Returned by the selectmen as being on the quota of the town.

GEORGE GRAMBURG.

Enrolled from Hingham, age 19.

Mustered May 7, 1864, and discharged July 16, 1865, by reason of close of the war.

JOHN E. MORSE.

Transferred from Co. B, Fifteenth Regiment, which see for record.

* ALVIN TOWER.

Co. A.

TWENTY-FIRST REGIMENT.

This regiment, which was recruited at Camp Lincoln, Worcester, included two enlistments only, connected with the town of Hingham, viz. : —

GEORGE A. GROVER.

Enrolled from Hingham, age 18.

Mr. Grover was a volunteer member of the Lincoln Light Infantry, and left Hingham with the company, April 17, 1861, for Fortress Monroe, serving three months. Aug. 23 of the same year enlisted at Boston as private in Co. E, Twenty-first Regiment, M. V. I., three years, and was mustered out March 18, 1863, by reason of disability from wounds received in battle. He was in the engagements of Roanoke Island, N.C., Newbern, Camden, Second Bull Run, Va., Chantilly, South Mountain, Md., Antietam, and Fredericksburg, Va.

ANDREW JACOB.

Born in Hingham, Feb. 8, 1843.

Mustered in Co. G, of the Twenty-first Regiment, M. V. I., Aug. 23, 1861, having enlisted in Boston, in July, for three years.

Consigned to the Department of North Carolina, he was in the engagements at Roanoke Island, Newbern, and South Mills.

In January of 1863, by reason of sickness, he was sent to the hospital at Alexandria, and soon after transferred to Providence, R.I., where by virtue of surgeon's certificate of disability he was honorably discharged from service, March 16, 1863.

The Twenty-first was engaged at Roanoke Island, New-bern, Camden, Second Bull Run, Chantilly, South Mountain, Antietam, Fredericksburg, and Blue Spring, as well as at other localities after the above were mustered out of service.

TWENTY-SECOND REGIMENT.

The Twenty-second Regiment was organized by Hon. Henry Wilson at Lynnfield, Mass., and was mustered into the service of the United States Oct. 5, 1861. Beginning with the battles before Richmond, it was present in almost every prominent engagement up to that before Petersburg; the losses sustained being severe. During the campaign one hundred and forty-one were killed in battle, and one hundred and forty-three died from wounds and disease.

Of natives or residents of Hingham, it included the following, viz. : —

PRIVATES.

CHARLES F. ALGER.

Age 20.

Enrolled from Boston. Member of Co. K. Mustered Sept. 6, 1861, and discharged Oct. 17, 1864, by reason of expiration of term of service. A resident of Hingham since the war.

* JOHN B. CREASE.

Co. A.

WILLIAM B. CUSHING.

Co. D.

WILLIAM KIMBALL GOULD.

Co. F.

Afterwards in Fifth Battery, then in Thirty-second Regiment, where his general record will be found.

*SEWALL PUGSLEY.

Co. F.

TWENTY-THIRD REGIMENT.

This regiment left Massachusets Nov. 11, 1861, in command of Col. John Kurtz; and after being encamped for a time at Annapolis, Md., set sail for Pamlico Sound, where it became a part of the famous Burnside expedition to North Carolina. In this department it was engaged at Roanoke, Newbern, Rawles' Mills, Kinston, Whitehall, Goldsboro', Wilcox Bridge, and Winton, as well as in many important expeditions into the interior.

On the 17th of October, 1863, it re-embarked for Fortress Monroe, and subsequently was engaged in various undertakings with the Army of the James; was in the battle at Smithfield, Heckman's Farm, Arrowfield Church; and in the fight at Drury's Bluff, lost eighty-nine men, in killed, wounded, and missing, out a force of two hundred and twenty.

The Twenty-third was among the regiments detached from Gen. Butler's command, May 29, 1864, to re-enforce the Army of the Potomac, and was engaged at Cold Harbor, and other battles before Richmond.

Re-embarking for Newbern, N.C., Sept. 4, 1864, it was afterwards in the expedition to Kinston, March 8, 9, and 10, 1865, where the regiment lost, in killed, wounded, and missing, one officer and thirty men. It was mustered out as a regiment Sept. 25, 1864; but the re-enlisted men, and recruits whose term had not expired, remained in service under the same designation until June 25, 1865, when they were discharged.

The Hingham persons in this regiment were: —

SERGEANT

GEORGE EDSON HUMPHREY.

Born in Hingham, Jan. 4, 1839.

Mustered as private in Co. H, Sept. 28, 1861; promoted corporal at Newbern, N.C., May 1, 1862; sergeant at Newport News, Va., Nov. 28, 1863; mustered out Oct. 13, 1864, by reason of expiration of service.

Serg. Humphrey has a good military record. He participated in all the engagements and expeditions of the regiment during his connection with it. Was in the attack on the rebel fleet and the forts defending Roanoke Island, Feb. 7, 1862; also the day following (Feb. 8), when about three thousand prisoners, two thousand stand of arms, and forty guns were taken, the enemy capitulating to Gen. Foster. Also in the battles of Newbern, South-west Creek, Kinston, &c.

At Whitehall, N.C., Dec. 16, 1862, the regiment lost sixty-seven in killed and wounded. Serg. Humphrey was among the latter, having been shot in the leg. As the wound did not heal, he was granted a furlough of thirty days, and came to Boston, where he received surgical treatment in the hospital. He afterwards rejoined the regiment, and shared its hardships and privations, as well as its honors and victories.

At the commencement of the war, he went to Fortress Monroe with the Lincoln Light Infantry (Co. I, Fourth Regiment) of Hingham, having volunteered as a substitute for one of its original members.

CORPORAL

EDWARD CHURCHILL BLOSSOM.

Born in Hingham, Jan 30, 1838.

May 21, 1861, enlisted at Boston as private in Co. A (Wightman Rifles), Twenty-ninth Regiment, M. V. I., three years, temporarily connected with the Fourth Regiment, M. V. M. July 6, 1861, was discharged for impaired sight, and returned to Hingham.

Re-enlisted Sept. 28, 1861, and entered the service as private in Co. A, of the Twenty-third Regiment, M. V. I., three years, for quota of Hingham ; promoted corporal Sept. 25, 1862.

Mr. Blossom was among the first of our townsmen who enlisted for the term of three years, and his service was active and protracted. In the Wightman Rifles from Boston, he was at the battle of Big Bethel, Va., and with the Twenty-third shared in the long list of engagements allotted to this regiment in the Department of the Carolinas ; being present at Roanoke Island, South-west Creek, Kinston, Whitehall, Goldsboro', Trenton, the defence of Newbern, Morehead City, and numerous other localities, till February, 1864, when, being disabled by sickness, he was transferred to the Veteran Reserve Corps. From this time he was stationed at Point Lookout, Md., guarding prisoners till the expiration of his term of enlistment, Oct. 27, 1864.

PRIVATES.

ANDREW JACKSON CLARK.

Born in Hingham, Dec. 13, 1837.

Co. H.

Enlisted Sept. 28, 1861 ; mustered at Lynnfield, Oct. 9 ; discharged Oct. 13, 1864, by reason of expiration of term of service.

Mr. Clark served under Gens. Burnside, Foster, Butler, and Heckman ; participating in most of the River and Sound expe-

22

ditions of the first brigade, second division, Eighteenth Army Corps; was at the attack on Fort Sumter in Charleston Harbor by our monitors; at the rescue of Little Washington, N.C.; at Newport News, Norfolk, and Portsmouth, Va., and later with the Army of the James. He was also at Roanoke Island, Newbern, N.C., South-west Creek, Kinston, Whitehall, Goldsboro', Smithfield, Va., Heckman's Farm, Arrowfield Church, as well as at Petersburg, and other battles before Richmond.

Having joined the Lincoln Light Infantry as a volunteer at the first call of the president, Mr. Clark's entire service covers a period of about three years and four months. In this time he was neither wounded nor seriously ill. He had no furloughs.

* SAMUEL M. LINCOLN.

Co. H.

TWENTY-FOURTH REGIMENT.

This regiment was raised by Col., afterwards Brig.-Gen. Stevenson, and left the State Dec. 9, 1861, for Annapolis, Md., where it remained till January, 1862, when it joined the Burnside Expedition.

It was engaged in the Department of the Carolinas, for a time was stationed in Florida, and in 1864 was united with the Tenth Army Corps in the Virginia Campaign.

Its record of battles includes those of the Carolinas, as well as many in the Department of Virginia up to the siege of Petersburg, and the engagement at Four-Mile Run Church and Darby Town Road.

It was mustered out of the service at Richmond, Va., Jan. 20, and arrived in Boston Jan. 24, 1866.

Of enlistments from the town of Hingham, there were, so far as known, but five, viz. : —

GEORGE LINCOLN GARDNER.

Born in Hingham, Aug. 31, 1838.

Enlisted and was mustered into service at Boston, Sept. 30, 1861, as private in Co. E.

Re-enlisted Jan. 3, 1864. Detailed for the Pioneer Corps, he served in this capacity up to June, 1863, when he joined the regimental band. In the Department of the Carolinas he was present in the engagements at Rawle's Mills, Kinston, Whitehall, Goldsboro,' Morris Island, and the siege of Charleston.

During this time he was despatched to Long Island, Boston Harbor, for the charge of recruits and conscripts ; but, after a short service, applied for permission to rejoin the regiment, then stationed at St. Augustine, which was granted. It was at this locality he re-enlisted, and obtained the thirty-days' furlough allowed in consideration.

He was next in the Department of Virginia, under Gen. Butler. Was at Bermuda Hundred, Green Valley, Drury's Bluff, Bethesda Church, siege of Petersburg, besides other important engagements, and lastly sent to Bermuda Landing for provost duty, where he remained until the fall of Richmond. Proceeding at once to the captured city, he remained on duty here till Jan. 20, 1866, when by G. O., No. 2, Headquarters War Department of Va., he was discharged from service, four years and five months being included in his terms of enlistment.

Mr. Gardner adds, that whatever may have been the practice with other regiments, the band connected with the Twenty-fourth was required to bear its part in engagements. Pending these events, instruments were laid aside, stretchers for the conveyance of the wounded were shouldered, and the musician and soldier shared in the common danger of the conflict.

JOHN WARE LINCOLN.

Born in Hingham, age 26.

Enlisted first from Northborough, Sept. 28, 1861, as private in Co. C; discharged for re-enlistment Jan. 3, 1864; and was serving as principal musician at the time of final mustering out, Sept. 9, 1865.

PRIVATES.

ALBERT F. BARNES.

Born in Hingham, age 24.

Enlisted from Cohasset; mustered as private in Co. A, Aug. 14, 1862; discharged Dec. 4. 1864, by reason of expiration of term of service.

* WILLIAM HENRY BEAL.

Co. A.

JAMES BOOTH.

Age 21.

Enlisted from Hingham, and returned by the selectmen as upon the town's quota; mustered May 16, 1862. Unassigned recruit.

JUSTIN A. CARVER.

Age 22.

From Marshfield. Enlisted for the quota of Hingham; mustered Oct. 17, 1861, as private in Co. C; discharged on account of disability, Oct. 5, 1862, having been in service nearly one year.

THOMAS CONWAY.

Age 19.

Served for the quota of Hingham, and was mustered Oct. 22, 1861, as private in Co. F; mustered out by reason of expiration of term of enlistment, Oct. 22, 1864.

Mr. Conway had been in the country but a short time, and was employed at the Union House, when the war began. He has a good record.

TWENTY-SIXTH REGIMENT.

The Twenty-sixth Regiment was recruited at Lowell, and left Boston Nov. 21, 1861, the winter being spent at Ship Island.

In July, 1862, it was stationed at New Orleans City, performing provost duty, and remained there till June 20, 1863. Afterwards engaged at different points in the vicinity, and for a long time was connected with the Department of the Gulf. Served also in the Army of the Shenandoah Valley, subsequently at Savannah, Ga., where on the 26th of August, 1865, it was mustered out of service, and Sept. 12 embarked for Boston.

The enlistments from Hingham were four in number, as follows, viz. : —

CORPORAL

CHARLES BOLSTER.

Enrolled from Hingham, age 21.

Mustered April 14, 1864, and was corporal in Co. E. Mustered out Aug. 26, 1865, by reason of close of the war.

PRIVATES.

EDWIN BARR.

Enrolled from Hingham, age 18.

Private in Co. E, and was mustered May 1, 1864; discharged Aug. 26, 1865, by reason of close of the war.

JOHN O'BRIEN.

Enrolled from Hingham, age 26.

Was mustered as private in Co. B, May 7, 1864; discharged Aug. 26, 1865, by reason of close of the war.

NELSON T. WOOD.

Enrolled from Hingham, age 20.

Private in Co. E, and mustered May 1, 1864; mustered out Aug. 26, 1865, by reason of close of the war.

TWENTY-EIGHTH REGIMENT.

This regiment was mustered in the autumn of 1861, and left the State Jan. 11, 1862, assigned to the Department of Virginia. It was present in nearly all of the most noted engagements which there took place, from Second Bull Run to Petersburg, The casualties were very large, — the number killed in battle, or dying from wounds or disease, being three hundred and sixty-three. Of those connected with Hingham, it contained, so far as known, a single enlistment, viz. : —

PRIVATE

PETER READY.

Age 25.

Enlisted from Hingham, and served for the town's quota ; mustered as private in Co. F, Dec. 20, 1861, and was discharged by reason of disability, Feb. 18, 1863.

TWENTY-NINTH REGIMENT.

The companies composing this regiment were mustered into service, and left the State at different dates. Seven of the number were formed from among the first enlistments of three years' men. They were sent to Fortress Monroe, to fill up the ranks of the Third and Fourth Militia Regiments, the latter including the Lincoln Light Infantry of Hingham; and when these returned home, the seven companies were designated as the First Battalion Massachusetts Volunteers. Three new companies were afterwards sent to join it ; and the battalion was then regularly organized as the Twenty-ninth Regiment, M. V. I.

In the subjoined records will be found further interesting particulars with regard to this noted and truly excellent regiment. The names of five natives of Hingham, and of two of our recruits, appear upon its muster-roll, viz. : —

BRIGADIER-GENERAL

JOSEPH HENRY BARNES.

Born in Hingham, July 25, 1833.

Gen. Barnes raised a company in East Boston, Mass., in April, 1861. The actual date of his enlistment was May 18, and on the 22d he was mustered as captain at Fortress Monroe.

The company left Massachusetts as an independent organization. Upon arriving at Fortress Monroe, it was for a short time attached to the Fourth Massachusetts Regiment of Infantry, as Co. K, but subsequently became Co. K of the Massachusetts Twenty-ninth.

On the 16th of July, 1861, Gen. Barnes was assigned to the command of all the three-year companies of Massachusetts volunteers (seven in number) remaining in the Department of Virginia. When the Twenty-ninth, of which these seven companies were the nucleus, was formed (Dec. 28, 1861), he was commissioned lieutenant-colonel of this regiment, having retained command of the battalion during the interval.

Gen. Barnes participated in twenty pitched battles ; having fought in Maryland, Virginia, Kentucky, Tennessee, and Mississippi. He was actively engaged in the three great sieges of Richmond (under McClellan), Vicksburg, and Petersburg ; was in the first battle of the war at Big Bethel, and was present with his regiment, taking part in the famous encounter between the ram " Merrimac " and our vessels in the James River. He was also at the taking of Norfolk, at the battles of Gaines' Mill, Peach Orchard, Savage Station, and in all of McClellan's " seven days' battles ; " commanded his regiment at White Oak Swamp, Glendale, Malvern Hill, Second Bull Run, Antietam, Fredericksburg, at Vicksburg, and at Jackson, Miss. ; also at the battles in front of Petersburg, as well as in other engagements of lesser note.

In August, 1863, after the Vicksburg campaign, he received leave of absence on account of sickness, having served *two years and three months, without being absent a day for any cause whatever.* After returning to the army from sick-leave, he served on the staff of Gen. Willcox at Cumberland Gap, until December, 1863, when he rejoined his regiment in Tennessee.

March 12, 1864, Gen. Barnes was placed in command of a brigade of the Ninth Corps, and remained in that capacity until some time in the month of April. During this period the brigade marched from Morristown, East Tennessee, to Knoxville ; thence over the mountains, through Kentucky, to Cincinnati. In April, 1864, Gen. Barnes arrived in Boston with his regiment on " Veteran Furlough." They subsequently joined the army in Virginia under Gen. Grant, and participated in the battles of June 1st, 2d, and 3d.

Gen. Barnes commanded a brigade of the Ninth Corps, consisting of seven regiments, in a severe battle in front of Petersburg, June 17, 1864. He was also in the battle of July 30, the noted *mine explosion.* From July 31 to Sept. 16, 1864, he commanded the brigade, although ranking at the time as lieutenant-colonel.

For his services at the battle of Blick's Station, Weldon Railroad, Aug. 19, 1864, he was recommended by his corps commander for appointment as brevet brigadier-general. The recommendation begins thus : —

"VI.   Lt.-Col. Jos. H. Barnes, 29th Mass., lately commanding brigade, first division, Ninth Army Corps, for distinguished gallantry and success in action at Blick's Station, Weldon Railroad, resisting enemy's attack on 9th Corps' right," &c.

The Twenty-ninth Regiment was attached to the noted Irish Brigade for a period of five months, during which it participated with the brigade in the battles before Richmond under McClellan, and at Antietam and Second Bull Run.   Brig.-Gen. Thomas Francis Meagher, the commander of the brigade, in a letter to Gov. Andrew, published in the annual report of the Adjutant-general of Massachusetts, for 1862, says, " Lieut.-Col. Joseph H. Barnes is a soldier of the true type, in whom I have perfect and implicit reliance.   Brave and honorable, he is a credit to the State."

The following recommendations are copied from the original documents : —

Headquarters 3d Brig., 1st Div., 9th A. C.,
Dec. 10, 1864.

Brig.-Gen. L. Thomas, A. G. U. S. A.

Sir, — I have the honor to recommend for appointment in Gen. Hancock's new 1st Corps, Jos. H. Barnes, late Lieut-Col. Twenty-ninth Mass. Vols. He entered the service May 22, 1861, as captain, was promoted to lieut.-col. Dec. 13. 1861, and was mustered out by expiration of term, Oct. 11, 1864.

During his term of service, Lieut-Col. Barnes commanded his regt. nearly two-thirds of the time, and commanded a brigade for nearly two months in the present campaign.

I consider him a cool, reliable officer, courageous, and of good judgment and conduct, both in action, and in camp: a fine disciplinarian, and capable of commanding either a regiment or brigade.

I am Very Respectfully.
Your Obedient Servant,
N. B. McLaughlin,
Bvt. Brig.-Genl. Vols. Comdg. 3d Brig. 1st Div. 9th A. C.

Hd. Qrs. 3d Brig., 1st Div., 9th A. C., December 10th, 1864.
McLaughlin N. B., Bvt. Brig. Gen'l. U. S. V. Comdg.

Recommends Jos. H. Barnes late Lt.-Col. 29th Mass. Vols. for appointment in Genl. Hancock's new 1st Corps.   Entered the service as Capt., May 22, 1861, was promoted to Lieut.-Col. Dec. 13, 1861, and mustered out by expiration of term, Oct. 11, 1864. During his term of service Col. Barnes commanded his regiment nearly two-thirds of the time, and commanded a brigade nearly two months of the present campaign.

A True Copy.

Hd. Qrs. 1st Div., 9th Corps, Before Petersburg, Va., Dec. 12, 1864.

It gives me extreme pleasure most heartily to recommend Lt.-Col. Barnes for such an appointment. I consider him a man of great coolness and gallantry, considerable experience as a regimental and brigade commander, and every way qualified.

O. WILLCOX, *Brevet Maj. Gen.*

Hd Qrs. 9th Corps, Dec. 12, 1864.

I heartily indorse the within recommendation. I consider Col. Barnes a most excellent soldier, and very efficient commander. He is eminently qualified for command.

JNO. G. PARKE, *Maj. Gen.*

LIEUTENANT

WALDO FLINT CORBETT.

Born in Hingham, Jan. 4. 1843.

Enlisted at Charlestown, Mass., Nov. 5. 1861 ; mustered as corporal in Co. H, Dec. 23, 1861 : re-enlisted as veteran Jan. 1, and mustered Jan. 25, 1864 ; promoted second lieutenant of First U. S. Heavy Artillery (colored), April 16, 1864, and first lieutenant Jan. 25, 1865.

Lieut. Corbett was in active service during the Peninsular campaign in the summer of 1862 ; also in the Vicksburg and Jackson campaign, summer of 1863, and at East Tennessee in the autumn of that year ; siege of Knoxville, defence of Fort Saunders, &c.

He resigned, and his resignation was accepted, to date from Jan. 1, 1866, at Chattanooga, Tenn.

SERGEANT

CALEB HADLEY BEAL.

Born in Hingham, Jan. 15, 1833.

For record. see Co. K of the Thirty-fifth regiment, M. V. I.

CORPORAL

JOHN MANIX.

Age 24.

Accredited on Hingham quota; mustered as corporal in Co. I, Aug. 24, 1864; termination of service July 29, 1865.

PRIVATES.

EDWARD CHURCHILL BLOSSOM.

Born in Hingham, Jan. 30, 1838.

For record see Co. A, of the Twenty-third Regiment, M. V. I.

ROBERT GRACE.

Seaman, age 25.

Accredited on Hingham quota; mustered in unassigned recruits, May 9, 1864.

GEORGE THOMAS.

Born in Hingham, Nov. 2, 1841.

On the 18th of May, 1861, enlisted at Boston as private in the "Wightman Rifles," Capt. Thomas W. Clark, and was three months at Fortress Monroe.

After the departure of the Third and Fourth Regiments from Fortress Monroe, seven three-years' companies were made the basis of the Twenty-ninth Regiment, M. V. I., three years, the "Wightman Rifles" being Co. A.

The record of the Twenty-ninth is characterized by extended marches, numerous and trying privations, and a list of engagements among the most determined and destructive that occurred during the war. Private Thomas was present first at the battle of Great Bethel, then at Hampton Roads, Gaines' Mill, Savage Station, White Oak Swamp, Malvern Hill, Antietam, Fredericksburg, Vicksburg, and Jackson Miss., Blue Springs. E. Tenn., Campbell Station, and Siege of Knoxville, Tenn., Cold Harbor, Weldon Railroad, and Petersburg.

On the 30th of July, in the bloody struggle before Petersburg, during the charge following the Burnside Mine explosion, he was taken prisoner by the enemy, and sent by way of Richmond to Danville, Va., where he was confined in the noted " Tobacco Warehouse." This building, measuring forty by one hundred feet, four stories in height, contained at the time nearly eight hundred men. The quantity of food furnished was small, and the quality poor ; but, in consideration of services rendered as steward, our prisoner was allowed an extra ration of bread and meat. In the hands of the enemy, he remained at this place for a term of about seven months.

Returning from Danville to Richmond, he was here confined for three days in Libby Prison, and thence released on parole. Upon being granted a furlough of thirty-five days, he came to Hingham, where the time of absence was extended twenty days by his physician, Dr. Ezra Stephenson.

On the 10th of August, 1865, after the close of the war, he was mustered out at Readville, Mass., having been in the service more than four years.

THIRTIETH REGIMENT.

Organized as the Eastern Bay State Regiment, at Camp Chase, Lowell. It sailed from Boston Jan. 13, 1862, and arrived at Ship Island Feb. 12, having touched at Fortress Monroe on the passage out.

The regiment had an active experience, and was engaged in all the principal battles on the Lower Mississippi, including Vicksburg, Baton Rouge, Plains Store, Port Hudson, Donaldsonville, and also at Winchester, Cedar Creek, and Fisher's Hill, in Virginia. Twenty-seven were killed in action, and three hundred and forty-four died from wounds or disease.

So far as known, the number of enlistments from those connected with Hingham was four, as follows : —

SERGEANT

JACOB OURISH,

Of Hingham, born July 26, 1841.

Enlisted in Boston, Dec, 18, 1861, on Hingham quota ; mustered as private in Co. I, Dec. 28, 1861 ; re-enlisted at New Iberia, La., as veteran, Jan. 1, 1864 ; promoted sergeant Aug. 7, 1864, and July 5, 1866, was mustered out with the regiment at Charleston, S.C.

Sergeant Ourish was present at the siege of forts St. Philip and Jackson ; also at the taking of New Orleans, La. He participated in the engagement at Baton Rouge, Aug. 5, 1862 ; Plains Store, May 21, 1863; Siege of Port Hudson, May 25 to July 8, 1863 ; Kock's Plantation, La.; Opequan, Va. ; Fisher's Hill, Va. ; and Cedar Creek, Va.

While at New Orleans he was in the hospital with fever and ague for nearly a year; and at the battle of Cedar Creek, with Gen. Sheridan's forces, was severely wounded in the face by a musket-ball, which gave him five additional months of hospital experience, the latter being passed at Readville, Mass.

Sergeant Ourish entered the United States service May 18, 1861 ; and was sent to Fortress Monroe as a volunteer in the Lincoln Light Infantry, of Hingham, Co. I (Fourth Regiment). He was therefore a member of the first volunteer regiment mustered into service, as well as of the last volunteer regiment mustered out, — a circumstance with but few parallels during the war. His whole term covers a period of *four years and nearly nine months.*

CORPORAL

JOSEPH C. BURR.

Born in Hingham, Aug. 1, 1827.

Enlisted at Lowell, Mass, for three years ; mustered Oct. 15, 1861, as corporal in Co. C.

The regiment, after being on shipboard in Boston Harbor nearly a fortnight, took its departure for Fortress Monroe, Jan. 13, 1862. Soon after arriving there, it was ordered to Ship Island, and thence to New Orleans, La.

Mr. Burr was in the engagement at Baton Rouge, the enemy being under the command of Gens. Breckenridge and Van Dorn. At the siege of Port Hudson he was continually under fire, both day and night, until the surrender.

Subsequently the Thirtieth was ordered down the river to Donaldsonville; and, in the engagement at this place, the Union forces were driven back under cover of the gunboats. Here, from constant exposure, Mr. Burr became unfit for duty, and was sent to the hospital at Baton Rouge.

In September, 1863, he received a furlough, and came home. Reporting afterwards to Surg.-Gen. Dale, he was transferred to the Veteran Reserve Corps; and Dec. 1, 1864, was discharged from the Third Regiment, V.R.C., by reason of expiration of term of enlistment.

PRIVATES.

JOHN BROWN.

Age 23.

Farmer; enlisted from Boston for the quota of Hingham, and was mustered as private in Co. E, Nov. 4, 1861; date of discharge not recorded.

*WILLIAM J. STOCKWELL.

Co. I.

JOHN SULLIVAN.

Age 27.

Mustered Oct. 25, 1861, in Co. E; discharged, Nov. 5, 1863, on account of disability.

THIRTY-FIRST REGIMENT.

The Thirty-first Regiment was mustered into the service of the United States during the winter of 1861–2 ; left Massachusetts Feb. 21, 1862, and as a regiment was mustered out in December, 1864 ; leaving, however, several companies made up of re-enlisted men and recruits, which were all finally mustered out Sept. 9, 1865.

Its list of engagements includes Bisland, Port Hudson, Brashear City, Sabine Cross-Roads, Cane River Crossing, Alexandria, Gov. Moore's Plantation, Yellow Bayou, and the siege of Mobile.

Of enlistments from Hingham, the Thirty-first Regiment contained

LIEUTENANT

JOHN G. DAWES.

Born in Hingham, Mar. 13, 1832.

Enlisted in Boston for three years ; mustered at Lowell, Mass., Feb. 5, 1862, as private in Co. K, and accredited to the quota of Hingham ; promoted corporal, and afterwards sergeant.

Lieut. Dawes was with the Thirty-first at New Orleans, La., when that city surrendered to the Union forces. He afterwards rendered efficient service upon garrison and outpost duty.

Oct. 3, 1862, he was transferred to the Second Louisiana Volunteers, colored, and promoted second lieutenant ; was present at the battle of Port Hudson, &c. After serving under the last promotion about fifteen months, he resigned his position and came home.

Lieut. Dawes died in Hingham of consumption, Nov. 4, 1870, aged 38 years, 7 months, 21 days. He was a son of John P. and Juliet (Lincoln) Dawes.

CHAPTER X.

THIRTY-SECOND REGIMENT.

Organization — Recruiting by Capt. Stephenson at Camp Dimmick, Hingham — Thirty-
one men from Camp Cameron — Mustering Company — Leave for Fort Warren —
Recruiting by Lieut. Lyman B. Whiton, at Oasis Hall — Recruits leave Hingham for
Camp Cameron — Consolidation with Co. E — Co. F — Number of Hingham Enlist-
ments in the Thirty-second Regiment — List of Battles — Number of Killed and Wounded
— Sketch of the Battle of Laurel Hill.

SIX companies M. V. M., organized for garrison duty at Fort
Warren, constituted the basis of the Thirty-second Regiment.
Capts. Luther Stephenson, jun., of Hingham, and Cephas C. Bumpus of Braintree, had previously been connected with the Fourth
Regiment, M. V. M., and were three months at Fortress Monroe,
commanding companies I and C. Many of the enlistments
were also from those who had already been in the service, and
the battalion was regarded as one of the most efficient organizations in the State.

These several commands were not, however, recognized as a
regiment until May 25, 1862, when by telegraph despatch they
were ordered to report at the seat of war at the earliest possible
moment. In twelve hours from the time the despatch was
received, they were on their way for Washington. Shortly after,
the requisite number of companies was forwarded to join the
battalion, and the ranks were filled.

In November, 1861, Capt. Luther Stephenson, jun., entered
upon the work of recruiting a company, to be stationed at Fort
Warren, for the purpose before stated, and established his headquarters at the Town Hall, Hingham, designating the locality as
"Camp Dimmick," in honor of Col. Dimmick, then in command
at Fort Warren. In the prosecution of his labors, he had the
hearty sympathy and co-operation of his fellow townsmen, who
in various forms testified their interest, not only by acceptable

contributions for the happiness and comfort of those in camp, but by rendering every-other service in their power.

Enlistments came in rapidly, many from various towns in different sections of the State, as well as from among the citizens of Hingham; and shortly, by the accession of thirty-one men from Camp Cameron, including Lieut. Charles A. Dearborn of Salem, the requisite number was secured. Of natives or residents of Hingham, Co. A contained twenty-four.

On Monday, Nov. 26, 1861, all were mustered into the service of the United States; and on Tuesday, Nov. 27, left camp for Fort Warren, where the winter of 1861-2 was passed.

Immediately on the departure of Co. A, Lieut. Lyman B. Whiton opened a recruiting-office at Oasis Hall, for the purpose of obtaining enlistments, to be joined to a company then being raised by Capt. Bumpus of Braintree. · His enterprise was soon crowned with abundant success. More than fifty men were enrolled, nearly forty of whom were from the town of Hingham. A portion of these, however, were not mustered in, on account of excess of numbers, thirty-two being finally accepted. On Monday, Dec. 13, the recruits left Hingham for Camp Cameron, where they were consolidated with Co. E, Capt. Bumpus, and where they remained until Tuesday, Dec. 24, when all left for Fort Warren.

Co. F, gathered from different localities and by different recruiting agents, contained twenty-two men from Hingham; and there were six enlistments of this class in other companies, swelling the total of natives or residents of the town who were connected with this regiment to eighty-four.

In January, 1864, three hundred and thirty men of this regiment, having re-enlisted, were permitted to go to their homes in Massachusetts for thirty days. They arrived in Boston on Sunday, and received a most cordial welcome from Gov. Andrew, the mayor, and other officials. A salute was fired on Boston Common in honor of their arrival, and a collation provided at Faneuil Hall. The men from Hingham were sent home in carriages free of expense. Their visit here was made pleasant by a grand reception ball, as well as by other provisions for their gratification.

The list of battles of the Thirty-second is as follows, viz.: Malvern Hill, Gaines' Mill, Second Bull Run, Antietam, Shepardstown Ford, Fredericksburg, Chancellorsville, Gettysburg, Rappahannock Station, Mine Run, Wilderness, Laurel Hill, Spottsylvania, North Anna, Tolopotomy Swamp, Bethesda Church, Cold Harbor, Petersburg, Weldon Railroad, Vaughan Road, Dabney's Mills, Boydton Road, and White Oak Road.

The total number of killed and wounded, and of those who died from disease, was two hundred and seventy-seven. The regiment was mustered out June 29, 1865.

Gen. Luther Stephenson, jun., who at the time was lieutenant-colonel commanding the Thirty-second Regiment, has prepared for these pages the following vivid sketch of the battle of Laurel Hill. It will be read with peculiar interest by those who escaped the dangers of the day, and it will not fail to enlist the hearty attention of the general public.

THE BATTLE OF LAUREL HILL, VA.

The 12th of May, 1864, will long be remembered by the soldiers of the Thirty-second Massachusetts Regiment as a marked day in its history, because of the severe and disastrous battle in which it participated, which for severity of losses, when the numbers engaged, and the short, sharp conflict, are taken into consideration, can hardly be exceeded by the reports from any other regiment that was engaged during the war of the rebellion.

The regiment had met with severe losses and hard fighting in other battles, particularly at Fredericksburg and Gettysburg; but the number of killed and wounded, in proportion to the number engaged, at these places, fell far short of the casualties in the conflict known in the history of the regiment, and inscribed upon its battle-flag, as the "Battle of Laurel Hill."

In furnishing an account of this battle, I am compelled to relate my own personal experience on that day, and may be pardoned for the constant use of the personal pronoun, for the reason that I can better illustrate the action of the regiment by relating my own experience and action.

The regiment had crossed the Rapidan with the Army of the

Potomac under Gen. Grant, had been engaged with the enemy on the days of the 5th, 6th, and 7th of May, in the Wilderness, and, on the night of the 7th, marched to the left, arriving in the vicinity of a point known as Laurel Hill, which is near Spottsylvania, on the morning of the 8th, during which day we remained in position, supporting the Fifth Massachusetts Battery. On the morning of the 9th, we took our position near Laurel Hill, occupying some low earthworks which had been thrown up the day previous by troops who had taken the advance in the skirmishing when the van of the two armies came together, and Gen. Grant ascertained that his attempt to flank his skilful antagonist had been unsuccessful.

The appearance of the country in this locality is very similar to what may be seen in most parts of Virginia, — a succession of hills and valleys, admirably adapted for defence. Our position was in a valley near the foot of a hill, on which was stationed the Union picket-line; beyond, another eminence where the enemy's pickets were located; and still farther, Laurel Hill, occupied by a portion of the army under the command of Gen. Lee (this last locality being probably a distance of about one-fourth of a mile from our position). On the field between the two picket-lines, a skirmish had taken place on the 8th of May; and the dead bodies of our soldiers remained upon the ground, unburied, it being impossible to reach them in safety in the face of the enemy.

From the time we took this position, until the 12th, we remained inactive, with exception of duties upon the picket-line. Our situation, however, was unpleasant in the extreme, forced as we were to maintain a reclining position on account of the watchfulness of the enemy's sharpshooters, who made a target of every one who was reckless enough to stand erect. In addition to this annoyance, the weather was a succession of sunshine and showers, burning with heat, and then drenching us with rain. This operated fearfully upon the dead bodies of the slain left upon the field, filling the air with a stench disgusting and almost suffocating.

On the morning of the 12th, Gen. Griffin, commander of the first division, Fifth Corps, sent for me, and gave me orders to take command of the division picket detail, and advance it as a line of skirmishers upon the Confederate works, informing me that he should send after me, at once, the second brigade, consisting of the Sixty-second Pennsylvania and the Ninth and Thirty-second Massachusetts Regiments, for an assault upon the enemy's line directly in our front.

I proceeded at once to perform the duty required of me, and on arriving at the front found the picket-line (which consisted of details from a number of regiments belonging to the division), stationed in rifle-pits dug into the brow of the hill, a number of feet apart, three men occupying each pit.

This line was so extended, that some considerable time was consumed in communicating my orders to the officers in command of the several regimental details, which were, that at a given signal they should move forward at once from their position, deploying as they advanced. The preparations, however, for the advance of the main column had startled the enemy, who commenced a heavy fire of artillery, which swept the top of the hill where my line was stationed. This fire was so fierce, that the officers could not force their men forward as I desired. A few started, only to be shot, or to fall back again. In vain I expostulated, entreated, threatened. The men were so widely separated that it was impossible to control them. A few of the bravest would start forward, but would be compelled to return for want of support.

I recollect the action of the officer in command of the Ninety-first Pennsylvania detail, who, upon my threats of a court-martial for cowardice, sprang up, and, waving his sword, shouted to his men to come on; but unfortunately, a fresh volley of canister and shell came tearing over the hill, and he dropped into his hole again, from which no threats could remove him.

While striving to push my men forward, I looked back, and saw the assaulting columns, under the command of Col. Prescott, advancing in good order. It came over my picket-line, down the hill to the next, then forward to the foot of the next, when the men faltered under the terrible fire they encountered, and lay down within a short distance of the enemy's lines.

Looking over the brow of the hill, I saw with dismay that my own regiment was exposed to a terrible fire, not only in its front, but also to a cross-fire on its left flank, which must soon cut it to pieces ; and yet no effort was being made to relieve the brave men from their exposed position. With a thought only of the safety of the regiment, I started at once to join it. I can hardly find words to describe the fearful gauntlet I ran while making my way to the regiment. Exposed to the fire of the rebel line, the whizzing bullets, shot tearing up the ground all around me, shells bursting over my head, it seems a miracle that I reached my destination in safety, which, thank God, I did, after showing a rate of speed that would have astonished my friends at home, and suffering no injury excepting a rent in my coat made by a piece of shell.

Proceeding directly to the left, I inquired why they did not go forward, or at least do something to protect themselves from almost certain death. I recollect that Capt. —— answered that they were being cut to pieces without a chance of defending themselves. Directing the men to draw their bodies along on the ground, and get more under the protection of the hill, I turned, and saw that the regiments on the right had broken, and were falling back thoroughly disorganized ; and there was nothing left for the Thirty-second to do but to retreat. Calling upon the men to fall back and save themselves if possible, we started on our retreat, which was far more disastrous than the advance.

The rebels poured upon us an incessant fire of shot and shell, reaping down our noble soldiers like grass before the scythe men falling at almost every step, killed or wounded. In the Thirty-second, five color-bearers fell before the colors reached our old position behind the works. Once, looking back, I saw our flag had been left upon the field, and Col. Prescott and my-self turned to bring it off at all hazards, when another brave soldier took it only to fall in his turn. And here, I might add, that the rain commenced falling in torrents, while Heaven's artillery united with the cannon of the opposing armies, only to make the scene more fearful and terrific. I think no words can give so accurate an idea of the terrible fire to which we were subjected, as the statement that the Thirty-second took into that fight about one hundred and ninety men (a portion of the regiment being on picket-duty); and of this number one hundred and three were killed and wounded, all in the short space of less than *thirty minutes.*

Of the Hingham soldiers, we lost some of our best and bravest; Lieut. Geo. M. Hudson, being severely, and Washington I Stodder, Jacob G. Cushing, and Gardner Jones mortally wounded. Late in the afternoon I rode to the hospital of the first division, which was located some distance at the rear. The men who were wounded, and able to walk, were being sent forward to make their way to Fredericksburg; while those severely wounded were loaded into the heavy baggage wagons, lying upon a few pine boughs. When we consider that these poor men were transported in these vehicles, without springs to relieve the motion, to Fredericksburg, a distance of nearly fourteen miles, a considerable portion of which was over a corduroy road, made of logs, we can imagine the anguish and pain they endured during their fearful ride. Entering the hospital tents, I found six officers of my own regiment wounded, lying side by side: two of them, alas! I never saw again. On every side I found men of the Thirty-second. Washington I. Stodder had just breathed his last. I stopped to speak to Corp. Jacob G. Cushing, who, although seemingly dying, recognized me, calling me by name. My visit, however, was cut short by a message from the regiment, informing me that we had received orders to move; and, on hastening back, I found that we were to march at nightfall.

Silently we moved away from this place, leaving our dead and many wounded on the field to the tender mercies of strangers, and perhaps foes, and carrying with us, bitter, sad, recollections of the day and the locality. Our march was to Spottsylvania; there again to fight, only to move forward again, and again to fight, and so to continue until we had finished that terrible campaign, which might have been traced by a line of blood, extending from the Rapidan to the James.

GEN. LUTHER STEPHENSON, JUN.

Luther Stephenson, jun., was born in Hingham, April 25, 1830. At the commencement of the rebellion he held the position of first lieutenant in Co. I, Fourth Massachusetts Volunteer Militia. On the 17th of April, 1861, he received a telegram from the governor of the State ordering him to report with the company, by first conveyance, at Boston.

The order was received early in the forenoon, and at 5 o'clock, P.M., the company left Hingham. On arriving in Boston, it immediately joined the Fourth Regiment. Marching from the State House to the Old Colony Depot, the regiment took the train for Fall River, whence the steamer "State of Maine" transported it to Fortress Monroe, Va.

Lieut. Stephenson was elected captain of Co. I on the 18th, and on the 22d was mustered into the service of the United States at Fortress Monroe, Va.

He served with the regiment three months, returned home, and was mustered out on the 22d of July, 1861. Not content with this short term of service at the commencement of the country's perils, he immediately recruited the first Co. (A), of the Thirty-second Regiment Massachusetts Volunteers, and was again mustered into the United States service, Nov. 28, 1861, for three years, at Fort Warren, Boston Harbor, with the rank of captain. The regiment remained at the fort till May 25 1862, when it was ordered to Washington, and joined the Army of the Potomac at Harrison's Landing, Va., in June, 1862. With the rank of captain, he was in command of the regiment during the campaign under Gen. John Pope, which included the battle of Second Bull Run.

He was promoted to the rank of major, Aug. 18, 1862, and was present and took part in the battles of Antietam, Shepardstown Ford, and Fredericksburg.

Before the close of the year, Dec. 29, he was promoted lieutenant-colonel, and commanded the regiment at the battle of Chancellorsville.

At the battle of Gettysburg, July 2, 1863, he was severely wounded in the face by a rifle-ball. While thus disabled, he returned to his home in Hingham; and on recovering rejoined the regiment, Nov. 3, 1863, in time to participate in the battles at Rappahannock Station and Mine Run, Va.

He was with his regiment during the campaign under Gen. U. S. Grant, from May 5 till June 28, 1864, and took part in the battles of the Wilderness, Laurel Hill, Spottsylvania, North Anna, Tolopotomy Swamp, Bethesda Church, Cold Harbor, and Petersburg. He received slight wounds in the engagements of June 18 and 22, and on the 28th was discharged for disability caused by the wound received at Gettysburg.

By order of Gen. Grant, Lieut.-Col. Stephenson was brevetted colonel and brigadier-general, March 15, 1865, for "*gallant and meritorious services in the campaigns against Richmond, Va.*"

MAJORS.

EDWARD TRACY BOUVÉ.

For record, see Fourth Massachusetts Cavalry.

LYMAN BARNES WHITON.

For record, see Third Massachusetts Heavy Artillery.

CAPTAIN

GEORGE REUBEN REED.

Born in Hingham, Dec. 17, 1839.

Member of Co. I, of the Fourth Regiment, M. V. I., Lincoln Light Infantry, left Hingham with the first detachment, April 17, 1861, and was three months stationed at Fortress Monroe. Oct. 31, 1861, enlisted at Camp Dimmick in Co. A.

Sept. 1, 1862, he was promoted from sergeant to second lieutenant; Dec. 30, 1862, to first lieutenant; and July 20, 1864, was commissioned captain.

With the Thirty-second, in the Army of the Potomac, he bore a full part in all its marches, privations, and dangers, up to the month of August, 1864. Beginning at Malvern Hill, July 3, 1862, he was in the battle of Gaines' Mill, Second Bull Run, Chantilly, Antietam, Fredericksburg, Chancellorsville, Gettysburg, Rappahannock Station, Mine Run, Wilderness, Spottsylvania, North Anna, Tolopotomy, Bethesda Church, and Petersburg.

At Laurel Hill, Capt. Reed was in command of Co. I, Charlestown, consisting of forty-one men. In a charge on the enemy, covering scarcely more than fifteen minutes' time, twenty-five of these were killed or wounded.

At the battle of North Anna, while engaged on the skirmishline, he was for a short time a prisoner in the hands of the enemy, but, in the excitement and confusion of battle, fortunately succeeded in effecting his escape.

On the 3d of August, 1864, he was detailed as quartermaster at the Fifth Corps Hospital, City Point, Va., and continued at this post till the 25th of the following November, when he was mustered out at Petersburg by reason of the expiration of his term of enlistment.

In all the trying experience of the Thirty-second, Capt. Reed proved himself a good officer and true soldier.

LIEUTENANTS.

*GEORGE W. BIBBY.

Co. A.

* NATHANIEL FRENCH, Jun.

Co. A.

AMOS P. HOLDEN.

Age 38.

First enrolled from Hingham, subsequently from the town of Westminster. Was sergeant in Co. A at the time of enlistment, Oct. 31, 1861 ; promoted second lieutenant March 26, 1862.

2;

GEORGE MARTIN HUDSON.

Born in Hingham, March 29, 1829.

Enlisted Feb. 15, 1862; mustered Feb. 17, at Fort Warren, Boston Harbor, as private in Co. F, First Battalion, M. V. I., afterwards Thirty-second Regiment; appointed second sergeant March 1, first sergeant, Nov. 15, second lieutenant, Dec. 29, 1862, and First Lieutenant, Sept. 29, 1863.

Lieut. Hudson was in the battles of Antietam, Fredericksburg, Chancellorsville, Gettysburg, Bristoe's Station, Mine Run, the battles of the Wilderness, and Laurel Hill.

Severely wounded in both legs by a Minnie ball while bravely leading his men in a charge on the enemy's batteries at the battle of Laurel Hill, May 12, 1864, he was carried to Douglas Hospital, Washington, D.C., and, as soon as he was able to be removed, was brought to his home in Hingham.

He was mustered out at Boston, Feb. 18, 1865, by reason of expiration of term of service.

SERGEANTS.

THOMAS DAVIS BLOSSOM.

Born at Chicopee, Mass., April 29, 1842.

A resident of Hingham, he enlisted for the quota of the town as private, Jan. 21, 1862, at Fort Warren, Boston Harbor, Mass., and the same day was mustered into Co. E.

Nov. 28, 1864, promoted corporal; afterwards, March 1, 1865, sergeant; and again, April 25, 1865, orderly-sergeant.

He was discharged at Rappahannock Station, Va., for re-enlistment, and Jan. 4, 1864, enrolled to serve three years.

He shared in the engagement at Fredericksburg, Va., in December, 1862, and was in the battles at Antietam, Mine Run, and Petersburg, as well as in other engagements in which the Thirty-second took part.

Wounded at Petersburg, June 18, 1864, he was first sent to

the corps hospital; thence transferred to David's Island, and afterwards removed to Readville, Mass. Remaining here two or three weeks, he again joined his regiment for active duty; and on the 29th of June, 1865, after the close of the war, he was mustered out, having been in the service three years and six months.

LEONARD EDSON BUKER.

Born in Braintree, Mass., Dec. 9, 1836.

Resident of Hingham; enlisted at Boston, Feb. 15, 1862, and Feb. 19 was mustered as private in Co. F; promoted corporal March 1, 1863; and Nov. 1, 1863, promoted sergeant; Jan. 4, 1864, re-enlisted as veteran for three years.

Serg. Buker was present in the battles of Second Bull Run Antietam, Fredericksburg, Chancellorsville, Gettysburg, Rappahannock Station, Mine Run, Wilderness, Laurel Hill, Spottsylvania, North Anna, Petersburg, Weldon Railroad, Gravelly Run, and, with the exception of Five Forks, all other engagements and skirmishes set down to the Thirty-second Regiment.

At the battle of Gravelly Run he was wounded; and for two months was in the Army Square Hospital at Washington, D.C. Mustered out June 29, 1865, by reason of close of the war.

Serg. Buker's term of service included three years and four months. He was a faithful officer and soldier, and has an honorable record.

THOMAS ALONZO CARVER.

Born in Boston, May 20, 1832.

Enlisted at Hingham, Dec. 2, 1861, and was mustered as private in Co. E, Dec. 16, 1861; promoted sergeant Jan. 1, 1863; transferred to V. R. C. March 7, 1864.

Serg. Carver was in the engagements at Fredericksburg, Chancellorsville, and, lastly, at Gettysburg, where he was wounded in the arm, which occasioned a confinement of four months in the McClellan Hospital at Philadelphia, Pa. He was also four weeks at the hospital at Windmill Point from sickness. Mustered out at Washington, D.C., Dec. 16, 1864, by reason of expiration of term of service.

CHARLES CORBETT.
Enrolled from Hingham, age 37.

Mustered Nov. 10, 1861, as sergeant in Co. A ; was at Fort Warren in the winter of 1861-2, and shared in the general experience of the regiment in the Department of Virginia, until after the battle of Fredericksburg, when, taken sick and disabled, he was honorably discharged at Stoneman Station, Va., March 22, 1863.

Serg. Corbett was also one of the thirty-seven volunteers who left Hingham May 18, 1861, to join the Lincoln Light Infantry at Fortress Monroe.

JOHN WESLEY ELDREDGE.
Born in Hingham, June 3. 1843.

Was a volunteer in the Lincoln Light Infantry, and left Hingham with the company, April 17, 1861, serving three months at Fortress Monroe. Dec. 2, 1861, enlisted, and was mustered as private in Co. E of the Thirty-second Regiment. Mustered out for re-enlistment at Liberty, Va., Jan. 4, 1864. Promoted corporal, Dec. 4, 1863 ; and May 3, 1864, promoted sergeant.

From the battle at Malvern Hill to the surrender of Gen. Lee, sixteen of the engagements credited to the Thirty-second Regiment are included in the record of Serg. Eldredge.

At Laurel Hill he was wounded in the hand, and for a time was in the hospital at West Philadelphia. Mustered out at the end of the war, after a faithful service of nearly four years.

HENRY STURGES EWER.
Born in Hingham, Jan. 11, 1833.

Was a regular member of the Lincoln Light Infantry at the

outbreak of the war; and, leaving with the first detachment of the company, was three months at Fortress Monroe.

Enlisted Nov. 1, 1861, sergeant in Co. A, and was with the regiment at Fort Warren in the winter of 1861–2. In the Department of Virginia, he was present in the battles at Malvern Hill and Antietam; but, being disabled by sickness, he was honorably discharged near Falmouth, Va., March 22, 1863, having been in the service nearly sixteen months.

* JAMES MADISON HASKELL.

Co. A.

JAMES McCARTY.

Age 33.

Enlisted from Hingham, for the quota of the town Nov. 10, 1861, as private in Co. A; promoted corporal, afterwards sergeant. Mustered out for re-enlistment Jan. 5, 1864, and discharged June 29, 1865, by reason of expiration of term of enlistment or close of the war.

An incident from the record of Serg. McCarty will show at once his bravery and patriotism. At the battle of Laurel Hill, May 12, 1864, he was corporal in the color-guard. On the retreat which took place after the charge, he bore the national standard, — Stars and Stripes, — while a comrade carried the regimental flag of the State of Old Massachusetts. Missing his companion, he turned and saw that he had fallen. Planting his staff erect in the ground, he ran back, took the standard from beside the dying soldier, and retaking his own, brought both off safely together.

* CHARLES S. MEAD.

Co. A.

* PETER OURISH.

Co. E.

JOHN PARRY.

Age 25.

Enrolled from Weymouth, as corporal in Co. A; afterwards from
the town of Hingham, as sergeant in the same company.
Mustered Nov. 1, 1851. Discharged for re-enlistment Feb. 6,
1864. Mustered out June 29, 1865. by reason of close of the
war.

Serg. Parry was in nearly all of the battles in which the regiment took part.

ISAAC G. WATERS.

Age 20.

Sergeant in Co. F. Enlisted from Hingham for the quota of the
town, and was mustered Feb. 19, 1862.

Was in all the battles up to Gettysburg. Transferred to
Veteran Reserve Corps, Sept. 16, 1863. After this was assigned
for special duty.

Serg. Waters was connected with the Lincoln Light Infantry,
and as a volunteer left with the company on the afternoon of
April 17, 1861, and served three months at Fortress Monroe.

NATHANIEL WILDER, 2d.

Born in Hingham, Feb. 23, 1840.

Enlisted at Hingham, Dec, 2, 1861, as private in Co. E, and
Jan. 1, 1863, promoted sergeant; re-enlisted Jan. 4, 1864, at
Liberty, Va.; transferred to V. R. C., March 20, 1865.

Serg. Wilder was in the engagements at Second Bull Run,
Antietam, Shepardstown Ford, Fredericksburg, Chancellorsville,
Gettysburg, Rappahannock Station, and Mine Run.

While returning from the furlough granted on re-enlistment, he
was accidentally disabled at Baltimore, and was sent to camp
hospital at Liberty, Va., where he remained till the opening of
the Wilderness campaign, when he rejoined the regiment.

At Peebles Farm he suffered from sickness, and for a brief

period was in division hospital. After joining the regiment, he was again disabled, and sent to Lincoln Hospital, Washington, D.C., from which he was transferred to V. R. C., as before stated.

He was mustered out at Washington, D.C., Aug. 23, 1865.

CORPORALS.

JOHN CALVIN CHADBOURN.

Born in Effingham, N.H., July 8, 1838.

A member of Co. A ; enlisted as private at Hingham, Nov. 25, 1861, and the same day was mustered into service ; re-enlisted at Liberty, Va., Jan. 4, 1864 ; promoted corporal Dec. 4, 1864.

Corp. Chadbourn was in the employ of Mr. Erastus Whiton at the time of enlistment, and joined the Army of the Potomac at Harrison's Landing, July 3, 1862. With the exception of the surrender of Gen. Lee, and such of the engagements as occurred during his confinement in the hospital, he was in all the principal battles which took place in the Department of Virginia.

In the engagement at Cold Harbor he was wounded through the hips by a musket-ball, and afterwards conveyed to the hospital at York, Pa., where he remained until his recovery, a period of nine weeks. He was also at one time disabled by sickness, and came to Readville, Mass., where, after a stay of three months, he regained his health, and returned to active duty at the front.

His whole term of service included three years and six months ; mustered out by order of War Department, June 10, 1865.

SILAS HENRY COBB.

Born in Hingham, April 2, 1831.

Was corporal in Co. E ; enlisted Dec. 2, 1861. Soon after leaving the Peninsula, Corp. Cobb was taken sick and removed to the hospital; discharged· for disability, Dec. 23, 1862.

Mr. Cobb was one of the thirty-seven volunteers who went

from Hingham May 18, 1861, to join the Lincoln Light Infantry, then stationed at Fortress Monroe.

* JACOB GILKEY CUSHING.

Co. D.

THEOPHILUS CUSHING, Jun.

Born in Hingham, age 22.

Mustered Feb. 20, 1862; was corporal in Co. F; mustered out for disability, Jan. 23, 1863.

WILLIAM LORENZO DAWES.

Born in Hingham, April 10, 1842.

Enlisted from Hingham for the quota of the town, as private in Co. F, Feb. 3, 1862, and was mustered in Feb. 13; re-enlisted as veteran, Jan. 5, 1864; promoted corporal Co. F. After a faithful service of three years and four months, was finally mustered out June 29, 1865, by reason of the close of the war.

Corp. Dawes shared the fortunes of his regiment from first to last, being present in nearly all the engagements and skirmishes from Cold Harbor to Five Forks, leaving an honorable record. At the battle of Cold Harbor he was slightly wounded.

JOHN C. ELDREDGE.

Enrolled from Hingham, age 43.

Mustered Dec. 2, 1861, and was corporal in Co. E; service terminated Nov. 14, 1862, at which time he was mustered out for disability.

THOMAS L. FRENCH.

Age 31.

Was corporal in Co. F; enlisted from Hingham, Feb. 2, 1862, and Jan. 4, 1864, was mustered out for re-enlistment.

In the summer of 1863, Corp. French was confined by sickness at Convalescent Camp, near Alexandria, and for a time was detailed for hospital duty. Mustered out June 29, 1865, by reason of close of the war, having been in service three years and nearly five months.

HARVEY MANN PRATT.

Born in Cohasset, June 7, 1836.

Enlisted at Hingham, as private in Co. A ; re-enlisted Jan. 4, 1864 ; promoted corporal, May 25, 1865.

Corp. Pratt was in the battle at Second Bull Run, Fredericksburg, Chancellorsville, Gettysburg, Mine Run, Wilderness, and lastly at Cold Harbor in June, 1864, where, being wounded, he was sent to the United States Hospital at York, Pa., in which he was confined ten months.

Rejoining the regiment in the spring of 1865, he was mustered out at Gallop's Island, Boston Harbor, on the 29th of the June following. His whole term of service included three years and nearly eight months.

At the time of re-enlisting in January, 1864, Corp. Pratt availed himself of the privilege of coming home on a furlough. During his absence, however, his family had removed from Hingham to the town of South Scituate. But as he was counted on the quota of Hingham when he re-enlisted, he still claimed residence here, and accepted from our recruiting committee the bounty which was divided among the soldiers. Subsequently learning that the town of South Scituate could rightfully claim him on her quota, though bound by no legal obligation, the bounty money received from the town's committee was promptly and honorably restored.

Corp. Pratt was son-in-law of the late Nathaniel French, sen.

EDGAR P. STODDER.

Age 32.

Born in Hingham, and enlisted for the quota of the town, Dec. 2, 1861 ; mustered as private in Co. E ; promoted corporal ; mustered out for re-enlistment Jan. 4, 1864, and, according to the

26

report of the adjutant-general, discharged July 11, 1865, by reason of disability.

Corp. Stodder was in the service three years and seven months, and includes in his list the most noted engagements set down to the Thirty-second Regiment. He has a good record.

*WASHINGTON IRVING STODDER.

Co. F.

SUMNER A. TRASK.

Born in Boston, Feb. 1, 1835. A resident of Hingham.

Enlisted under Capt. Stephenson, at Camp Dimmick, Nov. 1, 1861, as private in Co A ; promoted corporal at Sharpsburg, September, 1862 ; was at Fort Warren until the defeat of Gen. Banks, when the regiment was sent to Harrison's Landing.

Corp. Trask participated in the battles of Fredericksburg and Antietam ; but soon after was taken sick with chronic diarrhœa, and April 27, 1863, was discharged on account of disability.

MUSICIANS.

EDWIN HERSEY.

Born in Hingham, March 14, 1842.

Enlisted on the quota of this town, and was mustered into service Dec. 2, 1861, as private in Co, E ; discharged at Liberty, Va., Jan. 4, 1864, to re-enlist as veteran ; final muster-out June 29, 1865, near Washington, D.C., by reason of special order No. 158, A. of P.

Mr. Hersey participated in the following battles, viz. : Malvern Hill, Va. ; Second Bull Run ; Antietam, Md. ; Blackburn's Ford, Md. ; Fredericksburg, Va ; Chancellorsville, Va ; Aldie, Va. ; Gettysburg, Pa. ; Bristoe's Station, Va. ; Rappahannock Station, Va. ; New Hope Church, Va. ; and Mine Run, Va.

He was one of those who re-enlisted in January, 1864, for a second term of three years. The hearty welcome extended to these veterans as they returned to their homes to enjoy the conditional furlough of thirty days, has been already noticed. . Mr. Hersey refers to these receptions as among the most pleasant memories of his soldier-life.

After rejoining the army, he was detailed as musician, and performed the service required until May, 1864. He was then assigned to hospital duty under Surg. William L. Faxon of the Fifth Corps Hospital; subsequently was appointed hospital nurse; afterwards, ward-master, and finally to the trying and responsible position of division dresser. In the latter situation he was called to the care of nearly one hundred per day of the most seriously wounded, — a service requiring skill and good judgment, as well as firmness of nerve.

In May, 1865, the war being over, and most of the wounded sent North, he returned to his regiment, which in July was ordered to Gallop's Island, Boston Harbor, where it was discharged.

Mr Hersey was also a volunteer member of the Lincoln Light Infantry at Fortress Monroe.

CHARLES H. F. STODDER.

Age 24.

Of Hingham; mustered as musician in Co. E, Dec. 2, 1861; mustered out for re-enlistment Jan. 4, 1864; re-enlisted Jan. 5, 1864; mustered out June 29, 1865, by reason of close of the war. Whole term of service, three years and nearly seven months.

Mr. Stodder was with the Lincoln Light Infantry at Fortress Monroe, and was one of the volunteers who left Hingham on the 18th of May.

PRIVATES.

EPHRAIM ANDERSON.

Age 35.

Born in Hingham, and enlisted Feb. 20, 1862, for the quota of the town, as private in Co. F; mustered out Jan. 4, 1864, for re-enlistment; finally mustered out June 29. 1865, by reason of close of the war, having been in the service three years and four months.

OTIS LINCOLN BATTLES.

Born in Hingham, Feb. 20, 1843.

Enlisted at Hingham, and was mustered at Camp Cameron, Cambridge, Mass., as private in Co. E, Dec. 2, 1861. Discharged at Liberty, Va., Jan. 4, 1864; and Jan. 5, re-enlisted as veteran for three years, or during the war.

With the exception of Gettysburg. when he was detailed for special service, Mr. Battles was present in every engagement set down to the Thirty-second Regiment. At the battle of Cold Harbor he was wounded and disabled, and for a time was in the hospital at Davis Island, N.Y. He subsequently was taken to Readville, Mass., and for a short time, in the summer of '64, was at home in Hingham. On regaining health, he left for City Point, Va., and rejoined the regiment in season to commence the campaign of the spring following, and was then in active service to the time of the surrender of Gen. Lee and the close of the war, when he was mustered out at Washington, D.C., June 29, 1865.

* DANIEL LEAVITT BEAL.

Co. F.

LABAN O. BEAL.

Enrolled from Hingham. age 26.

Enlisted for the quota of the town, and was mustered Feb. 20, 1862, as private in Co. F; Jan. 30, 1863, was discharged for disability.

* WILLIAM BREENE.

Co. A.

HENRY F. BINNEY.
Co. E.

PATRICK CALLAHAN.
Enrolled from Newton, Mass., age 29.

Returned by the selectmen of Hingham as serving on the quota of the town; mustered as private in Co. K, Aug. 16, 1862. Service terminated March 9, 1863, by reason of disability.

ICHABOD W. CHANDLER.
Age 31.

Enlisted from Hingham for the quota of the town, Dec. 2, 1861, as private in Co. E; transferred March 11, 1864, to Veteran Reserve Corps. After a service of more than three years, was mustered out by reason of close of the war.

MOSES RITTER CHURCHILL.
Born in Hingham, June 10, 1846.

Enlisted as private in Co. F, and was mustered March 4, 1865.

Leaving Gallop's Island, he joined the regiment with the Army of the Potomac, was in the engagement at Petersburg and other battles of the Thirty-second; and June 29, 1865, by special order of War Department, was mustered out of service.

RUFUS CHURCHILL.
Age 35.

Born in Hingham, and enlisted Feb. 20, 1862, as private in Co. F. Becoming disabled, he was detailed for special duty, and finally discharged for disability, May 30, 1863; having been in service one year and three months.

GUSTAVUS P. CORTHELL.
Age 18.

Enlisted from Hingham, Feb. 20, 1862, as private in Co. F.

Being unfitted for service, by reason of sickness, he was discharged May 28, 1863, one year and three months from the time of mustering in.

WILLIAM FARDY.

Enrolled from Hingham, age 18.

Private in Co. E, and was mustered Dec. 2, 1861 ; discharged for disability Oct. 27, 1862, having been in service nearly eleven months. Served for the quota of Hingham, and is included in the official list returned by the selectmen.

GEORGE FRENCH, JUN.

Born in Hingham, Nov. 6, 1822.

Enlisted in Hingham, and was mustered as private in Co. A, Nov. 2, 1861 ; was sick after the regiment left Harrison's Landing, and confined in Camp Convalescent a year ; sent to Washington, D.C., and there transferred to the Invalid Corps. Discharged for re-enlistment in the Veteran Reserve Corps, and accredited to Worcester, Mass., May 5, 1864. Mustered out at Washington, D.C., Nov. 15, 1865.

HENRY GARDNER.

Born in Hingham, Oct. 6, 1840.

Enlisted at Fort Warren, Boston Harbor, Feb. 17, 1862, as private in Co. F, and was mustered the same day. After joining the Army of the Potomac, he remained with the regiment up to Sept. 17, 1862, and was in the seven days' fight in July, and also at the battle of Antietam in September. Disabled by sickness, he was sent to the hospital at Philadelphia, where he remained for one year. On the 30th of September, 1863, he was transferred to Co. D of the Sixteenth Regiment Veteran Reserve Corps, and Nov. 30, 1864, at Hollidaysburg, Pa., was promoted sergeant. After the expiration of his term of enlistment, he was mustered out at Harrisburg, Pa., March 20, 1865.

STEPHEN PUFFER GOULD.

Born in Hingham, age 34.

Private in Co. E; mustered Dec. 2, 1861. Feb. 5, 1863, he was honorably discharged on account of disability caused by accidental injury.

WILLIAM KIMBALL GOULD.

Born in Medford, Mass., July 9, 1838.

A resident of Hingham, he was drafted at Taunton, Mass., July 30, 1863, to fill the quota then required from the town.

First assigned to Co. F of the Twenty-second Regiment, M. V. I., three years, he was conveyed to Long Island, Boston Harbor, and after a brief stay, with a small detachment of troops, joined the regiment, then in camp at Bealton Station, Va. A few weeks were here spent in scouting and skirmishing, when he was transferred to Co. D of the Fifth United States Battery, with which he remained for ten months. From the commencement of this term, his service proved an active one; North Anna, Spottsylvania, Wilderness, Petersburg, Weldon Railroad, and other engagements, being included in the record of battles in which the Fifth Battery sustained an important and honorable part.

He was next assigned to Co. L, of the Thirty-second Regiment, M. V. I., with which he continued up to the time of the surrender of Gen. Lee, and the close of the war. His entire term of service includes nearly two years; during which he was at no time absent from disease, and his place in the ranks was broken for a few days only, from the effects of a slight accidental injury.

It may be proper to repeat in this connection what will be found under other records in succeeding pages of the volume, that of the entire number who entered the service, either as natives of Hingham or who were embraced in the quota of the town, three only did so under decree of a draft. These were drawn at Taunton, July 20, 1863, viz.: Dr. Don Pedro Wilson, Sewall Pugsley, and William Kimball Gould, the latter being now the sole survivor.

At the time of the draft, the purchase of commutation or the procuring of a substitute, Mr. Gould believed he could not well afford, and at once magnanimously accepted what his fortune seemed to have appointed. Entering the army under circumstances calculated to chill patriotism and depress the spirit, his ready acquiescence and loyal fidelity can scarcely be too highly commended. That he evaded no duty, fought bravely, and cheerfully endured exposure, fatigue, and privation, is the noble record he bears on his return to his home and the pursuits of peace.

WARREN HATCH, Jun.

Born in Hingham, Jan. 7, 1843.

Mr. Hatch enlisted at Hingham, Oct. 30, 1861, as private in Co. A, and was mustered the 24th of November following.

Called to active service at the front, he took part in the battles of Malvern Hill, Gainesville, Second Bull Run, Chantilly, and Antietam.

During the autumn and early part of the winter of 1862, he suffered severely from chronic diarrhœa, and finally through the effects of this disease became entirely disabled. Leaving the regiment, he was conveyed to the Patent Office Hospital on the 31st of December. After remaining here a few weeks, he was next taken to the Carver United States General Hospital at Washington, and finally, from continued sickness and disability, was granted a furlough of sixty days.

At the expiration of this time, he returned to Washington with health little, if at all, improved. Being reported unfit for the field, he was detailed as clerk in Carver Hospital, and continued to act in this capacity till the expiration of his term of enlistment, when, by order of the War Department, he was mustered out of service at Boston, Mass.

SAMUEL JAMES HENDERSON.

Born in Boston, July, 1828.

Enlisted at Hingham, Oct. 25, 1861, as private in Co. A, and was mustered Nov. 25, 1861.

Mr. Henderson left for the seat of war May 26, 1862, and was in active service till Aug. 15, when, on leaving Harrison's Landing, he was detailed as nurse in the brigade hospital, under surgeon Z. B. Adams. Capable and reliable, he quickly proved the wisdom of the appointment; and as experience soon gave efficiency, he became almost indispensable, and was finally retained for duty in the hospital department until the expiration of his term of enlistment. Mustered out Nov. 25, 1864, at Petersburg, Va.

* JOHN QUINCY HERSEY.
Co. E.

WILLIAM HARRISON HERSEY.
Born in Hingham, Nov. 27, 1840.

Enlisted at Hingham, Feb. 15, 1862; and Feb. 19 was mustered as private in Co. F.

Mr. Hersey was in the following battles: Second Bull Run, Antietam, Fredericksburg, Chancellorsville, and Gettysburg, where he left the regiment for the hospital, remaining from July 3 to Aug. 3, 1863; when he was removed to the hospital at Alexandria, where he continued until Oct. 21, 1863, when he was discharged for disability.

WILLIAM HERSEY, Jun.
Born in Hingham, Jan. 27, 1820.

Enlisted at Hingham, Dec. 2, 1861, and on the 17th of the month was mustered at Camp Cameron as private in Co. E.

Mr. Hersey was with the regiment in the engagements connected with its earlier history. Afterwards disabled by sickness, he left the ranks Sept. 14, 1862, at Sharpsburg, and was confined six months in the hospital at York, Penn.; mustered out by reason of disability, April 15, 1863, having been in the service sixteen months.

27

SYLVANUS H. HIGGINS.

Age 23.

Enrolled Feb. 20, 1862, from Hingham, in Co. F; Jan. 4, 1864, mustered out for re-enlistment; Jan. 5, 1864, enlisted as veteran from Charlestown, Mass.; and June 29, 1865, was mustered out by order of War Department.

* WALLACE HUMPHREY.

Co. E.

JOSHUA JACOB, Jun.

Born in Hingham, Feb. 6, 1843.

May 26, 1862, enlisted at Fort Warren, Boston Harbor, as private in Co. D, and the same day was mustered into service.

After joining the Army of the Potomac, he was with the regiment up to the time it left Sharpsburg to cross Harper's Ferry, when, being disabled by sickness, he was obliged to "fall out," and make the best of his way alone. Placed in the hands of a physician, he was conveyed to Camp Convalescent at Alexandria, Va., where he remained until Dec. 23, 1862, when by virtue of surgeon's certificate of disability, he was mustered out of service.

FRANK JERMYN.

Born in May, 1832, at Cavan, Delincose County, Ireland.

January, 1862, enlisted at Hingham as private in Co. F, and was mustered Feb 10, 1862.

He was with the Army of the Potomac on the Peninsula till disabled by fever and chronic diarrhœa, when he was conveyed to the Fairfax Seminary Hospital, where he was finally discharged for general disability, Dec. 31, 1862.

* GARDNER JONES.

Co. F.

MORALLUS LANE.

Born in Hingham, March 10, 1839.

Mustered in Co. F, Feb. 15, 1862; confined by sickness in hospital at West Philadelphia from Aug. 10, 1862, to Oct. 18, 1862, and then and there discharged for disability.

ALFRED AUGUSTUS LINCOLN.

Born in Hingham, Sept. 25, 1838.

Was one of the thirty-seven volunteers who left Hingham on the 18th of May, 1861, to join the Lincoln Light Infantry, then stationed at Fortress Monroe; re-enlisted as private, Dec. 2, 1861, in Co. E, Thirty-second Regiment; being disabled by sickness, was sent from Harrison's Landing to Blackwell's Island, New York Harbor; then to Fort Hamilton; afterwards to Camp Convalescent, Alexandria; and thence to Lincoln Hospital at Washington, where on the 14th of February, 1863, he was mustered out of service by reason of surgeon's certificate of disability.

MELTIAH LORING.

Born in Boston, March 23, 1837.

Enlisted at Hingham, Oct. 31, 1861, and was mustered as private into Co. A, Nov. 25, 1861.

Spending the winter at Fort Warren, Boston Harbor, he left with the regiment for the front, May 26, 1862, and was in the battles of Chancellorsville, Gettysburg, Second Bull Run, Cold Harbor, Weldon Railroad, and Petersburg.

Though fortunate in passing through these different engagements uninjured, he suffered at one period from sickness, and was confined by fever for some months in the Emory Hospital at Washington, D.C.

During the summer of 1863 he was detailed for the charge and conducting of conscripts to the seat of war, and in the course of the year came repeatedly to Massachusetts for this purpose.

His discharge was obtained near Petersburg, Va.; and he left the service Nov, 24, 1864, having been in the army three years, — the full term of enlistment.

FRANK HARLEY MILLER.

Born at Salem, Mass., Oct. 3, 1843.

Enlisted at Hingham, Dec. 2, 1861, and Dec. 12 was mustered as private in Co. E; re-enlisted as veteran at Liberty, Va., Jan. 4, 1864.

Included in his record are the following engagements: Antietam, Chancellorsville, Gettysburg, Rappahannock Station, Wilderness, Laurel Hill, Spottsylvania, Cold Harbor, Petersburg, and others. At the battle of Hatcher's Run, Feb. 6, 1865, he was wounded in the fore-arm by a gun-shot, and taken to the field hospital. Returning to Massachusetts, he was discharged June 25, 1865, by reason of disability from wound, having been in service three years and nearly seven months.

PAUL McNEIL.

Born in Edinburgh, Scotland, May 8, 1812.

Enlisted at Hingham, and Nov. 12, 1861, was mustered as private in Co. A.

Served as steward at Fort Warren, and at the request of Col. Dimmick, and by consent of Col. Parker, remained at the fort after the departure of the battalion. Discharged in December, 1862. Re-enlisted Nov. 27, 1863, at Concord, N.H., as private in Co. F, of the Second Regiment, N. H. I., three years. Under the second enlistment was mostly employed in hospital service, and for ten months was himself confined by sickness at the hospital at Point Lookout.

Served six months after peace, engaged in provost-guard duty at Richmond and Fredericksburg. Mustered out Dec. 18, 1865.

HENRY G. MORSE.

Age 30.

Enrolled from the town of Weymouth ; mustered in Co. F, Feb. 24, 1862, and discharged April 19, 1865, by reason of expiration of term of service. Returned among the names certified by the selectmen as being upon the quota of Hingham.

*HIRAM NEWCOMB.

CO. E.

JOHN M. NOLAN.

Age 25.

Enlisted from Hingham for the town's quota, and was mustered Oct. 31, 1861, as private in Co. A. Discharged Nov. 24, 1864, by reason of expiration of term of enlistment.

Mr. Nolan shared in the general experience of the Thirty-second from first to last, did his duty faithfully, and retired from the ranks with a good record.

NATHANIEL BLAISDELL PEARE.

Born in Greene, Me., Jan. 18, 1831.

Enlisted at Hingham, Dec. 2, 1861, and the same day was mustered as private in Co. E.

Mr. Peare was in the engagement at Malvern Hill, and was mustered out by reason of impaired sight, at Harrison's Landing, Va., Aug. 14, 1862.

GEORGE M. PROUTY.

Age 30.

Returned by the selectmen of Hingham as upon the quota of this town. Mustered Feb. 24, 1862, as private in Co. F. Mustered out Jan. 4, 1864, for re-enlistment. Finally mustered out by reason of close of the war, July 19, 1865.

JAMES B. PROUTY.

Enrolled from Hingham, age 28.

Mustered Dec. 2, 1861, as private in Co. E; discharged for disability, July 1, 1862, after a service of seven months.

THOMAS RAFFERTY, Jun.

Born in Hingham, age 18.

Enlisted for the quota of the town, Dec. 2, 1861, as private in Co. E; discharged by reason of disability, Jan. 8, 1863, after a service of thirteen months.

FOSTER REMINGTON.

Born in Hingham. July 9, 1836.

Enlisted Dec. 2, at Oasis Hall, Hingham, and was mustered as private in Co. E, Dec. 17, 1861, at Camp Cameron.

Mr. Remington was in the battles of Antietam and Second Bull Run, but shortly after was taken sick, and sent to the general hospital at Fairfax, Va. Thence he was transferred to Fort Schuyler Hospital, N.Y., and detailed to act as nurse. From there he was transferred to Bedloe's Island Hospital, and appointed assistant steward, serving as such until Dec. 17, 1864, when he was mustered out by reason of expiration of term of enlistment.

WILLIAM F. RILEY.

Age 30.

Enlisted for the quota of Hingham, and was mustered Dec. 2, 1861, as private in Co. E; Jan. 4, 1864, mustered out for re-enlistment; finally mustered out June 29, 1865 by reason of close of the war.

Mr. Riley was in the service three years and nearly six months.

JOHN ELLESON SNELL.

Born in New Albany, County of Annapolis, N.S., June 17, 1822.

Enlisted at Hingham, Nov. 30, 1861, and Dec. 16 was mustered at Camp Cameron as private in Co. E.

Was present in battles from Second Bull Run to Gettysburg, inclusive : also engaged at Petersburg.

In the fight at Gettysburg he was wounded in the leg, and, being disabled, was conveyed to division hospital, where he remained for several weeks. Afterwards he was taken to hospital at York, Penn., and in March, 1864, was transferred to Philadelphia, where, suffering from the effects of protracted marches, a portion of his foot was amputated. Following this, was taken to McClellan Hospital, where he continued till October, when he reported for duty, and rejoined his regiment, having been confined by wounds and sickness fourteen months.

Mustered out at Petersburg, Va., by reason of expiration of term of service.

JOHN SPRAGUE SOUTHER.

Born in Hingham, Jan. 29, 1819.

At the outbreak of the war he enlisted for three months in the Lincoln Light Infantry, and left Hingham with this company on the afternoon of the 17th of April, 1861. Entering service for the second time, he enlisted Jan. 20, 1862, in Co. A, of the Thirty-second Regiment.

Unable to withstand continued exposure, and the fatigue attendant on frequent and protracted marches, his health continued to fail until he became entirely disabled. Six weeks were spent in the hospital at Washington, D.C.; and from this institution he was discharged for disability, Nov. 10, 1862.

* DEMERICK STODDER.

Co. F.

FRANKLIN A. STODDER.

Age 18.

Enlisted in Hingham. Mustered Oct. 25, 1861. Afterwards transferred to Veteran Reserve Corps.

*HORACE L. STUDLEY.

CO. E.

WILLIAM TAYLOR.

Born at Sterling, Mass., July 22, 1818.

Enlisted in Hingham, Feb. 13, and was mustered in Co. F, Feb. 21, 1862; was with the regiment until Aug. 25, when, being unable to march, was ordered by Capt. Cunningham to convalescent camp in the field ; afterwards placed on detached service by order of the War Department ; discharged at the general hospital, Nov. 25, 1863, by reason of surgeon's certificate of disability.

Mr. Taylor was a volunteer in the Lincoln Light Infantry, and left Hingham for Fortress Monroe, May 18, 1861.

WILLIAM HENRY THOMAS.

Born in Hingham, June 12, 1845.

Enlisted Oct. 31, 1861, and Nov. 25 was mustered as private in Co. A.

Taking part in the early experience of the Thirty-second, he left Fort Warren, Boston Harbor, May 26, 1862, and, with the exception of Antietam, was with the regiment until after the battle of Fredericksburg, when, being disabled by chronic diarrhœa, he was sent to Emory Hospital, Washington, D.C., April 19, 1863. Detailed first as a nurse, and afterwards as ward-master, he remained at this place until the expiration of his term of enlistment.

Aug. 10, 1864, he was transferred to the Veteran Reserve

Corps, from which he was finally mustered out, at Emory Hospital, Nov. 25, 1864.

*CHARLES E. WILDER.
CO. E.

EZRA WILDER, Jun.

Born in Hingham, Nov. 26, 1843.

Enlisted and was mustered into service, Dec. 2, 1861, at Hingham, as private in Co. E.

Left Fort Warren, Boston Harbor, in May, 1862, for Washington, D.C. After a short stay was ordered to the vicinity of Alexandria, Va., and thence to Harrison's Landing, where he arrived on the last day of the seven days' fight.

Here he became disabled by sickness, and was taken to the hospital at West Philadelphia, where he was confined for nearly three months. Having somewhat improved, he was transferred to the convalescent camp at Alexandria, and shortly after left to rejoin his regiment, then stationed at Sharpsburg.

For a time Mr. Wilder was in active field-service, and participated in the engagements at Malvern Hill and Fredericksburg. Disease, however, soon unfitted him for duty; and he was discharged for disability on the twenty-second day of March, 1863, at Potomac Creek, Va.

GEORGE WILDER.

Born in Hingham, July 9, 1833.

Private in Co. A. Enlisted from Hingham for the quota of the town, Nov. 3, 1861. Mustered Nov. 28, 1861; and March 7, 1863, after a service of one year and four months, was discharged on account of disability.

Mr. Wilder took part with the regiment in the battles at Antietam and Fredericksburg, and prior to being mustered out was sick at the regimental hospital, near Falmouth, Va., where he was confined about three months.

28

JOSHUA WILDER.

Born in Hingham, Dec. 19, 1813.

Enlisted as private in Co. A, and was mustered at Camp Dimmick, Nov. 2, 1861.

The following winter was spent at Fort Warren ; but having been detailed for duty in the Commissary Department, he remained at this post after the departure of the regiment, till the 29th of November, 1862, when he was discharged at Boston for disability.

*HORATIO PHILANDER WILLARD.

CO. A.

GEORGE ADAM WOLFE.

Age 45.

Enlisted for the quota of Hingham ; private in Co. E, and was mustered Dec. 2, 1861. Discharged for re-enlistment Jan. 4, and mustered as veteran Jan. 5, 1864. Discharged June 29, 1865, by reason of close of the war.

Mr. Wolfe's service included three years and nearly seven months. He was in several engagements, and served efficiently as a member of the pioneer corps.

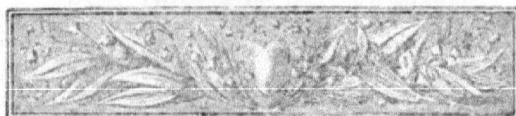

CHAPTER XI.

THREE YEARS' MEN CONTINUED.

Thirty-fifth Regiment — Thirty-eighth Regiment — Thirty-ninth Regiment — Fortieth Regiment — Fifty-fourth Regiment — Fifty-fifth Regiment — Fifty-sixth Regiment — Fifty-seventh Regiment — Fifty-eighth Regiment — Fifty-ninth Regiment.

THIRTY-FIFTH REGIMENT.

THE Thirty-fifth Regiment was mustered into the service of the United States Aug. 21, 1862, left Massachusetts the day following, and was mustered out June 9, 1865.

Few organizations from the State exhibit a more extended or a more severe experience. It rendered efficient service in Virginia, Kentucky, Tennessee, Arkansas, and Mississippi, and greatly distinguished itself at the taking of the City of Jackson, the capital of Mississippi. It was present at the battles at Antietam, Fredericksburg, Campbell Station, Siege of Knoxville, Spottsylvania, North Anna, Cold Harbor, Weldon Railroad, South Mountain, Vicksburg, Poplar Spring Church, Hatcher's Run, Fort Sedgwick, Fort Mahone, and Petersburg.

Of enlistments connected with Hingham, the regiment included the following, viz.: —

LIEUTENANT

OLIVER BURRILL.

Born in Hingham, July 2, 1835.

Enlisted at Weymouth, Aug. 2, and was mustered in Co. H, Aug. 11, 1862, with the rank of second lieutenant.

He left the State with the regiment, Aug. 22, and went directly to the field of active service, taking part in the battle of

South Mountain, Sept. 14.   He commanded the company at the
battle of Antietam, was in the battles of Fredericksburg and
Sulphur Springs, and received promotion to rank of first lieutenant Dec. 15, 1862.   Lieut. Burrill was sick with fever in camp in
front of Fredericksburg, and, before recovery, chronic diarrhœa
prevented a return to active service.   He was in hospital at
Fortress Monroe about four weeks, and discharged Oct. 6, 1863,
for disability.

GEORGE MARTIN ADAMS.

Born in Hingham, Oct. 20, 1840.

Enlisted at Weymouth, Aug. 6, 1862, as sergeant in Co. H, and
was mustered Aug. 12, 1862.   He was in the engagements at
South Mountain, Antietam, and Fredericksburg, and was
slightly wounded.

He was also confined in a Baltimore hospital for two months;
then transferred to the Veteran Reserve Corps.   Mustered out
June 27, 1865, at Washington, D.C., by reason of expiration of
term of service.
Serg. Adams was a volunteer in the Lincoln Light Infantry;
left Hingham on the afternoon of April 17, 1861, and was three
months at Fortress Monroe and vicinity.

MUSICIAN

JASON GARDNER.

Born in Hingham, Nov. 28, 1828.

Enlisted at Weymouth, on the quota of that town, Aug. 6, and
was mustered in Co. H, as musician, Aug. 11, 1862.

Mr. Gardner went with the regiment directly to the seat of
war, and shared the duties of his office at the battles of South
Mountain, Antietam, and Fredericksburg.   Also accompanied
the regiment through the Mississippi campaign, and was present
at the surrender of Vicksburg, the capture of the City of Jackson, and the siege of Knoxville, Tenn.

While in Tennessee, January, 1864, he received orders to report to the brigade band-master for duty. The corps afterwards left Tennessee, and went to Annapolis, Md., where it was re-organized, and marched to the front in time to take part in the battle of the Wilderness. Here the band was ordered to the hospital, where it remained till January, 1865. Orders were then received to move with the regiment to the lines before Petersburg.

Mr. Gardner was in the service till the close of the war, and was mustered out June 9, 1865.

PRIVATES.

CALEB HADLEY BEAL.

Born in Hingham, Jan. 15, 1833.

At the commencement of the war he was employed as book-keeper in the city of New York, and enlisted May 23, 1861, as private in Co. H, Fourteenth Regiment Regular State Militia, Brooklyn, N.Y., — afterwards designated the Eighty-fourth New York Volunteers. Commissioned second lieutenant, Co. E, One Hundred and Seventh New York Volunteers, and mustered in after the battle of Chancellorsville, where he was in command of the color-division of the regiment. Resigned his commission as second lieutenant, Dec. 20, 1863. Re-enlisted June 7, 1864, as prvate in Co. K of the Thirty-fifth Regiment, M. V. I., three years.

His list of engagements includes first and second Bull Run, South Mountain, Antietam, Fredericksburg, Rappahannock Station, Chancellorsville, Spottsylvania, Gettysburg, Mine Explosion, Weldon Railroad, Hatcher's Run, and siege of Petersburg. Finally transferred to Co. I of the Twenty-ninth Mass. Volunteers, and mustered out from this regiment at Readville, July 29, 1865, as sergeant.

*DAVID W. CUSHING.

CO. H.

*WILLIAM DUNBAR, Jun.

CO. A.

* PEREZ L. FEARING, Jun.

CO. I.

HIRAM THOMAS.

Born in Hingham, April 13, 1843.

Enlisted as private in Co. D, Aug. 16, 1862, and accredited to Waltham, Mass.

At the battle of Antietam, on the 17th of September, one month from the time of enlistment, he was accidentally disabled, and sent to the hospital for treatment. After a confinement of several months, his health being restored, he was detailed for clerical services, a situation for which he was well qualified. Lastly transferred to the hospital department at Philadelphia, where he remained until his discharge, May 11, 1865.

THIRTY-EIGHTH REGIMENT.

Seven companies of the Thirty-eighth Regiment were recruited at Camp Stanton, Lynnfield, and three (Cambridge companies) at Camp Cameron. It was mustered into the service Aug. 24, 1862, left the State Aug. 26 for Baltimore, and Nov. 10, embarked for New Orleans. In March, 1863, it joined the brigade at Baton Rouge, and on the 13th marched to Port Hudson to assist in the demonstration made to aid Admiral Farragut in passing the batteries. It was in the Western Louisiana campaign under Gen. Banks, and afterwards took part in all the assaults upon Port Hudson, suffering a heavy loss. It also shared in the Red River Expedition, under Banks.

The regiment returned to Virginia in the summer of 1864, and went through the Shenandoah Valley campaign under Sheridan; and was for a time under the command of Sherman in Georgia and North Carolina. After an extended, wearisome, and perilous experience, it was mustered out at Savannah, June 30, 1865, by reason of the close of the war, and finally reached home and was discharged July 13, 1865, eleven months' pay being then due the regiment.

The Thirty-eighth was present in the engagements at Bisland, Port Hudson, Cane River, Mansura, Opequan, Fisher's Hill, and Cedar Creek.

The following are the enlistments of natives or residents of Hingham : —

CAPTAIN.

JAMES A. WADE.

Age 22.

Served for quota of Hingham. Enrolled from Boston, and mustered as captain, Aug. 20, 1862. Resigned March 3, 1863.

LIEUTENANT.

LOUIS T. (V.[1]) (Z.[2]) CAZAIRE.

Accredited to the first quota of Hingham; was mustered as first sergeant in Co. I, Aug. 21, 1862, being at that time eighteen years of age; promoted second lieutenant, June 16, 1863. Not mustered.

Lieut. Cazaire, while in Louisiana with his regiment, performed his duties with credit to himself and the town he represented. April 19, 1864, he was discharged to receive a commission in the Eighty-ninth U. S. Colored Troops.

From the printed history of the Thirty-eighth Regiment, we learn that " Lieut. Cazaire afterwards distinguished himself for bravery and coolness on the occasion of the disaster to the steamship, 'Great Republic,' and his old companions of the Thirty-eighth have been gratified to see the public commendation of his conduct." He was on the staff of Gen. Canby when that general was killed by the Modocs, and is now military instructor in a college in Maine.

[1] Adjutant-general's Report.
[2] History of Thirty-eighth Regiment.

SERGEANT

BILLINGS MERRITT.

Age 31.

Resident of Scituate; served for the quota of Hingham. Sergeant in Co. D. Mustered Aug. 20, 1862, and discharged June 30, 1865, by reason of the close of the war.

PRIVATES.

HENRY BROWN.

Age 29.

Resident of Scituate; served for the quota of Hingham. Mustered as private in Co. D, Aug. 20, 1862. Transferred to the navy July 13, 1864.

CYRUS H. CHASE.

Age 29.

Enlisted from Hingham, and included in the town's quota. Mustered as private in Co. I, Aug. 24, 1862.

*THOMAS HERVEY.

CO. I.

*JOSHUA ROACH.

CO. H.

CUSHMAN ROUNDS.

Enlisted for the quota of Hingham; town papers say, "Thirty-eighth regiment; Capt. Wade — three years."

PETER H. ROYAL.

On authority of town documents, enlisted in Thirty-eighth regiment.

THIRTY-NINTH REGIMENT.

The Thirty-ninth Massachusetts Infantry was recruited principally from Bristol, Essex, Middlesex, Norfolk, Plymouth, and Suffolk Counties. Of those from Plymouth County, a large proportion were from the towns of Hingham, Scituate, and South Scituate.

The regiment was organized at Lynnfield, Mass., but for a short time before leaving the State was located at Camp Stanton, in the town of Boxford. It was mustered into the United States service Sept. 4; arrived at Washington, D.C., Sept. 8, 1862; and June 2, 1865, was mustered out by reason of close of the war.

The Thirty-ninth served upon picket-guard duty in the Department of Defences of Washington until July 12, 1863, when it joined the Army of the Potomac. It did not, however, take part in any engagement until May 5, 1864, when, being ordered out on the Brock Pike, it advanced in line of battle through the woods to the support of a body of troops in front, then being hard pressed by the enemy. From that time it was in nearly, if not all the conflicts that took place between the Army of the Potomac and the Confederate forces in Virginia. The last year of its history was marked by heavy losses in killed, wounded, and prisoners; Col. Davis, the commander of the regiment, being among those who were killed.

The battles in which it was engaged occurred in rapid succession. They were Mine Run, Wilderness, Spottsylvania, North Anna, Tolopotomy, Bethesda Church, Petersburg, Weldon Railroad, Dabney's Mills, Gravelly Run, and Five Forks.

Of the thirty-eight persons in the regiment who were connected with the town of Hingham, thirty-seven were in Co. G; and fourteen of the number gave up their lives for the preservation of the Union before the regiment was mustered out.

The Thirty-ninth was present at the surrender of Gen. Lee, and also was among the military organizations that participated in the grand review at Washington, D.C.

The names of the persons referred to as being connected with the town of Hingham are, —

29

THADDEUS CHURCHILL.

Born in Hingham, age 39.

Enlisted from the town of Quincy, Mass., and was sergeant in
Co. D; mustered Aug. 4, 1862; discharged from Thirty-ninth
regiment Oct. 18, 1863, for promotion as second lieutenant
in Third Regiment (colored), United States Army.

JOHN H. PROUTY.

Age 23.

Resident of South Scituate; served for quota of Hingham;
sergeant in Co. G, and was mustered Sept. 2, 1862; promoted
second lieutenant; discharged after close of the war, June 2,
1865, having served two years and nine months.

Lieut. Prouty was one of the thirty-seven volunteers who left
Hingham May 18, 1861, to join the Lincoln Light Infantry then
stationed at Fortress Monroe.

JOHN W. BAILEY.

Age 19.

Enrolled from Hingham, and served for the quota of the town;
was sergeant in Co. G, and mustered Sept. 2, 1862; discharged June 2, 1865, by reason of close of the war, having
had a service of two years and nine months.

Serg. Bailey shared in all the experience of his regiment,
from first to last.

*HENRY C. FRENCH.

Co. G.

WILLIAM HENRY JACOB.

Age 31.

Enlisted from Hingham for the quota of the town ; was sergeant in Co. G, and mustered Sept. 2, 1862 ; was detached for guarding rebel prisoners from Fortress Monroe to Washington, and similar services.

At the battle of Weldon Railroad he, with others, fell a prisoner in the hands of the enemy, and was sent to Richmond, Va. After remaining here a few weeks, he was put on board the cars, destined to some point in the State of Georgia. While on the road, Serg. Jacob determined to avail himself of the first opportunity which might offer to attempt his escape, however small the prospect of final success might be. Accordingly as the cars were on their way through North Carolina, favored by the darkness of the night, he leaped from the train and fortunately alighted without essential injury. With no other guide save the north star, he started for the Union lines, which, after a long, wearisome, and most perilous journey, he finally succeeded in safely reaching.

CORPORALS.

CHARLES CUSHING BAILEY.

Born in Hingham, Sept. 2, 1842.

In August, 1862, he enlisted as private in Co. G, and was mustered Sept. 2, 1862 ; promoted corporal.

Participating in the general service to which the regiment was called, he was engaged in picket-duty along the Potomac, and also in provost-guard duty until Dec. 28, 1863, when he was discharged for re-enlistment as hospital steward at Washington, D.C. Being an accomplished penman, he was detached for clerical duty in the office of the surgeon-general, — a position which was retained till the autumn of 1865, when he was mustered out of service.

His connection with the army covered three years; four

weeks having been spent in Judiciary Square Hospital, Washington, D.C., where he was confined by pneumonia.

* BENJAMIN CURTIS LINCOLN.

Co. G.

* HENRY FELT MILLER.

Co. G.

CHARLES C. YOUNG.

Age 32.

Enlisted on the quota of Hingham. Corporal in Co. G; mustered Sept. 2, 1862, and discharged June 2, 1865, by reason of close of the war, having served two years and nine months.

PRIVATES.

* CHARLES EUGENE BATES.

Co. G.

TIMOTHY B. CHAPMAN.

Resident of South Scituate, Mass., age 31.

Reckoned on the quota of Hingham, and was mustered as private in Co. G, Sept. 2, 1862.

Discharged June 2, 1865, by reason of close of the war. Time of service two years and nine months.

ELEAZER CHUBBUCK.

Age 18.

Enrolled from Hingham, and served for the town's quota; mustered Sept. 2, 1862, as private in Co. G, and was discharged June 2, 1865, by reason of the close of the war. Term of service two years and nine months.

* JAMES T. CHURCHILL.

Co. G.

JOHN CRESWELL.

Born in Londonderry, Ireland, July 23, 1833.

A volunteer in Co. I, Lincoln Light Infantry, Fourth Regiment, M. V. M., April 16, 1861, and was three months at Fortress Monroe; Aug. 9, 1862, enlisted at Hingham as private in Co. G, Thirty-ninth Regiment, and was mustered Sept. 2, 1862.

Beginning at Brock Pike, Mr. Creswell took part in all the battles that followed, including Wilderness, Spottsylvania, North Anna, Bethesda Church, and White Oak Swamp, up to the 19th of June, when being accidentally disabled, at the Norfolk Railroad, before Petersburg, he was removed to the Judiciary Square Hospital, at Washington. Remaining here a short time, he was granted a furlough, and returned to his home at Hingham. On rejoining his regiment, he was sent to Harewood Hospital, from which, after a stay of about ten weeks, he again reported for duty. From this time was in active service until the close of the war, when he was mustered out with the regiment, June 2, 1865.

* ANDREW J. DAMON.

Co. G.

* CHARLES E. FRENCH.

Co. G.

* GEORGE D. GARDNER.

Co. G.

ALVIN R. GLINES.

Age 21.

Enlisted from Hingham, and reckoned on the quota of the

town; mustered Sept. 2, 1862, as private in Co. G; mustered out June 2, 1865, by reason of close of the war. Service included two years and nine months.

For a portion of the time Mr. Glines was detailed as teamster, and served in quartermaster's department.

* ALBERT S. HAYNES.

Co. G.

ALBERT HERSEY.

Co. G.

Born in Hingham, age 29.

Enlisted for the quota of the town, and was mustered as private in Co. G. Sept. 2, 1862; mustered out with the regiment, June 2, 1865, having served two years and nine months. Was detailed for special service as teamster.

GEORGE LORING HERSEY.

Born in Hingham, July 18, 1830.

Enlisted for the quota of Hingham, Aug. 11, 1862, and was mustered as private in Co. G.

Mr. Hersey was with the regiment, and shared in its general experience, to the time of mustering out, June 2, 1865. Term of service, two years and nearly ten months.

HENRY FOSTER HERSEY.

Born in Hingham, July 20, 1833.

Enlisted under recruiting officer Edward Cazneau, for three years, Aug. 11, and was mustered Sept. 2, 1862, as private in Co. G, at Lynnfield, Mass.

Mr. Hersey was in the battles of Mine Run, Wilderness, Laurel Hill, Spottsylvania, North Anna, Bethesda Church,

Petersburg, and Weldon Railroad. On the second day of the last named engagement, Aug. 19, 1864, he, with a large number of the men of the Thirty-ninth, including several from Hingham, was captured and sent to Richmond, where he was confined in Libby Prison. Subsequently transferred to Belle Isle, and thence to the Stockade Prison at Salisbury, N.C. He was paroled at Wilmington, March 1, 1865, having been an inmate of these noted places for six months and ten days.

During this period, Mr. Hersey witnessed much suffering among his prison companions from a want of proper food and shelter; and his account of the treatment they received, and of the indignities heaped upon them by the prison officials, is far from flattering to those who were in authority.

He describes some of the punishments inflicted upon our soldiers as barbarous in the extreme. At Libby men were "bucked and gagged" for the most trifling offences. At Belle Isle a cruel punishment was practised upon those who presumed to stand up for their rights, or complained when robbed of their watches, rings, and mementos. The victim was first placed upon a horse made of joist; both legs and arms were fastened in a semi-horizontal position, and there kept for perhaps an hour. When released, after the most excruciating sufferings, the victim would frequently fall to the earth like a dead person. Prisoners were sometimes shot down by the guards. Mr. Hersey witnessed a number of such instances; among them a fellow-townsman, the late Mr. Henry C. French, who was killed in this way without the slightest provocation.

At Salisbury the prisoners were turned into an enclosed pen of several acres, very much the same as cattle are turned into a field, without shelter from the rain or sun. Strict guard was kept along the boundaries of the stockade, and the whole enclosure was commanded by batteries. Those who were well and strong found partial shelter for themselves by digging holes in the ground. Rations, consisting of half a loaf of bread, "blackbean soup," made from a few Mississippi *peas*, and yellowish, rancid pork, were served once a day.

Of a cheerful disposition, and possessing a vigorous constitution, Mr. Hersey was enabled to retain a fair degree of health, while many around him were dying from hunger, exposure, and despondency. After being released from prison he came home. He was discharged from the service June 2, 1865, by reason of general order No. 26, to the Army of the Potomac, dated May 17, 1865.

CHARLES LEROY.

Age 22.

Enlisted from Hingham, served for the quota of the town, and was mustered as private in Co. G, Sept. 2, 1862.

Mustered out June 2, 1865, by reason of close of the war. Term of enlistment two years and nine months. Was in nearly every engagement of the regiment.

* JOHN S. NEAL.
Co. G.

LEVI CROWELL NEWCOMB.
Born at Vinalhaven, Me., Oct. 4, 1813.

Enlisted Aug. 13, 1862, as private in Co. G, and served for the quota of Hingham. Was connected with the Department of Defences for Washington, D.C., up to Jan. 1, 1863; afterwards stationed at Poolsville; but becoming sick, and unfit for duty, he was transferred to the Army Square, Hospital at Washington, where he was finally discharged from service, June 11, 1863, on account of deafness and general disability.

CHARLES HENRY POOLE.
Age 18.

Enlisted from Hingham, and returned by the selectmen as reckoned on the quota of the town.

Mustered as private in Co. G, Sept. 2, 1862, and was discharged for disability Dec. 17, 1864. Term of service, two years and three months.

BENJAMIN W. PROUTY.

Age 34.

Resident of South Scituate; mustered Sept. 2, 1862, as private in Co. G; served for the quota of Hingham.

Mustered out on account of disability, Sept. 12, 1864, after a service of two years. Was sun-struck and disabled in the summer of 1863, and for a time confined in Kent Hospital at Washington, D.C.

* ELIJAH PROUTY.

Co. G.

ISAAC PROUTY.

Age 44.

Resident of South Scituate; and Sept. 2, 1862, was mustered as private in Co. G; Sept. 7, 1863, transferred to Veteran Reserve Corps.

WILLIAM PROUTY, Jun.

Age 28.

Resident of South Scituate, private in Co. G, and was mustered Sept. 2, 1862. Served for quota of Hingham. Mustered out June 2, 1865, by reason of close of the war, his whole period of service including two years and nine months.

Mr. Prouty was a volunteer member of the Lincoln Light Infantry, and left Hingham for Fortress Monroe with the second detachment, May 18, 1861.

* JOSEPH SIMMONS.

Co. G.

* EDWARD A. F. SPEAR.

Co. G. *

* THOMAS SPRAGUE.
CO. G.

SETH MELLEN SPRAGUE.

Born in Hingham, Nov. 16, 1843.

Enlisted at Hingham, Aug. 11, 1862, as private in Co. G.

Mr. Sprague entered the service when but nineteen years of age, and, during the time for which he enlisted, was called to bear a full measure of the trials and exposures of a soldier's life. He was in the battles of Mine Run, Wilderness, Spottsylvania, North Anna, Tolopotomy, Bethesda Church, Petersburg, Weldon Railroad, Dabney's Mills, Gravelly Run, and Five Forks.

Mustered out June 2, 1865, by reason of close of the war.

ALONZO G. STOCKWELL.

Born in Hingham, Sept. 11, 1840.

Enlisted for the quota of Hingham, and was mustered as private in Co. G. Sept. 2, 1862.

Mr. Stockwell was in the battle of the Wilderness, and others in which the regiment shared. During the engagement at Weldon Railroad, he was severely wounded in the foot, and confined nearly five months in the hospital, a portion of the time being spent at City Point, Va., and at Bristol, Pa. In the autumn of 1864, he came home on a furlough; and in June, 1865, absent from wound, he was honorably discharged from service by reason of close of the war.

CHARLES H. TISDALE.

Age 29.

Enlisted from Hingham for the quota of the town, and was mustered as private in Co. G, Sept. 2, 1862.

Mustered out Nov. 4, 1862, by reason of disability.

FRANKLIN JACOB TORREY.

Born in Hingham, Oct. 19, 1835.

Enlisted at Hingham, Sept. 2, 1862 ; was mustered as private in Co. G, and left the State for the seat of war Sept. 6, 1862.

His first engagement occurred at Brock Pike, May 5, 1864. The battle of Mine Run followed ; and, on the 7th, the march was made to Laurel Hill. In the battle which took place early on the following morning (Sunday, May 8), Mr. Torrey was severely wounded by a musket-ball. Being entirely disabled, he was removed to the Camden Hospital at Baltimore. After a short stay here, he was taken to New Haven, Conn. ; and lastly to the hospital in Pemberton Square, Boston, Mass., where he obtained his discharge by reason of disability, and was mustered out Dec. 10, 1864. Whole term of service two years and three months.

* ALBERT WILDER.

Co. G.

FORTIETH REGIMENT.

The Fortieth Regiment was recruited at Camp Stanton. It was mustered into the service Sept. 5, left Massachusetts Sept. 8, 1862, and was mustered out June 16, 1865. Of enlistments connected with Hingham, it included two only.

PRIVATES.

* JEREMIAH J. CORCORAN.

Co. A.

ENSIGN LINCOLN.

Born in Hingham, Jan. 15, 1841.

Enlisted in Co. I, at Sandwich, Mass., July 22, 1862, with the rank of private, and was mustered July 29, following, for three years' service.

He performed soldier's duty till January, 1863, and then was detailed as baker and cook at brigade headquarters, for Brig.-Gen. Robert Cowdin and staff.

On the march to Gettysburg, he was taken sick with intermittent fever, and sent to the U. S. Hospital at Frederick City, Md., where he remained till sent to convalescent camp at Alexandria, Va., Dec. 20, 1863. On the 11th of January, 1864, he received his discharge on surgeon's certificate of disability.

FIFTY-FOURTH REGIMENT.

This was the first colored regiment recruited in Massachusetts. It was mustered into service May 13, left the State May 28, 1863, and was mustered out Aug. 20, 1865.

The Fifty-fourth took an important part in the siege of Charleston, S.C., and had the advance at the assault on Fort Wagner. Besides these engagements, it was present at Olustee, James Island, Honey Hill, and Boykin's Mills.

The enlistments from Hingham were the following : —

CORPORAL

DAVID HENRY CHAMPLIN.

Born in Norwich, Conn., April 18, 1835, resident of Hingham.

Enlisted at Taunton, Mass., Aug. 25, 1863, as private in Co. B, and was mustered at Long Island, Boston Harbor. Promoted corporal March 1, 1864.

With a small body of troops, he joined the regiment at Morris Island, Charleston Harbor, S. C. The last of January left for Hilton Head, and thence sailed with the expedition to attempt the capture of Jacksonville, Fla. Arriving at that place, the Fifty-fourth was the first to land. The fire of the pickets was received with unflinching bravery, and the enemy was driven before them.

On the 20th occurred the battle of Olustee, where this regiment "made the reserve in the fight, and was the last to leave the field ; and it also covered the retreat."

Returning to Jacksonville, the company had marched one hundred and twenty miles in one hundred and two hours.

In the battle of Olustee, the fighting was continued from four o'clock of the afternoon until eight o'clock of the evening, with a total of seventy-nine killed and wounded. The regiment entered the fight with "three cheers for Massachusetts and seven dollars a month !"

The next battle was at John's Island, and James Island, after which Corp. Champlin was stationed at Folly Island and other places in the vicinity of Charleston, S.C., performing garrison duty or skirmishing with the enemy, until the advent of peace.

Mustered out Aug. 20, 1865. Whole term of service, two years.

Up to September of 1864, no compensation for services had been received by the men of the Fifty-fourth. "During the sixteen months prior to this, the regiment had been seven times mustered for pay. Seven dollars per month had been tendered the men on each occasion, in the place of the thirteen dollars monthly pay of the white soldiers; and on each occasion had the men refused to take it." But on the 28th of September, — pronounced by the adjutant-general "a memorable day in the history of the Fifty-fourth Regiment," — the United States acknowledged the men as "soldiers," and paid them, as such, thirteen dollars per month from the time of enlistment.

PRIVATE

LOUIS LEGARD SIMPSON.

Resident of Hingham, age 22.

Enlisted Nov. 25, 1863. Mustered in Co. G, Dec. 10, 1863. Wounded at Honey Hill, S.C., Dec, 10, 1864. Removed to hospital at Beaufort, and was there confined for six months. Mustered out May 25, 1865, by reason of disability caused by wound.

FIFTY–FIFTH REGIMENT.

This regiment was mustered into the service of the United States June 22, 1863, and left camp at Readville, Mass., on the morning of the 21st of July.

Its service was in the Carolinas, where it was present at the siege of Charleston, and in the engagements at James Island and Honey Hill. Of those connected with Hingham, this regiment included, —

LIEUTENANTS.

ALPHONSO MARSH.

Born in Hingham in 1839, but resided at Fitchburg when commissioned.

Enlisted as private in the Twenty-first Massachusetts Infantry, July 19, 1861. Promoted second lieutenant, in the Fifty-fifth Massachusetts Infantry, Aug. 21, 1863; first lieutenant July 9, 1864. Resigned Sept. 29, 1864. Has since resided at Philadelphia, and been in the employ of the Pennsylvania Central Railroad Company.

PETER NICHOLS SPRAGUE.

Born in Hingham, Dec. 16, 1826.

Sergeant in Co. I, Fourth Regiment, M. V. M., — Lincoln Light Infantry, — and was three months at Fortress Monroe and vicinity, April to July, 1861.

Removing to Weymouth, he was commissioned, Aug. 20, 1864, as second lieutenant, Co. A, in the Fifty-fifth (colored) Regiment, M. V. I., three years. Sept. 12 left for Hilton Head, where on the 26th he was mustered into service.

During the winter he was employed in garrison and picket duty; and he also took part in the engagement at James Island, besides joining the expedition under Gen. Potter to attempt a landing at Bull's Bay.

On the 19th of February, news was received of the evacuation of Charleston, and the next day the Fifty-fifth entered the city. Boats from the fleet had landed, and a few soldiers had come over; but the Fifty-fifth was the first body of troops that entered the town after its evacuation.

As they moved up King Street, a voice from an upper window called to know who they were. On being told that they were the Fifty-fifth from Massachusetts, he replied " God bless Gov. Andrew !"

From this time Lieut. Sprague was engaged in numerous expeditions at various points in the vicinity of Charleston, doing guard-duty, constructing bridges, &c., and on the 15th of May was promoted first lieutenant, the commission to date from April 1.

On the 5th of June, Companies A and I were ordered to leave Orangeburg for Fort Motte, and moved the day following. Remaining at this post till about Aug. 20, Lieut. Sprague returned with the company to Orangeburg, and thence to Charleston. On the 29th of August, after the close of the war, he was mustered out of service at Mount Pleasant, S.C., and finally discharged at Gallop's Island, Boston Harbor, Sept. 25, 1865.

PRIVATE

JOHN T. TALBOT.

Enlisted from Hingham, age 36.

Mustered into Co. B, Oct. 8, 1864, as private, and was mustered out after close of the war, Aug. 29, 1865.

FIFTY-SIXTH REGIMENT.

This regiment was organized at Readville, Mass., by Col. Charles E. Griswold. It was mustered into the service of the United States Feb. 25, left the State March 21, 1864, and was mustered out July 12, 1865.

It was present in the following engagements : Wilderness, Spottsylvania, North Anna, Cold Harbor, Petersburg, Weldon Railroad, Poplar Spring Church, Hatcher's Run, and siege of Petersburg.

Of those connected with the town of Hingham, the Fifty-sixth included the following : —

CORPORAL

* GEORGE BAILEY.

Co. I.

PRIVATE *

GEORGE A. CLAPP.

Enrolled from Hingham, age 28.

Mustered into Co. H, Jan. 27, 1864; mustered out by close of war, July 12, 1865.

31

FIFTY-SEVENTH REGIMENT.

The Fifty-seventh regiment was organized in Worcester County, during the autumn of 1863 and the winter and spring of 1864. It was mustered into the service April 6; left Massachusetts April 18, 1864, and was mustered out July 30, 1865.

Served in the Department of Virginia. In its list of engagements are the Wilderness, Spottsylvania, North Anna, Cold Harbor, Petersburg, Weldon Railroad, Poplar Spring Church, and Hatcher's Run.

So far as known, the following were the only enlistments from Hingham.

· MUSICIAN

EDWARD O. GRAVES.

Resident of Hingham, age 44.

First in Co. K, Twentieth Regiment; enlisted Jan. 14, 1864, in Co. C of the Fifty-ninth Regiment, and transferred to the Fifty-seventh, Co. C, June 1, 1865; June 22, 1865, discharged for disability.

PRIVATE

JOHN WELSH.

Enrolled from Hingham, age 20.

Enlisted as private in Co. G, May 16, 1864, and transferred June 1, 1865, to Co. G of the Fifty-seventh Regiment; mustered out July 30, 1865, by reason of close of the war.

FIFTY-EIGHTH REGIMENT.

The formation of this regiment was commenced in the autumn of 1863, and eight companies were organized April 25, 1864.

These companies left Readville April 28, under command of Lieut.-Col. John C. Whiton, for Alexandria, Va., which they reached Saturday, April 30. Of enlistments of natives or residents of Hingham, the number included in the Fifty-eighth was limited.

The regiment was in active service for nearly fifteen months. The nature of this service the following statement of the killed and wounded will show : —

Killed, eight commissioned officers and fifty-four enlisted men. Died of wounds, one commissioned officer, and forty-two men. Fifteen commissioned officers were wounded, and two hundred and eighty-four enlisted men ; making the total of wounded two hundred and ninety-nine.

The regiment was mustered out July 14, 1865. Further particulars of the service rendered will be found in the annexed record of Col. Whiton, who, as will be seen, also served nine months with the Forty-third Regiment in the Department of the Carolinas.

COLONEL.

JOHN CHADWICK WHITON.

Born in Hingham, Aug. 22, 1828.

Early in life Col. Whiton removed to Boston, and at the time of the outbreak of the civil war was in command of the "Tigers," one of the most noted and best disciplined of the military organizations of that city. As captain of Co. A, of the Second Battalion, M. V. M., he was with the first garrison at Fort Warren, Boston Harbor, remaining there from the 29th of April to May 21, 1861, when the battalion was relieved.

On the 27th of August, 1862, as captain of the same battalion, went into camp at Readville, for the purpose of recruiting a regiment, having command of camp and recruits. This regiment was designated the Forty-third, M. V. M., nine months,

and left Massachusetts Oct. 24, for the Department of North
Carolina, where the full term of enlistment was spent. Col.
Whiton was here present in the expedition to Goldsboro',
engaged at Kinston, Whitehall, Springbank Bridge, Blount's
Creek, and also at Little Washington ; in addition to which the
regiment performed its full measure of garrison duty, construction of roads, building of fortifications, &c.

At the expiration of his term of enlistment, he left with the
regiment for Fortress Monroe, and thence embarked for Baltimore. Some disaffection was here manifested on the part of the
soldiers at the delay in mustering out ; and an order was issued,
"leaving it optional with the men to go to the front or return
home." It was a season of peculiar peril, and the need of the
additional strength was urgent. Two hundred and three officers
and men, including Col. Whiton and all those from Hingham,
voted "to go to the front." Lieut.-Col. Whiton was in command ;
and proceeding at once to Sandy Hook, the regiment remained
at this point until July 18, when all embarked for Boston, and
were mustered out at Readville on the 30th, complimented for
the faithful manner in which their duties had been performed,
and commended for their bravery and patriotism.

Oct. 23, 1863, Col. Whiton was appointed superintendent of
recruiting for Plymouth County, and served in this capacity
until April of 1864.

During the winter of 1863-4 the Fifty-eighth Regiment,
M. V. I., three years, had been organizing at Readville ; and on
the 28th of April, under the command of Lieut.-Col. Whiton,
left Massachusetts for Alexandria and the Department of
Virginia. An active service followed. In eight days from the
time of leaving home they were engaged with the enemy ; and
from this time until August there were but few days when the
Fifty-eighth was not under fire. In the list of engagements are
included the Wilderness, Spottsylvania, North Anna, Tolopotomy, Bethesda Church, Cold Harbor, and the siege and capture
of Petersburg.

At the battle of Bethesda Church Col. Whiton was struck in
the side by a musket-ball, which fractured one of his ribs, and
was the cause of a brief confinement.

After the engagement at Preble's Farm, nearly all of the regiment had either been killed, wounded, or taken prisoners. Of those who actually participated in this battle, only one officer and about ten men escaped. The Fifty-eighth appeared to be almost extinct. Additional recruits, the return to duty of the convalescent, as well as of escaped prisoners, afterwards swelled the number to three hundred or more.

At the evacuation of Petersburg the regiment marched over the enemy's works, through the city, and joined in the pursuit of Lee's retreating army.

On the 10th of May, after the news of the surrender of Gen. Lee, the return march was commenced.

The Fifty-eighth was present in the grand review at Washington, D.C., on the 23d of May; and July 15, broke camp and returned to Readville, Mass., where it was regularly mustered out of service, July 26, 1865, by reason of close of the war.

SERGEANT

WILLIAM M. CARTER.

Enrolled from Hingham, age 23.

Co. H.

Mustered April 18, 1864; discharged July 14, 1865, by reason of close the war.

In the battle at Cold Harbor, Serg. Carter was wounded, and came home, where for some months he remained disabled. On being mustered out, he had the hearty commendation of those in command.

PRIVATES.

JOHN McDONALD.

Enrolled from Hingham. age 44.

Co. A.

Mustered Jan. 14, 1864.

JAMES L. LITCHFIELD.

Enrolled from Hingham, age 22.

Co. D.

Mustered March 1, 1864.

FIFTY-NINTH REGIMENT.

The Fifty-ninth was the last of the regiments raised for a service of three years. It was mustered by companies; left the State April 26, 1864, and was mustered out July 30, 1865.

Its list of engagements includes the Wilderness, Spottsylvania, North Anna, Cold Harbor, Petersburg, Weldon Railroad, Poplar Spring Church, Hatcher's Run, and Fort Stedman.

Among its enlistments were the following : —

CORPORAL

ALFRED TYLER.

Enrolled from Hingham, age 22.

Co. F.

Mustered Feb. 20, 1864 ; discharged by order of War Department, June 2, 1865. Town records say he resided at Bath, Me., and was a shoemaker by trade.

MUSICIAN

EDWARD O. GRAVES.

Co. C.

Transferred June 1, 1865, to Fifty-seventh Regiment, Co. C.

WILLIAM C. TORREY.

Born in Hingham, age 36.

Enlisted from Dedham, as private in Co. G, and was mustered March 4, 1864.

JOHN WELCH.

Enrolled from Hingham.

Co. G.

Transferred June 1, 1865, to Co. G, Fifty-seventh Regiment.

CHAPTER XII.

THREE YEARS' MEN CONTINUED.

First Regiment Heavy Artillery — Third Do. — First Battery Light Artillery — Third Do. —
Tenth Do. — List of Men in Regiments of Artillery and Batteries.

FIRST REGIMENT HEAVY ARTILLERY.

THE basis of this regiment was the Fourteenth Regiment Infantry. It was mustered into the service of the United States, July 5, and left Massachusetts July 7, 1861.

By order from the War Department, it was changed to a heavy artillery regiment, Jan. 1, 1862.

In 1863 the regiment re-enlisted for an additional term of three years, and was mustered out Aug. 16, 1865, making its complete period of service more than four years.

Its record includes the following engagements, viz. : Spottsylvania, North Anna, Tolopotomy, Cold Harbor, Petersburg, Strawberry Plains, Deep Bottom, Poplar Spring Church, Boydton Road, Hatcher's Run, Duncan's Run, and Vaughan Road. Of enlistments connected with Hingham, it included the following : —

CORPORAL

WEBSTER A. CUSHING.

Mustered in Co. D, Aug. 1, 1862. Mustered out April 2, 1865, by reason of close of the war.

PRIVATES.

WILLIAM CARTER.

Age 43.

Enrolled from Hingham. Member of Co. G, and mustered Sept.

28. 1864.   Discharged May 3, 1865.   Enlisted for one year.
Transferred from Fourteenth Regiment Infantry.

ANTON TAPP.

Age 35.

Enlisted from Hingham for the quota of the town.   Private in
Co. L.   Mustered Dec. 31, 1861.   Re-enlisted Jan. 1, 1864,
Mustered out June 7, 1865, by reason of close of the war.
Transferred from Fourteenth Regiment Infantry, where he
was private in Co. L.

THIRD REGIMENT HEAVY ARTILLERY.

The Third Regiment of Heavy Artillery was formed from
the Third, Sixth, Seventh, Eighth, Ninth, Tenth, Eleventh,
Twelfth, Thirteenth, Fourteenth, Fifteenth, and Sixteenth Unattached Companies of Heavy Artillery.

The eight companies first mentioned were originally raised
for the coast defence of the State of Massachusetts, and for a
time were so employed.

The new organization was directed by order of the War
Department; and the regiment was forwarded to Washington
in the autumn of 1864.

From this time to the expiration of its term of enlistment,
it was stationed at different points in the vicinity, for the defence
of the national capital.

The regiment included twenty enlistments from Hingham.
Of these, seventeen were members of Co. A, originally Third
Unattached.

32

MAJOR

LYMAN BARNES WHITON.

Born in Hingham, Jan. 17, 1834.

Was first corporal, then sergeant, in the Lincoln Light Infantry; left Hingham with the first detachment, April 17, 1861, and was with the company three months at Fortress Monroe and vicinity. Mustered out at expiration of term of service, July 22, 1861.

Commissioned second lieutenant in Co. I, First Battalion Infantry, M. V. Promoted first lieutenant May 26, 1862, then of Thirty-second Regiment. Resigned on account of disability, July 20, 1862. Commissioned second lieutenant in Third Unattached Company Heavy Artillery, Nov. 26, 1862. Promoted captain, Dec. 31, 1862, and Sept. 8, 1864, commissioned major in the Third Regiment, Mass. Heavy Artillery. Sept. 18, 1865, mustered out by reason of expiration of term of service.

When the Lincoln Light Infantry was called into service at the commencement of the war, Major (then Corporal) Whiton took an active part in obtaining volunteers to fill the ranks, and in making the necessary arrangements for joining the Fourth Regiment in Boston. The time for preparation was short; the needs of the hour pressing ; and it was through the hearty co-operation of Corp. Whiton and another officer, now deceased, that the company was enabled to appear with as full ranks as it did at the time of departure.

Early in December, 1861, Major (at that time Sergeant) Whiton opened a recruiting-office in Hingham, at Oasis Hall, for the purpose of obtaining enlistments for a company then being raised under Capt. Cephas C. Bumpus. Within ten days from the time the office was opened, fifty-seven recruits were procured ; and, before the month ended, all were sworn into the United States service at Fort Warren, as members of Co. E, of the First Battalion Infantry, M. V., afterwards Thirty-second Regiment, M. V. I. This, undoubtedly, was the most successful recruiting in Hingham during the war.

At the draft-riot in Boston, July 14, 1863, Major (then Captain) Whiton and his company came up from Fort Independence with a company of the Eleventh Infantry U. S. Regulars, for duty in support of law and order; the battalion being under command of Captain Whiton. The night was passed on guard in the city. The following night the company, with other troops, was ordered to the arsenal at Watertown, to protect that place against an apprehended attack; the entire force being in charge of Capt. Whiton.

While in Washington, D.C., his military record was closely identified with the history of the Third Regiment. A portion of the time, however, he was detached for special duty. Serving as judge advocate, on a general court-martial, he was highly complimented through special orders issued from headquarters.

CAPTAIN

EDWIN THOMAS.

Born in Hingham, age 26.

On the 28th of February, 1852, enlisted at Boston as private in the First Unattached Company Heavy Artillery. In January of 1863 was promoted second lieutenant; May 25, 1863, first lieutenant; and Sept. 8, 1864, captain.

Up to the time of his first promotion, he remained with the company in which he originally enlisted. By virtue of his first commission he was transferred to the Third Unattached Company Heavy Artillery; and here he remained until promoted captain, when he was again transferred to the Ninth Company Unattached Artillery (so designated at the time of its formation). Previous to his appointment as captain of this company, it had been consolidated with others, and was recognized as Co. K of the Third Regiment Heavy Artillery, M. V.

Capt. Thomas enlisted for the quota of the town of Weymouth; resigned, and was mustered out at Washington, D.C., June 25, 1865, having been in service three years and four months.

EDWIN F. TIRRELL.

Resident of Hingham, age 26.

Enlisted from Weymouth, as first sergeant in Co. B, and was mustered May 25, 1864. Promoted second lieutenant.

SERGEANT

FRANCIS K. MEADE.

Age 43.

Enlisted at Hingham, and Dec. 30, 1863, was mustered as quartermaster sergeant in Co. A. Mustered out Sept. 18, 1865, by reason of expiration of term of service.

CORPORALS.

FRANZ BURHENNE.

Born in Germany. Thirty-two years of age, and at the time of entering the service was in the employ of Mr. Alfred Loring, at South Hingham.

Mustered Dec. 30, 1863. Was corporal in Co. A ; mustered out after the close of the war, Sept. 18, 1865.

ISAIAH WILDER LORING.

Born in Hingham, Nov. 10, 1832.

Enlisted at Hingham, and Feb. 29, 1864, was mustered at Fort Independence, Boston Harbor; was corporal in Co. A ; mustered out Sept. 18, 1865.

ARTIFICER

JOHN BRIGGS BATCHELDER.

Born in Baldwin, Me., Sept. 19, 1829; enlisted from Hingham, Dec. 2, 1863, and served for the quota of the town. Artificer in Co. A, and was mustered Dec. 29, 1863. Mustered out after the close of the war, Sept. 18, 1865.

JONATHAN B. ACKERMAN.

Age 37.

Enlisted from Hingham, and included in the town's quota ; mustered Dec. 30, 1863, as private in Co. A. Mustered out after the close of the war, Sept. 18, 1865.

FIELDER BOTTING, Jun.

Born in Hingham, age 21.

Enlisted for the quota of Hingham, and was mustered as private in Co. F, originally Tenth Unattached, Sept. 16, 1863 ; mustered out by reason of disability, Aug. 26, 1864.

GEORGE ANTHONY CHUBBUCK.

Born in Scituate, July 9, 1844.

Enlisted at Boston, May 16, 1863, as private in the Third Unattached Company, Massachusetts Heavy Artillery ; July 5, 1864, transferred to Navy, which see for further particulars of his record.

JOSHUA CROSBY, Jun.

Born in Cohasset, age 23.

Enlisted from Hingham, and Sept. 1, 1864, was mustered as private in Co. A ; mustered out June 14, 1865, by reason of expiration of term of service.

FRANCIS MAYHEW.

Born in Hingham, age 18.

Enlisted from Hingham ; and mustered as private in Co. A, Sept. 10, 1864. Discharged June 14, 1865, by reason of close of the war. Enlisted for one year.

DANIEL H. MILLER.

Age 35.

Private in Co. A ; mustered Jan. 10. 1863, and discharged April 24, 1863, by reason of disability. Served for quota of Hingham.

LEVI HANSCOM DOW.

Born in Boston, Oct. 3, 1840.

First, a volunteer member of the Lincoln Light Infantry, Co. I, Fourth Regiment, M. V. M. Left Hingham May 18, 1861, and was three months at Fortress Monroe and vicinity.

Second, enlisted July 7, 1863, as private in Co. E, Third Regiment Massachusetts Heavy Artillery ; and was mustered out Sept. 18, 1865, by reason of close of the war.

Third, re-enlisted Nov. 11, 1867, for three years, in the Seventeenth Regiment, Co. E, Capt. Edward Collins, of the regular army of the United States, as artificer, and was mustered out Nov. 11, 1870, by reason of expiration of term of enlistment.

In the Army of the Potomac, Mr. Dow was employed in field and garrison duty, and shared in the engagements at Spottsylvania, Wilderness, Cold Harbor, North Anna, Petersburg, and in other battles of minor importance.

Afterwards, while in the regular army, was stationed for a time in Texas, and next in Dacotah Territory, engaged in border service.

JOSEPH HENRY NOYES.

Born in Boston, May 7, 1835.

Died May 18, 1872, at Peabody, Kansas.

Previous to the time of the rebellion, Mr. Noyes was connected with the United States Army, and with the First Regiment Mounted Rifles spent five years in frontier service in New Mexico, engaged in subduing the Indians of the Territory.

After the outbreak of the civil war, and having refused a lieutenant's commission tendered him in the rebel service, he enlisted from Hingham Dec. 4, 1863, in the Third Unattached

Company Heavy Artillery, afterwards Co. A, and was mustered at Fort Independence, Boston Harbor.

He was on duty in the defences of Washington until mustered out of service at Fort Totten, Sept. 18, 1865, by reason of the close of the war.

It is just to add, that the discharge papers of the deceased from the regular service of the United States bear the unsolicited testimonial of the officer in command to his character as a good soldier, and commending him for bravery and fidelity.

GEORGE PEACOCK.

Age 20.

Private in Co. A, and enlisted from Hingham; mustered Sept. 28, 1864, and discharged June 14, 1865, by reason of close of the war. Enlisted for one year.

GEORGE E. RICHARDSON.

Age 25.

Enrolled from Boston, and served for the quota of Hingham; mustered as private in Co. A, Jan. 10, 1863; transferred to Navy April 15, 1864.

JOSEPH ROLLINS.

Age 27.

Enlisted for quota of Hingham; mustered Dec. 10, 1862.

CHARLES EDWARD SPURR.

Born in Lowell, Mass., June 3, 1833.

Enlisted at Boston as private in the Third Unattached Company of Heavy Artillery, Nov. 25, 1863. Was clerk in the hospital at Fort Independence, Boston Harbor; discharged at Fort Berry, Va., July 11, 1864; served on the quota of Hingham.

AARON D. SWAN.

Age 40.

Enrolled from Hingham, and returned by the selectmen in the list of persons serving on the quota of the town; mustered Aug. 27, 1864, in Co. M, and discharged June 17, 1865; enlisted for one year.

HENRY WHITMAN.

Age 21.

Enlisted from Hingham, and mustered as private in Co. A, Dec. 20, 1862.

FIRST BATTERY LIGHT ARTILLERY.

The First Battery Light Artillery, also designated as Porter's Battery, was mustered at Camp Cameron. It left Massachusetts Oct. 3, 1861, and was mustered out Oct. 19, 1864.

Connected with the Army of the Potomac, it was in nearly all the noted engagements that occurred in the Department of Virginia during the civil war, from the battle at West Point to those of Petersburg and Fisher's Hill.

It contained one enlistment from Hingham, viz. : —

PRIVATE

JAMES RUSSELL FRENCH.

Born in Hingham, Oct. 23, 1816.

Enlisted at Boston Aug. 28, 1861, and was mustered at Camp Cameron the 6th of September following.

This battery was the first artillery organization raised in Massachusetts for three years. It joined the Army of the Potomac early in 1862, and was engaged in the following battles and skirmishes, viz.: West Point, Mechanicsville, Gaines' Mill, Charles City Cross-Roads, Malvern Hill, Second Bull Run, Crampton's Pass, South Mountain, Antietam, Fredericksburg, Chancellorsville, Gettysburg, Sander's House, Wilderness, Spottsylvania, North Anna River, Cold Harbor, and in front of Petersburg. It served under Gen. Sheridan in his advance up the Shenandoah Valley, and took part with the Sixth Corps in the battles of Winchester and Fisher's Hill.

Private French participated in all these engagements. He was not absent from duty a day; and his record for bravery and power of endurance stands among the first on our list of soldiers who were natives of Hingham. He was mustered out Oct. 19, 1864, by reason of expiration of term of enlistment, having served upwards of three years.

THIRD BATTERY LIGHT ARTILLERY.

This battery was mustered into the service of the United States Oct. 5, 1861, left Massachusetts, Oct. 7, and was mustered out Sept. 16, 1864.

The report of the adjutant-general states, that, connected with the Army of the Potomac, it took part in twenty-four engagements.

Among the enlistments was, —

GEORGE FRANKLIN TOWER.

Born in Hingham, April 13, 1834.

Enlisted at Boston July, 1861, and was mustered Sept. 5.

After the seven-days' battle, was taken sick, and transferred to the Harewood Hospital; from which, after a confinement of two months, he was honorably discharged Oct. 30, 1862, having been in the service fourteen months.

Mr. Tower was in all the engagements with the Army of the Potomac, until the battle of Gettysburg.

33

TENTH BATTERY LIGHT ARTILLERY.

* HOSEA ORCUTT BARNES.

List of men in regiments of artillery and in batteries : —

Jonathan B. Ackerman.
Hosea O. Barnes.
John B. Batchelder.
Fielder Botting, jun.
Franz Burhenne.
William Carter.
George A. Chubbuck.
Joshua Crosby, jun.
Webster A. Cushing.
Levi H. Dow.
James R. French.
Isaiah W. Loring.
Francis Mayhew.

Francis K. Meade.
Daniel H. Miller.
Joseph H. Noyes.
George Peacock.
George E. Richardson.
Joseph Rollins.
Charles E. Spurr.
Aaron D. Swan.
Anton Tapp.
Edwin Thomas.
Edwin F. Tirrell.
George F. Tower.
Henry Whitman.

Lyman B. Whiton.

CHAPTER XIII.

THREE YEARS' MEN CONCLUDED.

First Regiment of Cavalry — Second Regiment Do. — Fourth Regiment Do. — Fifth Do. — List of Men in Cavalry Service.

FIRST REGIMENT OF CAVALRY.

BUGLER.

WILLIAM ALDEN DAGGETT.

Born in Randolph, Jan. 5, 1846: resident of Hingham.

Was three months at Fortress Monroe, in Co. C, Fourth Regiment, M. V. M., Capt. Bumpus of Braintree. Afterwards enlisted as bugler in Co. K of the First Mass. Cavalry, for three years. Mustered Sept. 17, 1861. Transferred to Fourth Mass. Cavalry, Co. K; mustered out at expiration of term of enlistment, Sept. 14, 1864.

*CHARLES DAMON KILBURN.

CO. B.

SECOND REGIMENT OF CAVALRY.

According to the report of the Adjutant-general of Massachusetts, this regiment was mustered into the service by companies, at dates varying from January to April, 1863. The first detachment left Massachusetts Feb. 12, 1863, and the main body in the following May.   Mustered out July 20, 1865.

Beginning with South Anna Bridge, it was present in twenty-six battles, including Fort Stevens, Poolsville, Opequan, Winchester, Cedar Creek, White Oak Road, Five Forks, and others. The enlistments from Hingham were, —

THOMAS T. BARNES.

Age 34.

CO. B.

Was mustered Jan. 13, 1863. Discharged by reason of disability, Jan. 2, 1864.   Enlisted from Hingham, and included in the town's quota.

EBEN HART.

Age 19.

Enrolled from Hingham, and Oct. 24, 1864, was mustered in Co. L.   Discharged July 17, 1865, by reason of close of the war.

JOHN McLAUGHLIN.

Age 21.

Enlisted from Hingham, and served on the town's quota. Mustered Feb. 25, 1864; and May 18, 1865, discharged for disability.

FOURTH REGIMENT OF CAVALRY.

This regiment was organized by special order from the War Department, and was composed of the Independent Battalion, formerly Third Battalion, First Regiment of Cavalry, M. V., and two new battalions recruited in Massachusetts.

At the time of its organization, the First Battalion, Major Stevens, was stationed in South Carolina.

The Second Battalion left the State March 20, 1864, and the Third, April 23, 1864.

With full complement of men, the regiment consisted of twelve squadrons, each one hundred strong, and was fully recruited March 1, 1864.

A portion of the regiment was present in the engagements at Gainesville, Fla., Drury's Bluff, and also in several of the battles before Petersburg and Richmond.

Mustered out Nov. 14, 1865.

So far as known, the regiment included nineteen enlistments connected with Hingham, as follows: —

MAJOR

EDWARD TRACY BOUVÉ.

Born in Hingham, Aug. 14, 1841.

Enlisted, and mustered as second lieutenant in Co. G, Thirty-second Regiment, M. V. I., at Boston, June 30, 1862. Promoted first lieutenant Sept. 1, 1862, and was in active service in the Army of the Potomac from July until attacked with typho-malarial fever ; was then sent to the U. S. military hospital at Point Lookout, Md. Discharged Dec. 29, 1862, for disability.

With returning health, Lieut. Bouvé re-enlisted, and was appointed captain in the Fourth Regiment, Mass. Cavalry, Jan. 22, 1864.

He was in the Army of the James, and shared its fortunes

from April, 1864, to April, 1865, participating in the battles of Fredericksburg, sieges of Petersburg and Richmond, guerilla fights at Cove River, Unionville, and various other places. He was promoted major in the Twenty-sixth Regiment, New York Cavalry, commanding the Mass. Battalion of the regiment, Feb. 28, 1865.

From April to July, 1865, he was stationed on the New York frontiers, in command of the posts of Champlain and Malone, as a protection against rebel raiders from Canada.

Discharged July 7, 1865, on account of the regiment being disbanded.

LIEUTENANT

BENJAMIN THOMAS.

Born in Hingham, March 14, 1832.

In November, 1863, Mr. Thomas received an appointment as recruiting-officer ; and, in the following December, was commissioned second lieutenant. Located at the time in Boston, he continued the work of enlistment ; and, being quite successful, was commissioned Jan. 1, 1864, as first lieutenant, and assigned to the Fourth Mass. Cavalry as quartermaster.

In April, 1864, with the regiment, was ordered to report to Gen. Gilman, then in command of the Department of the South, with headquarters at Hilton Head, and three days after again embarked under orders to report at Fortress Monroe. His next destination was City Point, for the purpose of co-operating, under Gen. Butler, with all the armies of Virginia, in the "on to Richmond" movement of that year. Being the advance guard to City Point, the duties were numerous and the labor severe. Mr. Thomas, as quartermaster, was required to be constantly on the move. Besides being responsible for the supply of rations for men and horses, and other material for the general prosecution of the war, a further duty was imposed as "ordnance officer," by appointment of the colonel commanding.

Soon after there came an acceptable change, in being detailed as A. A. Q. M. of the Tenth Army Corps, under Gen. Terry. Here he continued his labors until, by order of Gen. Butler, the corps was disintegrated, and united with others.

Following this movement, Quartermaster Thomas, with other staff-officers, was ordered to report to Gen. Weitzel, who had just been placed in command of the Twenty-fifth Corps, composed of twenty-five thousand colored troops. Some disaffection was created with respect to the classing of white troops with colored ; but good feelings had the ascendency, and better judgment prevailed. Mr. Thomas affirms, that, during his entire experience, he found neither better nor braver men.

In November and December of 1864, he aided in fitting out the noted Fort Fisher expedition under Gen. Butler, the result of which is well known. At the close of the year, he resigned his situation on account of repeated domestic affliction.

Mr. Thomas retired from the service, having acceptably performed his multiplied and often perplexing duties.

LIEUTENANT

THOMAS HICKEY.

Born in Hingham, Jan. 14, 1841.

Enlisted at Waltham, Mass., and was mustered as private in Co. M, First Regiment Cavalry, M. V., Sept. 23, 1861.

Re-enlisting at Hilton Head, S.C., Jan. 28, 1864, on the quota of Hingham, he was transferred the 16th of April following to Co. M, Fourth Regiment Cavalry, M. V., and on the same day promoted successively to rank of corporal, sergeant, and color-sergeant, and subsequently appointed second lieutenant, his commission dating from Aug. 9, 1865.

Lieut. Hickey's military career was an eventful one. After sharing the dangers of many sanguinary engagements with the enemy at various points in South Carolina and Florida, including the battles of James Island, Olustee, and Three Mile Run, the regiment was divided, and several companies, including the one to which Lieut Hickey belonged, were ordered to Virginia, where they were attached to the Army of the James River, and took part in the contests in front of Petersburg.

Late at night, April 5, 1865, Col. Washburn of the Fourth

Regiment received orders to proceed with a small force of cavalry and two regiments of infantry, and destroy High Bridge, at that time of great importance to the army of Gen. Lee, then on the retreat from Richmond.   It was a hazardous expedition, and its immediate results disastrous ; but "it was to the sharpness of that fight," says one of Lee's staff to Gen. Ord, " that the cutting off of Lee's army at Appomattox Court House was probably due."   So fierce were the charges of Col. Washburn's men, and so determined their fighting, that Gen. Lee received the impression that they must be supported by a large part of the army, and that his retreat was cut off.

An officer of another cavalry regiment, in giving an account of this engagement, says, " In that handful of heroes was one among the enlisted, Color-sergeant Thomas Hickey, towards whom the heart of every man in the regiment thrills with gratitude to this day, not alone for the bravery with which he bore the standard through the thickest of the fight, but because, when all hope of victory was gone, he had the presence of mind to so utterly destroy it before he was surrounded and taken, that the touch of rebel hands never polluted its blue folds."

Just before Lieut. Hickey was captured, he dismounted from his horse in a valley, and, taking the regimental colors, made haste to reach a neighboring cabin, hotly pursued by rebel cavalry.   Gaining access to the dwelling, amidst a shower of bullets, he immediately thrust the standard into the fire and destroyed it.   He was at once made prisoner, and taken with Lee's army in its retreat.

He was deprived of most of his clothing, and received for rations but half a pint of Indian meal per day, which he was obliged to eat uncooked.   Four days after his capture, he was released by the surrender of Lee's army to the national troops under Gen. Grant.

Lieut. Hickey was in the service four years and about two months, and was discharged at Richmond, Va., Nov. 14, 1865, by reason of close of the war.

SERGEANTS.

FRANK H. GILMAN.

Age 23.

Sergeant in Co. B, enlisted from Hingham, and was mustered Dec. 28, 1863; discharged Nov. 14, 1865, by reason of close of the war.

ARVANDER MERROW.

Age 2?.

Enlisted from Hingham. Was sergeant in Co. B, and mustered Dec. 28, 1863; discharged Nov. 14, 1865, by reason of close of the war.

CORPORAL

* JAMES G. RAYMOND.

Co. D.

MUSICIANS.

THOMAS CLONEY.

Age 18.

Bugler in Co. F, and enlisted from Hingham; mustered Jan. 27, 1864, and discharged Nov. 14, 1865, by reason of close of the war.

WILLIAM A. DAGGETT.

Resident of Hingham. See First Regiment Cavalry.

PRIVATES.

ORIETES L. BAILEY.

Enlisted from Weymouth, age 18.

Mustered as private in Co. C, Jan. 6, 1864, and discharged Nov.

14, 1865, by reason of expiration of term of service ; recruited for Hingham.

CHARLES CAMPBELL.

Born in Boston, July 26, 1826.

Private in Co. D, and enlisted from Hingham, Dec. 31, 1863 ; mustered Jan. 9, 1864, and on the 9th of the June following was transferred to the Navy ; served on the quota of Hingham.

CORNELIUS CONNELL.

Enrolled from Hingham, age 23.

Mustered as private in Co. D, Jan. 9, 1864 ; discharged Nov. 14, 1865, by reason of expiration of term of service.

Mr. Connell was taken prisoner, and confined at Florence, Ala.

SAMUEL N. CORTHELL.

Age 21.

Was private in Co. D, and enlisted from Hingham ; mustered Jan. 9, 1864, and discharged Nov. 14, 1865.

Mr. Corthell, with many of his company, was taken prisoner at Gainesville, Fla., and conveyed to Florence. He was previously a member of Co. K, Seventh Regiment.

WILLIAM L. CUMMINGS.

Age 30.

From Weymouth, on the quota of Hingham, and was mustered in Co. D, Jan. 9, 1864 ; discharged June 24, 1865, by reason of close of the war.

ALFRED GARDNER.

Born in Hingham, July 15, 1812.

Enlisted February, 1863, as private in Co. C, and was mustered in March following.

CHARLES GARDNER.

Born in Hingham.

Enlisted from Brighton.

GEORGE W. FARRAR.

Age 38.

Enlisted from Hingham, and Dec. 28, 1863, was mustered in Co. B; mustered out by reason of expiration of term of service, May 23, 1865.

JAMES HICKEY.

Enlisted from Hingham, age 26.

Member of Co. C, and mustered Jan. 6, 1864; discharged Nov. 14, 1865, by reason of close of the war.

* WILLIAM HENRY JONES.

Co. C.

JOSEPH SMITH MILLER.

Born at Salem, Mass., May 20, 1847.

Co. F.

Enlisted from Hingham, and was mustered Jan. 27, 1864. Struck in the hand by a bullet, at Deep Bottom, Va., and honorably discharged by reason of disability from wound, May 20, 1865.

SAMUEL NEWCOMB, 2D.

Born in Hingham, July 9, 1825.

Co. D.

Enlisted from Hingham, Dec. 22, 1863; mustered Jan. 9, 1864; transferred to the Navy at Hilton Head, on the 9th of the following June.

THOMAS RAFFERTY, Jun.

Age 20..

Enlisted from Hingham, and was mustered in Co. F, Jan. 27, 1864.

*DENNIS SCULLY.

Co. D.

EDMUND SPELLMAN.

Age 22.

For quota of Hingham. Mustered Dec. 26, 1863, in Co. A.

*FRANK H. TILTON.

Co. C.

PHILO C. WINSLOW.

Age 36.

Co. A.

Enrolled from Hingham, and mustered Dec. 26, 1863.

FIFTH REGIMENT OF CAVALRY.

This regiment was composed of colored men, and was the only regiment of colored cavalry organized in Massachusetts.

It was mustered into the service of the United States by companies, at different times in the early part of 1864, and was mustered out Oct. 31, 1865.

Its field of service was principally in the Department of Virginia, and it was present in the engagement at Bailor's Farm, Va. At the date of mustering out, it was located at Clarksville, Texas.

The official record shows the following enlistments from Hingham : —

PRIVATES.

RUFUS CLARK.

Age 22.

Co. B.

Enlisted for the quota of Hingham, and mustered Jan. 29, 1864; discharged June 5, 1865, by reason of close of the war.

THOMAS DAVIS.

Age 18.

Mustered in Co. I, March 26, 1864; discharged by reason of expiration of term of service, Oct. 31, 1865.

GEORGE JONES.

Age 37.

Enlisted for quota of Hingham in Co. G, and was mustered May 7, 1864; discharged Oct. 31, 1865, by reason of close of the war.

MATTHEW H. LUCAS.

Age 21.

Enlisted for quota of Hingham ; mustered Jan. 29, 1864, in Co. B, and was discharged Oct. 31, 1865, by reason of expiration of term of service.

JOSEPH NATHAN.

Age 24.

Co. · B.

Enlisted Jan. 29, 1864 ; discharged Oct. 31, 1865, by reason of expiration of term of service ; enlisted for quota of Hingham.

LIST OF MEN IN CAVALRY SERVICE.

Orietes L. Bailey.

Thomas T. Barnes.

Edward T. Bouvé.

Charles Campbell.

Rufus Clark.

Thomas Cloney.

Cornelius Cornell.

Samuel N. Corthell.

William L. Cummings.

William A. Daggett.

Thomas Davis.

George M. Farrar.

Alfred Gardner.

Charles Gardner.

Frank H. Gilman.

Eben Hart.

James Hickey.

Thomas Hickey.

George Jones.

William H. Jones.

Charles D. Kilburn.

Matthew H. Lucas.

John McLaughlin.

Arvander Merrow.

Joseph S. Miller.

Joseph Nathan.

Samuel Newcomb, 2d.

Thomas Rafferty, jun.

James G. Raymond.

Dennis Scully.

Edward Spellman.

Benjamin Thomas.

Frank H. Tilton.

Philo C. Winslow.

CHAPTER XIV.

MANY of the names of the soldiers and sailors here included, will be found among the papers of the town relating to the war. In a majority of instances they were recruited, and probably served, for the quota of Hingham. All that could be obtained with regard to age, residence, time or place of enlistment, or the nature of their service, is embraced in the brief records which follow : —

EDWIN ALLEN.

Three years; served for quota of Hingham.

LOUIS ANDERSON.

A Recruit.

CALVIN R. BAKER.

A Recruit.

JOHN BAKER.

Three years, enlisted for quota of Hingham.

JOSEPH BARSTOW.

Of Hingham.

Served with Kit Carson.

GEORGE W. BOEN.

Three years; included in the list returned by town authorities as serving for the quota of Hingham.

GEORGE H. BONNEY.

Three years; returned by the selectmen as serving for the quota of Hingham.

EDWIN BOOTH.

JOHN BROWN.

Three years; enlisted from Hingham, and included in the official list returned by the selectmen as serving on the quota of the town.

MELZAR W. CLARK.

A resident of Hingham. Mr. Clark rendered important service, first as nurse, and afterwards as ward-master, in the United States Hospital at Point Lookout.

JOHN COLLINS.

Three years; served for the quota of Hingham.

THOMAS COLLINS.

Recruit; three years.

WILLIAM COLMAN.

BARNEY CONALEY.

Age 22.

Tailor. Enrolled from Hingham, Jan. 6, 1864.

CHARLES COOK.

Three years; enlisted for quota of Hingham.

HENRY DAGGETT.

Enlisted for three years, and served for the quota of the town.

HORATIO M. DALLAS.

On authority of town documents, enlisted Jan. 2, 1865, for one year, and served as captain in frontier service.

THOMAS D. DALTON.

Three years; served for the quota of Hingham.

ALBERT DAMON.

JAMES DEMPSEY.

Three years; and enlisted for quota of Hingham.

HENRY B. DOWNES.

On town's quota ; enlisted for three years.

JOSIAH EDSON.

WEST D. ELDREDGE.

Enlisted for three years, and served for the quota of Hingham.

LENDAL HANSCOM EWELL.

Born in Hingham, Sept. 7, 1841.

Served at Fortress Monroe, Va., with the Fourth Regiment Infantry, M. V., as volunteer member in Co. H, Hancock Light Guard, of Quincy. Enrolled May 22, 1861 ; mustered out with the regiment July 22, 1861.

Mr. Ewell died at Williamsburg, N.Y., Oct. 2, 1870, and was buried in the Fort Hill Cemetery in this town.
He was a son of Jacob A. and Sarah C (Barnes) Ewell.

THOMAS M. FARRELL.

JOHN G. GORHAM.

Age 43.

Farmer. Recruited for quota of Hingham, and, according to town documents, enrolled in the Fifty-sixth Regiment. Subsequently rejected.

TIMOTHY GORDON.

A native of Hingham; resident of Taunton, Mass.; was captain of the Taunton Light Guard, Co. G, Fourth Regiment, M. V. M., and left Boston April 17, 1861, for Fortress Monroe, where he shared in the general experience of the regiment during its service of three months.

Capt. Gordon was present in the engagement at Big Bethel, Va.

JAMES GORMAN.

Age 23.

Cigar-maker. Town papers say of the Twenty-first Regiment. Enrolled Feb. 24, 1864, from Providence, R.I.

THOMAS GRIFFIN.

Three years, and reckoned on the quota of the town.

EDWARD HACKETT.

Enlisted for three years, and reckoned on the quota of Hingham.

MARK HALL.

Age 35.

Laborer. Heavy Artillery; enrolled from Hingham, and enlisted Dec. 18, 1863, on the quota of the town; afterwards rejected.

OTIS C. HARDY.

Enlisted for three years; served for quota of Hingham.

JAMES HAYES.

WILLIAM HILLARSTON.

Recruited by Col. Edward Cazneau; enrolled from Gloucester, and mustered Jan. 5, 1864.

EDWARD BOURNE HINCKLEY.

Age 35.

Clergyman; enlisted Aug. 22, 1862.

HENRY A. HITCHCOCK.

Three years; served for the quota of Hingham.

JEREMIAH HURLEY.

Returned by town authorities in the list of persons serving for the quota of Hingham.

EDWARD KELLEY.

Returned by town authorities as serving on the quota of Hingham.

JOSEPH B. KELSEY.

—— KITTREDGE.

Quota of Hingham.

WILLIAM H. LANE.

Three years; served on quota of Hingham.

JACOB LOWE.

Age 34.

Served with the United States Colored Troops, and was mustered from Hingham in Fifth Artillery, Feb. 25, 1865.

JOHN C. MAGUIRE.

Born in Hingham, age 25.

Removed to Monson, Mass., and enlisted there October, 1862, as private in Co. G of the Forty-sixth Regiment, M. V. M., nine months ; mustered out at Springfield, Mass., July 29, 1863, by reason of expiration of term of service. In the Department of North Carolina it was present at the battles of Kinston, Whitehall, and Goldsboro.'

PATRICK MAHONY.

MICHAEL McGRANE.

Nine months ; served for second quota of the town.

CHARLES H. MUSCHATT.

Three years ; served for quota of Hingham.

GEORGE H. OSBORN.

Enrolled from Quincy, age 19.

EDWIN POINEY.

Enlisted for three years, and reckoned on the quota of the town.

EDWARD L. PRESTON.

A recruit. Town papers say "laborer ; Co. A, Fifth Cavalry ;" enrolled Jan. 2, 1864.

WILLIAM RANDALL.

Recorded in town papers as "moulder; Fourth Battalion;" enlisted Aug. 18, 1862.

EDWARD ROACH.

Enlisted for three years, and served for the quota of the town.

DAVID P. ROBINSON.

ALBERT SAWYER.

Returned by the selectmen as serving for the quota of Hingham.

FRANKLIN SIMMONS.

Served for the quota of Hingham, and included in the list returned by town authorities.

WILLIAM T. SPRAGUE.

Three years; served for quota of Hingham.

WILLIAM THOMPSON.

Son of Mr. Finton Thompson of this town; was in artillery service.

CLASSED AS ADDITIONAL ENLISTMENTS.

Edwin Allen.
Louis Anderson.
Calvin R. Baker.
John Baker.
Joseph Barstow.
George W. Boen.
George H. Bonney.
Edwin Booth.
John Brown.
Melzar W. Clark.
John Collins.
Thomas Collins.
William Colman.
Barney Conaley.
Charles Cook.
Henry Daggett.
Horatio M. Dallas.
Thomas D. Dalton.

Albert Damon.
James Dempsey.
Henry B. Downes.
Josiah Edson.
West D. Eldredge.
Thomas M. Farrell.
Timothy Gordon.
James Gorman.
Thomas Griffin.
Edward Hackett.
Mark Hall.
Otis C. Hardy.
James Hayes.
William Hillarston.
Edward B. Hinckley.
Henry A. Hitchcock.
Jeremiah Hurley.
Edward Kelley.

Joseph B. Kelsey.

—— Kittredge.

William H. Lane.

Jacob Lowe.

John C. Maguire.

Patrick Mahony.

Michael McGrane.

Charles H. Muschatt.

George H. Osborn.

Edward Poincy.

Edward L. Preston.

William Randall.

Edward Roach.

David P. Robinson.

Albert Sawyer.

Franklin Simmons.

William T. Sprague.

William Thompson.

CHAPTER XV.

VETERAN RESERVE CORPS.

In addition to those included in the general records as having been transferred to the Veteran Reserve Corps, the official list contains the following, viz. : —

MICHAEL CARR.

Age 28.

Enlisted for the quota of Hingham ; mustered Oct. 13, 1863 ; discharged by order of War Department, Nov. 30, 1865.

MICHAEL CASEY.

Enlisted from Hingham, age 24.

Mustered July 3, 1863 ; discharged by order of War Department, Nov. 30, 1865 ; served for quota of the town.

JOHN DOLAN.

Age 40.

Mustered Oct. 2, 1863 ; served on quota of Hingham ; discharged by order of War Department, Nov. 30, 1865.

PATRICK DONNELIN.

Age 45.

Recruit ; enlisted from Boston ; mustered Aug. 11, 1864 ; discharged Aug. 11, 1866, by reason of expiration of service.

MOSES FAIRFIELD.

Age 55.

Enlisted for quota of Hingham ; mustered July 29, 1863 ; discharged Nov. 30, 1865, by order of War Department.

MICHAEL FLEMMING.

Age 26.

Mustered Nov. 4, 1863 ; discharged Nov. 30, 1865, by order of War Department ; served for quota of Hingham.

THOMAS FOLEY.

Age 49.

Enlisted for quota of Hingham ; mustered Oct. 28, 1863, and discharged by order of War Department, Nov. 30, 1865.

PETER FORRESTER.

Age 25.

Enlisted from Hingham for town's quota ; mustered Oct. 31, 1864.

EDWARD GALVIN.

Age 23.

Enlisted for quota of Hingham ; mustered May 10, 1864.

LAWRENCE HICKS.

Age 53.

Enlisted from Hingham for quota of the town ; mustered Aug. 18, 1863 ; discharged by order of War Department, Nov. 30, 1865.

JOHN KEEFE.

Age 48.

Enlisted from Hingham for the town's quota ; mustered July 25,

1863, and discharged by order of War Department, Nov. 30, 1865.

*HENRY B. LIVINGSTON.

JAMES McGREGOR.

Age 46.

From Chelmsford, Mass.; enlisted July 23, 1864; included in town papers as recruited for Hingham.

EDWARD McLAUGHLIN.

Age 23.

Mustered Sept. 29, 1863, and discharged by order of War Department, Nov. 30, 1865; served for quota of Hingham.

JAMES TETTLER.

Age 40.

Quota of Hingham; mustered July 29, 1863; discharged Nov. 30, 1865, by order of War Department.

CHARLES TINMONS.

Age 37.

Quota of Hingham; Mustered Nov. 1, 1863; discharged by order of War Department, Nov. 30, 1865.

36

REGULAR ARMY.

The enlistments from Hingham, in the Regular Army of the United States, were few in number.

The following records are all that could be obtained : —

* RICHARD J. FARRELL.

DENNIS MULLIAN.

Age 21.

Of the Nineteenth Infantry, and mustered May 10, 1864.

JOSEPH HENRY NOYES.

See Third Regiment Heavy Artillery.

WILLIAM PERKINS.

Age 22.

Mustered in the Nineteenth Infantry, May 10, 1864.

* MICHAEL FRANCIS THOMPSON.

JOSEPH W. WELSH.

Age 32.

Mustered Sept. 24, 1864, and was detailed as hospital steward.

JAMES H. WILLIAMS.

Age 24.

Nineteenth Infantry, and mustered May 10, 1864 ; served for quota of Hingham.

VETERAN RESERVE CORPS.

Michael Carr.
Michael Casey.
John Dolan.
Patrick Donnelin.
Moses Fairfield.
Michael Flemming.
Thomas Foley.
Peter Forrester.

Edward Galvin.
Lawrence Hicks.
John Keefe.
Henry B. Livingston.
James McGregor.
Edward McLaughlin.
James Tettler.
Charles Tinmons.

REGULAR ARMY.

Richard J. Farrell.
Dennis Mullian.
Joseph H. Noyes.

William Perkins.
Michael F. Thompson.
Joseph W. Welsh.

James H. Williams.

CHAPTER XVI.

COLONEL

HAWKES FEARING, JUN.

Born in Hingham, May 20, 1826.

AT the outbreak of the war, resided at Manchester, N.H. Being connected with the Fourth Regiment, M. V. M., as lieutenant-colonel, he at once responded to the call of Gov. Andrew, and reported for duty at the State House at Boston, where a council of war was being held on the 16th of May, 1861. At the close of the session he came to Hingham, took part in calling together the members of the Lincoln Light Infantry, as well as shared in the deliberations of the meeting, and the next day returned to Boston. Leaving the city with the Fourth Regiment at 6 o'clock, P.M., of the 17th, he was three months at Fortress Monroe and vicinity.

On the 24th of September, 1861, he was commissioned colonel of the Eighth Regiment New Hampshire Volunteers, then being gathered at Manchester. This regiment was organized in December, and left the State Jan. 5, 1862. It was assigned to the New England Division, intended for operation in the Department of the Gulf.

After being in camp three weeks at Fort Independence, Boston Harbor, it embarked for Ship Island, and was there attached to Phelps's brigade. The summer was spent at Camp Parapet, eight miles above New Orleans ; Col. Fearing in this time being eight weeks in the regimental hospital from fever.

Its first engagement was at Georgia Landing in the following October.

In the engagements at Bisland, in April, 1863, Col. Fearing was wounded.

In command of the second brigade, Emory's division, from May to the time of the surrender of Port Hudson, in July, a period of forty-nine days, he was actively engaged in the siege of this stronghold of the enemy. Here the services of the Eighth New Hampshire Regiment were such as to render its history one of renown. Twice it led the assaulting column. It is a fact worthy of mention, that, during the severe struggle of the 27th of May, the regiment, in its eagerness to grapple with the enemy, charged its way through three of our own lines, falling upon the foe, and driving him from his strongly intrenched position to a point within his main works. At the close of the attack, one hundred and three of the two hundred and ninety-seven men engaged were either killed, wounded, or missing.

At the second assault by this regiment on the 14th of June, the loss was one hundred and twenty-two of the two hundred and seventeen engaged.

From this time the besiegers lay momentarily expecting to be called for an advance on the foe known to be in front, or to be attacked by a large force supposed to be in the rear.

On the 3d of July, came the news of the surrender of Vicksburg ; upon which Gen. Gardner, then in command of Port Hudson, at once proposed terms of capitulation ; the New Hampshire Eighth having the honor of first entering the place after its surrender.

In the following autumn Col. Fearing was detailed for recruiting service, and came to Concord, N.H., returning to New Orleans in November, in command of six hundred men, recruited for different regiments then in the service.

The winter was spent in organizing the regiment as a cavalry corps, intended for the Red River Expedition, the following spring. This being accomplished, he was next detailed for court-martial duty, during the summer of 1864, in New Orleans and vicinity. With the close of hostilities, the Eighth was assigned to provost-guard duty at Natchez, Miss., and was mustered out in October by order of War Department.

Aside from the battles before mentioned, fifty-three distinct skirmishes, some of which in former times would have been classed as important battles, are included in the record of the regiment.

The Eighth was also one of the regiments which comprised the expedition under Gen. Butler, the success of which wrested from the enemy one of the most important cities of the South.

Gen Davis, commanding fourth brigade, cavalry division, affirms that "not only the success, but the safety, of the entire command had in many instances depended on the steady bearing and dauntless bravery of the New Hampshire Eighth. Its gallant and heroic conduct, its fearlessness and impetuous daring in the hour of battle, have been conceded by friends and foes." Brevet Maj.-Gen. James McMillan adds, that "To say, I am a soldier of the Eighth New Hampshire, is sufficient to command honor and homage."

* JAMES BALLENTINE.

Fifteenth Independent New York Volunteers.

LIEUTENANT

WILLIAM BARNES.

A native of Hingham, son of William and Abigail (Osborn) Barnes. Enlisted in New York as private; afterwards promoted lieutenant, and served through the war. Lieut. Barnes was at one time a prisoner in Andersonville, Ga.

GEORGE BICKNELL.

Son of Leavitt L. and Harriet E. Bicknell, was born in Hingham, May 4, 1842; enlisted in the Second Regiment, New York Volunteer Infantry; was wounded in the first battle of Bull Run, by a musket-ball passing through the fleshy part of the arm; taken prisoner and confined for ten months in Salisbury and other Southern prisons. He was exchanged with others, and returned to New York, where he soon after enlisted in a New York Regiment of heavy artillery, in which, and in the invalid corps, he served during the remainder of the war.

MARTIN CUSHING.

Born in Hingham.

Enlisted from Pittsburg, Pa., and was in cavalry service.

CAPTAIN

HENRY HOWARD CUSHING.

Was quartermaster in the Eighty-eighth Illinois Volunteers; afterwards captain, and served in Rosecrans's Army. Since deceased, and buried in the Hingham Cemetery. Was son of Mr. George Cushing of this town.

SERGEANT

DAVID P. ELDREDGE.

Born in Hingham. Nov. 29. 1822.

Son of Reuben and Sally Eldredge; was a resident of Kansas when the war broke out. Soon after the call for troops in 1861, Mr. Eldredge left his farm to join the military service, and was mustered as orderly sergeant of Co. G, of the Seventh Kansas Cavalry. In 1864 he re-enlisted as veteran, and received promotion.

Serg. Eldredge was in all the battles and skirmishes in which his regiment engaged. He also performed effective service as a Union spy.

July 17, 1873, David P. Eldredge died at his home in Kansas, aged fifty years, seven months, and eighteen days.

JOHN J. L. FRENCH.

Son of the late Brosard French, was born in Hingham, August, 1824.

Resident of Concord, N.H.; mustered Sept. 5, 1864, as artificer in Co. E, First Regiment N. H. Heavy Artillery; discharged June 23, 1865, by reason of close of the war.

* CALEB GILL.

SERGEANT

JOHN GORMAN.

Born at St. John, N.B., April 1, 1842.

Enlisted at New York, and was mustered as private in Co. K, Thirty-sixth Regiment, N.Y. Vols., Feb. 14, 1862 ; discharged from Bellevue Hospital on account of wounds, Jan. 5, 1863 ; re-enlisted in Co. K, Twenty-fifth N. Y. Cavalry, for three years, or during the war, July 19, 1864 ; promoted sergeant Sept. 1, 1864; mustered out June 16, 1865, by reason of close of the war.

Mr. Gorman served with the Army of the Potomac under Gen. McClellan, at the battles of Yorktown, Williamsburg, Fair Oaks, Gaines' Mill, Savage Station, and Malvern Hill. He was also with Gen. Sheridan, at Winchester, Cedar Creek, Fisher's Hill, and through the valley campaign.

Wounded by a gun-shot through the right lung at Malvern Hill, July 1, 1862, he was captured and carried to Libby Prison ; not, however, until he had lain exposed and uncared for upon the battle-field until July 4. After being confined for six weeks, during which time he was relieved of the greater part of his clothing, he was exchanged, and sent to the Bellevue Hospital, where he remained until discharged. Mr. Gorman still retains the bullet which disabled him. It was extracted at the New England rooms in New York City, by Dr. Edward Herrick, fifteen months after the battle. He is now, and has been since the close of the war, a resident of Hingham.

HOSEA HARDEN.

Born in Hingham. March 8, 1839.

Mustered June 21, 1861, at Yonkers, N.Y., as private in Co G, Fortieth Regiment, N. Y. V. I.

Was in the Army of the Potomac, and had the general experience of infantry service. Engaged at the siege of Yorktown, battle of Williamsburg, Fair Oaks, and in the retreat to James River ; also in the engagement at Malvern Hill, Va.

In the summer of 1862 was sick in camp and general hospital at Harrison's Landing, and Aug. 11 removed to hospital at Philadelphia, where he remained till Nov. 20 of the following autumn, when he was discharged for disability.

CAPTAIN

*ELIJAH HOBART.

Co. B, Ninety-third Regiment, N. Y. Volunteers.

ALLEN G. JENNINGS.

Born in Stratford, Fulton County, N.Y., Jan. 28, 1843.

Resident of Hingham, and pastor of the Second Unitarian Society; enlisted Aug. 21, 1862, for three years, in Co. H, One Hundred and Twenty-first Regiment, N. Y. Vols.

In consequence of severe marching and exposure, nearly one-half of the men became disabled; Mr. Jennings being of the number. After a short time spent in the hospital at Frederick, Md., he was discharged and sent home. While absent, he was in the battle of South Mountain, but, as he states, "did but little *fighting*, as all their strength was spent in *marching*."

At home he soon recovered his health, and resolved to go again. Accordingly, on the 13th of September, 1864, he re-enlisted, and was in the field about two months with the One Hundred and Seventy-fifth Regiment, N. Y. Vols. He was in the battle of Cedar Creek; after which, having had some experience in medicine and surgery, was transferred to the U. S. General Hospital at Frederick, Md., where he served as clerk and assistant to the executive officers until the close of the war.

Whole time of service about fourteen months, "with the general experience that usually falls to the lot of a soldier."

COLONEL

CHARLES BRADFORD LEAVITT.

Born in West Randolph, Mass., Jan. 16, 1842.

Resident of Hingham; enlisted Oct. 16, 1863, at Memphis, Tenn., and Oct. 20, was mustered as first lieutenant in Co. M, of the sixth Regiment, U. S. Colored Heavy Artillery.

March 13, 1864, promoted lieutenant-colonel, Seventieth U. S. Colored Infantry. This organization was consolidated with the Seventy-first U. S. Colored Infantry, Nov. 7, 1864. Being then the junior lieutenant-colonel, he was transferred Dec. 14, 1864, as major of the Twelfth U. S. Colored Heavy Artillery.

Was present at several engagements in Mississippi, Louisiana, Arkansas, and Tennessee, and at the battle of Pleasant Hill (Red River), and Nashville, Tenn.

In one of the skirmishes received two wounds, and for two months was in hospital at Natchez, Miss.

Mustered out at Louisville, Ky., April 24, 1867.

While lieutenant-colonel, he was appointed on Gen. Lorenzo Thomas' staff as inspector of colored troops from Cairo, Ill., to New Orleans. In the spring of 1865 commanded the Post of Bowling Green, Ky.; afterwards at Mumfordsville, then at Muldraugh's Hills, and lastly commanded the Military Prison Department at Louisville, Ky., from July, 1866, till the time of mustering out.

SERGEANT

BEZA H. LINCOLN.

Son of the late Rufus W. Lincoln, and a native of Hingham. Enlisted from Concord, in New Hampshire First Heavy Artillery, Co. E, as quartermaster-sergeant. Mustered Sept. 5, 1864; discharged June 23, 1865, by reason of close of the war.

SERGEANT

JOHN LINCOLN, Jun.

Born in Hingham, Oct. 24, 1837.

Jan. 8, 1862, enlisted at Hebron, Conn., as private in Co. G of the Thirteenth Regiment Connecticut Infantry Volunteers, three years. In March promoted corporal; re-enlisted Feb. 7, 1864, at Thibodeaux, La., as veteran volunteer, and July 6 promoted sergeant.

Sergeant Lincoln was in active service during more than four years of the time covered by the rebellion. He was in the engagement at Georgia Landing, Irish Bend, Cane-river

Crossing, Mansura, La., Opequan, Fisher's Hill, Cedar Creek, Va., and was wounded near Winchester Va., Sept. 19, 1864.

In April, 1863, he was sick with typhus fever at Washington, La.; and May 1, conveyed to the Marine Hospital at New Orleans : there he remained until the 20th of September, when, having regained his health, he was discharged, and again reported for duty.

After the battle of Cedar Creek, he was in different places in the Shenandoah Valley, from Staunton to Martinsburg, up to January, 1865, when he went to Savannah, after Sherman had reached the sea.

In March he was at Morehead City, Newbern, and Kinston, N.C., and in May returned to Savannah. From this time he was stationed in different localities in the State, from Augusta to Rabun County, until ordered to Fort Pulaski, where he was mustered out in April, 1866.

SERGEANT

* LEAVITT LINCOLN.

Sixty-first Illinois V. I.

GENERAL

ALLYNE C. LITCHFIELD.

Born in Hingham, July 15, 1835.

Removed to Boston with his parents in 1844.

· At the commencement of the war he was a resident of Michigan; and in 1862 raised a company for the Fifth Michigan Cavalry, in which his zeal and organizing skill soon attracted the attention, and gained the favor, of superior officers. Before the regiment left the State, Mr. Litchfield was transferred to the Seventh Cavalry as lieutenant-colonel. With the Seventh he took the field with the Michigan Cavalry Brigade, under the gallant Custer, who subsequently said of him, " I regard Col. Litchfield as one of the most efficient officers of his rank in the service." His regiment between April and November, 1863, was in sixteen battles and skirmishes in Virginia and Maryland ; also in the battle at Gettysburg, Pa., July 3 of that year, in which its losses were eighty-one in killed, wounded, and missing.

As commanding officer of his regiment, he was appreciated and respected. At Gettysburg his horse was shot under him; and he narrowly escaped capture, while doing effective service, as the official report says, with a Spencer carbine. At Falling Waters, Col. Litchfield, with a single battalion, captured an entire rebel regiment, numbering four hundred men, with a stand of colors.

In the famous Kilpatrick-Dahlgren raid on Richmond, the colonel was captured, with others, by the enemy, and sent to Libby Prison, where he was kept in close confinement with negroes for four and a half months, and for six weeks of the time on *one-third of a prison ration.* From Richmond he was taken to Macon, Ga., and thence to Charleston, S.C., where he and some hundreds of prisoners were stockaded by the rebels under fire of the federal guns. At the end of a year he was exchanged. On his return from prison he was brevetted brigadier-general.

Gen. Litchfield is a son of Dea. Nichols Litchfield, formerly of this town, but now of Boston. In 1871 he received and accepted from the United States government the position of consul-general to Calcutta.

JAMES LOWRY.

Resident of Hingham.

Served in the Third District Columbia Regiment; was in numerous severe engagements, in one of which the regiment was nearly destroyed. He has a good record.

* DANIEL MURPHY.

WILLIAM L. NEAL.

Sixth New Hampshire Infantry; formerly resided at South Hingham; now deceased.

CHARLES REMINGTON.

Served in the Lincoln Body Guard at Washington, D.C.

JOHN FEARING ROGERS.

Born in Stonington, Conn., May 5, 1841.

Formerly a resident of Hingham, son of the late Dr. Edward
C. and Lydia Cushing (Gilkey) Rogers. Enrolled from the
State of Illinois under Col. Jefferson C. Davis ; was present,
and took part, in the battles of Pittsburg Landing, Chickamauga, Lookout Mountain, Chattanooga, siege of Knoxville, Missionary Ridge, Murfreesboro', Cumberland Gap, and was with
Gen. Sherman at Atlanta, Ga.

Mr. Rogers served through the war, and received an honorable discharge from Co. A of the Seventy-fourth Regiment
Illinois Volunteers.

HENRY E. SPAULDING.

Born in Lyndeboro', N.H., Sept. 24, 1843.

A resident of Hingham ; physician ; served in the Thirteenth
Regiment New Hampshire Volunteer Infantry. Enlisted
1862, was in the battle at Fredericksburg, and discharged
May 14, 1863, for disability.

CAPTAIN

ISAIAH FEARING TOWER.

Born in Hingham.

Enlisted at Dayton, Montgomery Co., Ohio, and was mustered
as private in Co. A of the Ninety-third Regiment, Ohio Volunteer Infantry, Aug. 22, 1862.

Promoted first to sergeant ; second to sergeant-major ; third
to first lieutenant, and adjutant ; and in 1863 to captain of
Co. G.

Capt. Tower had an active service from the time of mustering in. He was in the battles of Lawrenceburg and Richmond,

Ky.; Nashville, Tenn.; Stone River, Perryville, Ky.; Tallyhoma, Chickamauga, Buzzard's Roost, Rocky Face Ridge,
Dallas, New Hope Church, Kenesaw Mountain, Cassville,
Atlanta, Ga.; and at Nashville, Tenn., on the 15th and 16th
of December, 1864.

In the last engagement, he received a serious wound. His
left arm was broken above the elbow, and the use of the hand
entirely lost. Capt. Tower states that he entered the field at
the time with but fifteen men and two officers. During the
charge, the sergeants and both of the officers were killed, and
he was wounded as described. Whole term of service, three
years and four months. To these incidents of personal experience, he adds the following complimentary note: "No Hingham boy is known to me, and there were many of them in the
Army of the Cumberland, that behaved discreditably to his
native town or State, — a record I doubt not you will duly
appreciate."

LIEUTENANT

BENJAMIN SHURTLEFF WHITING.

A native of Hingham.

Enlisted in the State of Ohio, where he resided. Was also
lieutenant in the Seventieth United States Infantry, and has a
good record.

CAPTAIN

WEBSTER A. WHITING.

Born in Hingham.

Moved to the West some years before the war, and was captain
of a company in the celebrated "Board of Trade Regiment,"
from Chicago. With the Eighty-eighth Illinois Volunteers,
served in Rosecrans's army, and was an efficient and valiant
officer.

*CONRAD P. YÄGER.

NATIVES OR RESIDENTS OF HINGHAM ENLISTED IN OTHER STATES.

James Ballentine.
William Barnes.
George Bicknell.
Martin Cushing.
Henry H. Cushing.
David P. Eldredge.
Hawkes Fearing, jun.
John J. L. French.
Caleb Gill.
John Gorman.
Hosea Harden.
Elijah Hobart.
Allen G. Jennings.
Charles B. Leavitt.

Beza H. Lincoln.
John Lincoln, jun.
Leavitt Lincoln.
Allyne C. Litchfield.
James Lowry.
Daniel Murphy.
William L. Neal.
Charles Remington.
John F. Rogers.
Henry E. Spaulding.
Isaiah F. Tower.
Benjamin S. Whiting.
Webster A. Whiting.
Conrad P. Yäger.

CHAPTER XVII.

THE NAVY.

Number of Massachusetts Men in the Navy — Number of Hingham Men in the Navy — Naval Records.

H INGHAM was well represented in this arm of the service.

Congress passed an act July 4, 1864, allowing all men in the Navy to be credited on their proper quotas. The whole number who had enlisted in Massachusetts to date of March, 1864, and whose names were on the books of the receiving-ship "Ohio," was twenty-two thousand, three hundred and sixty. These were apportioned among the cities and towns of the State, under the same rules governing credits for enlistments in the army. The portion received by Hingham under this act was a timely contribution towards filling the quota then required from the town.

The number of natives or residents of Hingham serving in the Navy, so far as known, was thirty-five; as follows : —

CHIEF ENGINEER

CHARLES HARDING LORING.

Born in Boston, Mass., Dec. 26, 1828; resident of Hingham.

Feb. 26, 1851, appointed third assistant engineer, in the U.S. Navy.

May 21, 1853, promoted second assistant engineer.

May 9, 1857, promoted first assistant engineer.

January, 1861, stationed at the U.S. Navy Yard, at Charlestown, Mass.

March 25, 1861, Mr. Loring was promoted to chief engineer.

May 10, 1861, ordered to the U. S. steam-frigate "Minnesota," forty-eight guns, as first engineer, attached to the North Atlantic blockading squadron.

Aug. 27 to 29, 1861, this vessel was flag-ship in the attack at Hatteras Inlet.

Sept. 2, 1861, the "Minnesota" arrived at New York with rebel prisoners.

March 8 and 9, 1862, Mr. Loring, in this vessel, took part in the engagement with the rebel ram "Merrimac," during which the U. S. ships "Cumberland" and "Congress" were sunk.

March 8, 1862, participated in the engagement at Sewell's Point.

Oct. 10, 1862, ordered to Cincinnati on special service.

In January, 1855, he was on special duty at St. Louis, Mo.

In January, 1867, on board the U. S. steam-frigate "Susquehanna," fourteen guns, he was engaged in special service.

In January, 1868, again on board the "Minnesota."

During 1868 and 1869, he was waiting orders; and April 6. 1869, was assigned to the U. S. Navy Yard, at Washington, D.C., in charge of the engineer's department.

He is still in the service.

ACTING-MASTER

*THOMAS ANDREWS.

ACTING ASSISTANT PAYMASTER.

ANDREW TOWER.

Born in Hanover, Mass., May 26, 1829.

July 2, 1863, appointed acting assistant paymaster in the U. S. Navy, and ordered to Philadelphia.

July 24, 1863, reported for duty at Philadelphia, and was ordered to the U. S. schooner "Norfolk Packet," five guns attached to the South Atlantic blockading squadron; and while in this vessel also had charge of the paymaster's department of the U. S. schooners, "C. P. Williams," four guns, and "Para," three guns.

Dec. 25, 1863, he took part in the attack up Stono River, in the "C. P. Williams."

July 11, 1864, shared in the joint army and navy attack up the same river in the " Para."

Aug. 29, 1864, ordered to the U. S. ironclad " Passaic," four guns.

Sept. 4, 1864, ordered back to the " Norfolk Packet."

Dec. 10, 1865, he was honorably discharged from the U. S. Navy.

ACTING ASSISTANT SURGEON.

FRANKLIN NICKERSON.

Born in Hingham, Sept. 8, 1838.

Nov. 16, 1863, he was appointed acting assistant surgeon in the U. S. Navy, and ordered to the U. S. steamer "Shokokon," six guns, attached to the North Atlantic blockading squadron, stationed in the rivers and sounds of North Carolina and Virginia. In this vessel he took part in picket-duty, and in covering the movements of troops.

August, 1864, ordered to the U. S. steamer " Britannia," five guns, attached to the same squadron, and stationed off Wilmington, N.C. While in her, he was engaged in enforcing the blockade.

Nov. 5, 1864, resigned his position in the Navy, which resignation was accepted.

ACTING ENSIGNS.

* EDWARD WELLES HALCRO.

CHARLES MASON FULLER.

Born in Hingham, Feb. 17, 1844.

Jan. 14, 1863, he was appointed acting master's-mate in the U. S. Navy, and ordered to the U. S. school-ship " Macedonian," stationed at Boston, for instruction.

March 14, 1863, ordered to the West Gulf blockading squadron.

March 30, 1863, ordered to the U. S. iron-clad "Essex," twelve guns, attached to the Mississippi squadron. While here he was engaged in the dangerous duty of removing torpedoes from the river; also in command of several foraging parties, one of which captured seventeen men and a set of colors of the First Louisiana Cavalry, near Tunica Bend.

May 23 to June 26, 1863, he took part in the siege of Port Hudson, on the "Essex;" and while thus engaged, the vessel was struck twenty-three times by shells from the batteries of the enemy.

June 15, 1863, was bearer of despatches from the "Essex" to Adm. Farragut. In the discharge of this duty he passed under a heavy fire for a distance of two miles, in a small boat, manned by four negroes, during which the stroke-oar was shot away.

Feb. 24, 1864, promoted acting ensign.

March, 1865, ordered to the U. S. iron-clad "Ozark," seven guns, attached to the Mississippi squadron.

Sept. 5, 1865, received an honorable discharge.

CHARLES ANDREW STEWART.

Resident of Hingham; born in Beverly, Mass., Aug. 19, 1833.

May 3, 1862, he was appointed acting master's-mate in the U. S. Navy, and ordered to the U. S. school-ship at New York, for instruction.

June, 1862, ordered to take passage on the U. S. supply steamer "Magnolia," to Hampton Roads, to report for duty on board the U. S. screw-sloop "Wachusett," ten guns, attached to the James River squadron.

July, 1862, ordered to the U. S. steamer "Southfield," four guns, then repairing at Norfolk Navy Yard.

November, 1862, "The Southfield" was ordered to the Sounds of North Carolina.

January, 1864, ordered to the U. S. steamer "Underwriter," four guns.

Feb. 1, 1864, the "Underwriter" was boarded by an over-whelming force, and after an obstinate resistance captured. Mr. Stewart, with the rest of the officers and crew taken prisoners, came to Richmond. After being conveyed from one locality to another, he was finally placed under fire at Charleston, S.C.

Oct. 26, 1864, exchanged at Richmond, and, on his arrival North, was granted one month's leave. At the expiration of this time, he was ordered to the U. S. steamer "Muscoota," ten guns, and in her went to Fortress Monroe, Beaufort, and Key West.

March 16, 1865, promoted to acting ensign.

The "Muscoota" sailed for Brazos Santiago, Texas, where some of the crew were taken with yellow fever, and she was ordered North, arriving at Portsmouth, N.H., in August, 1866.

Oct. 12, 1866, ordered to the U. S. steamer "Saco," ten guns ; and in her visited the principal ports in the West Indies, and finally was stationed at Aspinwall.

Sept. 21, 1867, granted four months' leave, and a passage home.

Jan. 21, 1868, he received an honorable discharge.

ACTING THIRD ASSISTANT ENGINEER.

JOHN MEANS TRUSSELL.

Born in Belfast, Me., Aug. 16, 1832 ; resident of Hingham.

Aug. 26, 1864, shipped in the United States Navy, at Boston, as first-class fireman, and was sent to the United States receiving ship "Ohio."

Sept. 15, 1864, ordered on board the United States supply-steamer "Connecticut," and made the trip in her from Boston to Mobile, stopping at Hilton Head, Key West, Pensacola, and intermediate ports ; leaving supplies and mails for the different ships stationed at these points, and returning to Boston in about six weeks.

Nov. 1, 1864, sent on board the United States steamer " Iuka," seven guns, then fitting out at Boston for the East Gulf blockading squadron, where she went, and was employed in cruising from Key West to Havana, along the coast of Cuba, and Mexico as far as the Rio Grande, and return.

March 18, 1865, promoted to acting third assistant engineer, and ordered to the United States steamer "Clyde," two guns, and on this vessel was employed in cruising between Key West and St. Marks, stopping at Tampa Bay and Charlotte Harbor.

July, 1865, the "Clyde," was ordered to New York, where she arrived early in August.

Aug. 16, 1865, granted one month's leave.

Sept. 16, 1865, received an honorable discharge.

CAPTAIN'S CLERK

AUGUSTUS BARNES.

Born in Hingham, March 7, 1839.

June 5, 1863, appointed paymaster's steward of the United States Sloop "Marion," practice-ship of the Naval Academy, and in this capacity served until the end of the cruise in the following November.

Dec. 21, 1863, appointed paymaster's clerk of the United States steamer "Pocahontas," six guns, fitting out at Philadelphia for the West Gulf blockading squadron.

July 11, 1864, appointed captain's clerk on the same vessel.

March 21, 1865, resigned at New Orleans, La., for a clerkship on shore. This resignation was regretfully accepted by his commanding officer.

MASTERS-AT-ARMS.

FREDERICK CLINTON BLAIR.

Born in Pittsford, Rutland Co., Vt., Sept. 5, 1842. A resident of Hingham.

Sept. 5, 1861, shipped in the United States Navy, at Boston, as ordinary seaman, one year, for duty on board the United States barque "W. G. Anderson," seven guns, then fitting out at Boston for the West Gulf squadron, with headquarters at

Key West, for which place she soon sailed. Shortly after leaving Boston, Blair was rated master-at-arms, which rating he held to the end of the cruise.

Nov. 12, 1861, took part in the capture of the rebel privateer " Beauregard," which was conveyed to Key West. The " Anderson " was then employed in cruising in the West Indies, and finally returned to Boston in the following March, when Blair was allowed twenty-four hours' leave.

As soon as the " Anderson " could be got in readiness for sea, she was loaded with ammunition, and sailed a second time for the West Gulf blockading squadron, then having headquarters at Ship Island under command of Rear-admiral Farragut. On her arrival, she was employed in cruising, and enforcing the blockade, and in various special expeditions, among which was the cutting out of the rebel schooner " Montebello."

While cruising, they fell in with and captured three blockade-runners ; one of which was the " Reindeer," loaded with cotton.

Arriving at Pensacola, Blair was transferred, with twenty others, to the prize steamer " Arizona," as a crew to bring her North. On board this vessel he served as fireman, and came to Philadelphia.

Nov. 12, 1862, his term of service having expired, he was discharged.

eturning to Pittsford, and then removing to Brandon, he was there drafted, and entered the army as a private. While in this b a h of the service, about eight months, he was detailed as guard to transport substitutes and bounty-jumpers to Washington ; after which, by general orders, he was transferred to the United States Navy at Boston, and sent on board the United States receiving-ship " Ohio " as seaman.

Shortly after he was forwarded, with a large number of men, by transport to the United States receiving-ship " Potomac," of the West Gulf blockading squadron, stationed at Pensacola. From the " Potomac " he was sent on board the United States steamer " Metacomet," ten guns, then on the blockade off Mobile, where he received the rate of quartermaster Aug. 5, 1864. On this vessel, which was lashed to the flagship " Hartford," he took part in the memorable entrance into Mobile Bay by Rear-admiral Farragut, resulting in the capture of the rebel ram "Tennessee," steamer " Selma," the sinking of the steamer " Gaines," and capture of Fort Gaines and Powell.

He was then transferred to the now United States steamer "Selma," four guns, as one of a prize-crew, and here rated chief boatswain's-mate. On the " Selma " he assisted in reducing Fort Morgan, and was engaged in blockading Dog River Bar, and the still more hazardous duty of removing torpedoes.

The " Selma " was finally ordered to New Orleans, where Mr. Blair, being sick with chronic diarrhœa, was placed in the Naval Hospital, and then sent North on the United States steam-sloop " Richmond," to the Naval Hospital at Chelsea, Mass.

His term of service having expired, he was honorably discharged, Aug. 1, 1865.

ALFRED B. WHITING.

Born in Hingham.

Jan. 21, 1861, shipped in the U. S. Navy, at Boston, as landsman for three years, and was sent on board the U. S. receiving-ship "Ohio."

Soon after assigned to the U. S. steam-frigate " Colorado " fifty-two guns, and there rated master-at-arms.

The " Colorado " was sent to Ship Island to take part in the capture of New Orleans ; but, owing to the great draft of water required, she was unable to pass the bar at the mouth of the Mississippi River.

Feb. 10, 1864, his time of service having expired, he was discharged at Portsmouth, N.H. ; since deceased.

GUNNER'S MATE

CHARLES CAMPBELL.

A resident of Hingham ; born in Boston, July 26, 1826.

June 8, 1864, transferred from the U. S. Army to the Navy at

Hilton Head, S.C., and sent on board the U. S. store-ship "Vermont," where he was on the sick-list for three months.

Sept. 15, 1864, ordered to the U. S. schooner "Para," three guns, and on this vessel was engaged in bombarding, enforcing the blockade, and in guard-duty.

Dec. 1, 1864, rated to quarter-gunner.

Mar. 1, 1865, rated to gunner's mate, in charge.

Aug. 7, 1865, discharged at Charlestown, Mass., his term of service having expired.

PAYMASTER'S STEWARD

HENRY WINSLOW HERSEY.

Born in Hingham, Aug. 16, 1823.

June 2, 1862, shipped in the U. S. Navy at Boston, as landsman, for three years.

July 8, 1862, sent on board the U. S. steamer "Sachem," five guns, attached to the West Gulf blockading squadron.

July 15, 1862, rated paymaster's steward.

Aug. 12 to 16, took part in the engagement at Corpus Christi, and capture of the rebel armed schooner "Breaker," destroying two others.

Dec. 16, 1862, took part in the capture of a schooner block-ade-runner.

Jan. 1, 1863, the "Sachem" was present in the engagement at Galveston, Texas, when the rebels captured the U. S. steamer "Harriet Lane," and two coal-barks, and when Com. Renshaw blew up the U. S. steamer "Westfield," to prevent her falling into the hands of the enemy.

Jan. 8, 1863, transferred to the U. S. steamer "Diana."

March 28, 1863, the "Diana," while making a reconnoissance on Atchafalaya River, was fired upon by a concealed battery ; and after a fight of two hours and forty-five minutes, with all but one officer and a large portion of her crew killed or wounded, being entirely disabled, she drifted ashore and was captured. Hersey, though unhurt, was taken prisoner, and, with the rest of the crew, paroled, and sent to New Orleans.

May 16, 1863, sent North, on the U. S. transport "Kensington," to the U. S. receiving-ship "North Carolina," at New York.

July 10, 1864, exchanged, and sent to the U. S. iron-clad "Onondaga," four guns. After about three weeks' service on this vessel, he was taken sick, and sent to the Naval Hospital at New York.

Sept. 6, 1864, having recovered, was sent to the U. S. steamer "Otsego," ten guns, attached to the North Atlantic blockading squadron.

Nov. 12, 1864, took part in the reduction of the forts and capture of Plymouth, N.C.

Dec. 9, 1864, the "Otsego" was sunk by a torpedo in the Roanoke River. Hersey, from exposure, was again placed on the sick-list, sent to the Naval Hospital at Newbern, N.C., and thence to New York.

April 24, 1865, his term of service having expired, he was discharged at New York.

SIGNAL QUARTERMASTER.

ELKANAH BINNEY.

Born in Hingham, Oct. 18, 1813.

Jan. 6, 1862, shipped in the U. S. Navy, at New York, as seaman for three years. Sent on board the U. S. steamer "Oneida," ten guns, and joined the fleet off the mouth of the Mississippi River.

April 18 to 24, 1862, took part in the famous passage of the Mississippi and bombardment and capture of Forts Jackson and St. Philip, the Chalmette Battery, and New Orleans.

April 25, rated signal quartermaster.

May 18, 1862, the "Oneida" arrived off Vicksburg, Miss., and demanded its surrender.

June 28, 1862, he took part in the engagement at Vicksburg, passing up the river.

July 15, 1862, took part in the passage of the Vicksburg batteries, going down the river, and engagement with the rebel ram "Arkansas."

September, 1862, the " Oneida " was ordered to the blockade off Mobile.

Aug. 5, 1864, this vessel, lashed beside the U. S. steamer "Galena," took part in the memorable entrance into Mobile Bay by Rear-admiral Farragut, and capture of the rebel ram " Tennessee," steamer " Selma," the sinking of the steamer " Gaines," and capture of Forts Gaines and Powell.

The " Oneida" was struck a number of times, and finally received a shot in her starboard boiler which disabled her, causing the steam to escape, and scalding several of the officers and crew. The commander was very severely wounded.

In this engagement Binney was slightly wounded. Feb. 25, 1865, his term of service having expired, he was discharged.

SIGNAL QUARTERMASTER.

SAMUEL NEWCOMB, 2D.

Born in Hingham, July 9, 1825.

June 8, 1864, he was transferred from Co. D, Fourth Regiment Mass. Cavalry, at Hilton Head, S.C., to the U. S. Navy, as seaman, and sent on board the U. S. receiving-ship "Vermont."

July 8, 1864, ordered on board the U. S. barque " Braziliera," eight guns, of the South Atlantic blockading squadron, then stationed on the blockade off St. Andrew's and St. Simon's Sounds. Shortly after joining the " Braziliera," he was rated captain of the after-guard. October, 1864, again rated to signal quartermaster, and served in this capacity until the end of the cruise.

March, 1865, the " Braziliera" was ordered North.

April, 1865, Newcomb was sent, with the rest of the crew, on board the U. S. receiving-ship " Princeton," at Philadelphia, from which he was granted leave, and came to Hingham. After a short stay at home, he returned to the " Princeton," and was sent on board the U. S. supply steamer "South Carolina," and made the trip to Pensacola and return, stopping at intermediate ports.

Aug. 26, 1865, his term of service having expired, he was discharged at Philadelphia.

FIRST-CLASS FIREMAN.

ALDEN LINCOLN.

Born in Hingham, March 13, 1829.

June 25, 1862, shipped in the U. S. Navy, at Boston, for three years, as first-class fireman, and was sent the U. S. receiving-ship "Ohio."

July 3, 1862, ordered to the U. S. steamer "Genesee," eight guns, attached to the North Atlantic blockading squadron, stationed on the James River.

Sept. 1, 1862, the "Genesee" was stationed on the blockade off Wilmington, N.C.

February, 1863, the "Genesee" was ordered to the West Gulf blockading squadron.

March 13, 1863, she arrived at Profit Island, Mississippi River.

March 17, 1863, at night, this vessel, lashed to the U. S. steam-sloop "Richmond," attempted the passage of the Port Hudson batteries. On this occasion the officers and crew of the "Genesee" were especially commended, in the official despatches, for rescuing the officers and crew of the U. S. steam-frigate "Mississippi" (burned), and saving the "Richmond" from sharing a like fate, after her engines were disabled.

From this time until Port Hudson surrendered, the "Genesee" took part in the various engagements for its reduction.

Aug. 15, 1863, the "Genesee" was sent to the blockade off Mobile; where she remained until the passage of the forts in August, 1864, when she was stationed outside in reserve, to prevent rebel vessels from escaping seaward.

July 13, 1865, Lincoln was discharged at New Orleans, La., and granted passage North, his term of service having expired.

GEORGE ALEXANDER GROVER.

Born in Charlestown, Mass., Jan. 24, 1846; a resident of Hingham.

Oct. 21, 1863, shipped in the U. S. Navy, at Boston, as second-class fireman for one year, and was sent on board the U. S. receiving-ship "Ohio."

Dec. 6, 1863, ordered to the U. S. steamer "Acacia," four guns, attached to the East Gulf blockading squadron.

Jan. 1, 1864, rated to first-class fireman.

Dec. 23, 1864, took part in the capture of the blockade-runner "Julia," loaded with cotton, in Alligator Creek, S.C. On this vessel he came North, as one of the prize-crew, and acted in the capacity of engineer.

Jan. 21, 1865, his term of service having expired, he was discharged at Boston, Mass.

* DANIEL STODDER LINCOLN.

SEAMAN.

WILLIAM ELDREDGE.

Born in Provincetown, Mass., Sept. 25, 1809; a resident of Hingham.

Shipped June 8, 1861, in the U. S. Navy, at New Bedford, Mass., as seaman for three years, and was sent on board the U. S. ship "Vincennes," ten guns, attached to the West Gulf blockading squadron.

In March, 1863, he was ordered to the U. S. Naval Hospital, at New Orleans, and thence North to New York City, where, on the 29th of May, 1863, he was discharged for disability.

* JOHN WILLIAM GARDNER.

GEORGE E. RICHARDSON.

Served for the quota of Hingham.

Transferred at Boston, Mass., April 15, 1864, from the Third

Mass. Heavy Artillery, to the U. S. Navy, as seaman, and was
sent on board the U. S. steamer "Massasoit," ten guns,
attached to the North Atlantic blockading squadron.

GEORGE ANTHONY CHUBBUCK.

Born in Scituate, July 9, 1844; a resident of Hingham.

Transferred July 25, 1864, from the Third Unattached Company
Massachusetts Heavy Artillery, at Fort Berry, Va., to the
United States Navy, as ordinary seaman, and was sent on
board the United States receiving-ship "Princeton," at Philadelphia.

About three weeks after, was removed to the United States
steamer "Glaucus," nine guns, employed in convoying the Cali-
fornia mail-steamers through the West Indies. Returning North,
the "Glaucus" struck on Molasses Key, and was got off after
throwing overboard the guns and a portion of the cargo. She
then put into Inagua for repairs. Shortly after leaving this port,
she lost her rudder, and with some difficulty succeeded in reaching Key West.

July, 1865, Chubbuck was assigned to the United States
schooner "Mather Vassar," two guns.

Discharged at Philadelphia, Aug. 19, 1865, by reason of expiration of term of enlistment.

WILLIAM GRAY CUSHING, Jun.

Born in Hingham, Nov. 7, 1836.

Aug. 15, 1861, shipped in the United States Navy, at Boston, as
ordinary seaman, for one year, and was sent on board the
United States barque "Gemsbok," seven guns.

On the 22d of September, 1861, the "Gemsbok" captured the
schooner "Mary E. Pindar." On the 3d of October she captured the schooner "Beverly," and on the 20th of the same
month the brig "Ariel."

April 25, 1862, in the same vessel. Cushing was present in the bombardment and capture of Fort Macon and Beaufort, N.C.

April 26, 1862, the " Gemsbok " captured the ship "Gondor" and barque " Glenn." Cushing continued in the service till August 1862.

BENJAMIN HATCHFIELD.

July 27, 1861, shipped in the United States Navy, at Boston, as ordinary seaman, for three years, and was sent on board the United States receiving-ship " Ohio."

In August, 1861, he was taken to Washington, D.C., and in the December following was assigned to the United States iron-clad "Louisville," thirteen guns, attached to the Mississippi squadron.

Jan. 10 and 11, 1863, on board this vessel, took part in the bombardment and capture of the rebel works at Arkansas Post, Arkansas River.

April 17, 1863, was present in the bombardment and passage of the Vicksburg batteries.

April 29 to May 3, he shared in the bombardment and capture of the rebel works at Grand Gulf, Mississippi River.

Discharged at Mound City, Ill., Aug. 24, 1864, by reason of expiration of term of service.

DANIEL STODDER.

Shipped in the United States Navy, at Boston, June 24, 1862, as ordinary seaman, for two years, and was sent on board receiving-ship "Ohio." From this vessel he was shortly transferred to the United States steamer " Conewaugh," nine guns, stationed off Charleston, S.C., engaged in enforcing the block-ade.

In March, 1864, the " Conewaugh " was sent to join the West blockading squadron, stationed off Mobile. Discharged July 22, 1864, by reason of expiration of term of service.

THOMAS R. MURPHY.

Shipped at Boston, May 19, 1863, in the United States Navy, as ordinary seaman, for one year, and was sent on board the receiving-ship "Ohio." Shortly after, transferred to the United States barque "Ethan Allen," nine guns, attached to the West Gulf blockading-squadron.

Discharged at Philadelphia, June 29, 1864, his term of service having expired.

COAL-HEAVER.

ISAAC MURRAY DOW.

Born in South Boston, Oct. 3, 1839; a resident of Hingham.

Shipped Jan. 2, 1864, in the United States Navy, at Boston, as coal-heaver, and was sent on board United States steamer "Massasoit," four guns, then fitting out at Boston for the North Atlantic blockading squadron.

May 2, 1864, he was removed to the United States Naval Hospital at Chelsea, Mass.

LANDSMEN.

DANIEL DALEY.

ROBERT FRANCIS HARDY.

Born in St. Johns, Newfoundland, Sept. 8, 1846; a resident of Hingham.

Shipped at Boston, Mass., Nov. 16, 1863, in the United States Navy, as landsman for one year, and was sent on board the United States receiving-ship "Ohio," being shortly after transferred to the United States transport "Queen," seven guns, then fitting out at New York.

Feb. 11, 1864, on board this vessel he took part in the capture of the schooners "Louisa" and "Cosmopolite," off Brazos River Bar.

In March of the same year, he was sent on board the United
States iron-clad " Passaic," two guns, stationed off Charleston,
S.C., and participated in numerous engagements with the ene-
my's forts and batteries.

His term of service expired Jan. 6, 1865, and he was discharged at Philadelphia.   Since lost at sea.

EDWARD GOTTCHELL.

Born in Ireland, Aug 17, 1845; a resident of Hingham.

Shipped in the United States Navy, Nov. 28, 1863, at Boston, as
landsman, for one year, and was sent on board the United
States receiving-ship " Ohio."

Soon after was assigned to the United States transport
" Queen," seven guns, at New York City.

Feb. 11, 1864, took part in the capture of the schooners
" Louisa" and " Cosmopolite," off Brazos River Bar.

In the following March he was placed on board the U. S.
iron-clad " Passaic," two guns, stationed off Charleston, S. C.,
and here shared in numerous engagements with the forts and
batteries of the enemy.

Discharged Jan, 7, 1865, at Philadelphia, his term of service
having expired.

BENJAMIN LINCOLN JONES.

Born in Hingham, Nov. 22, 1832.

Shipped Aug. 9, 1862, in the U. S. Navy, at Boston, Mass.,
for one year, as landsman, and was taken on board the U. S.
receiving-ship " Ohio."

Shortly after, with others, was transferred to the U. S. receiving-ship " North Carolina," at New York, and in about four
weeks was again transferred to the U. S. receiving-ship
" Brandywine," at Hampton Roads.

In November, 1862, was assigned, with others, to the U. S.
steamer " Hetzel," and in her sailed for Little Washington,
N.C., where he was taken on board the U. S. steamer " Louisiana," five guns.

April 1 to 18, with the "Louisiana," he shared in repulsing the attack and siege of Little Washington.

Sept. 9, 1863, his term of service having expired, he was discharged at Little Washington, and granted passage North.

*GEORGE HOWARD MERRITT.

DANIEL JOSEPH THOMPSON.
Born in Hingham, March 12, 1849.

Jan. 28, 1864, shipped in the U. S. Navy, at Boston, for one year, as landsman, and was sent on board receiving-ship "Ohio."

March 24, 1864, Thompson was discharged by special order, upon requisition of his father, he being under age.

HENRY TROWBRIDGE.
Born in Hingham, July 14, 1842.

Shipped Aug. 9, 1862, in the U. S. Navy, at Boston, for one year, as landsman, and was sent on board the U. S. receiving-ship "Ohio."

Soon after, with others, was transferred to the U. S. receiving-ship "North Carolina," at New York, and in about four weeks was assigned to the U. S. receiving-ship "Brandywine," at Hampton Roads.

In November, 1862, again changed to the U. S. steamer "Hetzel" he sailed for Little Washington, and was there transferred to the U. S. steamer "Louisiana," five guns.

From the 1st to the 18th of April, 1863, he took part in repulsing the attack and siege of Little Washington.

Sept. 9, 1863, his term of service having expired, he was discharged at Little Washington, and granted passage home.

WILLIAM BURTES.

HINGHAM MEN IN THE NAVY ACCORDING TO RANK.

OFFICERS.

Charles Harding Loring.   Edward Welles Halcro.
Thomas Andrews.   Charles Mason Fuller.
Andrew Tower.   Charles Anderson Stewart.
Franklin Nickerson.   John Means Trussell.
                  Augustus Barnes.

WARRANT OFFICERS.

Frederick Clinton Blair.   Elkanah Binney.
Alfred B. Whiting.   Samuel Newcomb, 2d.
Charles Campbell.   Alden Lincoln.
Henry Winslow Hersey.   George Alexander Grover.
                  Daniel Stodder Lincoln.

SEAMEN.

William Eldredge.   John William Gardner.
                  George E Richardson.

ORDINARY SEAMEN.

George Anthony Chubbuck.   Benjamin Hatchfield.
William Gray Cushing, jun.   Daniel Stodder.
                  Thomas R. Murphy.

COAL-HEAVER.

Isaac Murray Dow.

LANDSMEN.

Daniel Daley.   Benjamin Lincoln Jones.
Robert Francis Fardy.   George Howard Merritt.
Edward Gottchell.   Daniel Joseph Thompson.
                  Henry Trowbridge.

UNKNOWN.

William Burtes.

CHAPTER XVIII.

IN MEMORIAM.

Soldiers and Sailors who were Natives, Residents, or otherwise connected with Hingham, who died in the Service, or Prior to the Erection of the Monument — Biographical Sketches.

TO perpetuate the names of those persons who were accredited to the quota of Hingham, and of those natives of the town serving elsewhere, who lost their lives in battle or by disease contracted in the service during the late civil war, is the special object of the present chapter. To this end, the leading circumstances and events of their early history have been obtained, as far as possible, and, with their military record and heroic self-sacrifices, are introduced in brief biographical sketches, in the hope of making bright in the eyes of future generations their example of ardent patriotism and of devotion, even unto death, to the principles of human rights and freedom.

There is a voice in the memory of the dead who have died in a noble cause, and an influence in their history, however humble, which thrill and inspire us at the mention of their acts of heroism and valor. They may linger, perhaps, only in the name of a revolutionary patriot, like Warren; or they may fade into the mist of legend and tradition like the grand story of Thermopylæ; yet they are the natural sources from which flow the poetic animation, the national pride, and the patriotic fire, that mark and make an advanced, high-minded, and spirited people with firm principles and lofty aims.

With this thought, we have placed on record the story of men, who, from the everyday walks of life, rose by the glorious steps

of service and sacrifice to the exalted rank of a nation's heroes.
They sleep in quiet graves. Their lives were cut off like early
blossoms. With a pale face and quickly beating heart the quiet
citizen, the eager schoolboy, the son of fond father and mother,
enlisted. A waving of the hat, the brushing aside a tear, were
all that marked the parting. There was the lithesome step on
the march, the buoyant spirit in the camp, the gallant bearing on
the field of battle. But with the blight of disease or the crack
of the rifle, all was over. Some are resting in Southern dust.
The remains of others were tenderly brought home, and by loving hands committed to their native turf. All was over in one
sense; but in another and a grander sense, life only passed into
a more glorious life, into the fabric of a higher national life, into
the temple of a loftier national virtue and purity, into the very
arch of the cause of Christian humanity, cemented with their
sacred blood.

> Patriots have toiled, and in their country's cause
> Bled nobly; and their deeds, as they deserve,
> Receive proud recompense. We give in charge
> Their names to the sweet lyre. The historic Muse,
> Proud of her treasure, marches with it down
> To latest times: and Sculpture, in her turn,
> Gives bond, in stone and ever-during brass,
> To guard them, and immortalize her trust."

JOHN ALBION ANDREW.

[Communicated.]

Hingham has the proud distinction of having been the home of John Albion Andrew, governor of Massachusetts during the entire period of the rebellion, and of now, in accordance with the wish he once expressed before the citizens of Hingham, tenderly cherishing in her soil his sacred ashes. It is fitting that his name should stand at the head of the list of her heroic dead.

It is unnecessary, in the scope of the present work, to give more than the barest biographical outline of one whose life and services are already a part of the national literature, imprinted on its brightest pages. He was born, of worthy New England stock, at South Windham, in the State of Maine, May 31, 1818. The comfortable circumstances of his father procured him a good academical education and a collegiate course at Brunswick. He was a glad, wholesome, noble boy, with open face and curly head, and a brave, generous, and buoyant heart, fond of history, reading widely, with a taste for poetry and elegant literature, with no exalted rank as a plodding scholar, but with always a tendency towards broad views and humane sentiments. Even in those days, the anti-slavery cause had touched his heart ; and the faint whisper of the approaching storm was awakening his pulses to that love of freedom and respect for human rights which so signally found expression in his later life.

In 1837 Andrew entered the law-office of Henry H. Fuller, Esq., of Boston. He there pursued for twenty years the ordinary course of his profession, making now and then a stump-speech or a literary oration, and constantly rising in practice and reputation. In December, 1848, he married Eliza Jones Hersey of this town, whom he had met at an anti-slavery fair in Boston ; and from that period, for a great part of the time, he resided in Hingham. Here was his home, here children were born unto him, here he walked to church, and sang the familiar hymns, and taught the Sunday-school. Here his rare and sweet social qualities surrounded him with friends who loved and admired him ;

and here his generous nature, his fondness for natural scenery, his love of children, and his strong social attachments, brought him some of the happiest hours of his life.

While residing in Hingham, Andrew was nominated for State senator, but defeated. He had as yet had no entrance into political service. Nevertheless, he was daily becoming better known as an intelligent advocate of progress, and for his strong anti-slavery sentiments. In 1854 he bravely defended the parties arrested for the rescue of Anthony Burns, and in 1857 was chosen to the General Court as representative of the Sixth Ward of Boston. In this arena he rose at once to distinction. Brought into conflict with Caleb Cushing, one of the astutest and most powerful debaters and thinkers of the whole country, he carried off the victory in the bitter struggle over the removal of Judge Loring. In 1859 he unflinchingly presided at the stormy meeting in Tremont Temple, for the relief of John Brown's suffering family, declaring, that, whether Brown's enterprise at Harper's Ferry were right or wrong, "John Brown himself is right." In 1860 he was a delegate to the Chicago presidential convention, and contributed all his influence to the nomination of Abraham Lincoln; and in 1861, having been elected by a sort of spontaneous impulse of the heart of the Commonwealth, as the one fit man for its magistracy, took his seat as governor of the State. In April, the rebellion already at its outburst, came the call for arms; and, as if Providence had raised him up for the place, Andrew responded to it with that electric promptness, that magnetic fervor, that soulful devotion, which, from that day forward till the end of the war, animated him under all circumstances, and imparted to the people at large the enthusiasm of his own ardent nature. His great heart breathed in that now historic telegram to the Mayor of Baltimore, "I pray you to let the bodies of our Massachusetts soldiers, dead in Baltimore, be laid out, preserved in ice, and tenderly sent forward by express to me."

Unsuspected powers at once put forth in him, his public addresses thrilled with loftier notes, his executive energies expanded to the widest limit of his countless duties and labors; the quiet citizen and plodding lawyer budded in a day into the grandest measure of the statesman and leader ; and it seemed almost a dream that our good-humored neighbor was indeed the foremost governor in the Union, the most chivalrous, if not the greatest, civilian of the war.   At the assembling of loyal governors at Altoona, Pa., Sept. 24, 1862, his was the leading spirit that urged new vigor in the prosecution of the campaign. When negro regiments began to be formed, he was among the first to organize them, prescient of their efficiency and gallantry in the field.   In all that could stimulate the soul of the nation, in all that could wake its patriotic fire, yet none the less in the most watchful care of the home interests of the State, of its institutions of charity and correction, he was always foremost; and the activity of his life and labors was almost superhuman. Says the Rev. Dr. Clarke, " He worked like the great engine in the heart of a steamship."

With the war, his term of office as governor expiring, he resumed the practice of the law.   In 1866 he was chosen president of the New England Historic-Genealogical Society.   In 1867, with the same bravery and heroism that had marked him thitherto, though against the judgment of many of his friends, he began his strenuous and able assaults upon the prohibitory law of the State.   All this time his broad national reputation, his great popularity, his sound judgment, his conciliatory and liberal sentiments, were marking him as the coming man in the national councils.   It seemed as if years of new usefulness lay before him. But he had finished his work.

On the 30th of October, 1867, he died at his residence in Boston.   His remains were afterwards brought to Hingham ; and on the 30th of October, 1869, after solemn services in the New North Church, at which he had formerly been an attendant, his Boston pastor, James Freeman Clarke, pronouncing the address, he was buried in our cemetery, near its crest, and not far from the Soldiers' Monument.   At his feet are the village he loved, the branches under which he sauntered, and the picturesque stretch of the bay over which he had so many times gone to and from his home.   He rests at scarce the distance of the sound of the voice from the threshold on which he stood, when on the 3d of September, 1860, he addressed his fellow-citizens of Hingham,

who had come to congratulate him on his nomination as governor, and in the course of his remarks spoke these hearty words:

"I confess to you, my old neighbors, associates, and kins-people
of Hingham, that I could more fitly speak by tears than by words
to-night. From the bottom of my heart for this unsought, enthusiastic, and cordial welcome, I thank you. I understand—
and this thought lends both sweetness and pathos to the emotions of the hour,—I am here to-night among neighbors, who for
the moment are all agreed to differ and all consenting to agree.

"How dear to my heart are these fields, these spreading trees,
this verdant grass, this sounding shore, when now for fourteen
years, through summer heat and sometimes through winter
storms, I have trod your streets, rambled through your woods,
sauntered by your shores, sat by your firesides, and felt the warm
pressure of your hands, sometimes teaching your children in the
Sunday-school, sometimes speaking to my fellow-citizens, always
with the cordial friendship of those who differ from me oftentimes in what they thought the radicalism of my opinions. Here
—here I have found most truly a home for the soul free from
the cares and turmoil and responsibilities of a careful and anxious
profession. Away from the busier haunts of men, it has been
given to me here to find a calm and sweet retreat. Here too,
dear friends, I have found the home of my heart. It was into
one of your families that I entered, and joined myself in holy
bonds of domestic love to one of the daughters of your town.
Here, too, I have first known a parent's joys and a parent's
sorrows. Whether you say Aye or No to my selection, John A.
Andrew is ever your friend."

Gov. Andrew, when in Hingham, lived on the east side of
Main Street, in the first house northerly from Water Street, in
the Hinckley house on the same and in the Thaxter house on
the opposite side of Main Street, in the old Hersey house on
Summer Street, overlooking the blue water and sweet with the
fragrance of clover fields, and also in the Bates house on South
Street. His habits, like his nature, were simple. He loved to
drive and walk; he enjoyed the breezy trips and neighborly chat
of the steamer; his heart went out to children and won them;
he was especially fond of conversation, full of anecdote and

story, and not averse to controversial discussion. His humor and cheer were always abundant. He sang old psalms, he recited noble poems that dwelt in his memory, he was running over with the quaint history of old times and odd characters, and to the last there never faded in his breast the warm, glad enthusiasm of boyhood. His sympathies were touched as quickly as a girl's : each year he went to Maine to stand beside the grave of his mother ; each day some sad woman or poor boy thanked him for his humanity, for in him the unfortunate always had a helper and a friend. No heart less generous could have uttered those memorable words that expressed his great and genuine humanity : " I know not what record of sin may await me in another world ; but this I do know, I never was mean enough to despise a man because he was poor, because he was ignorant, or because he was black." Add to all this his incorruptibility and honesty, his fiery patriotism, his unswerving sense of right and wrong, his pure glow in act and word, and we may trust, that, as his monument rises over his grave, it will point to the example of purposes so lofty, of a soul so magnanimous, and a mind so sound, that it will be like a beacon-light to guide the way of future generations to the like achievement of the fulness of a noble life.

J. D. L.

THOMAS ANDREWS.

Acting-master in the U. S. Navy, died at New Orleans, La., Feb. 27, 1865, of consumption, aged forty-eight years, eight months, eighteen days.

Thomas Andrews, born in Hingham, June 9, 1816, was the youngest son of David and Betsey (Sargent) Andrews, and a descendant from Thomas Andrews, an early resident of this town. Among his paternal ancestors were Capt. Thomas Andrews, of Sir William Phips's Canada expedition ; and Lieut.

Thomas Andrews, who was son of the captain. There also were patriotic families on the maternal side.

After receiving instruction at the public and private schools of the town, the subject of this sketch entered the merchant service, and before the expiration of his minority was appointed chief officer of a ship. He subsequently commanded several square-rigged vessels, in which he made voyages to the East Indies and other foreign countries.

Oct. 29, 1861, he was appointed acting-master in the U. S. Navy, and shortly after was ordered to the U. S. store-ship "Vermont," then fitting out at Boston. In the "Vermont" he made the memorable passage to Port Royal, S.C., during which, in a severe gale, the ship parted with two steamers sent to convoy her, and lost rudder and most of her sails. She was finally found, and towed into port, having been at sea over forty days.

Shortly after her arrival, Mr. Andrews was ordered to the command of the U. S. transport "Courier," then running between Port Royal and New York.

Jan. 1, 1863, finds him in command of the U. S. steamer "Crusader," seven guns, attached to the North Atlantic blockading squadron. In this vessel he was engaged in the arduous duty of enforcing the blockade, as well as in numerous other expeditions, including the attack on West Point, Va., April 15, 1863.

Jan. 1, 1864, he was doing duty on board the U. S. screw-sloop "Pensacola," twenty-six guns, attached to the West Gulf blockading squadron, and stationed at New Orleans, La.

In February he returned to Hingham in feeble health, and remained here several months incapacitated for active service.

Dec. 19, 1864, he was re-appointed acting-master in the U. S. Navy, and ordered to New Orleans for duty on the West Gulf blockading squadron. His health, however, continued to fail; and he died at the Naval Rendezvous, as previously stated.

His remains were embalmed, and sent to Hingham. Appropriate services were held at the New North Meeting-house, after which the body was buried in the family lot in the Hingham Cemetery.

He left a widow and two children.

GEORGE BAILEY.

Corp. George Bailey was a member of Co. I of the Fifty-sixth
Regiment, M. V. I., three years, and was mustered March 1,
1864.

In the absence of the details of his war-record, the following
facts make up all of his history which can now be given. He
appears to have enlisted from Boston for the quota of Hingham,
was about thirty years of age, and received the amount of bounty-
money paid to soldiers at the time of entering the service.

His career was brief. Joining the Army of the Potomac in
April, the regiment to which he was attached took part in the
battle of the Wilderness when Col. Griswold was killed; next at
Spottsylvania; then at North Anna, Bethesda Church, Cold
Harbor, and lastly at Petersburg, where on the 17th of June,
according to the report of the adjutant-general, in a brave and
successful charge on the enemy's line, he fell in the cause for
which he had imperilled his life to defend and preserve, having
had a short but active service of three months.

JAMES BALLENTINE.

The subject of this sketch was born in Roscommon County,
Ireland, April, 1842. His parents were William and Catharine
(Ward) Ballentine.

A laborer by occupation, and but eighteen years of age, he
left Hingham in May, 1860, prior to the outbreak of the rebellion, for the purpose of entering the regular service of the
United States. The officer under whom he enlisted was connected with the Third Infantry, then stationed at the Ringold
Barracks on the Rio Grande, Texas; and our young recruit was
ordered to this locality. Soon after the beginning of the war,
they were besieged by the enemy, and an effort was made to
escape by water. The vessel, however, was captured, and the
entire command taken prisoners.

An invitation to volunteer in the cause of secession was declined to a man, and all were paroled and sent to New York. From some cause, the parole was not recognized. The Irish Brigade was then recruiting; and an officer from Boston visited the regiment, and organized a body of men for a troop of dragoons to be attached to the brigade. No cavalry, however, being required, guns were furnished by the State, and the regiment, or brigade, was known as the Fifteenth Independent; Mr. Ballentine being of the number, and claiming that, though enlisted *in* the State of New York, he was serving *for* the State of Massachusetts.

After organizing, the battery joined the Army of the Potomac, and was in the battles of Antietam, Gettysburg, siege of Petersburg, and at other localities.

The battery was detailed for the purpose of cutting off the Weldon Railroad, and thus preventing the transport of supplies for the enemy. At the engagement which here occurred, young Ballentine was stationed at the extreme front, and the ranks suffered terribly. From early morning he worked steadily and bravely at his gun, notwithstanding the almost universal carnage; but at two o'clock of the afternoon he was stricken in the breast by a solid shot, and fell. His death was instantaneous, and without a struggle.

Capt. Hart, who commanded the battery, speaks in warm terms of the courage and bravery of this young soldier.

HOSEA ORCUTT BARNES.

Hosea Orcutt Barnes, whose name is upon the Soldiers' and Sailors' Monument, son of Elisha J. and Harriet A. (Peakes) Barnes of Boston, was born in Scituate, Mass., June 13, 1842. He joined the Tenth Light Battery, under Capt. J. Henry Sleeper, and was mustered as private, Sept. 9, 1862

During the time young Barnes was connected with the battery, it was engaged at Kelley's Ford, Mine Run, Po River, Spottsylvania, and North Anna.

May 30, 1864, the battery went into position on the south side of Pamunkey River, at a place called Jones' Farm, and was about to engage the enemy, when a detachment of four men was sent to cut down a tree which stood in a position that prevented accurate firing. The men returned, and reported that it could not be accomplished by reason of exposure to the enemy's sharpshooters. Private Barnes then *volunteered* to perform the duty, and had removed the obstruction when he received his death-wound.

He was a promising young man, and a favorite with all who knew him.

A marble tablet, erected over his remains in the Hingham cemetery, bears the inscription : —

HOSEA O. BARNES,

MEMBER OF

10TH BATT., MASS. VOLS.,

KILLED AT

JONES' FARM, VA.,

MAY 30, 1864.

AGED 21 YEARS 11 MONTHS.

—— —— — ·

OUR LOVED ONE SLEEPS
FOR HIS COUNTRY'S FLAG.

CHARLES EUGENE BATES.

Charles Eugene Bates, born in Cohasset, Dec. 16, 1837, was a son of Charles and Clara (Turner) Bates, and a descendant of Clement Bates, one of the first settlers of Hingham. He was a resident of Scituate at the time of enlistment, and by occupation a boatman.

Joining the first quota of Hingham, under recruiting-officer Edward Cazneau, he was mustered as a private in Co. G of the

Thirty-ninth Regiment. M. V. I., Sept. 2, 1862. This regiment was not brought into any general battle for more than eighteen months after it left Massachusetts, having been employed upon other important duties. Its first engagement, according to the annual report of the adjutant-general, was May 5. 1864. In its second engagement (Sunday morning, May 8, 1864), young Bates was wounded in the left arm during a charge upon the enemy's breastworks at the commencement of the battle of Laurel Hill. He was immediately taken to the field hospital, and thence to Jarvis Hospital, in Baltimore, Md., where, after partially recovering, he volunteered to serve as nurse for those who were greater sufferers than himself. In the performance of this duty, he contracted diphtheria, from which, on the 2d of November, he died. Dr. D. C. Peters, U.S.A., the surgeon in charge of the hospital, paid a warm tribute to his memory; and the nurses passed a series of resolutions expressive of sorrow and sympathy for the parents of the deceased.

Private Bates possessed many excellent traits of character. Brave and true as a soldier, thoughtful of others, forgetful of self, and patient when suffering, he has passed to the higher life. His remains were taken to Scituate for burial; and a headstone erected to his memory bears the following inscription : —

HE IS NOT HERE, HE HAS RISEN.

CHARLES EUGENE BATES,

DIED Nov., 1864,

IN THE SERVICE OF HIS
COUNTRY,

IN THE 39TH REGT., MASS. VOL.,

AGED 26.

HE WHO DESTROYETH OUR EARTHLY HOPE
CALLETH US TO A DIVINER TRUST.

DANIEL LEAVITT BEAL.

Private in Co. F, Thirty-second Regiment, M. V. I., three years; died July 29, 1864.

Daniel Leavitt Beal, son of Daniel and Hannah Leavitt (Burbank) Beal, was born in Cohasset, June 23, 1832.

On the 17th of March, 1862, he enlisted at Fort Warren for the quota of Hingham, and remained at his place till May, when he left with the regiment for Washington. June 25, under orders to join the Army of the Potomac, he was at Harrison's Landing, where the regiment was stationed in line of battle throughout the day.

On the 8th of July he was detailed as provost-guard at Gen. Potter's headquarters, where, acting as orderly for Gen. Sykes and Col. Locke, he remained till June 24, 1864, when, sick and disabled, he was sent to City Point Hospital, where he died of fever, aged thirty-two years.

In addition to the foregoing sketch, a brother of the deceased gives the following particulars. Early in May, 1864, he was attacked with night blindness, and also suffered at the time from diarrhœa. As surgeons were all engaged at the front, medical advice was not easily obtained; and it was not till the 24th of the following June, that the necessary papers for admission to the hospital were secured. After reporting from one hospital to another, he was at last transferred to the charge of the women of the Sanitary Commission. Steadily declining, he soon became entirely disabled, and finally, from the combined effects of typhoid fever and diarrhœa, died as before stated. His remains were brought home, and interred at North Cohasset.

From the diary of the deceased, it would appear that there was a lack of needed attention, want of proper treatment, and, at an earlier date, a degree of laborious service demanded which he had not the strength to perform.

WILLIAM HENRY BEAL.

Private in Co. K of the First Regiment, M. V. I., three years; mustered Aug. 13, 1862; mustered out May 25, 1864.

Re-enlisted from the town of Cohasset, 1864, in Co. A of the Twenty-fourth Regiment, M. V. I., three years; transferred to Co. K.

William Henry Beal was the eldest son of Robert and Chloe (Sprague) Beal, and was born in Hingham, Oct. 9, 1841.

Aug. 13, 1862, he enlisted from the town of Hingham, and was mustered as private in Co. K of the First Regiment, M. V. I., three years, as before stated. Connected with the Army of the Potomac, he was in the battle before Fredericksburg, took part in the engagement at Chancellorsville, and in the conflict at Gettysburg was severely wounded in the side by a musket-ball. After being in the hospital a short time, he was granted a furlough; and in August, 1863, returned to his home in Hingham, where, during the short respite allowed, his health was in some measured restored. Rejoining the army, he was discharged May 25, 1864, at the expiration of his term of enlistment.

He subsequently removed to Cohasset, and there in the summer of 1864 re-enlisted, entering the service as private in Co. A of the Twenty-fourth Regiment, M. V. I., three years.

After the close of the war, he still suffered from the effects of the wound received at the battle of Gettysburg, and, indeed, never regained the measure of health and vigor enjoyed at the time of entering the service.

Gradually failing, he died of consumption, at the residence of his father, at Hingham, Dec. 20, 1865, aged twenty-four years.

He was a laborer, and unmarried.

GEORGE W. BIBBY.

Member of Co. I, Lincoln Light Infantry, Fourth Regiment, M. V. I., and was three months at Fortress Monroe and vicinity, April to July, 1861 ; lieutenant in Co. A of the Thirty-second Regiment, M. V. I., three years ; killed while on picket-duty, May 30, 1864.

After returning from Fortress Monroe, Mr. Bibby enlisted at Hingham, Oct. 31, 1861, as sergeant in Co. A of the Thirty-second Regiment, as before stated, and the same day was regularly mustered into service.

Aug. 21, 1862, he was promoted second lieutenant ; and Aug. 22, 1863, commissioned first lieutenant.

In the Army of the Potomac with the Thirty-second, Lieut. Bibby fought in the battles at Malvern Hill, Gaines' Mill, Second Bull Run, Antietam, Fredericksburg, Chancellorsville, Gettysburg, Rappahannock Station, Mine Run, Wilderness, Spottsylvania, North Anna, and lastly at Bethesda Church, where, at the head of the picket-line of the regiment, he fell mortally wounded by a ball from a rebel sharpshooter.

Gen. Stephenson, in a note to Mrs. Bibby, writes as follows: "Your husband was killed while in the discharge of his duty, in command of the pickets of the regiment. The ball passed through his arm into his body, and he lived but a short time after he was struck. I saw him but a few moments before he expired. He was buried near the residence of Dr. Brockenborough, on the road from Hanover Town to Richmond, about one mile and a half from Pamunkey River. . . . Lieut. Bibby had endeared himself to the whole command, and by his bravery won the respect of all."

In a similar note addressed to Mrs. Bibby, Col. Prescott bears testimony to his heroism and efficiency as an officer, tenders the bereaved the heartfelt sympathy of the entire regiment, and adds in closing, "You will have the satisfaction of knowing he died for his country."

Funeral services to his memory were held in the Orthodox Church at Hingham, Rev. Mr. Parker, Sunday afternoon, June 19, 1864.

Lieut. Bibby entered the service of his country, from motives of genuine patriotism, and his record of goodness and purity is one which will long live in the hearts of those who knew him.

42

JOHN H. BLACKMAN,

MEMBER OF

CO. H, 12TH REGT., M.V.

BORN IN DORCHESTER

JUNE 6. 1842,

KILLED AT THE BATTLE OF
FREDERICKSBURG, VA.,

DEC. 13, 1862.

LEMUEL S. BLACKMAN,

MEMBER OF

CO. K, 11TH REGT., M.V.,

BORN IN DORCHESTER

FEB. 18, 1840.

DIED

JUNE 13, 1870.

———

SONS OF LEMUEL S. AND ELIZABETH
BLACKMAN.

The above inscription is from a marble stone in the Hingham Cemetery, recently erected in memory of two patriotic brothers, who sacrificed their lives for the preservation of the Union ; and although not upon the quota of Hingham, it seems proper that a brief notice of them should appear in this connection.

John H. Blackman enlisted at Weymouth, and was mustered July 15, 1861. A printed report relating to his death says, " He was shot through the head, and instantly expired. His body was not recovered from the battle-field."

Lemuel S. Blackman was mustered June 13, 1861, and accredited upon the quota of Dorchester. He was discharged the 29th of August following for disability, but never regained his health. The mound which marks his grave is annually decorated with flowers by Post 104, G. A. R., of this town.

These young men were at one time residents here, and are remembered as grandsons of the late Mr. Ebed Hersey.

CHARLES WHITON BLOSSOM.

Son of Thomas Davis and Susan Allen (Whiton) Blossom was born at Chicopee, Mass., June 29, 1840, and died at Hingham, Aug. 26, 1862.

On the 12th of July, 1861, he enlisted from Boston as private, afterwards promoted corporal in Co. I, known as the Newton Guards, of the Sixteenth Regiment, M. V. I., three years, and was mustered into the service at Camp Cameron, Cambridge, Mass.

On the 17th of August he left for the seat of war. After a brief stay at Baltimore, he was ordered to Fortress Monroe, and the winter of 1861-2 was spent in Camp Hamilton.

In May, 1862, he was at Gosport, next at Suffolk, Va., and afterwards at Fair Oaks, where he took part in the skirmishes, and in the more important engagements which occurred from the 18th to the 28th of the month.

On the 29th he was again in conflict with the enemy at Glendale, and lastly took part in the battle at Malvern Hill. In these several engagements the Sixteenth sustained a loss of more than one hundred and fifty men.

But protracted marches and the privations of camp-life soon told on the strength and health of the young soldier and patriot; and early in August, after a few days spent in the hospital, he was discharged from service on account of disability. It was just one year from the time he left Massachusetts. Stopping a few days at Washington, for rest, he reached Hingham Aug. 20, 1862.

From the complete exhaustion that followed, he never rallied; and six days after his arrival home, he "fell asleep," at the residence of his father, aged twenty-two years.

At no time after his return did strength permit him to give any facts relating to his personal experience.

There can, however, be little doubt that his death was caused by complete prostration of the system induced by an attack of camp-fever, while in service on the Peninsula.

That he was a young man of exemplary character, dutiful as

a son, beloved as a brother, brave and patriotic as a soldier, and
as a friend respected and esteemed by all who knew him, is a
truthful and well deserved tribute to his memory.

He was buried in the Hingham Cemetery. The stone erected
to his memory bears the following inscription : —

IN MEMORIAM.

CHARLES W. BLOSSOM,

CO. I, 16TH REG., MASS. VOLS.,

DIED

AUGUST 26, 1862.

AGED 22 YEARS 2 MONTHS.

———

HE GAVE HIS LIFE TO HIS COUNTRY.

———

WILLIAM BREEN.

Corporal in Co. A of the Thirty-second Regiment; taken pris-
oner at Petersburg; and died at Salisbury, N.C., Nov. 5, 1864.
Corp. William Breen was born in Hingham, March 12, 1842.
His parents were John and Susan (Joyce) Breen.

On the 31st of October, 1861, young Breen enlisted for three
years in the defence of the cause of freedom and the Union.
To say that he was connected with the Thirty-second Regiment
would alone indicate the nature of the service in which he was
afterwards engaged. The battles of Malvern Hill, Gaines' Mill,
Second Bull Run, Antietam, Fredericksburg, Chancellorsville,
Gettysburg, Rappahannock Station, Mine Run, Wilderness,
Spottsylvania, North Anna, Tolopotomy, Bethesda Church, and
Weldon Railroad, as a class the most severe that occurred dur-
ing the war, are included in his brilliant record. At Gettysburg

he escaped unharmed, though repeatedly struck by musket-balls in his equipments and clothing; but at the battle of Weldon Railroad he fell a prisoner into the hands of the enemy, and was conveyed to Salisbury, N.C., where he died Nov. 5, 1864, at the early age of twenty-two years.

Bravery and fidelity were prominent characteristics of young Breen, and he was often detailed for service where these qualities were indispensable. His death was a deep sorrow to relatives and friends, who saw in him the promise of a noble manhood and a career of honor and usefulness.

DANIEL HORACE BURR.

Private in Co. K, Eleventh Regiment, M. V. I.; killed at the battle of Gettysburg Pa., July 2, 1863.

Daniel Horace Burr, the only son of Daniel and Lucy Lane (Andrews) Burr, was born in Hingham, Feb. 19, 1838. Residing at Dorchester, Mass., where he worked at his trade of a wheelwright when the war broke out, he enlisted in April, 1861, for three years; and June 13, was mustered as private in Co. K, of the Eleventh Regiment, M. V. I.

He participated in all the engagements of the regiment during his connection with it; including the first battle of Bull Run, Yorktown, Williamsburg, Fredericksburg, Chancellorsville, and Gettysburg.

In the engagement at Williamsburg, May 5. 1862, he received a wound in his thigh which disabled him for duty. He was removed to Chesapeake Hospital, Fortress Monroe, and remained there until the middle of June, when, to make room for other patients, he was sent to Dorchester.

Rejoining his regiment in September, he faithfully performed the duties required of a soldier, until he fell at Gettysburg.

The colonel of the regiment, in a communication to Gov. Andrews, said, " Daniel Horace Burr died like a true soldier, with his face to the foe."

His body was never recovered.

JAMES THOMAS CHURCHILL.

Private in Co. G, Thirty-ninth Regiment, M. V. I., died at Andersonville Prison, Ga., June 23, 1864, aged twenty-three years.

> " Oft o'er that fair and sunny clime the gale hath borne
> The sighs of exiles never to return."

James Thomas Churchill, the eldest son of James and Cynthia (French) Churchill, was born in Hingham, May 9, 1841.

Leaving his employment of painter and glazier to join the first quota of Hingham, he enlisted Aug. 11, 1862, under recruiting-officer Edward Cazneau, and was mustered at Lynnfield, Sept. 2, as private in Co. G of the Thirty-ninth Regiment, M. V. I.

The regiment left Massachusetts early in September for Washington, D.C., and during a part of the year following was engaged in guard and picket duty in the vicinity of the Potomac. July 26, 1863, it became a part of the first brigade, second division, First Army Corps.

When the Army of the Potomac fell back before the enemy, Oct. 11, 1863, young Churchill, being sick, was left behind with others to follow the next day; but during the night was taken prisoner near the Rapidan, and carried to Richmond, thence to Belle Isle, and subsequently to Andersonville, Ga.

Of delicate constitution, he was unable to endure exposure and privation, and early fell a victim to the harsh treatment to which during his prison-life he was subjected.

One of his Andersonville companions, in a communication to the relatives of the deceased, writes as follows : " We told him of his approaching dissolution ; and though he was too weak to move on his hands and knees, yet he was full of faith that he should live to reach home, and enjoy the society of his relatives and friends.

He left a widow, but no children.

THOMAS CHURCHILL.

Thomas Churchill, born in Hingham, Feb. 5, 1808, was a twin son of Jesse and Annie (Barrell) Churchill. While a lad he lived with Col. Joseph Cushing of this town; and afterwards with Mr. John Leavitt, of whom he learned the trade of pump and block maker. At a later period he removed to Boston.

In the summer of 1861, he enlisted for three years under Capt. Lewis N. Tucker of Boston, and Sept. 13 was mustered as private in Co. A of the Eighteenth Regiment, M. V. I., in which he served principally in the commissary department.

Before Yorktown, in the expedition under Gen. Stoneman, on the march, or in the camp, he filled acceptably the position assigned him.

At Harrison's Landing, Va., he was sick with diarrhœa, from which he died on the 7th of August, 1862, aged fifty-four years and six months.

JEREMIAH J. CORCORAN.

Private in Co. I, Lincoln Light Infantry, Fourth Regiment, M. V. I., three months. Private in Co. A of the Fortieth Regiment, M. V. I.; three years.

Private Jeremiah J. Corcoran resided on Fort-hill Street, and was one of the thirty-seven men who enlisted to fill the quota required for the Lincoln Light Infantry, and who left Hingham on the 18th of May, 1861, to join this company, then stationed at Fortress Monroe.

Aug. 23, 1862, he again entered the service, enlisting as private in Co. A of the Fortieth Regiment, M. V. I.; three years. During the autumn he was in the Department of the South; was present in the expedition to Kraivah and the Seabrook Islands; took part in the bombardment of Sumter and Wagner; and in the State of Florida was in the battle of Olustee and at Jacksonville.

He afterwards joined the Army of the James, was at Drury's Bluff, Bermuda Hundred, and afterwards in other engagements prior to that of Cold Harbor. Here on the 3d of June, in a determined, but sharply contested advance of the regiment on the enemy's lines, he was mortally wounded, and conveyed to the hospital, where, lingering till Friday, June 10, he died at twenty-eight years of age.

With the exception of Private Corcoran, the Fortieth Regiment contained few enlistments from Hingham. Of the severity of the service it is not necessary to speak. In South Carolina, Florida, and lastly in the Army of the James and the Potomac, engagements with the enemy were numerous and severe. Through all "Jerry" evaded no duty. His daring, almost reckless bravery constantly impelled him to the front. Fear to him was a stranger; and, be the situation what it might, he was one of the last to yield.

"He was a good soldier," is the testimony of his comrades; and as such he fell in the cause of the Union.

NELSON FRANCIS CORTHELL.

Corporal in Co. A of the Eighteenth Regiment, M. V. I., died of wounds received at the second battle of Bull Run, Va., Aug. 30, 1862, aged twenty-four years, five months.

> "No pomp, no funeral rites, no weeping eyes,
>   To grace thine obsequies."

Nelson Francis Corthell, the eldest son of Nelson and Margaret (Overton) Corthell, was born in Hingham, April 1, 1838. He was a cooper by trade. Leaving his employment to respond to the call for troops, he enlisted under Capt. Lewis N. Tucker of Boston, and was mustered at Camp Brigham, Readville, Aug. 27, 1861.

Mr. Corthell participated in all the marches, privations, and exposures of the regiment. During the siege of Yorktown, he was constantly under the fire of the enemy's batteries.

At the second battle of Bull Run, Mr. Corthell was fatally wounded during a charge made by the regiment. His comrades made an effort to remove him to a place of safety; but the repulse of our forces obliged them to abandon the undertaking. The next day search was made for the body by private William W. Robinson of Hingham, and other members of Co. A, but without success.

He left a widow.

JOHN BROWN CREASE.

John Brown Crease, whose name is upon the Soldiers' and Sailors' Monument, son of Rev. Robert and Helen (Brown) Crease, was born at Leeth Lumsden, Scotland, May 26, 1839.

He came to the United States a few years prior to the commencement of the war, and soon found employment in Hingham. Possessed of a fine disposition and attractive manners, he rapidly made friends in the circle in which he moved. His strong religious tendencies and social nature, inherited from good family connections, and early nurtured by pious home influences, drew him towards good society in pursuit of social intercourse. While here he united with the Baptist Church by baptism; the pastor, Rev. Jonathan Tilson, being one of his most intimate and valued friends.

Shortly before the war, he went to Boston, where he made the acquaintance of Rev. Phineas Stowe and other distinguished men, and was an active member in the Young Men's Christian Association.

He joined the Twenty-second Regiment (Havelock Guards) at its organization, and was mustered as private in Co. A, Oct. 4, 1861. As a soldier of the army, as well as a follower of his religion, he was constant at the post of duty, and served faithfully.

He was taken sick with typhoid fever before Yorktown, and died at Bedloe's Island Hospital, New York Harbor, May 16, 1862, aged nearly twenty-three years. Some time after, his

43

remains were disinterred, and brought to Boston, where appropriate services were held. They were subsequently deposited in the Hingham Cemetery.

In addition to the foregoing, Rev. Jonathan Tilson of this town furnishes the following : —

"John Brown Crease was an only son. His father designed that he should follow the same holy calling as himself. He gave him the rudiments of the Greek and Latin and Hebrew languages. But his father died when he was but thirteen years of age, leaving him and his widowed mother and two younger sisters, to the care of a kind Providence.

He was the *great grandson* of John Brown of Haddington, whose able writings are circulated in all parts of the Christian world.

This fatherless boy came to this country, to seek a fortune for himself and the dependent ones of the family. After spending a short time in the city of New York, he came to Hingham, and lived here for a few years. During this time he made a public profession of religion, and united with the Baptist Church in this place.

He was distinguished for his Christian principles and consistent life. He was active and useful as a soldier of Christ at all times. One of his regiment says of him, "He was never known to do any thing he thought to be wrong, and he was the means of doing much good in the army ; and some were induced to become Christians through his faithful labors."

In his regiment he was called "*the little gospel*," he was so upright and so free from the vices of camp-life. But few gained such a victory as did this young man in our late war. The manner of his life and labors and death has been a great comfort to his deeply afflicted mother and sisters. He has a noble record, and died in a good cause. "*He fought a good fight,*" and has received his crown. His remains now repose in our beautiful cemetery, and his memory is fondly cherished by many who knew him and loved him when in life."

DAVID W. CUSHING.

The remains of this soldier repose in the cemetery at Fort Hill ; and although not on the quota of Hingham, his former residence at the West End of the town, where he was employed as stitcher, renders a notice of him here not inappropriate.

He enlisted at Weymouth, and was mustered, Aug. 19, 1862, as private in Co. H of the Thirty-fifth Regiment, M. V. I. Proceeding immediately to the seat of war, he was killed by a shell in the battle of Antietam on the 17th of September following.

Private Cushing was born in Weymouth, Dec. 8, 1831. His parents were Mager, and Susan (Cook) Cushing.

He left a widow and two children.

JACOB GILKEY CUSHING.

Member of Co. I, Lincoln Light Infantry, Fourth Regiment, M. V. I., three months ; corporal in Co. D. Thirty-second Regiment, M. V. I., three years ; wounded at Laurel Hill, May 12, and died, May 14, 1864.

Corp. Jacob Gilkey Cushing was the only son of John and Harriet Jacob (Gilkey) Cushing, and was born in Hingham, Oct. 8, 1836. At the outbreak of the war, he was a regular member of the Lincoln Light Infantry, and with this body was among the first to take the field for the defence of the Union. After returning from the three months' service at Fortress Monroe, he enlisted, Dec. 27 of the same year at Fort Warren.

In the Army of the Potomac, with the Thirty-second, he was present in the engagements at Antietam, Fredericksburg, Chancellorsville, Gettysburg, Rappahannock Station, and lastly in the bloody struggle at Laurel Hill. Here, on the 12th of May, the regiment was ordered to make a bayonet charge on the enemy. The advance was in a single line, exposed to a destructive fire of musketry and artillery. Corp. Cushing was color-guard, always a position of peculiar peril, and one demanding a large degree of true courage and heroism.   Such a soldier could not be insensible to the fact, that he —

> " Who bears the standard on the battle's tide,
>   Oft bears it in his shroud."

In the carnage that attended the disaster of the day, he fell mortally wounded, and was taken to the camp hospital, where he survived until May 14, when he died at twenty-eight years of age.

His loss was great to parents and friends at home, as well as to comrades in the field.   As a citizen, he bore a character of the strictest integrity; as a son, he was dutiful and exemplary; while as a soldier, he was equally faithful, brave, and patriotic.

The father, with that genuine, consistent, heartfelt devotion to the cause of liberty and universal freedom, a cause which through life had never ceased to be his earnest hope and labor, " kept not back" in the trying hour, but gave for the sacrifice what most he loved and prized.

An only son, a soldier, for his country he fell.

> " Patriot. — lay thy weapon down,
>   Quit the sword, and take thy crown."

WILLIAM BRADFORD CUSHING.

Private in Co. D of the Twenty-second Regiment, M. V. I., three years; died Aug. 8, 1862.

William Bradford Cushing, the youngest son of Laban and Alice (Ferguson) Cushing, was born in Hingham, Aug. 16, 1836.   On the 6th of September, 1861, he enlisted at Boston, and after spending a few weeks in camp at Lynnfield, Mass., left for the seat of war, arriving at Washington on the 11th of October.

The winter was spent at Hall's Hill, Va., and preparations

for hostilities were commenced early in the following spring. The year proved an eventful one. At Alexandria he was engaged in provost-duty, and thence embarked for Fortress Monroe; took part in the reconnoissance towards Big Bethel, and was also in the engagement in front of Yorktown, when being detailed for picket-duty, he was among the first of the troops to enter the works and town just deserted by the enemy, and to plant therein the Stars and Stripes of the United States. He next left for West Point, Va., and from thence, *via* White House Landing, Gaines' Mill, and Hanover Court House, took up his weary march towards Richmond.

After the skirmish at Hanover Court House, he was detailed as teamster, and was employed in this capacity up to the month July. While in camp at Harrison's Landing, he was sick and disabled; and, after a sickness of one week, died of typhoid fever at this place, on the 8th of August as before stated, aged twenty-six years.

Scarcely a year in service, and just entering on the full strength and vigor of manhood, he was thus early removed by death, — death from disease, but death for the defence of his country. He left a widow and son.

ANDREW JACKSON DAMON.

Andrew Jackson Damon enlisted in Hingham, under recruiting officer, Edward Cazneau, Aug. 8, 1862. He was from Scituate (son of John C. and Polly (Mayo) Damon), and was born in that town, June 14, 1843.

A mason by trade, he left a good employment to join the Union army. Young Damon came forward at a time when enlistments were slow, and when the prospect of obtaining a sufficient number of men to avoid a draft in this town was far from promising. Accepted as a recruit by the proper officials, he was mustered into the U. S. service, Sept. 2, as private in Co. G of the Thirty-ninth Regiment, M. V. I., and accredited to the quota of Hingham. The regiment arrived at Washington, D.C., Sept. 8, and was immediately ordered to an important duty near the Potomac River.

But the change of climate and the exposures of camp-life soon brought disease to many of our soldiers, young Damon being among the number. Without witnessing the clash of 'arms, or having suffered to any extent from long marches or military discipline, he became a victim to diarrhœa soon after leaving Washington; and the 10th of October, 1862, about five weeks after leaving Boston, he entered the hospital at Seneca Mills. Thence he was removed to Muddy Creek Hospital, Oct. 17, 1862; next to Patent Office Hospital, Washington, D.C., Nov. 5; and then to Continental Hospital, Maryland, Nov. 24, 1862. Subsequently, he was at convalescent camp; afterwards at Kalorama Hospital, and thence sent back to convalescent camp, April 5, 1863.

July 31, 1863, he was discharged from the U. S. service at Boston for disability, and the record says, died at Scituate, of consumption. Thus was a young life given for the preservation of the Union as really as though it had been sacrificed after many years of hard service.

In the cemetery at North Scituate, a small marble stone bears the following inscription : —

ANDREW J. DAMON,

30TH REGT., MASS. VOLS.,

DIED

Oct. 27, 1863.

ÆT 20 YRS.

———

A SOLDIER'S GRAVE.

WILLIAM DUNBAR, Jun.

William Dunbar, jun., son of William and Sarah W. (Groce) Dunbar, was born in Hingham Nov. 2, 1828.

Being employed as a farmer in Scituate, he enlisted upon the quota of that town, for three years, as private in Co. K, Seventh Regiment, M. V. I., June 15, 1861 ; discharged on account of disability, March 17, 1862; re-enlisted in Co. A, Thirty-fifth Regiment, M. V. I., and mustered Aug. 9, 1862.

Mr. Dunbar shared the duties of the regiment while serving with the Ninth Army Corps in East Tennessee, through the severe weather and dearth of food that followed the siege of Knoxville. The history of the regiment during his connection with it is an eventful one, and doubtless his personal experience was extensive and interesting ; but it is almost entirely involved in obscurity, no friend or relative being able to communicate the facts of his toil, hardships, and dangers.

He died of wounds received at the battle of Weldon Railroad, Aug. 19, 1864, aged thirty-five years, nine months.

HELEN AURELIA DYER.

It would be ingratitude were the name and services of this self-sacrificing and truly patriotic young lady omitted in our record of the heroic dead. She was the eldest daughter of Rev. E. Porter Dyer, formerly pastor of the Congregational Church at Hingham, and was born at Stowe, Mass., March 17, 1844.

Her father having removed to this town in 1847, she was for several years a pupil in one of the schools at South Hingham, but finished her education in the high school at Medford, of which her uncle was principal. On returning home, she taught a private school at South Hingham, where she will be remembered by all who knew her for her happy disposition, her gentle demeanor, and the sweet Christian spirit she manifested in all her intercourse.

In 1852 her oldest brother, who had been sent to South Carolina by the Freedmen's Aid Society, and was employed by the government as superintendent of abandoned plantations and contrabands on Port Royal Island, had gathered a school on the plantations; but finding his active duties so burdensome that he could not give proper attention to his pupils, he suggested to his sister to come and take charge of the school.

The Freedmen's Aid Society was calling for help of this kind; and though the remuneration offered was scarcely more than enough to furnish the necessaries of life, yet Miss Dyer gladly accepted the suggestion; and, before her brother was aware of her decision, he was informed of her arrival in Beaufort. She immediately took up her residence on the plantation with her brother, where, outside the picket-lines that guarded the town of Beaufort, and amid many discomforts and even dangers, and with very little society, save that of her poor colored *protégés*, she taught her little school for several months.

After the removal of her brother to the army post-office at Hilton Head, she received an invitation to teach in a larger school of colored children in the town of Beaufort. Her success in this work was only equalled by the delight she felt in its prosecution.

While on the plantation she became acquainted with Mr. B. N. Lee, paymaster in Gen. Saxton's civil department, and afterwards postmaster of Port Royal. This acquaintance ripened into an engagement; and in the autumn of 1864 Miss Dyer returned north to make preparations for marriage. She was married to Mr. Lee early in December, 1864, and Jan. 6, 1865, sailed from New York on her return to the South, by the steamer "Melville." This was just after Sherman's march through Georgia, and the government had assumed control of the steamers plying between New York and Port Royal. "The Melville" was an old, and, as it proved, an utterly unseaworthy vessel; but it was the only means of conveyance at the time, and delay seemed to offer nothing better. On the 7th of January, The "Melville" was struck by a heavy sea in a snow-squall, her quarter-bow was stove in, and at eleven o'clock of the next morning she went down, bride and husband, with a large number of passengers, who soon perished in the wintry waters. But one passenger and two or three of the crew were saved alive to tell the story.

Thus perished one of Hingham's fairest volunteers, who, though she bore no arms of conflict, yet "endured hardness as a good soldier" for the benefit of poor, down-trodden humanity.

RICHARD JAMES FARRELL.

Died in Hingham, of wounds and chronic diarrhœa, March 24. 1864, aged twenty-three years, two months, fourteen days.

Richard James Farrell was born in Dungarvan, County of Waterford. Province of Munster, Ireland, Jan. 10. 1841. His parents were Richard and Mary (Landers) Farrell.

After he came to Hingham with his parents, he attended the public schools of the town, and at a later period was in the employ of the Hingham Cordage Company. When the war broke out, he went to Boston with his associate, Michael Thompson, for the purpose of joining the regular army; and on the 10th of June, 1861, enlisted as private, and was mustered for five years, under J. Hartwell Butler, first lieutenant commanding Co. G. Second Regiment U. S. Artillery.

Concerning the personal experience of this soldier during the war, but little is known, except that he took part in the seven-days' fight, and was in McClellan's retreat on the Peninsula. Being wounded in the head, and afflicted with chronic diarrhœa, he was confined for some time in the hospital near White Oak Church, and from that place was discharged by reason of surgeon's certificate of disability, dated Dec. 8, 1862.

After returning to Hingham, he was sick and delirious till his decease. He was a man of fine disposition, and the officer commanding the company speaks of him, in his discharge papers. as bearing an excellent character.

14

PEREZ FRANCIS FEARING.

Private in Co. I of the Thirty-fifth Regiment, M. V. I., three years; died of wounds in Poplar Lawn Hospital, Aug. 15, 1864.

Perez Francis Fearing, son of Perez Lincoln and Margaret (Corthell) Fearing, was born in Hingham, Aug. 19, 1842. In August, 1862, he enlisted at Dover, Mass., and on the 16th was mustered into service. On the 14th of September he was engaged at South Mountain; Antietam followed. At the decisive moment of this great battle, he was called to aid in a charge upon the enemy, which, notwithstanding exposure to a most destructive cross-fire, was bravely carried through. In these two battles the loss of the regiment, in killed and wounded, was two hundred and sixty-seven.

Next came the battle of Fredericksburg, in which the position of the regiment was much exposed, and where the loss sustained was again heavy. In two months from the date of his first engagement, the number of killed and wounded in the Thirty-fifth was three hundred and twenty-seven.

In 1863 he shared in the privations and extended marches of the Mississippi Campaign. Kentucky, Tennessee, Ohio, Indiana, Illinois, Arkansas, Louisiana, and Mississippi were severally traversed during the year.

The taking of Jackson, the capital of Mississippi, was preceded by numerous and rapid marches. The weather was intensely warm, and many of the men were sun-struck, or disabled by heat.

From the time of the capture of the city of Jackson to the close of the year 1863, ever changing from one point to another throughout the South and West, his experience was one of peculiar trial and danger. He passed through Cumberland Gap, participated in the engagement at London Bridge, was besieged at Knoxville by Longstreet, relieved by Sherman, and afterwards, in the winter of 1863-4, at Blain's Cross Roads, East Tenn., suffered greatly from lack of food and clothing.

In March, 1864, he left Tennessee to rejoin the Army of the Potomac, and took part in the advance through the Wilderness

under Gen. Grant.   He was in the battles at Spottsylvania, North
Anna, Cold Harbor, and other localities on the rout to James
River, crossed the stream on pontoons June 15, and moved on
Petersburg.   Up to the 29th of July, he was employed at the
front in the construction of earthworks and batteries, often exposed to the fire of the besieged by day, and burying the dead
at night.   On the 30th, in an advance at the Mine explosion,
he was mortally wounded, and taken prisoner by the enemy, who
conveyed him to Poplar Lawn Hospital, where he lingered till
Aug. 15, 1864, when he was released by death, having been in
the service two years.

The record of this young soldier has few parallels in our local
history.   In wearisome marches, suffering from intense heat in
summer, destitute of food and clothing, and exposed to the cold
of winter, continually in contact with the enemy, mortally
wounded almost at the moment of the final triumph of the great
cause he had endured so much to sustain, taken prisoner, helpless, and dying, and at last giving up his life surrounded by his
foes, the hand of war had scarcely more to add : his cup was full.

MICHAEL FEE.

Private in Co. F, Sixteenth Regiment, M. V, I., three years ; died
Sept. 26, 1863, at Stanton Hospital, of disease contracted in
the service.

Michael Fee was born in Ballinamore, Leitrim County, Ireland,
December, 1820.   His parents were Patrick and Rose (Dolan)
Fee.   Resided on Cedar Street, Hingham, at the time of entering
service.   Enlisted at Boston, Dec. 1, 1861, and was mustered the
January following.   Joining the regiment at Fortress Monroe,
he remained there until May, 1862, when the march was made
into Norfolk and Portsmouth, "the Sixteenth being one of the
first Union regiments which entered these cities.

On the 13th of June, he joined the Army of the Potomac, and
on the 18th the regiment sustained its first loss in a skirmish at

Fair Oaks. Peach Orchard, Malvern Hill. Second Bull Run. Fredericksburg, Chancellorsville, and other battles, followed, not omitting Gettysburg, where the loss of the regiment, in killed and wounded, was nearly one-third of the whole number engaged.

In the last battle he was wounded, and taken a prisoner to Richmond. After being exchanged, he was removed to Stanton Hospital at Washington, D.C., where he died of chronic diarrhœa, Sept. 26, 1863, aged forty-three years. He left a widow and six children.

JAMES FITZGERALD.

James Fitzgerald, or James Fitz as the name appears in a portion of the State papers, was born in Nova Scotia, in 1841. The father dying while the son was quite young, mother and child removed to Boston; and in 1854, when about thirteen years of age, the youth came to this town, where at South Hingham he served an apprenticeship with Mr. John Cushing, remaining with this gentleman until 1859.

June 10, 1861, close upon the opening of the war, he enlisted as private in Co. G of the Twelfth Regiment, M. V. I., three years; and on the 26th was mustered at Long Island, Boston Harbor. During the following year, he took part in some of the most noted battles which were fought during the rebellion. He was first engaged at Cedar Mountain, next at Second Bull Run, and lastly at Antietam, in the famous "Cornfield Battle," fought at that place on the 17th of September. The conflict was continued throughout the day; the scale of victory turning doubtfully, first to the one side, and again to the other, until Lee, pressed by the persistent courage and bravery of the loyal troops, was obliged to commence a retreat, and re-cross the Potomac.

In the prolonged struggle, both armies had suffered extremely. Among the seriously injured was the subject of this sketch, young Fitzgerald. A musket-ball had entered his leg; and thus disabled, he was removed to the hospital at Smoketown, where in the hope of arresting disease, and preserving life, he suffered amputation of the limb. No favorable results followed; and gradually sinking, he died at this place, Nov. 6, 1862, aged nearly twenty-one years.

The record left by this young soldier is a noble one. He was faithful, unflinchingly brave in seasons of greatest peril, was a general favorite, performed his duty to the end, and patriotically laid his life on the altar of his country.

CHARLES EDWIN FRENCH.

Charles Edwin French, the youngest son of Nathaniel and Lydia (Burrill) French, was born in Hingham, Aug. 2, 1842.

He enlisted for the quota of Hingham, and was mustered into service as private in Co. G, of the Thirty-ninth Regiment, M. V. I., Sept. 2, 1862. At the battle on the Weldon Railroad, he was taken prisoner with others of the regiment, and conveyed to Salisbury, N.C.; where, from the best information that can be obtained, he died Nov. 28, 1864, from privation and exposure, aged twenty-two years.

Young French was the third of the patriotic sons of this family who died in the service of their country.

HENRY CHUBBUCK FRENCH.

Sergeant in Co. G, Thirty-ninth Regiment, M. V. I.,; killed while a prisoner at Belle Isle, Va., Aug. 26, 1864, aged twenty-eight years, one month, twenty-six days.

"Yet another crime,
Another woe, must stain the Southern clime."

Henry Chubbuck French, the second son of Nathaniel and Lydia (Burrill) French, was born in Hingham, June 30, 1836. He was brother of the late Lieut. Nathaniel French of the Thirty-second Regiment, and also of the late Charles E. French of the Thirty-ninth Regiment, both of whom gave up their lives while in the service of their country.

Serg. French was a sailmaker by trade. Early in May, 1861, he joined the volunteers who went from Hingham to fill the ranks of the Lincoln Light Infantry, Co. I, Fourth Regiment, then at Fortress Monroe, Va. Returning with the company, July 24, 1861, he remained at home until August, 1862, when he again enlisted, and was mustered, Sept. 2, as sergeant in Co. G of the Thirty-ninth Regiment, M. V. I., three years.

He participated in all the engagements of the regiment, up to the time of his capture, viz.: Mine Run, Laurel Hill, North Anna, Bethesda Church, White Oak Swamp, Petersburg, and Weldon Railroad. With several comrades, including his brother Charles, he was taken prisoner in the last named battle, on the Weldon Railroad, Aug. 19, 1864, and carried to Libby Prison, where he was subjected to the wicked usage which characterized this notorious place of confinement. At the time of his capture, he was so enfeebled by disease, as to be scarcely able to walk, and in this condition was transferred with others across the River to Belle Isle.

He had been at this place but two or three days, when, tottering to his miserable quarters, the order was given him to move quicker. His weakness and bodily sufferings rendered it impossible to comply with this command. A boy sentry, represented as one of the most desperate fellows on guard, then raised his gun, and deliberately shot him through the heart. The position of the sentry was such that the prisoner's back was towards him, and he had, of course, no intimation of the horrid fate that awaited him. Thus foul murder finished what disease had begun; and the life of this brave young soldier was laid on the altar of his country under circumstances of the most cruel barbarity.

War in its best aspect is horrible enough. The falling of a soldier on the field of battle, amid whistling bullets and shrieking shells, is a scene sufficiently dreadful to contemplate; but the savage butchery of the unarmed and feeble, possessing neither means nor strength for resistance, with the avenues for retreat closed on every hand, furnishes an instance of human depravity which must be condemned throughout the civilized world.

By permission, the body of Serg. French was buried in another part of the island, under the supervision of his comrade and friend, Sergt. William Henry Jacob.

He left a widow and three children.

NATHANIEL FRENCH, Jun.

Nathaniel French, jun., the oldest son of Nathaniel and Lydia (Burrill) French, was born in Hingham, April 7, 1828. He was a painter and glazier by trade.

When the Lincoln Light Infantry was organized, Oct. 9, 1854, he joined the company as private ; and May 18, 1857, was promoted corporal ; Aug. 21, 1860, sergeant ; and April 19, 1861, was commissioned second lieutenant.

On the breaking out of the war in 1861, he took an active part in obtaining volunteers to fill the ranks of the company ; and partly through his energy and popularity, it was enabled to respond so promptly, and in point of number so creditably, to the call issued by the governor of the Commonwealth.

At Fortress Monroe, Lieut. French shared in the general experience of the company.

Shortly after, returning to Hingham, he opened a recruiting-office in Oasis Hall, for the purpose of obtaining recruits for a company in Boston.

Nov. 16, 1861, he was commissioned second lieutenant of Co. A, First Battalion, M. V., then stationed at Fort Warren ; and March 7, 1862, was promoted to first lieutenant. Subsequently, May 25, 1862, the battalion was ordered to Washington,

D.C., and was afterwards known as the Thirty-second Regiment. With the change of organization, he was assigned to Co. D ; and at Capitol Hill, Alexandria, Fairfax Seminary, &c., he performed all the duties of his position with efficiency and zeal.

To a pleasing address, and thoughtful care of those under his charge, he added abilities, which, had he lived, would undoubtedly have insured him further promotion.

While in camp near James River, Harrison's Landing the last of July, he was attacked with intermittent fever, and removed to the General Hospital early in August.

From a letter written by the captain of Co. D to a near relative, we make the following extract.

HARRISON'S LANDING VA., Aug. 9, 1862.

DEAR MADAM, — Lieut. French is no more. He died this morning about ten minutes before one o'clock at the General Hospital. He received all possible medical attendance, and the best of nursing. His last few days were clouded in delirium ; and he did not seem to realize his situation or recognize those who faithfully watched over him. He died like one going to sleep, without a struggle. His body will be embalmed, and sent to Boston by express, directed to the care of Gov. Andrew. I need not say to you, that the loss falls heavily upon me and my command, as he was beloved as a brother by the officers of the company. The regiment has lost one of its most efficient men. His life was given to his country, and his name will ever be revered as one of the many who have fallen in this mighty struggle. In behalf of his comrades, I tender you and his surviving relatives and friends our sincere sympathy, ever mourning the loss and cherishing the memory of a brave officer and kind friend.

[Signed]   JAMES P. DRAPER,
          Captain Co. D, Thirty-second Regiment, M. V. I.

The remains of Lieut. French were brought to Hingham for interment ; and appropriate services were held on Sunday afternoon, Aug. 17, 1862, first at the former residence of the deceased, and at a later hour in the meeting-house of the First Parish, Rev. Dr. Stebbins of Woburn, and Rev. Robert Collyer of Chicago, officiating. A large concourse of people was present to show their respect for the patriotism of the deceased, and to sympathize with the family in their bereavement.

A marble stone in the Hingham Cemetery bears the inscription, —

IN MEMORIAM.

LIEUT. NATHANIEL FRENCH, Jr.

CO. D. 32D REG., MASS. VOLS.

DIED AT

HARRISON'S LANDING, VA.

AUG. 9, 1862.

AGED 34 YEARS 4 MONTHS.

HIS COUNTRY CALLED, HE OBEYED

GEORGE DOANE GARDNER.

Aug. 9, 1862, enlisted at Hingham as private in Co. G of the Thirty-ninth Regiment, M. V. I., three years, and was mustered Sept. 2, 1862 : died Aug. 4, 1864.

George Doane Gardner was the son of Enoch Whiton, and Orra (Amadon) Gardner, and was born in Boston, Mass., Aug. 27, 1828.

Mr. Gardner entered the service in August of 1862, a time when the real magnitude of the conflict began to be realized; and during the two following years shared in the privations and exposures, as well as in the numerous engagements, allotted to this portion of the army. At Brock Pike, Mine Run. Laurel Hill, Spottsylvania, North Anna, Bethesda Church, and in all the prominent battles before Petersburg up to the 20th of July, he was present, and took part. A few days after this date, being taken severely ill, he was conveyed to the Fifth Corps Hospital, at City Point, Va., where he died of inflammation of the bowels, aged thirty-six years.

He is commended by his companions in arms as one who never evaded a duty, and as being a true soldier.

45

JOHN WILLIAM GARDNER.

First, private in Co. I, First Regiment, M. V. I., three years;
second, in the Navy on board gunboat "Hartford;" third,
private in Co. I of the Twelfth Regiment, Maine Vol. Inf.,
three years; died at New Orleans, June 24, 1863.

John William, more familiarly known as William, Gardner,
was the youngest son of Hosea and Sophia (Cole) Gardner, and
was born in Hingham, Aug. 17, 1820.

He entered the service May 24, 1861, and was among the first
of the three-years' men who left the State, as he was also
among the first in the service of the United States. Leaving
camp on the 15th of June, he reached Baltimore on the 17th,
and marched through the city; Col. Cowdin's regiment being
the first that had passed through the place since the attack on
the Sixth Regiment on the memorable 19th of April. At
Washington they were reviewed by the president.

" On the morning of the 17th of July, orders were received to
make an advance for the purpose of attacking the enemy. The
battle of Bull Run followed in the afternoon. Detailed as
"pioneer" on the occasion, the duties of this exposed and truly
perilous position were well performed. Referring to the disas-
ters of the day, it was remarked that "the Massachusetts
First, from the beginning to the end, bore itself gallantly; and,
if all had done equally well, a different result would have
happened."

On the 19th and 20th he was engaged with the enemy; and
on the 22d was one of the rear-guard that covered the army in
its retreat to Washington. A service so active soon induced
disease, and finally disability, for which he was discharged,
Sept. 2, 1861.

Dec. 14, 1861, with the partial return of health, he shipped in
the U. S. Navy, at Boston, as seaman, and was assigned to
the U. S. steamer "Hartford," twenty-two guns, and on board
this vessel sailed to join the Gulf squadron.

On the 3d of February, 1862, the "Hartford" left Hampton
Roads for the mouth of the Mississippi River, under command
of Flag-officer Farragut, and Feb. 20 arrived at Ship Island.

From the 16th to the 25th of April, he shared in the bombardment and passage of Forts Jackson and St. Philip, and the capture of New Orleans, during which the "Hartford," while accidentally aground, was set on fire by a fire-raft, and was struck thirty-two times by shot from the guns of the enemy.

June 28, 1862, took part in the passage of the Vicksburg batteries, going up the river; and on the 15th of July was present in a like engagement at the same point on the passage down, attacking also the rebel ram " Arkansas."

In the autumn of 1862, being enfeebled and almost disabled by severe rheumatism, he left the "Hartford" while at New Orleans, and for the second time entered the land service, enlisting in the Twelfth Maine Volunteer Infantry, as before stated.

In January, 1863, this regiment was stationed at Plaquemine, a small town on the west bank of the Mississippi, about a hundred miles above New Orleans. The New Hampshire Eighth, happening to halt at this place, Col. Hawkes Fearing states that he was agreeably surprised to meet and take by the hand the subject of this sketch. Neither age nor the vicissitudes of war had done much to change the man; and his form and manner awakened recollections of youthful days, and pleasant scenes at home in younger years. It was probably his last interview with one of his fellow-townsmen. Disabled by disease, he was removed to the St. James Hospital at New Orleans, where his death took place from chronic diarrhœa, June 24, 1863, aged forty-two years.

He was unmarried. Much of his early life was spent as seaman. During the war with Mexico, though not in the regular service of the United States, which he never entered except as a volunteer soldier in the civil war, he was employed in the quartermaster's department; and in the transportation of provisions and general supplies rendered important assistance, proving capable, faithful, and efficient.

While connected with the First Regiment, he " performed his duty well, fought well," and had the commendation of the officers generally, as being a good and brave soldier. His life,

varied and eventful, was closed in the service of his country.
Who thus dies, dies not in vain.

CALEB BEMIS GILL.

Died of consumption at Norris, Fulton County, Ill., April 24,
1867, aged twenty-seven years and ten months.

Caleb Bemis Gill, whose name is upon the Soldiers' and Sailors'
Monument. son of Dixon Lewis and Eliza (Fuller) Gill, was
born June 29, 1839, while his parents were temporarily residing
at Fitchburg, Mass.   They afterwards removed to Hingham, and
he was a pupil in our public schools.   At a later period he was
employed as clerk at Cincinnati, Ohio.

The family removed to Hagerstown, Ind., early in the year
1859 ; and Caleb enlisted at Richmond, in that State, Oct. 8, 1861,
and was mustered Oct. 10, as sergeant in Co. I, Fifty-seventh
Regiment, Indiana Foot Volunteers ; promoted second lieutenant
at Murfreesborough, Tenn., April 3, 1863.

Lieut. Gill was assistant quartermaster about two years, and
served on Gen. Wood's staff about one year.

He was in the battles of Fort Donelson, Stone River, Murfreesborough. Chickamauga, Lookout Mountain, and at the siege
of Vicksburg.

The disease that caused his death was the result of hardship
and exposure while in the service of his country.

He left a widow and one child.

ELIJAH B. GILL, Jun.

[From the Massachusetts Register of 1862.]

Elijah B. Gill, jun., was born in Hingham, Mass., April 24,
1833 : but had resided in Boston for several years.   When

the proclamation for troops was issued, he promptly came forward, and enlisted in Co. I, First Regiment of Massachusetts Volunteers, and was chosen a lieutenant of the company. He entered upon his duties with a patriotic pride and satisfaction, cheerfully sharing in the dangers and privations of a soldier's life.

A part of the regiment to which he belonged was engaged in the battle of Bull Run, in July, 1861; and his company was detailed, with others, for especial duty, on the 21st instant; and it was in the gallant discharge of this dangerous duty, that young Gill heroically fell, mortally wounded by a bullet through the breast. His comrades tenderly bore his body from the field, and buried it that night at Centreville, with feelings of keen sorrow for their loss, and regret that the body could not be conveyed to his native State.

. . . .

One of the officers of the regiment writes, "My recollections of him are of a pleasant nature. He was one of my favorites. In scenes of anxiety and danger, I learned his fine qualities, and contracted a strong friendship for him.

"His deportment was gentlemanly, his habits good, and, as an officer and soldier, he was kind and efficient. His men loved him, his officers esteemed him, and his memory will ever be cherished by his friends."

Lieut. Gill was the first native of Hingham whose life was sacrificed in the late civil war.

NATHANIEL GILL.

Nathaniel Gill, son of Leavitt and Susannah (Stowell) Gill, was born in Hingham, July 29, 1832.

After completing his studies in the public schools of this town, he learned the trade of carriage-painter, and at the time of enlistment was employed at his occupation in Boston.

Aug. 3, 1861, he joined the military band of the Eleventh

Regiment, M. V. I., and was mustered into the United States service as private.

During the battles of the Peninsula under Gen. McClellan, Mr. Gill served with his associates in carrying the wounded to the hospital from the different parts of the battle-field.

He was mustered out Aug. 8, 1862, by reason of an order from the War Department, dispensing with regimental bands.

In 1865, while residing in Boston, he became insane, and was sent to the Boston Hospital, and afterwards to the Taunton Lunatic Asylum, where he died Dec. 31, 1865, aged thirty-three years and five months.

EDWARD WELLES HALCRO.

Born in the city of Hamburg, Jan. 24, 1836. His parents were George Wright, and Annie (Wright) Halcro, both natives of Sunderland, Eng.

The death of the mother was soon followed by the death of the father, leaving Halcro an orphan six years of age. Returning to Sunderland, he remained there till 1857, when he emigrated to the United States, became a legal citizen, and resided in Boston.

Entering the Navy May 5, 1862, he was appointed acting master's-mate, and ordered to the United States steamer "Genesee," eight guns, attached to the North Atlantic blockading squadron, taking part in the memorable passage of the Port Hudson batteries on the night of March 17, 1863. The officers and crew of this vessel were especially commended for the service rendered on that occasion. The "Genesee" not only saved a large portion of the crew of the United States steam-frigate "Mississippi (burned), but also rescued the United States sloop "Richmond" from a like fate, after her engines had become disabled. Mr. Halcro is particularly mentioned by his commanding office in the official despatches.

Dec. 15, 1863, he was promoted acting ensign ; June 27, 1864, sent to Pensacola Hospital, where a board of medical examiners ordered him North to the hospital at Chelsea, Mass.

In September, having regained his health, he was sent on board the United States schooner "Ovetta," three guns, as executive officer attached to the South Atlantic blockading squadron.

May 19, 1865, ordered to the United States schooner "Sarah Bruen," two guns, went to New York, and was there detached, and granted leave. Dec. 26, 1865, received an honorable discharge.

Jan. 11, 1866, he was re-appointed acting ensign in the United States Navy, and ordered to the United States steamer "Idaho," then building at New York. On the 16th of June, 1866, he was ordered to the United States receiving-ship "New Hampshire," stationed at Norfolk, Va.

Feb. 6, 1867, his appointment was revoked, and he was sent to Norfolk Hospital, where he died of consumption, April 5, 1867. His remains were subsequently deposited in the cemetery at Hingham Centre. For some years prior to his decease, he resided in this town, and was esteemed for his strict integrity and consistent Christian character.

> "How deep the calm! The haven reached,
> Nor storms, nor fear of shipwreck, now are thine."

JAMES MADISON HASKELL.

Volunteer in the Lincoln Light Infantry, afterwards in Co. A, Thirty-second Regiment, M. V. I., three years.

Promoted first to corporal, second to sergeant. Wounded at Gettysburg, July 2, 1863, and died Aug. 26, 1863. aged twenty-six years.

Serg. James Madison Haskell, son of William and Rachel (Turner) Haskell, was born at Augusta, Me., in 1837. He early removed to Hingham, and was a resident here at the breaking out of the rebellion. On the 17th of April, 1861, he left town as a three months' volunteer, in the Lincoln Light Infantry; and in October following enlisted for three years, and joined the Army of the Potomac, sharing in the numerous as well as severe engagements allotted to the Thirty-second Regiment. At Gaines' Mill, Malvern Hill, Second Bull Run, Chantilly, Antietam, Fredericksburg, and Chancellorsville, he fought with manly courage, and escaped unharmed ; but in the terrible struggle at Gettysburg, he was wounded in both legs, and conveyed in a helpless condition to the general hospital. Here, after most intense suffering, he found partial relief through amputation of one of the limbs, but it was soon apparent that he had passed beyond the reach of human skill.

At one period of the war, six brothers of the deceased were enlisted in the service, actively engaged in the cause of freedom and the support of the Union.

Capt. George R. Reed speaks in the highest terms of his excellent qualities as a soldier. At the hospital he bore his misfortune with gentle resignation, and as a true Christian.

A dutiful son, kind brother and friend, he died universally esteemed and lamented.

ALBERT STANLEY HAYNES.

First, a volunteer in the Lincoln Light Infantry ; second, private in Co. G of the Thirty-ninth Regiment, M. V. I., three years. Wounded at Laurel Hill, May 8, 1864, and died the 11th of the June following, aged twenty-one years.

Albert Stanley Haynes was born in Hanover, Mass , September, 1843. His parents were John and Persis (Whiting) Haynes. At the beginning of the national struggle, and then but nineteen years of age, he enrolled his name as a member of the Lincoln Light Infantry, and was one of the thirty-seven men who left Hingham on the 18th of May, 1861, to fill the quota of this company, then stationed at Fortress Monroe.

While connected with the Army of the Potomac, he was called to no general engagement prior to 1864, a year most eventful in the history of the Thirty-ninth. The winter and early spring had been spent at the front. On the 6th of May the great struggle was fairly begun; and, for weeks after, one engagement followed another in rapid succession. They were the decisive battles of the rebellion.

At Laurel Hill, during a charge on the enemy's lines, young Haynes was unfortunately wounded in the foot by a musket-ball, and, being disabled, was conveyed to the Judiciary Square Hospital, Washington, D.C. Having been granted a furlough of thirty days, he returned to Hingham. Here his situation became critical, and finally hopeless. Amputation of a portion of the limb was followed by no favorable results; and he died from the effects of the wound, at the residence of Mr. Dexter Whiting, at South Hingham.

An orphan, without brother or sister, almost alone in the world, young Haynes early enlisted for the defence and support of the Union. His record has no blemish, and the pages of our history will contain few instances of greater fidelity or nobler heroism.

HIRAM WILLEY HENDERSON.

Enlisted in the town of Gray, Me., and was connected with the Twenty-fifth, and also with the Thirtieth Maine Regiments, both under Col. Fessenden. He entered the service as private, and was promoted corporal. Died of disease contracted in the service.

Corp. Hiram Willey Henderson, whose name is upon the Soldiers' and Sailors' Monument, was born in Boston, in March, 1826. His parents were Timothy B. and Nancy (Neale) Henderson.

After joining the army, he was with Gen. Banks on the Red River Expedition, and participated in all the engagements of the Thirtieth Regiment during the three years it was in the field.

His experience was long and severe, covering as it did a period of forty-five months. Escaping death and wounds, he was mustered out at the end of his term of enlistment in August, 1865.

Just before leaving the army, he was attacked by chronic diarrhœa; and returning to his family in the town of Gray, Me., he there died, on the 24th of March, 1866, at forty years of age.

The deceased was a brother of Mr. Samuel J. Henderson of this town, and for some years followed his trade at Hingham Centre, where he will be remembered by many early friends and associates.

DANIEL DUNBAR' HERSEY.

Private in Co. F, Thirty-second Regiment, M. V. I., died of chronic diarrhœa, at Weymouth, Mass., Oct. 15, 1862, aged thirty-nine years, two months, fifteen days.

Daniel Dunbar Hersey, son of Peter and Mary (Dunbar) Hersey, was born in Hingham, July 31, 1823. By trade he was a shoemaker, although he followed packeting between Hingham and Boston during some portion of his life. At the time of entering the service he resided at Weymouth, and was accredited on the quota of that town. He enlisted Feb. 14, and was mustered Feb. 19, 1862, at Fort Warren, as private in Co. F of the Thirty-second Regiment, M. V. I.

But little is known of the military life of this soldier, except that he was discharged at Fortress Monroe, Sept. 30, 1862, for disability. He was very ill and weak at the time of leaving the fortress; but a strong affection for his friends and home, and the desire to reach them before his death, kept up strength and spirit. On hands and knees, he started for the depot to take the departing train; but, failing in the attempt, a negro kindly bore him on his shoulders to the place of destination.

Mr. Hersey reached home a mere skeleton, too weak to relate any of his experience, and died in two or three days.

HOLLIS HERSEY.

Hollis Hersey, son of Nathaniel and Priscilla (Stodder) Hersey, was born in Hingham, May 3, 1833.

On the 15th of August, 1862, he enlisted at Readville, Mass., and Sept. 16 was mustered as private in Co. K of the Forty-third Regiment, for nine months. In the department of North Carolina, where the regiment spent its term of service, Mr. Hersey was present in the engagements at Whitehall, Kinston, and Goldsboro'; but afterwards, being sick and disabled, he was conveyed to the camp hospital, then near Newbern. Remaining here till the close of his term of enlistment, he returned with the regiment to Boston, and was mustered out July 30, 1863.

In feeble health he came to Hingham, where he hoped a change of scene, and the invigorating air of his native town, might restore his wasted strength and health. No permanent improvement, however, followed; and lingering till the 30th of August, 1865, he died of hemorrhage of the stomach, aged thirty-one years.

JOHN QUINCY HERSEY.

John Quincy Hersey, born in Hingham, Sept. 23, 1829, was a son of William, 2d, and Elizabeth Burbank (Tower) Hersey.

He was a laborer.

Enlisting in this town under Lieut. Lyman B. Whiton, he was mustered Dec. 17, 1861 at Camp Cameron, Cambridge, as private in Co. E, First Battalion Infantry, M. V., afterwards Thirty-second Regiment. Dec. 23 following, he joined the regiment at Fort Warren, and shared its marches and dangers.

Mr. Hersey was at Harrison's Landing, and in the battles of Second Bull Run and Antietam. But the heat of summer, an unhealthy climate, and the hardships of the soldier, were too much for his physical strength; and he gave his life a sacrifice on the altar of his country early in her days of need.

He died of chronic diarrhœa, at Judiciary Square Hospital, Washington, D.C., Nov. 28, 1862, aged thirty-three years and two months.

THOMAS HERVEY.

Thomas Hervey was from Charlestown, Mass., and enlisted for the first quota of Hingham. He was mustered as private in Co. I of the Thirty-eighth Regiment. M. V. I., Aug. 21, 1862, and was killed April 13, 1863, at Bisland, La. He was a currier by trade, and thirty-seven years of age.

ALEXANDER HITCHBORN.

Born in Hingham, 1822.

His parents were Alexander and Cinderilla (Gardner) Hitchborn. At the commencement of the rebellion, he was a resident of North Bridgewater (now Brockton), to which place he removed about the year 1854, and where he had established himself as a physician.

June 26, 1861, he enlisted in Co. F of the Twelfth Regiment Massachusetts Volunteer Infantry, and the same day was commissioned captain. Resigned, and received his discharge May 13, 1862.

Soon after enlisted, or was appointed, as assistant surgeon in the Seventh Infantry of the Regular Army. At the battle of Chancellorsville, he pitched his hospital-tent in the rear, not far from the " Brick House " mentioned in the records of that engagement. The army was just moving into the fight which resulted so disastrously to the Union forces, when he was stricken by a stray bullet, as is supposed, and fell instantly dead. He was buried on the spot.

Dr. Hitchborn, while in North Bridgewater, stood well as a

physician, and gave promise of attaining a high position in his profession. To this it is proper to add, that he was a genial companion, possessed a most tenacious memory, and was gifted with conversational powers rarely allotted to an individual. With the exception of an adopted daughter, he left no family.

ELIJAH HOBART.

[Communicated.]

Elijah Hobart, son of Caleb and Mary (Lincoln) Hobart, grandson of Caleb Hobart, a Revolutionary soldier, was born in Hingham, Oct. 4, 1821; died near Point of Rocks, Va., July 4, 1864.

Capt. Hobart received his early education in the public schools and Derby Academy of the town. At the age of fifteen he left home for Boston, to learn the art of engraving, and continued there five years after the expiration of his apprenticeship; then went to Plymouth, Mass., to make a copy on steel of Sargent's "Landing of the Pilgrims." After more than two years of constant labor, he completed the work, and in February, 1850, received a copyright. The work became quite celebrated, and is well known in our vicinity. In 1850 he removed to Albany, N.Y., and devoted his time and talents to the engraving of bank-notes till war spread its dark cloud over the land.

Soon after the outbreak of the rebellion, and when the country still needed volunteers, Capt. Hobart, in writing to his friends, said, "Our country is worth defending: I shall prepare to enter the army."

Being skilled in the use of the rifle, he at once set about recruiting a company of sharpshooters for Berdan's regiment, then forming.

The company was organized and accepted Nov. 9, 1861; but, in consequence of not being able to supply the requisite arms, the destination of the company was changed by order of the government, and was assigned the position of Co. B, Ninety-third Regiment New York Volunteers; and was included in Gen. Casey's division, to go to the Peninsula with Gen. McClellan.

Capt. Hobart continued in command of his company, sharing its duties and perils, at Lee's Mills, White House, and Williams-burg; was detailed for the destruction of government stores at the evacuation of White House, and to convey prisoners to Fortress Monroe and Fort Delaware.

He received an honorable discharge from the service of the United States, dated June 12, 1862, and took an important position in the Treasury Department at Washington, where he had the general superintendence of the engravings for the fractional currency issued by the government.

On the Fourth of July, 1864, with a party of friends, he started for a day's sail on the river, with the intention of going to Harper's Ferry; but when near "Point of Rocks," Mosby's battery opened fire on them. They immediately changed their course, and ran into a creek near by, the party escaping to the woods. Capt. Hobart stood on the prow of the boat, watching the battery, and said to a friend near by, "They have our range: jump, and I will follow." Before they could do so, five men, who had left the battery and crept through the woods to their rear, fired upon their unconscious victim. He was instantly killed.

Of Capt. Hobart's devotion to duty, one associated with him while in the army thus writes, "Through the Peninsular cam-paign, one of the severest of the war, he led his company with a courage and devotion that never faltered; and when exposure and hardship were thinning our ranks faster than the bullets of the enemy, his own health giving way, he only spoke words of encouragement and cheer to his men; and when he left the regiment, it lost one of its best and bravest officers."

Another writes, "I was the first to enlist in his company, and never knew a truer, braver, or better man; and our greatest loss, as a company, was when he left us."

In his native town, in consecrated grounds, with kindred and friends, he sleeps.

H. G. G.

EDWIN HUMPHREY.

Captain of Co. A, Eleventh Regiment, M. V. I.; killed at the battle of Gettysburg, Pa., July 2, 1863, aged thirty-one years, nine months, twenty-six days.

> "Come from the heat of battle, and in peace,
> Soldier, go home ; with thee the fight is won."

Edwin Humphrey, second son of Leavitt and Meriel (Stodder) Humphrey, was born in Hingham Sept. 6, 1831. He was educated in the public schools of the town, and afterwards learned the trade of carriage-maker in Boston. At the termination of his apprenticeship, he commenced business on Chapman Street; but in 1858 returned to Hingham, and opened a carriage manufactory on Summer Street, near Commercial Wharf.

When the Massachusetts Sixth was attacked in Baltimore, Capt. Humphrey felt it his duty to join the forces then recruiting for the preservation of the Union ; and the next day, (April 20) went to Boston and enlisted. He had previously been connected with the military of the State, and was well qualified from experience to assist in organizing and instructing the new recruits.

June 13, 1861, he was commissioned first lieutenant of Co. G, Eleventh Regiment, M. V. I., then in camp at Fort Warren, Boston Harbor.

Oct. 11, 1861, Lieut. Humphrey was promoted captain, and assigned to Co. A.

He shared in the general experience of the Eleventh in all its engagements, marches, and privations ; was present with his command, and took an active part, in the battles of First Bull Run, Yorktown, Williamsburg, Fair Oaks, Savage Station, Glendale, Malvern Hill, Bristoe's Station, Second Bull Run, Chantilly, Fredericksburg, Chancellorsville, and Gettysburg. In the first day's fight at Gettysburg (July 2, 1863), he fell mortally wounded. He had evidently been picked off for his bravery by the enemy's sharpshooters, as upon examination the body was found shot in four places. He died the following night, at the field hospital, and was buried on the battle-field. His remains were subsequently brought to Hingham for interment.

Capt. Humphrey was the first person from this town who enlisted upon our quota for three years. His former military experience, good judgment, and quiet, unassuming manner, made him a favorite in the regiment. He was not only respected as an officer, but loved as a friend and brother. The colonel of the regiment, in a communication written on the battle-field, said of the deceased, " We feel deeply our loss of a brave and meritorious officer. Kind and forbearing in disposition, gallant in action, he combined the qualifications of the commander and the gentleman."

His funeral services were held Sunday afternoon, July 19, 1863, first at the family residence, and afterwards at the Universalist Meeting-House. An appropriate sermon was preached by the pastor, Rev. John E. Davenport. Rev. Daniel Bowen of the Third Parish, and Rev. Jonathan Tilson of the Baptist Society, took part in the exercises. The occasion called together a large number of relatives and friends to pay the last tribute of respect to his memory.

He left a widow and two children.

A marble tablet, since erected in the Hingham Cemetery, bears the following inscription : —

EDWIN HUMPHREY

CAPT. OF CO. A, 11TH REG.

MASS. VOLS. BORN SEPT. 6, 1831.

FELL AT THE BATTLE OF GETTYSBURG, PA.

JULY 2, 1863.

A hero sleeps beneath this stone,
A patriot firm and brave.
Through thirteen battles he had passed
His country's flag to save ;
Four bullets pierced his mortal frame ;
He fell, but left an honored name.

WALLACE HUMPHREY

Private in Co. E, Thirty-second Regiment, M. V. I., killed at Cold Harbor, Va., June 3, 1864, aged twenty-seven years and nine months.

Wallace Humphrey, son of Joshua and Mary (Hudson) Humphrey, was born in Hingham, Sept. 2, 1836. He was by occupation shoemaker.

Joining the Thirty-second Regiment at Fort Warren, Boston Harbor, he was mustered Dec. 2, 1861, as private in Co. E. He re-enlisted as veteran Jan. 4, 1864, and was mustered the day following.

Soon after the second battle of Bull Run, private Humphrey being sick, was sent to the United States Hospital at David's Island, N.Y., where he remained about eight months. Rejoining his regiment in April, 1863, he was present at the battles of Chancellorsville, Gettysburg, Rappahannock Station, Mine Run, Wilderness, Laurel Hill, Spottsylvania, North Anna, Tolopotomy Swamp, Bethesda Church, and Cold Harbor. A portion of this time he was detailed for duty on the baggage-train.

At Cold Harbor the regiment charged the enemy, and took the first line of earth-works and rifle-pits. Sharp skirmishing followed at intervals through the day; and while firing over the earth-works near Old Church, private Humphrey was struck in the head by a ball from the rear, and mortally wounded. He lived but two hours. His remains were buried at night, on Brokenboll's Farm, near the church, and the grave designated by the name, company, and regiment of its occupant.

Mr. Humphrey was a good soldier, remarkably brave, attentive to duty, and had the esteem of his comrades, and the confidence of his officers.

He left a widow.

47

GARDNER JONES.

Private in Co. F, Thirty-second Regiment, M. V. I., died of wounds at Campbell Hospital, Washington, D.C., June 1, 1864, aged twenty-one years, four months, and twenty-one days.

> "Thou art where friend meets friend,
>   Beneath the shadow of the elm to rest;
>   Thou art where foe meets foe, and trumpets rend
>   The skies, and swords beat down the princely crest."

Gardner Jones, second son of William Henry and Elizabeth (Glover) Jones, was born in Boston, Mass., Jan. 10, 1843. While an infant his parents removed to Hingham, and he afterwards was a pupil at the public schools of the town.

Following the occupation of shoemaker at the time of entering the service, he enlisted under recruiting-officer Edward Cazneau, Feb. 13, 1862; and Feb. 19 was mustered at Fort Warren as private in Co. F of the Thirty-second Regiment, M. V. I., for three years.

To relate his experience is to repeat the history of the regiment; for wherever ordered, or however great were its exposures, young Jones was ever at the post of duty. A youthful, joyous, enthusiastic soldier, full of hope in the future, and without a thought of danger, he went marching on.

During the year 1862 he was with the regiment in the engagements at Antietam, Shepardstown Ford, and Fredericksburg.

In 1863 he took part in the following battles and engagements, viz.: Chancellorsville, Aldie Gap, Gettysburg, Rappahannock Station, and Mine Run; and in 1864 he participated in the battle of the Wilderness.

On the removal to Laurel Hill, May 10, 1864, while the regiment was endeavoring to establish a new picket-line, young Jones, with two others, volunteered to perform a perilous duty, and with one of his comrades was severely wounded. Prompt measures were taken to lighten his distress, and to make his situation as comfortable as possible. But the nature of his injury was such that the most skilful surgeons could afford but temporary relief; and his name was soon added to that long list of heroes who gave up their lives for the Union of the States.

The following letter dated, June 8, 1864, was received by the mother of young Jones : —

DEAR MADAM, — Circumstances have not permitted me to write you before this time in regard to your son. Gardner Jones, of my company, who was severely wounded in the thigh, May 10, in a charge of the regiment upon the enemy's rifle-pits.

He was at first sent to the hospital at Fredericksburg, thence to Washington. I did not suppose he was dangerously wounded.

To-day I have received the sad intelligence that he died of his wounds June 1, in Campbell Hospital, Washington, D.C.

He behaved most bravely in all the battles up to the time he was stricken down, and I had determined to promote him for his good conduct.

I deplore his sad fate, and sympathize with you in your great loss. With kind wishes for you as the mother of Gardner, I remain yours truly,

[Signed]   E. O. SHEPARD,

Capt. Co. F, 32d Mass. Vols.

He was buried at Washington, D.C.

WILLIAM HENRY JONES.

The names of three brothers, sons of Nathaniel French of Hingham, who lost their lives in the service of their country, will be found among the heroic dead. Another instance in which three persons were taken from one family by the ravages of war occurs in connection with the record here given.

William Henry Jones, the father of William Henry, jun., and Gardner Jones, and son of Samuel Jones, was born in Boston, Mass., March 23, 1816. For nearly thirty years before the war he had resided in Hingham, at the west part of the town, where he followed the occupation of bootmaker. He was highly esteemed by those who knew him most intimately, for his kindness of heart, his noble impulses, and his energetic and intrepid traits of character. For many years he was an efficient member of the fire-department in this town, and held various responsible positions in that sphere of duty.

Mr. Jones entered the United States service at Readville, under Capt. Benjamin F. Meservey, and was mustered Aug. 24, 1861, as private in Co. K of the Eighteenth Regiment, M. V. I., and accredited on the quota of Hingham.

He was with the regiment in the skirmishes before York-town, and in the expedition to White House under Gen. Stone-man. But rapid marches, and exposures to a summer's sun, induced disease; and on arriving at Harrison's Landing, July 2, 1862, he was sent to Hampton Hospital, at Fortress Monroe, from which institution he was discharged March 6, 1863, for disability.

With the quiet of home life came returning health; and Jan. 6, 1864, he re-enlisted, and was mustered as private in Co. C, Fourth Regiment of Cavalry, M. V. While in this arm of the service, in the Department of the South, he went with the expe-dition to John's Island, S.C., participating in the engagements and skirmishes of the 2d, 5th, 7th, and 9th of July. He also was at Pilatka, Fla., and in the expedition up Ashepoo River; but whether he took part in any subsequent battles or skir-mishes does not appear. The adjutant-general, in his report, says William Jones died of wounds, Sept. 19, 1864, at Magnolia, Fla.

He was forty-eight years and six months old at the time of decease, and left a widow and eight children, all of whom were then under sixteen years of age.

In a letter written to Mrs. Jones by the captain of Co. C, relating to the death of her husband, occurs the following: —

HEADQUARTERS Co. C, 4TH MASS. CAVALRY,
MAGNOLIA, FLA., Sept. 20, 1864.

MRS. JONES, — I regret that it is my duty to be the bearer of sad tidings to you Your husband, William H. Jones, died yesterday at one o'clock, of inflammation and ulceration of the bowels.

He was ill but two weeks; and it was only within the last few days that we supposed he was in a dangerous condition. An intimate friend from Hingham has attended him, and he had the best care and medical skill that could be procured. His last words and thoughts were about his family, and what they would do after his death.

We buried him under the shade of a live oak, near our camp; and I will see that a head-board and fence are erected there.

It will doubtless be a satisfaction for you to know that he always did his duty promptly and well, and that he was a man upon whom I could always rely under any circumstances. He also was a favorite among his comrades.

[Signed] Very respectfully, your obt. servant,

EDWIN B. STAPLES,

Capt. Co. C, 4th Mass. Cavalry.

WILLIAM HENRY JONES, JUN.

Sergeant in Co. K of the Eighteenth Regiment, M. V. I.; died at Washington, D.C., Feb. 12, 1864, aged 23 years.

> "Leaves have their time to fall,
>> And flowers to wither at the north wind's breath,
> And stars to set; but all,
>> Thou hast all seasons for thine own, O Death!"

William Henry Jones, jun., son of William Henry and Elizabeth (Glover) Jones, was born in Weymouth, Mass., Jan. 26, 1841.

In early life his parents removed to Hingham, and he attended the public schools of the town. Subsequently he was in the employ of Rev. Calvin Lincoln; and at a later period worked at the trade of tinman with Charles Gill.

In May, 1861, young Jones joined the Lincoln Light Infantry at Fortress Monroe, as a volunteer. Returning with the company, he followed his trade for a short time in Boston.

Serg. Jones was among the first of those who re-enlisted in the service for Hingham, having been mustered at Readville, Aug. 26, 1861, under Capt. Benjamin F. Meservey, as private in Co. K of the Eighteenth Regiment, M. V. I., for three years. Sharing in all the engagements, marches, and privations of the regiment during his connection with it, he was promoted corporal, and afterwards sergeant, for bravery and good conduct. He was an especial favorite, and a peacemaker among his comrades.

As was not often the case, father and son were for a time

serving in the same company; and the constant and respectful care shown by the son towards the father had a good influence throughout the regiment.

His bravery before the enemy was in keeping with his moral character. At the battle of Second Bull Run, he was ordered to the rear with a wounded officer. Their route led them past Gen. King's division, just at the time it was attacked by the Confederate forces. Requesting permission of the wounded officer to join the fight, he placed his charge under a tree, and went into the engagement with a strange regiment to assist in repulsing the attack. Acts like these were characteristic of this soldier-boy.

After participating in many hard-fought battles, viz.: Second Bull Run, Shepardstown Ford, Fredericksburg, Chancellorsville, Gettysburg, Rappahannock Station, and Mine Run, he was taken sick, and sent to the regimental hospital. For nearly three weeks his health continued to fail, and finally he was removed to Washington.

The following extract relating to his death is from a letter written to his mother by one of the hospital stewards : —

WASHINGTON, D.C., Feb. 14, 1864, Carver Hospital, Ward 16.

. . . Although he had some fever, we did not consider him dangerously ill. During Friday, the 12th, he spoke to me about the approaching expiration of his term of enlistment, and of his prospects of soon obtaining a furlough. Towards night, however, he seemed to be more feeble, and expressed a wish to see his mother. "There is not a day," he said, "but that she thinks of me." Shortly afterwards he complained of nausea, and, in attempting to rise, fell back, as we supposed from faintness. We sent for the surgeons at once ; but they could do nothing, and he never spoke or moved again. This was at twenty-five minutes past eight o'clock on the evening of Feb. 12.

[Signed] J. A. SHAW.

The remains of Serg. Jones were brought to Hingham for burial. His funeral ceremonies took place at the Universalist Church, Sunday afternoon, Feb. 21, 1864; Rev. John E. Davenport, the pastor, making the address, and Rev. Calvin Lincoln of the First Parish assisting in the introductory and closing exercises. It was expected that the body would arrive in time for these services; but in this the relatives and friends were disappointed. The father and brother of the deceased (both soldiers) were present at the time, on furlough; and it was on their account that the ceremonies were not postponed, as their time for being absent had nearly expired. The body of young Jones was afterwards buried in the cemetery at Fort Hill.

CHARLES DAMON KILBURN.

Corp. Charles Damon Kilburn, whose name is on the Soldiers' and Sailors' Monument, son of George Harris and Adeline (Damon) Kilburn, was born in Boston, June 22, 1839.

On the 5th of September, 1861, he enlisted at Boston as private in Co. B of the First Regiment, Mass. Cavalry, and was subsequently promoted corporal.

The year 1863 was spent in the Department of Virginia; and from the beginning to its close, one engagement followed another in rapid succession. At the battle of Chancellorsville, Va., May 2 and 3, he was orderly for Major-Gen. Berry at the time this officer was killed, and was also orderly for Major-Gen. Sickles at the battle of Gettysburg, Va., when Sickles received the wound which deprived him of his leg.

At the close of November, 1863, Corp. Kilburn was severely wounded, near Hope Church, Va., and immediately conveyed to McVeigh Hospital, Alexandria, where he died Jan. 4, 1864.

The following tribute to his bravery and fidelity is taken from a Boston daily of Jan. 9, 1864 : —

"Corp. Charles D. Kilburn belonged to the First Mass. Cavalry, and bravely bore his part in the duties performed by this admirable corps. He was wounded in the shoulder last November, and his demise was hastened by a second hemorrhage. He had three brothers in the service, and leaves many friends in this vicinity who mourn his death."

PARKER EMERY LANE.

Born in Hingham, Oct. 19, 1840. His parents were Joshua Leavitt and Eliza (Shaw) Lane. At the outbreak of the war, he was a regular member of the Lincoln Light Infantry, and, leaving Hingham on the 17th of April, was three months with the company at Fortress Monroe. On being mustered out, he returned to Weymouth, where for some years he had resided, and where, after a protracted sickness, he died of consumption, Dec. 10, 1869. He left a widow.

The following incident, among others connected with the departure of the Lincoln Light Infantry, is given in the military record of the State for 1862 : —

A member of the company, calling to see his friends, and bid them adieu, was entreated by an aged relative to remain at home. Turning a deaf ear to her appeals, a liberal offer of money, much in excess of any sum he might expect to receive for his services in the field, was added as a persuasive. Although few in the ranks were really in greater need, all availed nothing. His answer was, " No, I cannot take it. I am a member of the Lincoln Light Infantry, and they are called for the defence of the country: where they go, I go."

It is only necessary to add that the facts as given are correct; the hero of the story being young Lane, whose history is briefly sketched above.

BENJAMIN LINCOLN.

Benjamin Lincoln, son of Benjamin S. and Mary (Anderson) Lincoln, was born in Hingham, Sept. 29. 1835.

He was a tinsmith by occupation.

On the 6th of February, 1864, he enlisted as private in Co. G, Fourth Regiment of Cavalry, M. V., was mustered into service March 1, left for the seat of war with the regiment, and was in active service until the 6th of June ; when, being sick and unfit for duty, he was sent to the hospital at City Point, Va. ; afterwards transferred to the hospital at Portsmouth, Va.; and lastly to Portsmouth Grove, R.I.

Sept. 6, 1864, he received a furlough of thirty days, and returned to Hingham, where he had the professional services of Dr. R. T. P. Fiske.

Shortly before the expiration of the furlough, his physician pronounced him too unwell to travel; and, believing he had the requisite authority, granted an extension of the time allowed. This act, though well intended, proved the cause of much anxiety and suffering for Mr. Lincoln. The second day after the expiration of his original furlough, he was waited upon at his home by a messenger from Major Clark of the Fourth Cavalry, and ordered to report at headquarters *forthwith.* Complying with this demand, he was retained at the office of the provost-marshal in Boston one day and night; was then taken without a hearing, and placed in a cell beneath the Court House, where, without food or bedding, he remained for nearly three days. At the end of this time he was returned to the hospital at Portsmouth Grove, and confined for seven days in the guard-house, suffering severely, and receiving daily visits from the surgeon. At the expiration of the week, he was ordered to report to the ward in the hospital, and there remained until released on a furlough for the purpose of attending the November election. Returning to the hospital, and being yet in feeble health, he was put upon light duty.

Dec. 26, 1864, Mr. Lincoln was sent to Gallop's Island, Boston Harbor, and Feb. 9, 1865, to Fortress Monroe. From this place he was conveyed to Bermuda Hundred, and after two days returned to the Distributing Barracks at Hampton.

March 9, 1865, he joined his company at Williamsburg, and remained with it until the 26th of November, when he was mustered out of service.

Mr. Lincoln came back to Hingham bearing the seeds of disease, which soon developed in the form of consumption. After a protracted and painful illness, which was patiently endured, he died March 29, 1866, aged thirty years and six months.

48

BENJAMIN CURTIS LINCOLN.

Major of the Second Regiment, United States Colored Infantry, died of wounds received in battle at a place called "Natural Bridge," between St. Marks and Tallahassee, Fla., March 9, 1865.

> " Now lies he low, no more to hear
> The victor's shout or clashing steel ;
> No more of war's rude cares to bear,
> No more kind sympathy to feel.

Benjamin Curtis Lincoln, son of Alfred and Mary Lee (Curtis) Lincoln, was born in Hingham, Aug. 12, 1840. Relinquishing a good situation to respond to the call for troops, he enlisted in Boston, Aug. 7, 1862, and was mustered Sept. 2, for three years, as private in Co. G of the Thirty-ninth Regiment, M. V. I. ; promoted corporal, Jan. 15, 1863; released from duty with the regiment, July 14, 1863, and ordered to report to Major-Gen. Silas Casey, U. S. V., commanding provisional brigades at Washington, D.C. ; honorably discharged July 31, 1863, to accept an appointment as captain of Co. B, Second U. S. Colored Infantry ; and July 20, 1864, commissioned major of the regiment.

While in the Massachusetts Thirty-ninth, he was detailed as clerk, and served in that capacity a large part of the time.

With the Second United States colored troops, stationed first at Ship Island, and subsequently at Fort Taylor, Key West, Fla., Major Lincoln devoted nearly every leisure hour at his command to the improvement of the men, teaching them to read, to write, and the use of money. At Key West he was attacked with yellow fever ; and, while many officers died of the disease, he lived, to fall afterwards on the field of battle.

A correspondent of "The Boston Journal," writing from Key West under date of March 12, 1865, closes an account of the engagement between the Union forces under Brig.-Gen. Newton, and a large body of the enemy commanded by Major-Gen. Smith, as follows : —

" We regret to say that the loss among officers is very heavy in proportion to the men.

" Major Lincoln was struck by a shell about noon of the 8th, and lingered to the 9th, when he expired. He was formerly in the employ of Haughton, Sawyer, & Co., of Boston, and had worked his way up from the ranks by untiring energy, intelligence, and force of character. He excelled as a disciplinarian, was thoroughly pure in his morals, and was ambitious as well as courageous. Major Lincoln is worthy to stand among the very few of New England's choicest sons who from principle have laid down their lives in battle. He had, it might be said, no faults ; and surely he had no enemies but his country's. His men loved him with unsurpassed devotion ; and his kindly, unselfish, and Christian character endeared him to all.

" His life was indeed a costly sacrifice."

DANIEL STODDER LINCOLN.

Daniel Stodder Lincoln, son of Daniel and Priscilla (Cain) Lincoln, was born in Hingham, July 8, 1841. He was a descendant of Serg. Daniel Lincoln, one of the early settlers of the town.

Shortly after the Lincoln Light Infantry arrived at Fortress Monroe, young Lincoln enlisted with the volunteers who went from Hingham to fill the ranks of the company, and was mustered into service May 18, 1861. Mustered out with the company, July 22, 1861.

In 1864, Aug. 1, he shipped in the United States Navy at Boston, as second-class fireman, for one year, and was sent on board the U. S. receiving ship " Ohio." From this vessel he was transferred to the U. S. iron-clad " Monadnock," for duty during her trial trip, after which he returned to the " Ohio."

Sept. 15, 1864, he was sent on board the U. S. supply steamer

"Connecticut," and in her made the trip from Boston to Mobile, stopping at Hilton Head, Key West, Pensacola, and intermediate ports, to leave supplies and mails for the different ships stationed at these points. Returning in about six weeks, he was again ordered to the "Ohio."

Nov. 1, 1864, transferred to the U. S. steamer "Iuka," seven guns, then fitting out at Boston for the East Gulf blockading squadron, where she went, and was employed in cruising from Key West to Havana, along the coast of Cuba and Mexico, up as far as the Rio Grande and return.

March 18, 1865, he was rated first-class fireman, and June 15, 1865, was discharged at Boston by reason of close of the war.

During the time young Lincoln was in the Navy, he filled his position so completely as to gain the approbation of those in command, and receive promotion.

Upon returning home after the war, he was employed as shoemaker, until stricken with scarlet fever. In his anxiety for the sufferings of another, he contracted this disease, and died May 28, 1869, aged twenty-seven years, ten months, twenty days.

He left a widow and one son.

LEAVITT LINCOLN.

Sergeant in Co. I, Sixty-first Regiment Illinois Volunteers; died at the general hospital, Duval Bluffs, Ark., Dec. 7, 1864, aged forty-one years, nine months.

Leavitt Lincoln, third son of Jotham and Meriel (Hobart) Lincoln, was born in Hingham, March 2, 1823. After completing his studies at school, he went to Boston, and was employed for some time in the store of Gedney King, mathematical instrument maker. Returning to Hingham, he learned the trade of printer, and worked with Jedediah Farmer, and also with William W. Wilder, in "The Hingham Patriot" office. He was next in New York, following his occupation, and afterwards removed to Wisconsin; thence he went to Pike's Peak, and at a later period came to Chicago, Ill., where he was employed in a printing-office when the war broke out.

He enlisted in Chicago, Dec. 27, 1861, for three years, and was mustered March 7, 1862, as private in Co. I, Capt. H. S. Goodspeed, of the Sixty-first Regiment Illinois Volunteers ; promoted sergeant Sept. 1, 1862.

Serg. Leavitt Lincoln was present, and took an active part, in the battle of Pittsburg Landing ; his regiment losing nearly five hundred in killed, wounded, and missing. He afterwards participated in other engagements, and shared the rough experience of a soldier's life until stricken by disease. His term of service had nearly expired, and he was anticipating a visit to his friends in the East, when the dread messenger came. He died of chronic diarrhœa.

Capt. Goodspeed, in a letter to the relatives of the deceased, said, —

" He was a good soldier, brave and generous, beloved by all."

SAMUEL MARSTON LINCOLN.

Died of yellow fever, at Newbern, N.C., Oct. 2, 1864, aged twenty-two years and nine months.

Samuel Marston Lincoln, brother of Major Benjamin C. Lincoln, and son of Alfred and Mary Lee (Curtis) Lincoln, was born in Hingham, Dec. 28, 1841.

Receiving his early education in the schools at the west part of the town, by good conduct, close application to study, and rapid progress, he invariably obtained the approbation of his teachers and school-officers. At a later period he was employed as salesman in Boston.

Ambitious to render such assistance as he was able to offer in support of the government, he entered the army, and was mustered Oct. 9, 1861, as private in Co. H of the Twenty-third Regiment, M. V. I.

Mr. Lincoln was detailed as clerk in the quartermaster's

department, at the time of enlistment, and filled the position so acceptably, that a discharge from the army was obtained for him on a surgeon's certificate of disability, dated May 28, 1863, in order to secure his further services in this capacity. After a short visit home, he returned to his clerkship in the department at Newbern, N.C., and remained there until his death.

During the prevalence of fever, scarcity of help brought increased duties; and, generously dividing his leave of absence among those more needy, he bore his own and others' hardships, and gave largely of his hours for rest to hospital labor, till the fatal disease seized him as one of its victims. He was taken sick on Thursday, and died the following Sunday.

WARREN PARKER LINCOLN,

Private in Co. A, Third Minnesota Cavalry, died at or near Fort Snelling, Minn., in the autumn of 1862, aged twenty-nine years.

Warren Parker Lincoln enlisted at Minneapolis, Minn., Oct. 10, and was mustered Oct. 28, 1861, as private in Co. A, Third Minnesota Cavalry.

For several months the regiment performed guard-duty at various Western posts. In March, 1862, it was ordered to more active service, and at the battle near Murfreesboro', Tenn., July 13, 1862, was captured, and all were made prisoners. They were soon paroled, and sent to Benton Barracks. Released in August, and ordered to Minnesota to fight the Indians. After several sharp conflicts with the enemy, a furlough of thirty days was obtained. It was during this furlough that private Lincoln received an accidental injury, which resulted in hemorrhage of the brain and death.

Warren Parker Lincoln was born in Boston, Jan. 31, 1833. He was son of Warren (born in Hingham, Dec. 6, 1801), and Nancy (Parker) Lincoln. His funeral services took place at Minneapolis; after which his remains were brought to this town, and buried in the Hingham Cemetery.

HENRY B. LIVINGSTON.

Concerning this soldier whose name is upon the Soldiers' and Sailors' Monument, the Committee on Publication have but little to offer. They have neither been able to ascertain the names of his parents, nor the place or date of his birth.

According to the printed record of the Massachusetts Volunteers, published by the adjutant-general of this State (See vol. ii. page 999), Henry B. Livingston was mustered as private in the Veteran Reserve Corps, Oct. 26, 1863, and accredited to the quota of Hingham. He was then forty-seven years of age.

From a communication furnished by Hon. B. W. Harris, we extract the following : —

WAR DEPARTMENT, ADJUTANT-GENERAL'S OFFICE,
WASHINGTON, D.C., March 25, 1874.

It appears from the records of this office, that Henry B. Livingston, Co. D, 13th V. R. C., died May 21, 1864, from injuries received on railroad track.

[Signed]   E. D. TOWNSEND, *Adjutant-General.*

JOHN LEWIS MANUEL.

John Lewis Manuel died suddenly at Fort Warren, Boston Harbor, Aug. 19, 1862, aged thirty-two years, six months, and sixteen days. He was the oldest son of John and Mary (Lincoln) Manuel, and a native of Hingham, having been born in this town, Feb. 3, 1830.

Residing at Green Hill, Hull, in the early part of the war, he left his occupation of shoemaker to enlist for duty at Fort Warren, and, with other young men from the adjoining village of North Cohasset, was mustered Feb. 5, 1862, as private in the First Unattached company of Heavy Artillery, and accredited to the quota of Cohasset.

This company was afterwards designated as Co. A, First Battalion Heavy Artillery, M. V. I.   It was raised for special garrison duty at Fort Warren, and was not called into active service in the field.   A portion of the company, however, was occasionally employed in guarding prisoners and conscripts to and from remote places.

Private Manuel was connected with one of these detachments in the summer of 1862, that was sent South to guard prisoners; and although his health seemed to be impaired after returning to the fort, yet he was able to report for duty until the day he died, as stated above.   His remains were buried in the village cemetery at North Cohasset.

He left a widow and five children.

CHARLES HENRY MARSH.

Private in Co. K, Eleventh Regiment, M. V. I., died May 6, 1862, from wounds received the day previous at the battle of Williamsburg, Va.

Charles Henry Marsh, the oldest son of Peter and Lydia (Hersey) Marsh, was born in Hingham, July 12, 1828.   He was a carpenter by occupation.   At the commencement of the war, and for several years previous, he resided in Dorchester, where he worked at his trade.   From this place he enlisted in May, 1861, for three years, and was mustered into the United States service at Fort Warren, Boston Harbor, June 13, as private in Co. K of the Eleventh Regiment, M. V. I.

The regiment left Fort Warren for Camp Cameron, Cambridge, June 17, thence, *via* New York City, Reading, Lebanon, and York, Pa., and Baltimore, Md., it arrived at Washington, D.C., July 3, and went into camp a short distance from the White House.

Mr. Marsh participated in all the expeditions and engagements of the regiment up to the time of his death.   At the first battle of Bull Run (July 21, 1861), he came near losing his life, but was spared to make the sacrifice on another field.

From a diary which he kept, commencing with the time of his enlistment, we make the following extracts : —

"Friday, May 2, 1862.

"Eleventh Regiment called up at half-past two this morning for fatigue-duty. At work on mortar batteries. One battery shelled out by the rebels. Cos. K and E continued at work in their position. Two men wounded. Rebels firing from heavy guns and field-pieces all day."

The following entries were made by Capt. Benjamin Stone, jun., of Co. K : —

"Sunday, May 4, 1862.

"Enemy evacuated Yorktown. Followed them as far as the works before Williamsburg, and camped.

"Monday, May 5, 1862.

"At 4, A.M., our brigade met the enemy, and fought all day. About 3, P.M., Charles H. Marsh, Co. K, 11th Mass. Regiment, was shot and left on the field.

"Tuesday, May 6, 1862.

"Marsh died at eleven o'clock in the forenoon, and was buried on the field, the spot well marked."

[Signed,]   B. STONE, JR., *Capt. Co. K.*

CHARLES SELDEN MEADE.

Charles Selden Meade, son of Francis K. and Clara Ann (Burn-ham) Meade, was born at Walpole, N.H., March 1, 1844.

While a lad, his parents removed to Hingham, Mass., and he attended the schools of the north and west districts. Subsequently he was employed a short time in the office of "The Hingham Journal," but soon gave his attention to the acquirement of a better education, and was admitted a pupil in Philips Academy, Exeter, N.H., where an elder brother was preparing for college. Learning, while there, that a company was being formed in Hingham, he hastened home, and enlisted

49

under Capt. Stephenson, at Camp Dimmick, and Nov. 12, 1861, was mustered into the U. S. service as private in Co. A, First Battalion, M. V., afterwards Thirty-second Regiment; promoted corporal Sept. 1, 1863, and sergeant Dec. 15, 1863.

Serg. Meade was one of the younger members of the Thirty-second, and a great favorite. He took part with the regiment in the engagements at Malvern Hill, Second Bull Run, Antietam, Shepardstown Ford, Fredericksburg, Chancellorsville, Gettysburg, Bristoe's Station, Rappahannock Station, and Mine Run. For his bravery and good conduct in battle he received promotion.

At Liberty, Va., Jan. 4, 1864, he re-enlisted as a veteran, and came home on a thirty-days' furlough. It was the last visit he was to enjoy with relatives and friends. In less than a month after returning to camp, he met with an accidental injury (March 3), which resulted in pleurisy, congestion, and death. He was sick but three days. The sad intelligence was at once communicated to the relatives in Hingham ; and letters expressing the most profound sorrow at the loss of one so young and promising were received from Cols. Prescott and Stephenson, Capts. Hamilton and Fuller, Lieuts. Reed, Drury, and others, offering words of comfort and consolation to the bereaved. To show the esteem in which this young patriot was held by the members of the regiment, we extract from the letters of our Hingham officers, Col. Stephenson and Lieut. Reed, the following : —

CAMP THIRTY-SECOND REG. MASS. VOLS., LIBERTY, VA., March 7, 1864.
MRS. MEADE.

Dear Madam, — I presume ere this you have received my telegram announcing the death of your son. The company to which he belonged has been detached from the regiment for some days, and I was not aware of his illness until an hour before he died. He was taken with pleurisy on Friday the 4th inst., and was not considered dangerously sick until last evening, when he was attacked with congestion of the lungs, and died about nine o'clock this morning.

It would be useless for me, in your bereavement, to attempt to alleviate your sorrow ; but I cannot refrain from giving my testimony to his worth as a soldier and a man. Always ready and prompt in the performance of his duties, fearless in battle, of correct habits, kind and pleasant, he won the love and respect of all ; and no greater testimony could be given of his worth than the sorrow evinced, and the sympathy expressed, not only among his immediate companions, but by all the officers and men of the regiment.

Please accept my kindest sympathy for your loss, and believe me with respect,   Yours truly,

LUTHER STEPHENSON, JR.,
Lieut.-Col. 32d Mass. Vols.

Lieut. Reed writes as follows : —

CAMP OF THE 32D REGIMENT, MASS. VOLS., LIBERTY, VA., March 8, 1864.

MY DEAR MADAM, — I hardly know what to write in connection with your and our sad loss, but feel that a few lines in regard to Charlie's last moments will interest you. Less than five days prior to his death he was in my tent, seemingly as well as usual. He was taken sick the same evening, but was not considered dangerous until Sunday evening: and before I could leave the regiment to see him, he had passed away. All was done to save him, and make him comfortable, that could be. At first the physician said he had pleurisy: but Monday morning at four o'clock, congestion of the lungs set in, and at nine o'clock he died. You know that I have been with him nearly every day since he joined the company: and I am happy to bear testimony to his kind and generous nature, and worth as a son, a brother, and a friend. Every one in the regiment seemed to like him. The colonel has spoken freely in his praise; and Capt. Hamilton esteemed him highly, promoting him at the first opportunity.

His body is being embalmed, and we hope to enable you once more to look upon his loved form. The company were energetic in taking measures to send his body to you; and although tearfully regretting the necessity, are grateful that it was their privilege to do even this in evidence of the affectionate regard they have ever cherished for him. Col. Stephenson has written you concerning the disposition of the body, which will be sent to the care of Mr. John Todd. . . . With much sympathy for you in this deep affliction, I am very respectfully yours,

GEORGE R. REED,
Lieut. Co. A, and Acting Q. M. 32d Mass. Vols.

The body of Serg. Meade was embalmed at Brandy's Station, and then sent to Hingham, the whole expense being paid by the company of which he was a member.

Impressive and appropriate funeral services were held over the remains in the Baptist meeting-house in this town on Tuesday, the day after their arrival. The exercises were conducted by Rev. Jonathan Tilson, assisted by Revs. Calvin Lincoln, Starr, and Davenport. A procession was then formed, and escorted

by a detachment from Capt. Lyman B. Whiton's company of
Heavy Artillery from Fort Independence, and the band of the
fort, proceeded to the Hingham Cemetery, where the remains
were deposited in the receiving-tomb. They were subsequently
removed to a lot selected for the purpose.

A marble stone erected at his grave bears the inscription, —

SERGT. CHARLES S. MEADE.

Co. A. 32D

REGT. MASS. VOLS.

DIED AT

BEALTON STATION, VA.,

MAR. 7, 1864.

AGED 20 YEARS.

IN YEARS A YOUTH,
A VETERAN IN THE
SERVICE OF HIS COUNTRY.

GEORGE HOWARD MERRITT.

Was born in Scituate, Sept. 11, 1842. His parents were Henry
and Isabel (Litchfield) Merritt.

He was a resident of Hingham, and Aug. 9, 1862, with others
from this town, entered the service of his country, enlisting in
the Navy as landsman for one year.

First taken on board the U. S. receiving-ship "Ohio," at the
Navy Yard in Charlestown, but soon transferred to the "North
Carolina," at New York City. After remaining on board five
weeks, was next sent to the U. S. receiving-ship "Brandywine,"
at Hampton Roads. Again changed, he was taken to the
"Heitzel," in which he embarked for the scene of active operations in the Sounds of North Carolina. Transferred to the
"Louisiana," five guns, he was engaged in cruising off and on
the seaboard, supporting land-forces, and in expeditions up the

rivers, co-operating in the general service, until stricken by disease, and unfitted for duty.

He died of swamp-fever, Feb. 7, 1863, at the early age of a few months more then twenty years, and was buried from the hospital at Little Washington, N.C.

A stone in the cemetery at South Scituate bears the simple record of the death of the young patriot; and the monument erected by the town of Hingham includes in its list of the heroic dead the name of the deceased.

> " Is his sleep less sweet in the land where the wild winds swept him,
> Than if soothed to rest at home, and kin and friends had wept him ? "

HENRY FELT MILLER.

Corporal in Co. G, Thirty-ninth Regiment. M. V. I., died of wounds at Washington, D.C., May 25, 1864, aged nineteen years, three months, twenty-six days.

> Soldier, rest ! thy warfare o'er,
> Sleep the sleep that knows not breaking,
> Dreams of battle-fields no more,
> Days of danger, nights of waking.

Henry Felt Miller, son of John and Martha (Elliot) Miller, was born at Salem, Mass., Jan. 30, 1845. Residing in Hingham, and following the trade of shoemaker, when the war broke out, he enlisted on the first quota of the town for three years, and was mustered at Lynnfield, Mass., Sept. 2, 1862, as private in Co. G of the Thirty-ninth Regiment, M. V. I. Promoted corporal in December, 1862, at Poolsville, Md.

Corp. Miller fell mortally wounded, by a musket-ball in the head, at the first battle of the regiment. It was on Sunday morning, May 8, 1864, during a charge made upon the enemy over an open field, at Laurel Hill. For a short time he received such attention as the field hospital afforded, and was afterwards removed to the Stanton Hospital, at Washington, D.C., where he died. When taken from the field, he was able to give his name, and the regiment to which he belonged ; but soon became unconscious, and continued so until death relieved him from suffering.

His remains were sent to Hingham for burial, and appropriate funeral services held at the Methodist Church, the pastor, Rev. William H. Starr, and Rev. Calvin Lincoln of the First Parish, officiating.

DANIEL MURPHY.

Daniel Murphy, son of Catharine (Creed) and the late John Murphy, was born in Boston, Mass., Nov. 22, 1840.

He was by occupation a shoemaker, and in early life worked at this calling in Marblehead and Woburn. He subsequently went to sea in the coasting-trade ; but afterwards came to Hingham, and was employed at his vocation in the south part of the town. At a later period he went to New York, and, on the breaking out of the war, enlisted in Co. C, Fifteenth Regiment, N.Y. V. (engineers). Mustered into service at Willett's Point, June 25, 1861, for two years.

Private Murphy was connected with the regiment, and shared its dangers and exposures, until Nov. 15, 1862, when he was " discharged at Camp Alexander by reason of general debility, in consequence of chronic diarrhœa." No further information in regard to him appears upon the official records. He died in Hospital at Washington, D.C., some time prior to Nov. 24, 1862, when letters were received from the Sanitary Commission giving information of his decease.

His mother is still living in Hingham, where she has resided for many years. Her claim that her son should be classed as a citizen of Hingham is certainly just; " for," adopting her words, " if Hingham was not his home, the young man had no home."

JOHN SPAULDING NEAL.

Private in Co. G, Thirty-ninth Regiment, M. V. I., died at Salisbury Prison, N.C., Jan. 16, 1865, aged thirty-three years and two months.

John Spaulding Neal, son of John and Sarah (Hazelton) Neal, was born at Hebron, N.H., in November, 1831. Removing to Hingham with his parents, he afterwards followed the occupation of shoemaker.

When the town was in need of men to fill its first quota, Mr. Neal came forward and enlisted under recruiting-officer Edward Cazneau; and Sept. 2, 1862, was mustered into service as private in Co. G of the Thirty-ninth Regiment, M. V. I.

Mr. Neal shared the experience of his regiment during the first two years of its history. He took part in the battles of Laurel Hill, North Anna River, Petersburg, and Weldon Railroad. Taken prisoner, with several others from Hingham belonging to Co. G, at the last-named battle, he was sent to Petersburg, and afterwards to Richmond, Va., where for a time he was confined in Libby Prison. Thence he was removed to Belle Isle, on the opposite side of James River; and subsequently to the stockade prison at Salisbury, N.C., where he died of diarrhoea, brought on by exposure, and the want of care and proper food.

In a letter written to Mrs. Neal by a prison companion of the deceased, occurs the following: —

"John was a good soldier and a much-loved comrade. His friends in the regiment were as numerous as the men, for he had no enemies. Ever kind to his companions and respectful to his officers, he was ready and willing to perform every duty imposed upon him. He deserved a better fate than that which has befallen him. But He who doeth all things well knows what is best for us, and to Him alone can we look in this hour of trouble for consolation.

[Signed]   ALPHEUS THOMAS,
2d Lieutenant Co. K, 39th Mass. Vols."

HIRAM NEWCOMB, 2D.

Hiram Newcomb, 2d, eldest son of Levi and Jane (Dawson) Newcomb, was born in Hingham, in January, 1842.

He was a seaman. In the winter of 1863-4 enlisted in Co. E of the Thirty-second Regiment, M. V. I., three years, and was mustered on the 17th of February, this being the date of the expiration of the furlough granted the three hundred and thirty men of the regiment who had re-enlisted. With this body of troops, on their return to duty, he at once became connected with the Army of the Potomac, and up to the close of the war had his full allotment of the labors, privations, and perils of a soldier's life.

He was in the battles of the Wilderness, Laurel Hill, Spottsylvania, North Anna, Tolopotomy, Bethesda Church, Petersburg, and Weldon Railroad.

On the 28th of June, 1865, he was mustered out at Washington, and the day following left for Boston, where he arrived Saturday, July 1, and where at Gallop's Island, July 11, he was honorably discharged, having been in the service one year and nearly five months.

Though in good health at the time of enlistment, it was evident, that, through exposure and privation, his native strength and vigor were rapidly departing. Consumption was gathering what the bullet had spared. Returning to Weymouth, where his family had resided during his absence, he there lingered until Oct. 15, 1867, when he died, at the age of twenty-five years and five months, leaving a widow and one son. His remains were interred in the Hingham Cemetery.

ANDREW P. OLSON.

From North Bridgewater (town authorities say resident of Hingham). Served for the second quota of this town. Was corporal in Co. C of the Forty-second Regiment, M. V. I., nine months; and was mustered Oct. 11, 1862, then twenty-eight years of age.

In the absence of the record of this soldier, few particulars of his history can be given. It appears from the report of the adjutant-general, that his death took place Aug. 9, 1863, in New York City. As scarcely four weeks had passed since the expiration of his term of enlistment, it seems probable that his death must have been the result of disease contracted while in the service.

Though the name is not found on the Soldiers' and Sailors' Monument, Mr. Olson enlisted under recruiting-officer Edward Cazneau, and received the bounty offered by the town.

PETER OURISH.

Sergeant in Co. E, Thirty-second Regiment, M. V. I., died of wounds at the Stanton Hospital, Washington, D.C., June 8, 1864, aged nineteen years, one month, and twenty-three days.

Peter Ourish, second son of Simon and Agnes (Hoser) Ourish, and brother of Jacob Ourish of the Lincoln Light Infantry, and Thirtieth Regiment, was born in Buffalo, N.Y., April 15, 1845. After the family removed to Hingham, he attended the public schools of the North Ward.

At the age of sixteen, he was a large, sturdy, well proportioned young man. Many of his older acquaintances had enlisted; the company under Capt. Stephenson had already left Hingham, and accessions were rapidly being made to another company at Oasis Hall by Lieut. Lyman B. Whiton, when young Ourish came forward to join the latter, and, giving his age as eighteen, was accepted as a recruit, and accredited to the quota of Hingham.

He was mustered into service as private in Co. E of the First Battalion Infantry, M. V., afterwards Thirty-second Regiment, Dec. 2, 1861; promoted corporal Oct. 14, 1862; re-enlisted as veteran volunteer, Jan. 5, 1864; promoted sergeant, and in this position continued to serve acceptably during the remainder of the time he was connected with the regiment.

The battles in which he took part were Malvern Hill, Second Bull Run, Antietam, Fredericksburg, Chancellorsville, Gettysburg, Rappahannock Station, Mine Run, Wilderness, Laurel Hill, North Anna, and Tolopotomy Swamp. In the last engagement he was seriously wounded in the shoulder, and, after a confinement of eight days, died at the Stanton Hospital, Washington, D.C.

Thus did another of our soldier-boys pass away. He fell at the post of duty, while gallantly fighting for the old flag ; and the testimony of all is, that he served his country nobly and well. By strict adherence to military discipline, he dignified his position, and won the respect of his comrades and the good opinions of his superiors. An officer of the same regiment says " He was not only a brave, conscientious, and faithful soldier, but a youth of pure character, one upon whom the vices and bad habits of camp-life made no impression."

His remains were brought to Hingham for interment ; and the funeral services were held at the meeting-house of the Third Parish, on Sunday morning, June 19, when the pastor, Rev. Joshua Young, delivered an appropriate address. Other clergymen also were present, and assisted in the exercises. The body was followed to its last resting-place, in the Hingham Cemetery, by a large number of relatives and friends.

He left a widowed mother, who has since died, and several brothers and sisters.

> " Freedom hallows with her tread
> The silent cities of the dead."

ALBERT L. PIERCE.

Age 21.

Was first a member of the Lincoln Light Infantry, and left Hingham, May 18, 1861, with the volunteers who had enlisted to fill up the ranks of the company, then in service at Fortress Monroe.

After returning home, he re-enlisted, and Nov. 1, 1861, was mustered as corporal in Co. A of the Thirty-second Regiment, M. V. I., three years. His connection with the army was brief. The regiment had but commenced its career, afterwards so signally active and eventful, ere disease obliged him to leave the field; and he was discharged from service by reason of disability, Aug. 2, 1862.

He died at Freedom, N.H., Dec. 6, 1864.

DANIEL W. PENDERGAST.

Resident of Hingham, age 27.

Private in Co. G of the Forty-fifth Regiment, M. V. M., nine months.

Enlisted as private Sept. 26, 1862, in Co. G. On the 5th of November, left Boston for Newbern, assigned to the Department of North Carolina. A short time was spent in camp on the banks of the Trent; after which Co. G was detached, and sent to Fort Macon to form a part of the garrison of that post. Towards the close of April, being relieved from duty at Fort Macon, he was transferred to Fort Spinola, and afterwards rejoined the regiment, which continued in camp near this place during the remainder of his term of enlistment.

In the course of his service, Mr. Pendergast was detailed for the corps of sappers and miners. Here periods of over-exertion were often followed by exposure to cold and wet, and he was mustered out sick and disabled. Returning home, he never recovered the health possessed at the time of joining the army, but, gradually failing, at last fell a victim of consumption.

Served for the quota of Hingham, and received the bounty offered by the town.

ELIJAH PROUTY.

From Weymouth, age 26.

Enlisted in August, 1862, under recruiting officer Edward Caz-neau, for the first quota of Hingham; and Sept. 2 was mustered as private in Co. G, Thirty-ninth Regiment, M. V. I., three years.

According to the report of the adjutant-general of Massachusetts, he died Dec. 9, 1863, at Washington, D.C.

Mr. Prouty was a volunteer in the Lincoln Light Infantry; left Hingham with the first detachment, April 17, 1861; and was three months at Fortress Monroe and vicinity.

Though not on the Soldiers' and Sailors' Monument, he was recognized as serving for the quota of Hingham, and received the bounty offered by the town.

SEWALL PUGSLEY.

Drafted at Taunton Mass., July 20, 1863, to fill the quota required at the time from the town of Hingham; mustered as private in Co. F of the Twenty-second Regiment, M. V. I., three years, on the 28th of the following August.

Sewall Pugsley was born in Hiram, Me., March 20, 1831. His parents were Seth and Jerusha (Hartford) Pugsley. After removing to South Hingham, he was employed in the factory of Messrs. Joseph Jacob & Son, and married a daughter of the late Henry Cushing, Esq.

At the time of the draft, he was in feeble health, as he had been for some years previous, and was evidently unfit for the service required. The authorities, however, thought differently, and declined to grant the exemption Mr. Pugsley earnestly desired, and which his condition really demanded. Not having the means to purchase commutation, and at the same time provide for the needs of his young family, he yielded to the destiny the draft seemed to have decreed, and gave his life a sacrifice for his wife and children.

Joining the Twenty-second Regiment at the seat of war, he was engaged for a few weeks in active duty along the Rapidan, and on one occasion took part in the capture of a large number of prisoners. Camp-life, however, soon developed anew the disease which even under the comforts of home often unfitted him for labor, and he was conveyed to the hospital at Mount Pleasant, Washington, D.C., where at the end of eight days, and but eleven weeks from the time of entering the army, he died of chronic diarrhœa, Nov. 12, 1863, aged thirty-two years.

Of the large number of natives or residents of Hingham who were engaged in the civil war, but three instances of involuntary service are known. In common with Mr. Pugsley, these instances were severally the result of the draft at Taunton on the 20th of July, 1863. Their story is briefly told. Escaping disease and the casualties of the field, one returned safely home. Of the second, nothing is known respecting his fate. Falling in battle, he probably filled the grave of an unrecognized soldier. And lastly the subject of this notice, dying from disease a few weeks only from the time of parting from his home and family.

In view of the liberality of our citizens exemplified shortly after in repeated and yet cheerful contributions of money adequate to whatever the needs of the hour demanded, the occurrence of these exceptional cases of coerced service, and their melancholy results, must be generally deplored.

JOSHUA ROACH.

Thirty-eight years of age.

Entered the service Aug. 21, 1862, as private in Co. H of the Thirty-eighth Regiment, M. V. I. Beyond the date of his decease, which took place on the first day of June, 1863, no further particulars with regard to his history can be given.

Enlisted for three years, to serve for the quota of Hingham.

JAMES G. RAYMOND.

From the town of Weymouth ; corporal in Co. D of the Fourth Regiment of Cavalry, M. V., three years.

He entered the service Jan. 9, 1864, then eighteen years of age, and died at Hilton Head, S.C., on the 24th of the following May.

The adjutant-general in his report erroneously gives the time of enlistment as Jan. 9, 1865.

Mr. Raymond was a farmer by occupation, and recruited by the citizens' committee of Hingham.

WILLIAM WESLEY ROBINSON.

William Wesley Robinson was the eldest son of Nahum, and Margaret (Roberts) Robinson, and was born in Hingham, April 14, 1835.

On the 17th of April, 1861, at Faneuil Hall, Boston, he joined Co. H of the Fourth Regiment, as private, and left at once for Fortress Monroe and vicinity, serving three months. Although quite deaf, he performed all the duties of a soldier in a faithful manner, and was honorably discharged at Long Island, Boston, at the expiration of his term of enlistment.

After a short stay at home, he again entered the service, enlisting at Readville, Mass., Aug. 24, 1861, as private in Co. K of the Eighteenth Regiment, M. V. I., three years. Being presented for examination, the surgeon pronounced his deafness a disqualification, and he was accordingly rejected. Disappointed and almost disheartened, he appealed to Capt., now Major Benjamin F. Meservey, under whom he had served while at Fortress Monroe, when, by virtue of the influence of this officer, added to the soldier's emphatic declaration that " he was not too deaf to fight," the surgeon at last granted a reluctant consent. Most faithfully was Mr. Robinson's part of the contract performed : a better or braver soldier was never passed by any surgeon.

He was in the engagement at Yorktown, on the Peninsula, at Second Bull Run, Shepardstown, Fredericksburg, Gettysburg, Rappahannock Station, Mine Run, and in most of the principal engagements in the Department of Virginia.

Of the whole regiment, he was notedly one of the most daring and desperate. He fought at all times in a spirit of the most determined bravery; and on several occasions was so utterly exhausted by the labor and excitement of the conflict, that the aid of others became necessary to enable him to leave the field.

Under an experience naturally marked out by a spirit such as his, physical strength and vigor began at last to yield; and on the 9th of March, 1864, he was transferred to the Veteran Reserve Corps for disability.

Entering the army in the possession of perfect health, he returned home after the expiration of his term of enlistment, bearing with him the seeds of death. For a time he feebly labored at his trade, gradually sinking under the influence of a disease nothing could stay or avert, and at last died at Braintree, Mass. He was buried in the cemetery at North Weymouth.

During his sickness, he was often urged by friends to apply for a pension; but this he steadily refused to do. Becoming however, entirely disabled, he at last sought assistance from the government he had sacrificed his life to preserve. The surgeons before whom he was brought for examination decided that " though evidently very sick, the disease might have been contracted before entering the service," and, notwithstanding the testimony of his officers to the excellence of his health and strength at the time of enlistment, declined to grant the aid desired. In four weeks from the time of this refusal, the applicant was dead.

Unquestionably many claims for pensions are made which are really groundless; but it is earnestly hoped there are few instances where so great an injustice has been done a brave and dutiful soldier as in this.

DENNIS SCULLY.

Private in Co. D, Fourth Regiment of Cavalry, M. V., died of small-pox, at the hospital, Beaufort, S.C., April 26, 1864, aged twenty-nine years, seven months.

Dennis Scully, son of Daniel and Margaret (Shea) Scully, was born in September, 1834, in the Parish of Eniscarra, County Cork, Ireland.

He became a resident of Hingham, Mass., some eight or nine years before the war, and was employed successively at South Hingham, in the cordage factory at Hingham Centre, and for several years in the foundry at the Harbor, where he was still in service at the time of enlistment.

Joining the camp at Readville, he was mustered the 9th of January, 1864, as private in Co. D, Fourth Regiment of Cavalry, M. V., and accredited to the quota of Hingham.

Leaving Massachusetts, the regiment was stationed in South Carolina, where Dennis died shortly after its arrival.

In a communication from Capt. Morton of Co. D, to the late Edward Cazneau, Esq., of this town, occurs the following: "Dennis Scully was a quiet man, of unassuming manner, a friend to every one, and was always ready and willing to do his duty. He died in the firm assurance that the faith which had been his guidance through life would maintain those whom he was to leave, and support him in that world which was fast opening to his view."

He left a family and an aged mother.

JOSEPH SIMMONS.

Joseph Simmons, born in Scituate, April 11, 1829, was a son of Peleg and Lucy (Damon) Simmons.

After completing his school studies in his native town, he learned the shoemaker's trade, and this occupation he continued to follow until failing health induced him to seek some out-door employment. At the time of enlisting, he was engaged in farming.

With several young men from South Scituate, he joined the first quota of Hingham, under recruiting-officer Edward Cazneau, and was mustered Sept. 2, 1862, as a private in Co. G of the Thirty-ninth Regiment, M. V. I. This regiment was not engaged in any general battle during the time he was connected with it. Like many of our brave soldier-boys, however, who were stricken with disease, he as truly gave his life to his country as did those who fell upon the battle-field. His comrades speak of him as a good and loyal soldier, who was earnestly devoted to the old flag, and to the preservation of the Union.

He was taken sick at Culpepper, in December, 1863, and sent to the regimental hospital. Thence he was removed to Washington, D.C., where he died. His remains were subsequently taken to South Scituate, and buried in the cemetery at Assinippi Village.

He left a widow and three children.

A marble stone erected to his, memory bears the inscription :

JOSEPH SIMMONS,

DIED

AT WASHINGTON, D.C.,

MARCH 3, 1864,

AGED 34 YR'S 11 MOS.

OUR LOVED ONE SLEEPS
FOR HIS COUNTRY S FLAG.

EDWARD AUGUSTUS FRANKLIN SPEAR.

Private in Co. G of the Thirty-ninth Regiment, M. V. I. Enlisted at Hingham Aug. 8, 1862 ; mustered Sept. 2 ; taken prisoner Aug. 19, 1864 ; and died at Salisbury, N.C.

The subject of this sketch was born at Norwich, Vt., March

51

13, 1828. His parents were Edward Spencer and Hannah (Bates) Spear.

Removing to Hingham, he married a daughter of the late Nathaniel French, sen., and after the outbreak of the war enlisted for three years, as before stated. He shared in the battles of Mine Run, Wilderness, Spottsylvania, North Anna, Cold Harbor, and also in different engagements about Petersburg, from June 21 to Aug. 19, 1864, when, at the battle of the Weldon Railroad, he was taken prisoner.

In the hands of the enemy, he was first removed to Belle Isle, and then to Salisbury, N.C., where he remained until death, which took place from pneumonia, on the 20th of January, 1865. He was thirty-seven years of age, and his term of service included nearly two and a half years.

Never remiss in duty, but always faithful to the cause of his country, he died a good citizen and a brave soldier.

SAMUEL SPENCER.

Resident of Hingham.

Mustered June 26, 1861, as private in Co. E of the Twelfth Regiment, M. V. I.

Young Spencer was among the first that entered the service for three years. His term of enlistment had almost expired, when he was mortally wounded, while on duty in the trenches, by a bullet from one of the enemy's sharpshooters.

He was about twenty years of age, and died at City Point, Va., June 25, 1864, the day preceding the expiration of his term of service.

> " He rests with those who every danger braved,
> Unmarked, untrophied, 'mid the soil they saved."

THOMAS SPRAGUE, 2D.

Private in Co. G, Thirty-ninth Regiment, M. V. I., three years; died April 29, 1864, of disease contracted in the service.

Thomas Sprague, 2d, a resident of Hingham, was the youngest son of Amos and Mary (Clark) Sprague, and was born Oct. 25, 1826.

On the 2d of September, 1862, he enlisted, as previously stated, and left for the seat of war in the vicinity of Washington, Sept. 6. After a brief period of service, he was detailed as pioneer; in which capacity his fidelity not only attracted the attention of his comrades, but was commended at headquarters.

In the winter of 1863–4, being disabled by disease, he was transferred to the Stanton Hospital at Washington, D.C., where he died April 29, 1864, aged thirty-seven years. Possessed of a large degree of physical strength and endurance, his sickness was severe and protracted.

It is due to the memory and character of the deceased, to add that he was honest, temperate, faithful. The duty assigned to him was never imposed on another; while to the cheerful, uncomplaining spirit with which he bore the trials and privations of camp-life, his companions bear their undivided testimony.

He was a laborer, unmarried, and at the time of joining the army left an aged widowed mother dependent on him for support.

WILLIAM JOHNSON STOCKWELL.

The subject of this memoir was a son of Otis and Elvira (Gilman) Stockwell, and was born in Hingham, Feb. 24, 1842. After receiving the educational advantages of the public schools, he found employment for a while in a lithographic printing establishment in the city of Boston, but subsequently was employed by Mr. David Cushing, jun., of Hingham, with whom he was engaged when news of the attack on Fort Sumter awoke the patriotic North to arms. The Lincoln Light Infantry promptly responded to the president's call ; and young Stockwell took his place as a volunteer in the ranks, April 17, 1861, to join the defenders of the nation. Serving the three months' term of enlistment, he returned home, and after a short stay again en. listed, and was mustered Nov. 29, 1861, for three years, as private in Co. I, Capt. Kelty, of the Thirtieth Regiment, M. V. I.

The regiment was attached to Gen. Butler's division, and did valiant service amid the scorching heat and pestilence-breathing bayous of Louisiana.

At the battle of Baton Rouge, and the prolonged conflict before Port Hudson, it bore a conspicuous part. For nearly six weeks it acted as sharpshooters, or was engaged in supporting batteries at the latter stronghold. A portion of this time, it lay during the day behind logs, exposed to the burning rays of the sun, which thinned its ranks more rapidly than the enemy's bullets.

After the battle of Port Hudson, while on the way to Donaldsonville, the regiment had a sharp engagement with the enemy ; and of the company to which young Stockwell belonged, only *nine* survived that battle. Nowhere during the war were fiercer conflicts fought, or more heroic bravery displayed, than during this campaign.

Exposed to the malarious influences of the climate, so fatal to Northern constitutions, subjected to the most arduous military duty, private Stockwell was one of the many who fell victims to disease engendered by the climate. He died of typhus fever, in the hospital at Baton Rouge, Aug. 9, 1863, after an illness of only three days, aged twenty-one years, five months.

His death was deeply lamented by his associates, to whom he had greatly endeared himself by his quiet and unobtrusive manners and kindness of heart.

His remains rest in the soil which he helped to redeem ; but in the home of his childhood his memory will be cherished and his name honored.

> " What though brief his date ?
> We reckon life by deeds, not years :
> That life is long which answers life's great end."

DEMERICK STODDER.

Private in Co. F of the Thirty-second Regiment, M. V. I.;
killed at the battle of Gettysburg, Pa., July 2, 1863, aged
twenty-three years, seven months, nine days.

> " How sweetly they sleep who have died for their country.
> And never will wake for the combat again;
> But mantled with glory they peacefully slumber,
> And rest from their toil in the graves of the slain."

Demerick Stodder, son of Demerick and Maria (Bassett)
Stodder, was born in Hingham, Nov. 23, 1839. He was by
occupation shoemaker, and a descendant from John Stodder,
who came to Hingham in 1638.

Private Stodder was one of the thirty-seven volunteers that
left Hingham May 18, 1861, to join the Lincoln Light Infantry
at Fortress Monroe, and returned with the company at the expiration of its service of three months.

Re-enlisting upon the quota of Hingham, he was mustered at
Fort Warren, Feb. 20, 1862, for three years, as private in
Co. F of the First Battalion Infantry, M. V., afterwards Thirty-
second Regiment ; and while connected with this organization,
shared its experience with the Army of the Potomac.

The battles in which he took part were Malvern Hill, Second
Bull Run, Antietam, Fredericksburg, Chancellorsville, and Gettysburg.

He was instantly killed by a shot in the forehead from a rifle,
at about sunset, on the first day of the fight at Gettysburg.

Private Stodder was a good soldier, always cheerful, and dis-
posed to make the best of circumstances, whether on the march
or in camp, and remarkably brave and impetuous in battle.
Gen. Stephenson says, " Demerick Stodder was one of our reliable men ;" and this statement is confirmed by the testimony of
Capt. Reed and other officers.

His remains were buried on the battle-field by his comrades,
the night of July 3, but, subsequently were deposited in the
National Cemetery at Gettysburg.

WASHINGTON IRVING STODDER.

Private in Co. F, Thirty-second Regiment, M. V. I., three years; promoted corporal; re-enlisted Jan. 4, 1864, for the remainder of the war; mortally wounded near Spottsylvania Court House, May 12, and died May 14, 1864.

Washington Irving Stodder, son of Caleb and Esther Saunders (Gardner) Stodder, was born in Hingham, Aug. 26, 1841.

Responding to the earnest appeals for aid in support of the cause of the Union, young Stodder enlisted at Boston on the 15th of February, 1862, and July 2 was promoted corporal. Continually at the front, his whole career was signally character- ized by constant exposure, long marches, and numerous engage- ments. Never discouraged, he cheerfully acquiesced in the for- tune of war, and looked bravely forward to the full triumph of the cause he had taken arms to sustain.

His list of battles includes nearly all set down to the Thirty- second Regiment. Beginning at Malvern Hill, he fought at Second Bull Run, Antietam, Fredericksburg, Chancellorsville, Gettysburg, Rappahannock Station, Wilderness (May 4, 5, 6, and 7), and many other less important engagements.

Never wounded nor disabled by sickness, he had escaped the perils incident to a soldier's life. But on the 12th of May, 1864, — a dark day in the history of our young patriot, — he entered the field for his last conflict. Stricken by a bullet in the strug- gle near Spottsylvania Court House, he fell mortally wounded, and was conveyed to the field hospital, where he died, aged twenty-three years.

HORACE L. STUDLEY.

Private in Co. E of the Thirty-second Regiment, M. V. I., three years; died at Hingham, April 1, 1864.

Horace L. Studley, son of Homer and Lydia (Jenkins) Stud- ley), was born in Scituate, Mass., Sept. 24, 1837. Leaving home, he came to Hingham, and was apprenticed to Samuel G. Bailey, housewright. After his majority he still remained in town, following his trade, until Dec. 2, 1861, when he enlisted at Hingham for three years.

From the 15th of August, 1862, he shared in the numerous rapid marches of the Thirty-second down the Peninsula to Newport News, and its progress towards Washington, until he reached the vicinity of Warrenton Junction. Before arriving here, and afterwards on the route to Manassas Gap, many of the men fell out utterly exhausted and disabled, Mr. Studley among the number. Removed to the regimental hospital near Fredericksburg, his health gradually declined up to the month of January, 1863, when a furlough was granted, and he left for home. Stopping at Hingham, and being too weak and exhausted to proceed further, he was removed to the residence of Capt. Thomas King, into whose family he was kindly welcomed, and whose generous hospitality made their house at once the invalid's home. After a lingering sickness of nine weeks, during which he was attended by those he most loved and esteemed, and provided with every comfort the hand of affection, or even parental kindness, could supply, death came to his release, April 1, 1863, at twenty-six years of age.

The record of private Horace L. Studley is unblemished. As a soldier he evaded no duty; as a citizen he was temperate, industrious, faithful, honest. As a Christian, exemplary and sincere. Quiet and unobtrusive in manner, uniformly kind and obliging, a man of strict integrity and purity of character, he died beloved and respected by all who knew him.

His life, though closed by disease, was the life of a patriot, nobly sacrificed on the altar of his country.

HENRY SWEARS.

Born in Hingham.

Son of William Swears.

Enlisted from Weymouth, to which place the family had removed some years before the occurrence of the war.

Mustered June 26, 1861, as private in Co. H of the Twelfth Regiment, M. V. I.

Killed Dec. 13, 1862, at Fredericksburg, Va.

Mr. Swears was about twenty years of age; and his name is found on the Soldiers' and Sailors' Monument of the town of Weymouth.

FRANCIS THOMAS.

[Communicated.]

Was the son of William and Rachel (Beal) Thomas, and was born in Hingham, Feb 1, 1844.

At the outbreak of the rebellion, he seemed to divine its magnitude, and intimated to his family his intention to enlist. Being expostulated with on account of his youth, he replied, " I can be better spared than those of you who have families."

Shortly after, on the 26th of June, 1861, he enlisted for the quota of the town of Weymouth, in Co. H of the Twelfth Regiment, M. V. I., three years ; and was the first of five brothers, natives of Hingham, who entered the field for the support of the Union. His rank at the time of joining the army was sergeant-major ; but his fidelity, added to manly courage, soon attracted the attention of his superior officers, and he was recommended for promotion. Complying with their request, Gov. Andrew, on the 9th of September, 1862, awarded him a commission as second lieutenant, and soon after promoted him to first lieutenant, finally appointing him as adjutant of the regiment.

In January of 1863, he was still further advanced by being commissioned inspector of the second brigade, second division, of the First Army Corps. Here he proved a competent, brave, and faithful officer, with every prospect of future distinction and usefulness, until the 3d of July, 1863, when, in mortal combat with the foes of his country, he fell in the struggle at Gettysburg. The promise of a brilliant and prosperous career went suddenly down in the death of the young soldier and patriot.

Said the colonel of his regiment, " I loved him as a son." The

general commanding his division says of him : " He was unwearied on the march, faithful and diligent in the performance of
his duties, fearless in action, and beloved by all who knew him.
Brothers and sisters should have been proud to call *him*
brother, and parents should thank God who gave them such a
son !"   Said Gen. Grant, " That man is every inch a soldier."

" But his duty to his country is done : his record is immortal.
Beneath the soil he so bravely defended, his body lies ; while
upon the slope of the eternal hills, let us believe his soul lives
sweetly on, tented in the folds of peace forever ! "

MICHAEL FRANCIS THOMPSON.

Michael Francis Thompson, son of Daniel and Mary (Brennan)
Thompson, was born in Mountrath, Queen's County, Ireland,
March 9, 1840.

While yet a boy, the family emigrated to this country, and
took up its residence in Hingham.   After receiving the benefit
of our public schools, he was employed in the spike-factory at
the harbor, and subsequently at the blind-and-sash factory on
South Street.

Mr. Thompson was among those who enlisted for three years
at the commencement of the war, having joined the regular
army of the United States as private, June 10, 1861.   He was
sworn in at the time of enlistment, and assigned to Co. D, Capt.
Charles Griffin, of the Fifth Regiment of United States Artillery ;
afterwards promoted corporal, and then sergeant, a position
which is considered highly honorable in the regular army.

He took an active part with the regiment at the battles
of Yorktown, Hanover Court House, Antietam, Fredericksburg, Chancellorsville, Gettysburg, Rappahannock Station, Mine
Run, Wilderness, Laurel Hill, Spottsylvania Court House, Jericho Mills, and Bethesda Church.

By his purity of life, even temperament, and unostentatious
manner, he endeared himself to a large circle of friends.   Com-

mander Rittenhouse of the Fifth United States Artillery wrote concerning his character as follows: " Serg. Michael Thompson is a good and honest soldier."

At the expiration of his term of enlistment, June 10, 1864, he returned to Hingham, and obtained work with a former employer. His health and strength, however, had been given to his adopted country ; and in about two years he was stricken with the disease which terminated his existence.

He died of consumption, at the residence of his parents in Hingham, Jan. 6, 1867, aged twenty-six years, nine months, and twenty-eight days.

The Army and Navy Association of this town, in a series of resolutions adopted Jan. 12, 1867, speaks of him in terms nearly as follows : —

Whereas, The death of Serg. Michael Thompson calls for some expression from this association for the loss of a worthy member, a faithful soldier, and an esteemed citizen, therefore,

Resolved, That . . . we will cherish in our hearts the memory of one whose life was the manifestation of those qualities that elevate and adorn human character.

FRANK H. TILTON,

Aged eighteen years. Accredited on the quota of Hingham, and mustered into the service Jan. 6, 1864, as private in Co. C, Fourth Regiment of Cavalry, M. V.

He was one of the thirty-eight recruits obtained by the Citizens' Committee in January, 1864, and received State Aid from the town, in addition to the sum paid him as bounty money.

Of the personal history of this soldier nothing is definitely known ; and but little can be said of his military record, except that he served several months with the Fourth Cavalry in the Department of the South, and died July 12, 1864, at Hilton Head, S.C.

" That glowing land was but his sepulchre."

THOMAS TINSLEY.

Private in Co. K, First Regiment, M. V. I., died at Washington, D.C., May 11, 1863, from wounds received at the battle of Chancellorsville, Va., aged forty-one years, nine months.

Thomas Tinsley was born at Foleshill, County of Warwick, England, Aug. 7, 1821. His parents were James and Hannah (Pickard) Tinsley. About the year 1847 he emigrated to the United States, and located in Hingham. Being a weaver by trade, he was employed for some time by the firm of Lincoln, Wilder, & Co. ; and afterwards, at the time of entering the service, by Messrs. Burr, Brown, & Co.

July 9, 1862, he enlisted on the first quota of Hingham, under recruiting-officer Edward Cazneau, and was mustered Aug. 14, as private in Co. K of the First Regiment, M. V. I.

While he was connected with the regiment, it took part in the battles of Kettle Run, Second Bull Run, Chantilly, Fredericksburg, and Chancellorsville. In the last named battle, he received a gunshot wound in the right lung, and was conveyed to the Carver Hospital, at Washington, D.C., where he died.

Private Tinsley was a brave and faithful soldier, a respected citizen, and a beloved husband and father. A diligent and accomplished student in the history of his own, he gave his life to enrich the page of his adopted country's history.

ALVIN TOWER.

Alvin Tower, youngest son of Asa and Ruth (Collier) Tower, was born in Cohasset, Sept. 13, 1832.

In April, 1861, he enlisted as private in Co. I, Lincoln Light Infantry, Fourth Regiment, M. V. M., three months, and was one of the number who left Hingham on the afternoon of the 17th for Boston, destined for Fortress Monroe.

At the end of the term he returned to Hingham, and, after a brief vacation, entered the service for the second time on the 27th of August, 1861, as private in Co. A of the Twentieth Regiment, M. V. I., three years.

On the 4th of September, he left Readville for the Department of Virginia, where, during the autumn and the following winter, which was spent at Camp Benton, near Poolesville, Md., he was employed as teamster and also as ambulance driver for the conveyance of the sick and wounded. Up to the close of May, 1862, his service in the ranks had been limited. On the 1st of June, in the battle of Fair Oaks, he found himself face to face with the foe; and at the close of the day, just as the enemy's lines began to give way, received a wound in one of his legs, from a musket-ball, which proved mortal.

His death took place June 8, 1862, at the General Hospital, Fortress Monroe; and at this locality he was buried.

Gen. Luther Stephenson states that he was the first Hingham soldier who died from the effects of wounds.

Mr. Tower was temperate, moral, a good citizen. and faithful soldier, and served his country well in all the situations he was called to fill.

ALBERT WILDER.

Albert Wilder, born in Hingham, Feb. 28, 1842, was a son of Albert G. and Elizabeth W. (French) Wilder; and a descendant from Edward Wilder, who in early life came to Hingham with his mother, and settled near Bull's Pond.

Albert was a shoemaker. He enlisted for three years under recruiting-officer Edward Cazneau, at a time when the town was in need of men to fill its first quota, and was mustered into service Sept. 2, 1862, as private in Co. G of the Thirty-ninth Regiment, M. V. I.

Through the month of February, 1863, young Wilder was sick with fever. and confined in the hospital at Poolesville, Md.

He afterwards shared in the general experience of the regiment until May 8, 1864, when, during a sharp engagement at

Laurel Hill, on Sunday morning, he was seriously wounded in his thigh. Every thing was done that could be to alleviate his sufferings, until he died at Harewood Hospital, Washington, D.C.

One who was in the company with him says, Albert was a good comrade and soldier.

> " He went with his noble heart unworn,
> And pure and high :
> A patriot stooping from the clouds of morn,
> Only to die."

His remains were brought to Hingham for burial ; and, in the cemetery at Liberty Plain, a marble headstone has been erected, which bears the following inscription : —

ALBERT WILDER

Co. G.

39TH REG. MASS. VOLS.

DIED

JUNE, 1, 1864.

AGED

22 YEARS 4 MONTHS.

HE DIED AWAY FROM HOME AND FRIENDS,
OUR LOVED ONE TRUE AND BRAVE ;
HE HAS FALLEN FOR HIS COUNTRY,
AND HE FILLS A SOLDIER'S GRAVE.

CHARLES EDWARD WILDER.

Charles Edward Wilder, born in Hingham, August, 1832, was a son of Caleb and Lydia (Damon) Wilder. Early in 1864 he enlisted in the service of his country, and was mustered the 17th of February, as private in Co. E of the Thirty-second Regiment, M. V. I. In the disastrous battle of Laurel Hill, May 12, 1864, private Wilder was wounded in the hand, while the regiment was bravely advancing on the enemy's breastworks.

Shortly after he was attacked by a bronchial trouble, which terminated in consumption and death. At the first symptoms of his illness, he was sent to the hospital at Point Lookout, and early in November obtained leave of absence, and came to his home in Hingham. All efforts of medical skill, and all the tender assiduities of loving friends, proved ineffectual in arresting the progress of the disease; and on the 23d of December, 1864, he died in the full meridian of manhood, honored for his noble self-sacrifice, and mourned for his many virtues. He left a widow and one child.

HORATIO PHILANDER WILLARD.

Enlisted at Hingham, Oct. 25, 1861 ; mustered Nov. 28, 1861 ; and died at Alexandria, Va., Nov. 6, 1862.

Horatio P. Willard was born at Ashburnham, Mass., Sept. 25, 1819. His parents were Philander Jacob and Hannah Parker (Snow) Willard. He was a harness-maker by trade ; and after removing to Hingham was in the employ of Mr. David A. Hersey and others, until the outbreak of the war, when, on the 25th of October, 1861, he enlisted as private in Co. A of the Thirty-second Regiment, M. V. I., three years, and was mustered at Camp Dimmick on the 25th of the following November. His subsequent history is embraced in the trials and hardships early put upon the body of troops to which he belonged. Extended marches and continued exposure, however, soon broke down a somewhat enfeebled constitution ; and in August of the same year he was conveyed to the Fairfax Seminary Hospital at Alexandria, Va., where, after eight or ten weeks, he died of chronic diarrhœa, Nov. 6, 1862, at forty-three years of age.

In common with many who entered the service from Hingham in the autumn of 1861, Mr. Willard enlisted in the belief, that, beyond the discharge of garrison duty, no more arduous labor would be imposed. The perils of the hour made the call for additional forces imperative ; and the regiment quickly found its way to the front, with its full measure of dangers and fatigues.

The natural result followed. Many who would have proved efficient soldiers, and survived their term of enlistment, if confined to garrison duty, soon fell victims to disease and death under the trials of the battle-field.

Just before leaving Fort Warren, the subject of this sketch remarked to a friend, that "all were willing, and even desired to be led to the front," adding, with a playful smile and in a significant undertone, "*except one.*"

DON PEDRO WILSON,

The son of Cyrus and Mary Wilson, was born at Dracut, Mass., Aug. 26, 1821. Having received a common-school education, he studied dentistry, and commenced practice on Boylston Street, Boston, but in 1853 removed to Hingham. In August, 1863, he was drafted, and sent to join Co. A of the Sixteenth Regiment, M. V. I. The printed report of the adjutant-general says of him : "Mustered Aug. 21, 1863. Prisoner Oct. 23, 1863, and supposed died."

In a letter written at Beverly Ford, Va., to one of his friends, he said that he was in the surgeon's department, and that his duty was to receive the medicine and to administer it.

A relative writes, "All the information we have been able to obtain is, that he was reported missing on the retreat from Culpepper, Va., at Barstow Station ; and, being sick and unable to keep up, it is thought that he was taken prisoner and died before any information could be obtained in regard to him."

Such, in brief, is the history of one whom many of our people remember as a man highly skilled and respected in his profession.

He was a lover of rural occupations, and somewhat of an enthusiast in horticulture. Being compelled to leave his home and profession for the stern realities of war, and called so soon to sacrifice his life, his death seems doubly sad. He stood side by side with the volunteer, defended his country's laws, and for her gave his all.

CONRAD P. YÄGER.

Conrad P. Yäger was born in Mergantheim in the kingdom of Würtemberg, about the year 1843. He was a son of Conrad and Elenora Yäger. After the death of his father, and when about ten years of age, he came with his mother to Hingham, and lived with his stepfather, Mr. Samuel Sherman.

Entering the West Grammar School as a pupil, his progress was quite remarkable; for although at first he knew but few English words. yet in six months he was able to be classed with boys of his own age. He evinced in his recitations an understanding of the subject matter studied which soon gave him high rank in the school. At fifteen years of age he left Hingham, and went to Newton Corner to learn the trade of a carver, and was subsequently in the employ of Dr. Lincoln of Boston.

He enlisted into the United States service at Boston, in 1862, and was mustered in Co. F of the Second Regiment, Lincoln Guard, at Washington, D.C., in February, 1863.

Shortly after the defeat of Gen. Pope, the regiment was ordered out to protect the forts around Washington, when, in consequence of exposure, he contracted a severe cold, and was sent to the hospital. The severity of the attack, heightened probably by constitutional tendencies to consumption, soon led to a fatal result. He died the 15th of October, 1863, not having quite completed his twentieth year.

He is remembered here as a lad of great promise, manly and courteous in his demeanor, possessing remarkable physical and intellectual vigor, and as one who, early consecrating himself to the service of his adopted country, sacrificed his life, and

> " Sank to rest
> By all his country's wishes blest."

P. B. M.

CHAPTER XIX.

FURTHER ENLISTMENTS.

THE names of the following persons were obtained while the
volume was passing through the press, viz. : —

ARTHUR BEAL.

Born in Hingham, July 8, 1846.

Enlisted for the quota of the town, and was mustered July 14,
1864, as private in Co. A, Forty-second Regiment, M. V. I.,
one hundred days. Termination of service, Nov. 11, 1864.

AUGUSTUS BOLLING.

Age 24.

Served for the quota of Hingham; mustered Oct. 11, 1862, as
private in Co. C, Forty-second Regiment, M. V. M., nine
months. Termination of service, Aug. 20, 1863.

SWAN P. COLBERG.

Age 28.

Corporal in Co. C, Forty-second Regiment, M. V. M., nine
months. Enlisted for the second quota of Hingham, and was
mustered Oct. 11, 1862; mustered out Aug. 20, 1863.

JAMES CORCORAN.

Age 30.

Private in Co. C, Forty-second Regiment, M. V. M., nine months.

Enlisted for the second quota of the town, and was mustered Oct. 11, 1862; mustered out Aug. 20, 1863.

WILLIAM OTIS LINCOLN, Jun.

Born in Hingham, April 20, 1838.

Mustered Dec. 24, 1861, as commissary sergeant in Co. A of the First Regiment Cavalry, M. V., three years. Served in the Department of the South; mustered out as regimental commissary sergeant, April 10, 1862.

PATRICK McCRANE.

Age 44.

Served for nine months on second quota of Hingham; mustered Oct. 11, 1862, as private in Co. C, Forty-second Regiment, M. V. M.; mustered out Aug. 20, 1863.

MICHAEL REARDON.

Age 35.

According to town documents, served on second quota of Hingham for nine months; enrolled Oct. 11, 1862, as private in Co. C, Forty-second Regiment, M. V. M.; termination of service, Aug. 20, 1863.

WILLIAM RICH.

Age 40.

Occupation farmer. Enlisted under recruiting-officer Edward Cazneau for the first quota of Hingham, three years. Thirty-eighth Regiment, Co. I.

JOHN RYAN.

Recruited for three years. Returned by the selectmen as serving for the quota of Hingham.

WARREN R. SPURR.

Age 32.

Resided in Hingham, and enlisted for the quota of the town. Mustered Dec. 30, 1863, as private in Co. A of the Third Heavy Artillery, M. V., three years. Service terminated Sept. 18, 1865.

SUMMARY.

Regular members and volunteers of the Lincoln Light Infantry who served at Fortress Monroe, not included in any quota 79

Number of soldiers and sailors, natives of Hingham, who served in the war, including enlistments in other States 243

Number of soldiers and sailors who served for the quota of Hingham 471

It should be understood that many of our soldiers and sailors served upon more than one quota of the town. In some instances, soldiers serving for short terms afterwards enlisted for three years. Others, at the expiration of their term of three years, or after being discharged for disability, re-enlisted upon new quotas, as required at the time.

The aggregate of the enlistments from Hingham during the war, and not including the members of the Lincoln Light Infantry, was 705

Number of soldiers and sailors connected with Hingham who died prior to the erection of the Monument . 87

LIST OF BATTLES AND SKIRMISHES

MENTIONED IN THE PRECEDING RECORDS, WITH THE
DATE OF OCCURRENCE.

Aldie, Va., June 21, 1863.
Alexandria, La., May 6–14, 1864.
Antietam, Md., Sept. 17, 1862.
Arrowfield Church (near Petersburg), Va., May 9, 1864.
Atlanta, Ga., July 22, 1864; surrendered to Gen. 'Sherman's
    army, Sept. 2, 1864.

Bachelder's Creek, N.C., Feb. 1, 1864.
Bailor's Farm, Va. (cavalry), June 15, 1864.
Ball's Bluff, Va., Oct. 21, 1861.
Baton Rouge, La., Aug. 5, 1862.
Bermuda Hundred, Va., attack at, May 16, 1864.
Bethesda Church, Va., June 2, 3, 1864.
Big Bethel, Va., June 10, 1861.
Bisland, La., April 12, 13, 1863.
Blackburn's Ford, Md. (sk.), July 18, 1861, and Sept. 20, 1862.
Blick's Station, Va. (see Weldon Railroad), Aug. 19, 1864.
Blount's Creek, N.C., April 9, 1863.
Blue Springs, Tenn., Oct. 10, 1863.
Boonsboro', Md.
Botler's Mill, Md. (see Shepardstown Ford), Sept. 20, 1862.
Boykins Mills, S.C., April 18, 1865.
Boydton Plank Road, Va., Oct. 27, 1864, and March 29, 1865.
Brashear City, La., June 26, 1863.
Bristoe's Station, Va., Oct. 14, 1863.
Brock Pike, Va. (sk.), May 5, 1864.
Bull Run, Va., first battle, July 21, 1861.
Bull Run, Va., second battle, Aug. 30, 1862.
Buzzard's Roost (near Resaca, Ga.), evacuated May 10, 1864.

Camden, N.C., April 19, 1862.

Campbell's Station, Tenn., Nov. 16, 1863.
Cane River, La., April 23. 1864.
Carsville, Ga., May 15, 1864.
Cedar Creek, Va., Oct. 13-19, 1864.
Cedar Mountain, Va., Aug. 9, 1862.
Chancellorsville, Va., May 1-4, 1863.
Chantilly, Va., Sept 1, 1862.
Charles City Court House, Va. (sk.), Dec. 13, 1863.
Charles City Cross Roads, Va., June 30, 1862.
Charleston, S.C., occupied by the national forces, Feb. 18, 1865.
Chattanooga, Tenn., occ. by the national troops, Sept. 9, 1863 ;
    battle near, Nov. 22-25, 1863.
Chickamauga, Tenn., Sept. 19, 1863.
Cold Harbor, Va., June 1-3, 1864.
Cove Creek, N.C. (sk.), May 22, 1863.
Crampton's Pass, Md. (see South Mountain), Sept. 14, 1862.

Dabney's Mills, Va., Feb. 6, 7, 1865.
Dallas, Ga., May 28, 29, 1864.
Darbytown Road (near Richmond), Va., Oct. 13, 1864.
Deep Bottom, Va., July 27 and Aug. 15, 16, 1864.
Donaldsonville, La., July 11-13, 1863.
Drury's Bluff, Va., May 12-16, 1864.
Duncan's Run, Va., March 25, 1865.

Fair Oaks, Va., May 31, June 1, 1862.
Falling Waters, Va.
Fisher's Hill, Va. Sept. 22, 1864.
Five Forks, Va., April 1, 1865.
Fort Donnelson, Tenn., Feb. 16, 1862.
Fort Mahone, Va., April 2, 1865.
Fort Saunders, Tenn., Nov. 29, 1863.
Fort Sedgwick (near Petersburg), Va., April 2, 1865.
Fort Stedman (near Petersburg), Va., March 25, 1865.
Fort Stevens, near Washington, D.C. (cav. sk.), July 11, 1864.
Fort Sumter, S.C., attack on, April 12, 1861 ; surrendered to the
    national forces, Feb. 17, 1865.
Fort Wagner, S.C., assault on, July 18, 1863.

Four Mile Run (near Richmond), Va., Oct. 27, 1864.
Fredericksburg, Va., Dec. 11–15, 1862.
Front Royal, Va., May 23, 1862.
Funkstown, Md. (sk.), July 12, 1863.

Gaines' Mill, Va., June 27, 1862.
Gainesville, Fla. (cav.), Aug. 17, 1864.
Gainesville, Va., June 29, 1862.
Gettysburg, Pa., July 2–3, 1863.
Georgia Landing, October, 1862.
Glendale, Va., June 29, 30, 1862.
Goldsboro', N.C., Dec. 17, 1862.
Goldsboro' Bridge, N.C. (sk.), Nov. 17, 1862.
Gov. Moore's Plantation (near Alexandria), La., May 3, 1864.
Gravelly Run, Va., March 31, 1865.

Hampton Roads, Va., March 8, 9, 1862.
Hanover Court House, Va., May 27, 1862.
Hatcher's Run, Va., Feb. 5, 6, 1865.
Hatteras Inlet, N.C., attack at, Aug. 27–29, 1861.
Heckman's Farm, Va., May 6, 7, 1864.
High Bridge, Va., April 6, 1865.
Honey Hill, S.C., Nov. 30, and Dec. 10, 1864.

Irish Bend, La., April 14, 1863.

Jackson, Miss., siege of, July 11–16, 1863.
Jacksonville, Fla., Feb. 5, 1864.
James Island, S.C., July 2–9, 1864.
Jericho Ford, May 23, 1864.
John's Island, S.C., July 2–9, 1864.
Jones' Farm, Va. (see engagement at Pamunkey River).

Kelley's Ford, Va., Nov. 7, 1863.
Kenesaw Mountain, Tenn., June 16, 22, 27, 1864.
Kettle Run, Va., Aug. 27, 1862.
Kinston, N.C., Dec. 14, 1862, March 8–10, 1865.
Knoxville, Tenn., siege of, Nov. 17 to Dec. 7, 1863.
Kock's Plantation, La. (sk. near), July 12, 1863.

Laurel Hill, Va., May 8 and 12, 1864.

Laurenceburg, Ky.

Lee's Mill, Va., April 16, 1862.

Little Washington, N.C., Nov. 3, 1862, and siege of, April 1–18, 1863.

Locust Grove, Va., Nov. 27, 1863.

Lookout Mountain, Tenn., Oct. 29, 1863.

Malvern Hill, Va., July 1–3, 1862.

Mansura, La., May 15, 16, 1864.

Mechanicsville, Va. June 26, 1862.

Mine Run, Va., Nov. 28–30, 1863, and Nov. 6, 1864.

Missionary Ridge, Tenn., December, 1863.

Mobile, Ala., occ. by Union troops, April 12, 1865.

Morris Island, S.C., July 10, 1863.

Murfreesboro,' Tenn., July 13, 1862, Jan. 1–3, 1863, and April 13, 1863.

NAVAL ENGAGEMENTS AND CAPTURES.

1861.

Aug. 28, Engagement at Hatteras Inlet, N.C.

Sept. 22, Capture of Blockade-runner " Mary E. Pindar."

Oct. 3, Capture of Schooner " Beverly."

Oct. 20, Capture of Brig " Ariel."

Nov. 12, Capture of Privateer " Beauregard."

1862.

March 8, Engagement at Sewall's Point.

March 8–9, Engagement with the ram " Merrimack " in Hampton Roads, and sinking of United States ships " Cumberland " and " Congress."

April 18–24, Engagement and capture of Forts Jackson, St. Philip, and the Chalmette batteries.

April 25, Engagement and capture of Forts Macon and Beaufort, N.C.

April 26, Capture of Ship " Gondor " and Barque " Glenn," blockade-runners.

HINGHAM IN THE CIVIL WAR.

May 1, New Orleans, La., captured.

June 28, Engagement with the batteries at Vicksburg, Miss.

July 15, Engagement with the Confederate Ram "Arkansas" and the Vicksburg batteries.

Aug. 12–16, Engagement at Corpus Christi. Capture of Confederate armed Schooner "Breaker."

Capture of Steamer "Arizona," blockade-runner "Reindeer," and Confederate Schooner "Montebello."

1863.

Jan. 1, Engagement at Galveston, Texas, capture by the enemy of United States Steamer "Harriet Lane," and blowing up of the United States Steamer "Westfield" by her commander.

Jan. 10–11, Engagement at Arkansas Post.

March 28, United States Steamer "Diana" captured by the enemy.

April 1–18, Attack at, and siege of Little Washington, N.C.

April 15, Attack on West Point, Va.

May 25 to July 8, The Navy co-operate with the army at the siege of Port Hudson.

Dec. 25, Attack at Stono River, S.C.

1864.

Feb. 1, United States Steamer "Underwriter" captured by the enemy.

Feb. 11, Capture of Schooners "Louisa" and "Cosmopolite."

July 11, A second attack at Stono River, S.C.

Aug. 5–8, Great Naval Engagement in Mobile Harbor; surrender of Forts Gaines and Powell, capture of the Confederate Ram "Tennessee," and Steamer "Selma," and sinking of the Confederate Steamer "Gaines."

Aug. 23, Fort Morgan, in Mobile Harbor, surrenders to Admiral Farragut.

Nov. 12, Capture of the Forts at Plymouth, N.C.

Dec. 23, Capture of blockade-runner "Julia."

Nashville, Tenn., taken by the National troops ab. Feb. 24. 1862.
  (Battle near, Dec. 15, 16, 1864.)
Natural Bridge (between St. Mark's and Tallahassee), Fla.. March
  8, 1865.
Newbern, N.C., March 14. 1862.
New Hope Church, Ga.. May 25, 1864.
New Hope Church, Va., November, 1863.
New Oak Church.
Norfolk, Va., surrendered to the national forces. May 10, 1862.
North Anna, Va., May 24, 1864.

Olustee, Fla., Feb. 20, 1864.
Opequan, Va., Sept. 19, 1864.

Pamunkey River, Va.. May 30, 1864.
Peach Orchard (Savage Station), Va., June 29, 1862.
Perryville, Ky., Oct. 8, 1862.
Petersburg, Va., siege of. June 16, 1864, to April 2, 1865.
Petersburg, Va., Mine Explosion, July 30, 1864.
Pittsburg Landing, Tenn., April 7, 1862.
Plains Store, La., May 21, 1863.
Pleasant Hill (Red River), La., April 9, 10, 1864.
Poolsville, Md. (cav. sk.), Sept. 5, 1862, and July 12, 1864.
Poplar Spring (or Grove) Church, Va., Sept. 30, 1864.
Po River, Va., May 10, 1864.
Port Hudson, La., siege of, May 25, to July 8, 1863.

Raleigh, N.C., occupied by Gen. Sherman, April 13–25, 1865.
Rappahannock Station, Va., Nov. 7, 1863.
Rawles Mills, N.C. (sk.), Nov. 2, 1862.
Richmond, Va., occupied by the national troops under Gen.
  Weitzel, April 3, 1865.
Roanoke Island, N.C., Feb. 7, 8, 1862.
Robertson's Tavern, Va., Nov. 27, 1863.
Rocky Face Ridge (See Dallas, Ga.).

Sabine Cross Roads, La., April 8, 1864.
Saunders House (Chancellorsville).

Savage Station, Va., June 29, 1862.
Shepardstown Ford, Va., Sept. 20, 1862.
Smitherick's Ford, N.C. (sk.), Nov. 2, 1862.
Smithfield, Va., engagement at, April 14, 1864.
South Anna Bridge, on the Pamunkey River, Va. (cav.), June
    26, 1863.
South Mountain, Md., Sept. 14, 1862.
South West Creek, N.C., March 7, 8, 1865.
Springbank Bridge, N.C. (sk.), Dec. 17, 1863.
Spottsylvania, Va., May 10, 12, and 18, 1864.
St. Mary's Heights (Fredericksburg), Va., Dec. 13, 1862, and
    May 3, 1863.
Stone River, Tenn., Jan. 2, 1863.
Strawberry Plains, Va. (sk. near), Jan. 16, 1864.
Sulphur Springs, Va. (cav.), Oct. 12, 1863.
Surrender of Gen. Lee, and the Army of Northern Virginia, to
    Gen. Grant, April 9, 1865.

Tallyhoma, Ga.
Tolopotomy Swamp, Va., May 31, 1864.
Trenton, N.C.

Vaughan Road, Va., March 29, 1865.
Vermilionville, La., Oct. 9, 1863.
Vicksburg, Miss., siege of, June 17 to July 4, 1863.

Wapping Heights, Va., July 24, 1863.
Weldon Railroad, Va., Aug. 18-25, 1864.
West Point, Va., May 7, 1862, and April 15, 1863.
Wheatland, Va.
Whitehall, N.C., Dec. 16, 1862.
White House, Va. (sk.), June 28, 1862.
White Oak Swamp, Va., June 30, 1862.
Wilcox Bridge, N.C. (sk.), July 7, 1863.
Wilderness, Va., May 5, 6, and 7, 1864.
Williamsburg, Va., May 3-5, 1862.
Williamsport, Md., evacuated, July 9, 1863.

Winchester, Va., at or near (cav.), March 23, and Dec. 3, 1862.
June 13, 14, 1863, and Sept. 19, 1864.
Winton, N.C. (sk.), July 27, 1863.

Yellow Bayou (near Simmsport), La., May 18, 1864.
Yorktown, Va., siege of, April 5 to May 3, 1862.

APPENDIX.

LIST OF PERSONS WHO CONTRIBUTED TOWARD THE
ERECTION OF THE SOLDIERS' AND SAILORS'
MONUMENT. ARRANGED BY FAMILIES.
(See pp. 20 and 21.)

Adams, Mrs. Ann Lizzie.
Amedy, Mrs. Deborah T.
Anderson, Alexander.
  Mrs. Alexander.
Andrews, Benjamin.
  Mrs. Benjamin.
  Benjamin, jun.
  Emma B.
Andrews, Lydia.
Andrews, Catherine A.
  Julia S.
Andrews, Mrs. Thomas.
  Sarah L.
  Harriet F.
  Willie B.
  Mary E.
  Addie L.

Bailey, Caleb.
  Mrs. Caleb.
Bailey, George.
  Mrs. George.
  Fanny D.
  Addie M.
  Lizzie N.
Baker, James L.

Baker, Mrs. Lydia J.
  Sarah F.
  Mary S.
Barnes, Adeline A.
Barnes, Edwin.
  John C.
Barnes, Elisha J., Boston.
  Mrs. Elisha J., Boston.
Barnes, Henry.
  Carrie P.
  Howard C.
Barnes, Isaac.
Barnes, Kilburn.
  Susan.
Barrett, Michael.
Bassett, John.
  Mrs. John.
Bassett, Daniel.
  Mrs. Daniel.
  D. Fletcher.
  Mary G.
  Wentworth A.
  Fannie W.
Bassett, Caleb T.
Bassett, George.
Barstow, Samuel B.

Barstow, Mrs. Samuel B.
Bartlett, Mrs. L. A.
 Edward W.
Bates, Amos.
 Mrs. Amos.
Bates, Amos B.
 Florence C.
Battles, Otis L.
Beal, Abner L.
Beal, Caleb.
Beal, Caleb G.
 Mrs. Caleb G.
Beal, Carrie M.
 Rachel B.
Beal, Elijah.
 Mrs. Elijah.
Beal, Ella C., North Cohasset.
 Isadora, North Cohasset.
Beal, Leavitt B.
 Mrs. Leavitt B.
 Oliver L.
 Henri L. F.
 Nettie F.
 Hubert.
Beal, Louise R.
Beal, Lizzie J.
Beal, Lucy.
 Martha B.
Beal, Wilbur F.
 Mrs. Wilbur F.
 Russell S.
 Wilbur, jun.
Beal, William.
Bicknell, Hannah.
 Quincy.
 Mrs. Quincy.
 Lincoln B.
 Hannah O.
 Quincy, jun.
Blossom, Thomas D.
 Mrs. Thomas D.
 Catharine W.
 Charles H.
Blossom, Edward C.
 Mrs. Edward C.

Brantley, Lorenzo,
Breene, Mrs. Susan.
 John J.
 Joseph.
 David.
Brett, Massena.
Bronsdon, Samuel.
 Mrs. Samuel.
 Emma F.
 Lizzie B.
Burbank, Samuel.
 Sarah B.
Burr, Joseph C.
Burr, Henry H.
 Anna E.
Burr, Mrs. Mary.
 Mary W.
 Maria S.
Burr, E. Waters.
 Mrs. E. Waters.
 William R.
 Henry W.
 Clarence S.
 Charles W.
 George W.
 Fannie H.
Burr, Charles T.
 Mrs. Charles T.
 Arthur W.
 Minnie F.
Burr, Fearing.
 Peter.
 Meriel.
 Margaret.
Burr, Mrs. Emma.
 Caroline A.
 Ellen L.
Burr, Brown. & Co.
Burrell, Lemuel.
Buttemore, Thomas.
Buttemore, John.

Cain, Daniel.
 Mrs. Daniel.
 Albion H.

Cain, Lucy A.
Cain, David.
   Mrs. David.
   David F.
Cain. Leonard O.
Casey, John.
Casey, George M.
Casey, Mary E.
Casey, Catherine W.
Cazneau. Mary B.
Clark. Andrew J.
   Harry L.
   Mary W.
   George F.
Clark. Ada A.
Clarey, George C., jun.
   Mrs. George C., jun.
Clement, James F.
   Mrs. James F.
Cobb. David, jun.
Cobb, Silas H.
Cook. James B.
Corbett, John M.
   Mrs. John M.
   Edith M.
Corthell, Sarah A.
Corthell, Loring.
   Mrs. Loring.
Corthell, John K.
   Mrs. John K.
   John G.
   Henry R.
   Joseph.
   Mary R.
   Ella J.
   Charles L.
Cowing, Edward.
Crehan, Lawrence.
   Thomas L.
   Mary A.
   James.
Crehan, Patrick.
Crosby, Samuel T.
   Mrs. Samuel T.
   Ellen L.

Crosby, Clara M.
   Samuel T., jun.
   Helen B.
Cross, Moses.
   Mrs. Moses.
   Walter I.
   William Davis.
   Harry Francis.
   Edward Gorham
Crowe, John.
   Mrs. John.
   Edmund T.
   Mary A.
   John, jun.
   William T.
Cushing, David, 2d.
   Mrs. David, 2 .
   Elizabeth B.
   Sarah.
Cushing. Leonard.
   Mary C.
Cushing. Mrs. Almira.
Cushing, Angelina H.
Cushing, William.
Cushing, Charles W.
   Mrs. Charles W.
   Charles O.
   Annie F.
   Virginia L.
Cushing. Elpalet L.
   Mrs. Elpalet L.
   Edna L.
   Maud Wales.
Cushing, David.
   Bella.
Cushing. John.
   Mrs. John.
   Fannie O.
Cushing. Loring H.
Cushing, Alonzo.
   Mrs. Alonzo.
   Alonzo F.
   Lizzie H.

Daley. John.

Damon, Catherine.
Damon, Isaac N.
    Abbie H.
    F. M.
Dana, Mrs. Lucy J.
Davis, Mrs. Deborah.
Davis, William.
Dawes, John P.
    John G.
Dawes, William L.
Dayton, Bela.
Donnelly John A.
Dow, Mrs. Susan P.
Drew, Phineas.
Dunbar, Andrew W.
    Mrs. Andrew W.
    Inez L.
Dunn, Alexander.
    Mrs. Alexander.
    Mary E.
    Matthew W.
    Charles.
Dupee, Lewis F.

Easterbrook, Joseph.
    Lizzie W.
Easterbrook, Samuel.
    Mrs. Samuel.
    Delia D.
Edes, Robert T.
    Annie B.
Eldredge, Eleanor W.
Eldredge, John W.
    Mrs. John W.
    Bessie C.

Farmer, Jedediah.
Fearing, Albert.
    Mrs. Albert.
Fearing, David, jun.
Fearing, William, 2d.
    Mrs. William, 2d.
    Willie B.
    Alice L.
Fearing, Abel.

Fearing, Arthur S.
    Watson B.
    Clarkson T.
Fearing, Mrs. Matilda.
    Leah L.
Fearing, Mrs. Priscilla.
    Emily.
Fearing, Perez L.
Fee, Peter.
Fee, James.
Fee, John.
    Peter.
    Mary E.
Fletcher, Henry L.
    Mrs. Henry L.
    Charles H.
    William O.
Fiske, Mrs. Annie F.
    Sarah D.
Foley, Cornelius.
    Catherine.
    Ellen.
    Mary.
    John.
    Cornelius, jun.
French, Mary E.
French, Lewis.
    Charles B.
    Edwin H.
    Carrie R.
French, Lydia.
Fuller, Tilson.
    Mrs. Tilson.
    S. Jenny.
    H. Adeline.
Fuller, Mrs. John E.

Gardner, Calvin.
    Isaac, 2d.
Gardner, Tobias O.
    Mrs. Tobias O.
    Carrie O.
Gardner, Andrew J.
    Mrs. Andrew J.
    Lucy S.

Gardner, Andrew W.
    Mrs. Andrew W.
    Albert S.
    Mrs. Albert S.
    John H.
Gardner, Isaac.
Gates, John D.
.   Mrs. John D.
    Lizzie.
    Cushing.
Gill, Caleb.
    Mrs. Caleb.
Gilman, William M.
Good, Charles E.
    Mrs. Charles E.
Goodrich, Hosah G.
Goodwin, Isaac F.
Gorman, Michael.
    Mrs. Michael.
    Mary I.
    Michael F.
    William I.
Gould, Lincoln.
Graham, Mary E.
Greely, William.
Groce, Mary L.

Hall, Miss Mary.
Halley, Patrick.
Harding, David.
    Henry C.
Harlow, Jonathan E.
    Mrs. Jonathan E.
Harris, Martha M.
Hawkes, James.
    Mrs. James.
Hersey, Albert F.
    Mrs. Albert F.
Hersey, Henry F.
    Mrs. Henry F.
    Ellen P.
Hersey, Ellen M.
Hersey, Isaac.
Hersey, Edwin.
Hersey, Caleb.

Hersey, Rosella F.
Hersey, Rachel.
    Hannah.
Hersey, Zadock.
    Mrs. Zadock.
    Susan W.
    Emma J.
Hersey, Isaac L.
    Mrs. Isaac L.
Hersey, Samuel.
Hersey, Edmund.
    Mrs. Edmund.
    Fanny.
Hersey, Cushing.
Hersey, Franklin H.
Hersey, Caleb S.
    Frances.
Hersey, William H.
Hersey, Gridley F.
Hersey, Maria S.
Hersey, Warren A.
    Mrs. Warren A.
Hersey, George W.
    Mrs. George W.
Hersey, William, jun.
    Leander C. T.
Hersey, Henry.
Hersey, Margaret.
Hersey, Francis H.
Hersey, Henry M.
Hersey, George.
Hersey, George, jun.
    Mrs. George, jun.
    Walter W.
Hersey, Edmund, 2d.
    Mrs. Edmund, 2d.
    Adelaide W.
    Howard P.
Hicky, Daniel.
    Susan H.
Hill, Daniel.
Hobart, Peter, jun.
Hobart, Henry.
    Mrs. Henry.
Hobart, Seth L.

Hobart, Mrs. Seth L.
   Ella M.
   Marion L.
   Mabel M.
Hobart, Leavitt.
   Mrs. Leavitt.
   George.
   Frank.
Hollis, John A.
   John C.
Hough, George F.
   Charles G.
   Ellen A.
Howard, Alfred.
   Hiram T.
Howard, Waters.
   Mrs. Waters.
   Sarah A.
   Elizabeth.
Howard, Charles.
Hudson, William.
Hudson, Eben H.
Hull, Thomas.
Humphrey, Mrs. Edwin.
   Mary C.
   Eddie D.
Humphrey, Leavitt.
Humphrey, Davis.
Humphrey, Marcellus.
   Amos C.
   Frederick.
Humphrey, Thomas C.
Humphrey, Charles.
Hunt, George.
   Mrs. George.
Hunt, Caleb S.
Hunt, James L.
Hyland, Mrs. Chloe S.

Jacob, Joseph.
   Mrs. Joseph.
   Sarah C.
   Frederick S.
Jacob, Joshua.
Jeffries, Mary T.

Jerald, Ora F.
   Mrs. Ora F.
Jernegan, William H.
   Mrs. William H.
   Lottie W.
Jones, William.
Jones, Gardner H.
Jones, Mrs. Moses.
Jones, Henry W.
Jones, Seaver.
   Mrs. Seaver.
Jones, Grace A.
   Lizzie M.
Jones, Henry.
   Mrs. Henry.

Kaliher, Ellen.
Kelsey, William P.
   John B.
   James M.
Kent, Maurice.
   Mrs. Maurice.
   Mary.
   John.
   Ellen.
   Honora.
Keshan, Mrs. John.
   Catherine T.
   Helen M.
   Anna M.
   Elizabeth J.
   John H.
King, George W.
   James S.
Kitterell, Jane A.
   Charles.

Lane, Rufus.
   Mrs. Rufus.
   Rufus A.
   Carrie L.
Lane, Mrs. Elizabeth.
Lane, Leavitt.
Lane, Morallus.
Lane, Ruth B.

Lane, Charles.
Leavitt, Abner L..
    Abner L., jun.
    William H.
Leavitt, Mrs. Almira.
    Sarah.
Leavitt, Elijah.
Leavitt, Thomas J.
    Mrs. Thomas J.
    Charles Thomas.
    Lilla M.
Le Baron, Russell.
Lewis, Mrs. Joanna K.
Lewis, James S.
    Mrs. James S.
    John B.
Lincoln, Bela.
    Mrs. Bela.
    Abby A.
    Bela F.
Lincoln, Calvin.
    Lydia L.
    Laurinda.
Lincoln, Calvin A.
    Mrs. Calvin A.
Lincoln, Charles, jun.
    Mrs. Charles, jun.
Lincoln, Charlotte C.
Lincoln, Charlotte L.
Lincoln, David.
    Mrs. David.
Lincoln, E.
Lincoln, George.
    Mrs. George.
    George M.
    Mercy W.
    Herman.
    Sarah J.
    Helen S.
    Alfred L.
Lincoln, Miss C. K. T.
Lincoln, Henry W.
    Henry W., jun.
    Lillie A.
Lincoln, Jairus B.

Lincoln, Mrs. Jairus B.
Lincoln, Joanna.
    Lucinda.
Lincoln, Mrs. Luther B.
Lincoln, Mrs. Marshal.
Lincoln, Mary C.
    Maria S.
    Ann S.
Lincoln, Mrs. Phœbe.
Lincoln, Robert W.
    Mrs. Robert W.
    Robert W., jun.
    William C.
    Marshal.
    James L.
Lincoln, Solomon.
    Mrs. Solomon.
    Solomon, jun.
    Arthur.
    Francis Henry.
Lincoln, Mrs. Susan N.
    George B.
    Frank R.
    Lydia W.
    Helen A.
Lincoln, Thomas H.
    Sarah F.
    Meriel F.
Lincoln, William O.
    Mary.
Litchfield, Franklin.
Loring, Albert B.
    Mrs. Albert B.
    Abner.
    Abbie W.
Loring, Alfred.
    Mrs. Alfred.
Loring, Mrs. Amelia B.
Loring, Enos.
    Ida W.
    E. Bradley.
    George A.
    Hattie A.
Loring, Isaiah W.
Loring, Mrs. Isaiah W.

Loring, Ida M.
 Francis W.
 Joseph J.
 Jennie R.
 Sarah J.
Loring, Zenas.
Lovett, John O.
 Mrs. John O.
 Mary E.
 Sarah F.
 John O., jun.
 Charles A.

McCarty, Catherine G.
 Catherine A.
 Mary E.
McDonough, Miss Caroline.
McNiel, Sarah.
 Hannah.
 Peter,
McKee, Mrs. Mary.
Mahoney, Helen.
 Maggie.
Marble, Demerick.
 Mrs. Demerick.
 Arthur D.
 Charles H.
Margett, Thomas.
Marsh, Caleb.
 Mrs. Caleb.
 George S.
 Lizzie M.
 Fred.
Marsh, Charles N.
 Mrs. Charles N.
 Ellen Billings.
 Ebed Hersey.
Marsh, Lydia L.
Marsh, Samuel W.
Marsh, Sarah L.
 Helen M.
Matthews, Henry A.
Maxim, Mrs. Lydia.
May, Hattie E.
May, Henry G.

Meade, Francis K.
 Mrs. Francis K.
Merritt, Henry L.
Merritt, Henry, jun.
 Mrs. Henry, jun.
Merritt, Paul B.
Meservey, Benjamin F.
 Mrs. Benjamin F.
 Manley, C.
 B. W.
Miller, Fred H.
Miller, Ellen C.
Moffitt, John.
Murphy, Jeremiah, jun.
Murphy, Mary E.
Muzzy, Julia A.

Nash, Reuben H.
 Frank W.
 Ellen M.
Nelson, Mrs. James.
Nelson, William J.
 Mrs. William J.
 Lois A.
 Lizzie P.
 Harry B.
 Willie B.
Nelson, William T.
Newhall, Joseph A.
 Mrs. Joseph A.
Nichols, Mrs. Alfred.
Nichols, George W.
 Mrs. George W.
Noyes, Joseph W.
Nye, Atkinson.
 Fanny L.
 William A.
Nye, Henry.
 Mrs. Henry.
 John H.
 Mary E.
 Sarah.
Nye, Lucy.
Nye, J. Sturgis.
O'Keefe, Patrick.

O'Keefe, Mrs. Patrick.
    Kate.
    Margaret.
    Caroline.
    Ellen M.
Osborn, Henry.
    Mrs. Henry.
Overton, Sarah E.

Palmer, Elizabeth B.
Palmer, Lydia B.
    Sarah A.
Park, Mary.
Parker, Benjamin.
    Mrs. Benjamin.
    Benjamin R.
    E. A.
Peare, Horace.
Peirce, Mrs. John W.
Perry, Seth W.
Poole, Joseph M.
Pyne, John.
    John W.
    David W.

Rafferty, John.
Reed, Horace F.
    Mrs. Horace F.
Remington, Bela C.
Remington, Hosea S.
Remington, John O.
    Mrs. John O.
    Otis L.
Remington, W. T.
Rich, B. W.
Rich, Alexander G.
Richards, I. D.
Riley, William.
Ripley, Mrs. Eben C.
    Charles H.
Ripley, George R.
Ripley, Levi B.
Ripley, Joseph.
    Mrs. Joseph.

Schmidt, Charles.
Seymour, Charles W.
    Mrs. Charles W.
    Mehitable W.
    Martha W.
Seymour, Charles W. S.
    Mrs. Charles W. S.
    Harriet L.
    Hubert.
Sherman, Samuel,
Shuck, Frederick.
    James B.
Shute, Elijah.
    Mrs. Elijah.
    Walter C.
Shute, Henry.
    Abigail B.
    Henry Leonard.
Siders, Henry.
    Mrs. Henry.
    Henry Francis.
    Sarah Davis.
    Elizabeth Blake.
Siders, John,
    Mrs. John.
Simmons, Samuel.
Snell, John E.
Snell, Thomas.
Snell, Margaret.
Spaulding, Henry E.
Spear, Sarah L.
    Adda F.
    Henry E.
Spencer, David.
    Mrs. David.
Spooner, George H.
Spooner, Leonore.
Sprague, Daniel W.
Sprague, Joseph.
    Mrs. Joseph.
    Thomas Loring.
    Joseph Sumner.
    Mary Eliza.
Sprague, Joseph C.

Sprague, Joseph T.
Sprague, Josiah.
    Freddie L.
Sprague, Leavitt, 2d.
Sprague, Peter N.
    Mrs. Peter N.
    Martha L.
Sprague, Widow Peter.
Sprague, Sally.
Sprague, Sidney W.
Sprague. Samuel.
Sprague, Sidney
    Mrs. Sidney.
Sprague. William B.
Spring, Charles.
    Mrs. Charles.
    Charles L.
    Lizzie H.
    Frederic W.
Stearns, Ella L.
    George W.
Stephenson, Ezra.
    Mrs. Ezra.
    William L.
    Ezra T. C.
    Levi T.
Stephenson, Henry.
Stephenson, John.
    Mrs. John.
    Susan A.
Stockwell, Otis.
    Mrs. Otis.
Stodder, Caleb S.
Stodder, C. H. F.
Stodder, John P.
Stodder, Martin.
Stodder, Martin L.
Stodder, Martin T.
Stodder, Mrs. R. L.
Stodder, Thomas.
Stodder, William T.
    Mary C.
    Albion T.
Stodder, William D.
    Henry L.

Southworth, Temperance.
Stowell, Hersey.
    Francis H.
    Martha.
    Helen M.
Stowell, Jared.
    Alice.

Taylor, A. C.
    Myra F.
Taylor, William.
    George H.
Thaxter, Mrs. Joseph B., sen.
    Lucy B.
    David.
Thaxter, Joseph B.
    Mrs. Joseph B.
    Joseph B., jun.
Thaxter, Anna O.
    Catherine K.
    Elizabeth K.
Thaxter, Norton O.
Thayer, Albert E.
    Mrs. Albert E.
    Edward W.
Thayer, Elihu.
    Mrs. Elihu.
    Charles M.
Thayer, Mrs. Jairus.
Thayer, Joshua.
Thomas, Mrs. David.
Thomas, Joseph.
    Mrs. Joseph.
    Fred W.
Thomas, Reuben.
    Mrs. Reuben.
Thomas, William.
    Mrs. William.
Thomas, William Henry.
    Mrs. William Henry.
    Widow Sally L.
Thompson, Catherine E.
Thompson. Domick.
Tilden, Elijah D.
    Mrs. Elijah D.

Tilden, Helen D.
    Mary E.
Tilson, Jonathan.
    Mrs. Jonathan.
Tinsley, Mrs. Hannah.
    Teresa.
    Jane.
    Mary A.
Tirrell, Sarah B.
Todd, John.
    Mrs. John.
    Oliver.
Tulley, Hubert J.
    Mrs. Hubert J.
    James W.
    John W.

Urie, John.
    Mary L.
    John F.
    George W.
    Robert.

Wade, John E.
Waters, George H.
Waters, John.
    Mrs. John.
Welch, John F.
Welch, John.
White, James P.
    Edward J.
Whiting, Amasa.
    Mrs. Amasa.
    Amasa J.
    Ada B.
    Widow Catherine B.
Whitney, George F.
    Mrs. George F.
    George E.
Whitney, Jason W.
    Mrs. Jason W.
    Everett E.
    Edward C.
    William C.
Whiton, Albert.
    Mrs. Albert.
    Albert H.

Whiton, Effie A.
    Eliza P.
Whiton, Bela.
Whiton, Adeline.
Whiton, Elijah L.
    Mrs. Elijah L.
    Dexter B.
    Mary L.
Whiton, Mary R.
Whiton, Thomas F.
    Mrs. Thomas F.
    Morris F.
Whiton, Royal.
    Sarah A.
Whiton, William.
    Fannie.
    Laura.
    Charles F.
Whittier, Mary A.
Wilder, Alden.
Wilder, Charlotte S.
Wilder, Edwin.
    Osgood.
Wilder, Edwin, 2d.
    Mrs. Edwin, 2d.
    Olive A.
    Edwin M.
Wilder, Elizabeth.
Wilder, Frederick S.
Wilder, Frederick.
Wilder, George.
Wilder, Henry.
    Isaac H.
    James H.
Wilder, Joseph H.
Wilder, Joseph.
Wilder, Martin.
Wilder, Nathaniel.
Wilder, William W.
    Lizzie May.
    Cordelia A.
Winslow, Isaac.
Woodward, Joseph.
Wolfe, David.
    Henry.
Wright, George.

OMISSION.

CHARLES HAYWARD BAILEY.

Born in Hingham, May 1, 1842.

Enlisted at Boston, Sept. 4, 1862, as private in Co. A, Forty-fourth Regiment, M. V. I., nine months.

Served in the Department of North Carolina, and was present . in the engagements at Rawle's Mill, Kinston, Whitehall, and Goldsboro'.

Returned with the regiment, and was mustered out at Readville, Mass., June 18, 1863, by reason of expiration of term of service.

ERRATA.

Page 213. — For Hiram Newcomb, *read* Hiram Newcomb, 2d.
Page 223. — For James A. Wade, *read* James H. Wade.
Page 228. — For Eleazer Chubbuck, *read* Eleazer Chubbuck, jun.
Page 287. — For Caleb Gill, *read* Caleb Bemis Gill.
Page 311. — For Robert Francis Hardy, *read* Robert Francis Fardy.
Page 322. — For Perez L. Fearing, jun., *read* Perez Francis Fearing.

INDEX.

GENERAL INDEX.

INDEX

TO NAMES OF SOLDIERS AND SAILORS.

www.ingramcontent.com/pod-product-compliance
Lightning Source LLC
Chambersburg PA
CBHW031823270326
41932CB00008B/526